The Visual Culture
of Women's Activism
in London, Paris
and Beyond

The Visual Culture of Women's Activism in London, Paris and Beyond

An Analytical Art History, 1860 to the Present

Colleen Denney

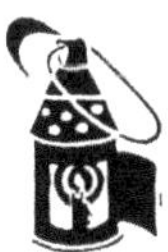

McFarland & Company, Inc., Publishers
Jefferson, North Carolina

Library of Congress Cataloguing-in-Publication Data

Names: Denney, Colleen, 1959– author.
Title: The visual culture of women's activism in London, Paris and beyond :
an analytical art history, 1860 to the present / Colleen Denney.
Description: Jefferson, North Carolina : McFarland & Company, Inc.,
Publishers, 2018 | Includes bibliographical references and index.
Identifiers: LCCN 2018020634 | ISBN 9781476671376 (softcover :
acid free paper) ∞
Subjects: LCSH: Feminists—Great Britain—History. |
Feminists—France—History. | Women political activists—Great
Britain—History. | Women political activists—France—History. | Social
justice—Great Britain—History. | Social justice—France—History. |
Art—Great Britain—History. | Art—France—History.
Classification: LCC HQ1191.G7 D45 2018 | DDC 320.082/0941—dc23
LC record available at https://lccn.loc.gov/2018020634

British Library cataloguing data are available

ISBN (print) 978-1-4766-7137-6
ISBN (ebook) 978-1-4766-3325-1

Front cover image of Artists' Suffrage League for NUWSS,
Justice at the Door: I, surely, am not excluded poster
designed by Mary Lowndes (1857–1929)
(Women's Library, London)

Printed in the United States of America

*McFarland & Company, Inc., Publishers
Box 611, Jefferson, North Carolina 28640
www.mcfarlandpub.com*

In memory of Whitney Leigh French,
fourth waver extraordinaire

Acknowledgments

I began working on this project in London in 2007 when I explored the visual imagery of Joan of Arc with the aid of a Basic Research Grant from the College of Arts and Sciences at the University of Wyoming for which I am extremely grateful. I thank Jolie Hughes as well as Marten Matthews for their continual hospitality on this occasion and during other research trips to London. Further work on suffrage archives was made possible through a grant from the Social Justice Research Center at the University of Wyoming.

Much of the research for this book came later, when I was awarded the Seibold Professorship from the College of Arts and Sciences at the University of Wyoming for 2013–14, which allowed me to spend extensive research time in London and Paris. I am honored and thankful for my university's support, and for the moral encouragement from Gabriel P. Weisberg. Further funding for images came from the Gender and Women's Studies Program, University of Wyoming; and the Caitlin Long Fund, College of Arts and Sciences Dean's Office, University of Wyoming.

I owe special thanks to Elizabeth Mansfield, for her early enthusiasm for the project and her encouragement; as well as my colleagues in the Wyoming Institute for Humanities Research, University of Wyoming, for their attention to the importance of this work; and to those amongst my students who have humored me as I nattered on about the importance of the first-wave women, whether it be in an art history class, a course on gender, or one on sex in the international city. I owe special gratitude to my helpers: Betsy Bress, Wendy Perkins, Crystal Hill, Carolyn Macdonald, and Shari Williamson.

I wish to thank all of the staff at various London libraries and museums who helped me with materials, particularly Beverley Cook at the Museum of London, Stefan Dickers at the Bishopsgate Institute, and the staff at the Women's Library and the British Library.

Table of Contents

Preface

The late 18th century witnessed the bifurcation synonymous with the modern world through the divisions that the Industrial Revolution created in the realms of private domestic space and public work space that are still strongly with us in the 21st century. This study examines those two realms and the interstices between them by focusing on ways that women enter the public arena while using the domestic politics of the private one to propel them forward in their cause for social justice, equality, and citizenship. My subject is unique not only in its focus on the visual culture of first-wave feminists in Edwardian England with a comparator analysis, where appropriate, on feminist developments in France, but also in its attention to women's movements into the public arena in the late 20th/21st century more globally in the context of how they continue to honor this first-wave suffrage history.

In some senses, I will be rightfully accused of inflecting a 21st-century view onto the circumstances of 19th- and early 20th-century women in an auto-ethnographic regard; that is, acknowledging their experiences through a relational narrative of my own. And that is largely my point: It is hard *not* to identify with women who struggled against isolation in marriage; the burden of numerous children and domestic duties; as well as the demands on their time, their energy and their physical bodies, that would make them either want to retreat into themselves or seek the larger world to put those issues right. These circumstances were hotly debated as "The Woman Question" during the 19th and early 20th century, reflecting a long history of women's dissatisfaction, in personal essays by single women such as the British writer Harriet Martineau, or the American writer Margaret Fuller in her feminist manifesto, *Women in the Nineteenth Century* (1845).[1] Both women prefigured the discourse that the French feminist Simone de Beauvoir took up in *The Second Sex* (1949) and Betty Friedan echoed for an American, middle-class public in *The Feminine Mystique* (1963).[2] Couple that suppression with the compositional devices and portrayal of a melancholic demeanor we find in the fine-art imagery of women in 19th-century interiors, seated in front of windows or sequestered in stifling interiors with seemingly no access to that exterior world, and then consider their situation in the context of the pokey-turtle move toward women's rights in Europe, and you have some inkling of an explanation for the reading I give here of such imagery as repressive, confining, and true to many women's real experience of both a mental and physical suffocation.

In this study, I hope to unravel the trajectory of their dissatisfaction and how they put it to good use in the visual materials that helped to bring their voices to the public arena. While women were moving in ever-larger public circles: in offices; at government gatherings; and into the streets; they held within them the respectability and sanctity that their more familiar domestic spaces symbolized.

In this context, the book addresses several themes in feminist work: (1) How do women begin to enter the public, political arena and what visual weapons do they use to promote their cause? (2) Why do they choose particular imagery and promote specific women as inspiration? (3) How do women's bodies in public spaces reflect attitudes about a woman's sexuality, historically and today? (4) Was the visual imagery effective in helping women gain political representation?

Of published work on the visual culture of women's activism, we owe a great debt to the groundbreaking work of Lisa Tickner in her feminist art history of the British suffrage movement between 1906–1914. Her book, *The Spectacle of Women*, began the necessary reclamation of suffrage ephemera, and its artists and designers.[3] Deborah Cherry has continued this recuperation in her book *Beyond the Frame* which focuses on England in the years of the early feminist movement, 1850 to 1900 and, like the present study and Tickner's, looks at the intertextuality of the material culture; that is, how messages in different media impact each other to create a significant dialogue. Cherry sets forth in her study to

> [shift] the ground of "Victorian" art to set painting alongside sculpture, graphic and decorative art, photographs and reprographic prints, illustrated magazines and the pageantry of demonstrations to argue that the elite forms of fine art were shaped by and understood within a visual culture in which art collided with politics, visual representation with political representation.[4]

The present project picks up that conversation where Cherry leaves off, investigating these material culture intersections within the Edwardian campaign for suffrage. It complements Tickner's study by offering an in-depth examination of representations of two historical women: Joan of Arc and the ancient Celtic Queen Bodica; as well as a dedicated critique of the role of representations of allegorical women within the movement: Britannia, Liberty and Justice. Further, it offers an opening stage for both Cherry and Tickner's scholarship by beginning with the frustrations of the domestic sphere as revealed in fine art imagery; and it provides a final curtain to these scholars' work through the epilogue's critique of women's continuing activist work in the public sphere globally, work that is heavily indebted to these brave first-wave women.

In preparations for a talk based on the research travel I did for this book, I was able to reflect on the fact that I have spent my entire career as a feminist art historian exploring what happens when women defy doing what their culture tells them to do; and how we learn to read their resulting resistant stories through their visual history. In the process, I have come to love and respect angry women because they're the ones who get things done.

In my sojourns through archives and public and private art collections in England, France, New Zealand and back in my resident state of Wyoming, as I learned more about women who fought for women's rights, I came to the revelation that women's anger is often coupled with desire: desire for change, for belonging, for love, for community, for purpose, for a place at the table. It is their expressive voices, passion, dedication, and unwavering courage—ones fueled by this longing—that I wish to share in this study.

Introduction:
Raise Your Banner High!

> What a lesson in self-denial, self-abnegation, self-discipline. The first time I took my place on the "Island" in Piccadilly Circus, near the flower sellers, I felt as if every eye that looked at me was a dagger piercing me through and I wished the ground would open and swallow me.—Kitty Marion, from her *Autobiography* (Suffragette Fellowship Collection)

> A banner is a thing to float in the wind, to flicker in the breeze, to flirt its colours for your pleasure, to half show and half conceal a device you long to unravel: you do not want to read it, you want to worship it.—Mary Lowndes, *The Englishwoman* (1909)

Women marching in public, waving elaborate banners that they have made, with big smiles on their faces, actively engaged in improving their own lives, well informed of their rights, their privileges and their lack of them, these are the women this book celebrates, honors and seeks to understand. The study analyses the British women's suffrage movement and its visual propaganda in London, with a comparator look at happenings in Paris and beyond, to determine how protest, a desire for change, and resistance to the status quo can be propelled through the persuasive impact of visual imagery. At the center of this debate, as Kitty Marion articulates, stands the culture's keen and constant surveillance of women in public.

In a study on male and female narratives of self-discovery, Jill Ker Conway's *When Memory Speaks* allows us to consider the role of memory in telling our stories.[1] Wrapped up with memory is an emphasis on nostalgia, but one of the original meanings of nostalgia was a longing for a *place* rather than a *time* in the past. In a feminist context, we can extrapolate *place* to mean many things: a place at the table in terms of having a voice; related to longing as in a sense of belonging to a group; and also, a longing, or belonging, to a home.

This longing for place is also at the heart of an ongoing feminist project: A tenacious concern with thinking through the "powers of desire"[2] and where such desire can take us, that binary of pleasure/danger always a space that women have to negotiate, "a moment to expand the potential for sexual and gender freedom and self-determination at the same time that we combat sadly persistent forms of sexual danger and violence."[3] Women's yearning to challenge the boundaries of their cultures often meant they met with violent confrontation, yet these women pushed on through to the other side, propelled by a need to be represented.

Such desiring suffrage women spoke from soapboxes; travelled the country in caravans to rally supporters for their cause; lectured across the country and abroad; chained themselves to government fences; and advertised the cause through pamphlets and through their various newspapers which they distributed from their own suffrage omnibuses, or on the streets of London, as Marion did. But, beyond those kinds of forays into the public, perhaps the most impacting way they demonstrated their collective desire for the vote was through a series of marches, pageants and pilgrimages. Millicent Garrett Fawcett, President of the National Union of Women's Suffrage Societies (hereafter NUWSS) organized several large London marches between 1907 and 1913. Perhaps the most spectacular London pageant was the 1911 Coronation Procession which comprised all of the women's suffrage groups, including the militant Women's Social and Political Union (hereafter WSPU), led by Emmeline Pankhurst and her eldest daughter Christabel. The procession encompassed women's achievements up to that date as well as celebrating women's history. For this purpose, many women dressed as important historical women who had provided them with inspiration. Among them were Queen Elizabeth I, Bodica, Lady Godiva, and, leading the march, Joan of Arc. Women surged forward in white dresses with sashes in the colors of their respective organizations, making a spectacular performance of femininity on parade. As Barbara Green suggests, "Although they resisted representing themselves as 'hyper-feminine' and saw limitations in the alignment of feminism with fashion culture, the suffragettes cultivated a delicate relationship between activism and fashionable femininity, developing … an ornamental body as civic body."[4] They literally walked a fine line between voicing their protests and representing themselves as respectable women deserving of citizenship.

In emulation of military parades, the WSPU trained a uniformed drum and fife band that frequently led local marches, sometimes for the purpose of advertising upcoming suffrage fairs. All of the organizers encouraged a sense of military order to the processions, including the use of sashes in society colors to identify the groups. Along with these demonstrations, beginning in 1908, the suffrage groups held large rallies in Hyde Park, sometimes led into the park by some forty bands announcing the individual groups. Other activities included celebratory parades to honor just-released prisoners from Holloway Prison.[5] Martha Vicinus stresses that "such huge public events … asserted the power of women to use public space for political purposes. Organized marches of uniformed or partially uniformed women were a show of strength as well as a means of developing self-respect and pride in women's history and culture."[6] Thus, in creating these large, moving displays they came to know themselves and how they were impacted by history.

Beyond these public displays, women also organized local branches of these larger organizations both around London and in over seventy cities in Great Britain. Each branch had its own banner and, often, its own shop, its windows filled with glamorous portraits of key women in the movement for purchase as post cards, as well as other propaganda for the cause, such as pins and china.

In addition, many of the women wrote confessional accounts—in letters, diaries, and speeches—as well as in suffrage fiction novels and plays that were staged in London and elsewhere. Further, they wrote autobiographical pieces, "confessions of the body," according to Green, that were published in the journals and newspapers of the cause.[7]

All of this dissemination is to suggest that theirs was no fly-by-night endeavor, but a huge undertaking for which many women fought their whole adult lives; it took considerable managerial, organizational and leadership skills, as well as the volunteer services of many women. That so many gave their time suggests what an incredibly passionate and spiritual quest they were on. And they were aware of women in the past that acted as strong and brave examples for them to emulate in their ensuing battle. But when I look at the suffrage women, in these images of their marches, their celebrations of released prisoners, or standing at their stalls or at their shops, what unites them for me is a kind of beatific expression; if sacrifice were necessary, they would not shirk it.

But, increasingly, the militant groups edged away from the more conservative NUWSS; the WSPU in particular separated themselves as early as 1905 when Christabel Pankhurst, along with Annie Kenney, her working-class associate, interrupted a Manchester election meeting to ask if they would sponsor votes for women; they ejected the two women from the hall, and Christabel committed a technical incursion on a police officer by spitting in his face which resulted in her arrest for assault and Kenney's arrest for obstruction. Refusing to pay the fine, they went to jail. This event set a pattern for the WSPU of agitation. Whenever suffragettes refused to pay their fines for such actions, they met with imprisonment, but this escalation of activities was still not enough to turn the heads of the government. More serious tactics were necessary; hence, we see suffragettes engaged in window smashing, arson, and other acts of destruction to property, perhaps the most symbolically placed being their literal attacks on works of art. While these activities landed them in prison and led to fractioning among the suffrage groups, it also kept them in the limelight, at the center of debate. As Vicinus summarizes:

> Militancy had not gained the vote or its long-range goal of a spiritually regenerated society. Yet it did not fail its participants. They had successfully brought before the eyes of the general public a new vision of what society could be—and of how women could behave. Women had sacrificed themselves in order to gain access to new spaces, public and spiritual, within themselves and the wider world.[8]

Hence, there were two sides to the suffrage struggle: One public, where they courted attention; the other private, a personal *mêlée* in prison, within themselves, in concert with other women with whom they created circles of camaraderie and with whom they worked for the common cause. While they sought control of the public gaze (not always successfully as Marion's account evinces), the private realm of the prison, as revealed especially in their personal confessions, magnified the ways that, in both realms, they were under constant scrutiny.[9]

This book determines how this imagery was impacted by the dialogue, battles and rhetoric amongst the British suffrage groups, focusing mainly on the NUWSS and the WSPU and the Women's Freedom League (hereafter WFL). It posits a comparator analysis, where relevant, to such activism among French groups. While the struggle for the women's vote in England was partially fulfilled in 1918 (for women householders over 30), it continued until 1928 (for all women 18 and over). In France, women were not enfranchised until 1945. Such a contrast in basic rights begs for such a comparative analysis. Further, because France experienced several types of government in the 19th century, its often-conflicted propagandistic imagery created an extended dialogue on depictions of women, particularly Joan of Arc, Marianne and Liberty. Such representations offered important examples for the later Edwardian suffragists.

Through this study, scholars and students will learn how women have been and continue to be empowered through the vehicle of artistic expression. No feminist art historian to date has examined the visual dialogue between the suffrage groups with regards to their evocation of the militant Joan of Arc; the historic Celtic military Queen, mother and warrior Bodica; the allegorical representations of Britannia, Liberty and Justice; nor in activist marches in terms of how using such representations as examples helped other women both then and now to gain control of their individual and collective bodies, ones that reflected their demand to be considered as a voting body or to demand basic human rights. This study redresses that gap by looking at the dialogue on feminist thought, sexuality and the body in terms of several threads: moral purity arguments; warrior symbolism; social justice; and transgressive gendered behavior.

My approach mirrors revisionist historians' arguments for a more fluid interpretation of suffrage dialogue between the major British groups rather than focusing on rigid-bound differences. In this regard, as a feminist scholar, I investigate how women's experiences help us illuminate the world in ways that sit differently from male narratives, responding to what we call an expansion of the "politics of knowledge" which traditionally has focused on white, male, privileged history, but which now has become more inclusive of women's roles. Feminist scholars also respond to the "politics of difference," that is, the ways women's lives differ from each other and hence offer up a rich tapestry of the myriad ways to challenge an often-unjust world.

Visual Culture in Early 20th-Century England

The visual culture of women's suffrage in England, and its counterpart in France, are part of a larger production that engages in contemporary debates which include ones concerning gender identities, as well as the role of institutions and cultural groupings and how they interact with and are represented by modes of production and consumption. In this regard, within suffrage visual discourse there are myriad examples of visual production: formal, photographic studio portraits; postcards of important activists often made from these formal portraits; imagery of marches, processions and meetings which appeared in the popular press as well as in the suffrage press; media stunts reported in the paper such as the Australian activist Muriel Matter's airship destined for Parliament with its large banner, "Votes for Women," or Flora Drummond on her barge on the River Thames outside Parliament with a loud speaker; political cartoons in the suffrage press and other British press outlets; suffrage posters and banners; as well as commemorative pins and other jewelry, along with china, linens, ribbons and the like. This study focuses on imagery of processions, marches and other media events; political cartoons; suffrage posters and banners.[10] There are three components to visual culture: the object itself, whether it is a painted portrait, cartoon or print, photograph, or text; the cultural institutions that create such a production; and the audience. Often the objects themselves were disseminated to an audience through reproduction or in photographic likenesses of the person in question in suffrage journals or British newspapers. Many suffrage women kept well-organized scrapbooks, which included such material, along with articles which they found of particular interest.[11]

But what I hope to show here is that there are not seamless, sealed-off differences between these kinds of visual production but rather connections; political cartoons, marches, posters, and banners worked in an intertwined fashion to create a comprehensive vision of the purposes of suffrage propaganda. Much of it was in response to the popular press's satirical images. Just as John Berger and Laura Mulvey claim that women adopt the male gaze,[12] so these suffrage women had to internalize the images of popular visual culture (low art prints for the trade and newspaper caricatures) in order to find ways to combat them in their own desire for a positive public message.

There is a discursive agenda at work here; we cannot separate out the different forms of ephemera necessarily as distinct genres just because one might be a print or a banner. There is instead an intertextuality at work in the imagery as a whole, the imagery building up its own history within the movement. One image and type of production cannot stand alone, but must be seen to be informed by others, both responding and reacting to them. In turn, there was a visual dialogue internationally that informed at least some of the imagery and its arguments, particularly between the U.S. and England, and between the British colonies of New Zealand and Australia and their mother country.[13] All such imagery, however, contested the status quo in images that created new representations of women, often as a way of countering existing stereotypes. As Deborah Cherry explains:

> Painting and drawing as much as comic drawings became a battleground for intense debates about the role of women in contemporary society which equally intruded into reviews and critical writing…. Visual culture as well as the mediating work of critics and writers acted as *loci* of interaction, points of production for the making of meaning. Artists who took up the challenge of imaging women as subjects who could claim political rights and visual representation were not unmindful of illustrations in the national press.[14]

Such representations are not just confined to the visual culture; indeed, I use many sources here to recreate and contextualize these women's lives so that, apart from the visual examples, I turn to these women's letters, diaries, memoirs and biographies in order to both inform the visual culture and to show how the visual culture might inform the writings.[15] All of these pieces of evidence—visual and textual—make up the raw material for this "battleground."

There were two specific suffrage artists groups, the Suffrage Atelier aligned with the WSPU and WFL, and the work it did for the WSPU Suffrage Shop; and the Artists' Suffrage League, most closely associated with the NUWSS.[16] Many individual artists also created political cartoons and drawings for the cause within the various journals: *The Vote* of the WFL; and *Votes for Women* edited by Emmeline and Frederick Pethick-Lawrence, originally for the WSPU, thereafter under their own steam in conjunction with the Votes for Women Fellowship and eventually with the United Suffragists. After this split, the WSPU under Christabel Pankhurst's editorship started *The Suffragette* which, with the onset of war, became *Britannia*; while the NUWSS published *The Common Cause*. Of particular importance is the work of the Australian artist Will Dyson who published posters and political cartoons in different suffrage journals, but also Alfred Pearse (publishing under the pseudonym A. Patriot) and Hilda Dallas for the WSPU.

Art as Propaganda

Related to this understanding of visual culture is the role of propaganda. Paula Hays Harper points out that the suffrage posters produced in Great Britain and America pre–First World War were the first publicity picture posters, noting that suffragists "were the first group to adapt this … art form to a political function and set the precedent that was so quickly followed on a massive scale, by the makers of official government propaganda posters."[17] She explains the long tradition in the graphic world to which such posters belong:

Both the government posters of World War I and the suffrage posters fall into the same general category in the history of the graphic arts, that of "popular prints," and both can trace their visual lineage back to the broadsheets of popular tradition, penny sheets combining printed text and pictures that first appeared in the later fifteenth century and flourished from the early sixteenth century onward. But the suffrage posters, unlike the war posters, carry on the traditional function of the broadsheets, which most often, when they were not simply reporting some sensational event, took a critical view of the political and social establishments and expressed minority opinions or individual viewpoints.[18]

Similarly, the suffrage banners belong to a long tradition of political agitation but, unlike the posters, the banner tradition was not a commercial one. Nonetheless, both banners and posters conform to Hays Harper's characterization of suffrage intent: They "were made by convinced individuals [and t]hey supported an antiestablishment cause and were directed to an audience that did not care so much about art as about the issues."[19]

Mary Lowndes designed the banners for the Artists' Suffrage League in concert, most often, with the NUWSS. When we consider the reclamation of quilts and embroidery within the women's liberation movement in the U.S. in the 20th century, we have to consider the strong precedent of such banner-making. Using what was considered a traditional women's craft, suffrage artists put it to artistic and political use in the same way that these later artists saw the very act of introducing traditional women's artwork into the high art forum as an activist move.[20] In this way, they challenged Hays Harper's characterization of politics trumping art; the medium was implicit to the message.

Banners were one means by which women entered the public field; these majestic swaths of cloth appeared swaying above the women within the processions but were also published in the suffrage journals; in the latter context, they sat alongside the public dialogue within the press in propagandistic cartoons both by the suffrage groups and by their enemies, the anti-suffragists. Lowndes wrote an article about the banners for the *Englishwoman* in 1909, in which she stated a recognition of the banners' broad reaching audience: "Banners ... have ... become associated with the appearance of women in public life, and it seems likely that they will continue to be so associated, to the great gain of our colourless streets and hitherto sober political gatherings." She was cognizant not only of their visual impact but also of their necessity to a political cause, stating that they were a visible expression of "the new thing," that is, being, "[p]olitical societies started by women, managed by women and sustained by women," and that, in that regard, the banner communicated the cause.[21] Like the political cartoon, it belongs to a long tradition of radical expression whose purpose was to persuade. In this regard, it was a key piece in the propagandistic arsenal of suffrage.

In coming to an understanding of such propagandistic materials, it is also important to note the spaces in which they appeared. Banners and posters were carried in processions, displayed in halls and branch shop windows, but were also plastered to walls around the city, as well as being hung as backdrops on platforms during speeches, rallies and meetings. Many women wore these images on their bodies in placard form or, even, apron form. Women walked the streets of London to sell the various suffrage newspapers, eliding themselves with the imagery on the page. Such activities gave new meaning to the body politic, a topic which I take up in the epilogue.

In terms of the style and approach of suffrage imagery, it was not uniform since all of the groups relied on individual artistic talents, some of whom belonged to different leagues but even within those leagues artists exhibited great variation in style and approach. That said, many suffrage artists made use of the then-current advertising styles, ones which stemmed from late 19th-century art production in both England and France of the Arts and Crafts/Art Nouveau period. While Hays Harper argues that their posters and banners are most important as "visual political documents"[22] they are also compelling works of art which had an impact upon their audience and whose style also sent particular messages about feminism and femininity working together.

General Themes of the Imagery

Iconic allegorical representations and homage to great women, both historically and from amidst the suffrage women's ranks, is the focus of the present study. My approach seeks to disrupt the dominant narrative of male representation of the female, so adequately expressed by Paule Vigneron:

> As long as there have been men who write and talk, they have heaped up their parchments and books, sprinkled the air with their words, lectures, and songs in order to pronounce their opinion of us, an opinion constructed most often from their poetic imaginations and always from the egotistical passions of their lives as men. They made us guardian angels like Antigone, flirts like Penelope, and traitors like Delilah.... They treated us as nonentities in fables, as perverts in the era of romanticism, as lunatics in contemporary novels, and nearly always as weak and limited in spirit. They have said that we were false, oh Machiavelli, oh Talleyrand; cowardly, oh Goethe ... nervous, oh Musset! They have even said that we were chatterboxes—they who invented parliaments, meetings, tribunals, clubs, cabarets, where they reserve for themselves the right to speak. Chatterboxes! When history is filled with only their sentences and their discourses! On the contrary, it is we who are "the great silent ones."[23]

Exploring the ways that imaging great women and evoking the powerful qualities of allegorical women gives focus and purpose to the women's suffrage cause involves this very kind of disruption. The chapters that focus on Joan of Arc, Bodica and allegorical examples will not take lightly the conflicts that arise in taking over imaging of women from men for women's sole purpose and voice.

Other themes that emerged as a form of protest against an unjust government were multifold and have been partially examined in the following: Hays Harper characterizes the British posters as being more often "on the attack rather than on the defense,"[24] and this estimation certainly speaks to the stance of some of the propaganda; in this regard, themes we see include women's intellectual achievements; working women's lot as doubly-burdened by domestic work and factory labor; motherhood and womanhood. Lisa Tickner groups the imagery into types and offers the only deep analysis we have in art historical suffrage scholarship; she examines the working woman; the modern woman; the hysterical woman and the shrieking sisterhood; the militant woman; and the womanly woman. She creates these types through an examination both of the suffrage material and the anti-suffrage imagery, the latter created both in response to the suffrage material and alongside it.[25] Hays Harper argues that, at least amongst the poster production, we see little direct strikes at the common enemy—Man. This stance is problematic for suffrage women since it was the men from whom they needed support to gain the vote. She asks, "But where ... is the suffragist poster depicting a monstrous male with his cruelly booted heel grinding down on the neck of the voteless, helpless female? Not to be found. The poster makers for women's suffrage avoid attacking men in favor of presenting a positive image of women."[26] While there are many such positive representations of women amongst the suffrage ephemera, there are many works that, as the agitation increased, became more hard hitting and hence give visual proof of the contrary, ones which this study will address alongside those positive ones, to lend a complete understanding both of the range of the visual protest and how it changed over time.

Theoretical Framework

Marion opens this introduction with a moment of surveillance that is symbolic of the entire battle suffrage women faced. Michel Foucault articulates the nature of their dilemma in *Discipline and Punish* with regards to his analysis of Bentham's Panopticon, from which he concludes that

> visibility is a trap.... The major effect of the Panopticon: to induce in the inmate a state of conscious and permanent visibility that assumes the automatic functioning of power. So to arrange things that the surveillance is permanent in its effects, even if it is discontinuous in its action; that the perfection of power should tend to render its actual exercise unnecessary; that this architectural apparatus should be a machine for creating and sustaining a power relation independent of the person who exercises it; in short, that the inmates should be caught up in a power situation of which they are themselves the bearers.[27]

The Pantopticon is a metaphor for power and, as in Marion's experience, it is omnipresent within the culture, exercising its value system on anyone who steps into the limelight and acts out, exhibiting transgressive behavior, as these women did. Whether they were in the papers, on the streets, or in prison, the cultural forces subjected them to this all-seeing Panopticonic eye and, in this regard, their visual productions both worked to extend that visible space and to respond to the powers in place. Hence, as Foucault characterizes the person within the Panopticonic vision:

> He who is subjected to a field of visibility, and who knows it, assumes responsibility for the constraints of power; he makes them play spontaneously upon himself; he inscribes in himself the power relation in which he simultaneously plays both roles; he becomes the principle of his own subjectivities.[28]

Throughout this text, then, we will see how the suffrage artists and activists both play into that responsibility and push at its boundaries. Alongside Foucault, this study recognizes the importance of symbolic inversions that belong to Mikhail Bakhtin's dialogue of the carnivalesque phenomenon.[29] While the processions of the British suffragists might look, to the untrained eye, like festivals, they were rather political protests. Nonetheless, public response to them can be couched in terms of carnivalesque language and expectations. Within this discourse, symbolic inversion

> may be broadly defined as any act of expressive behavior which inverts, contradicts, abrogates, or in some fashion presents an alternative to commonly held cultural codes, values and norms be they linguistic, literary or artistic, religious, social and political.[30]

The suffragists fought both the battle of stepping outside accepted norms, literally, in their marches, and the battle of contradicting accepted notions of feminine behavior. While their pageants were orderly, silent, and dignified, they were often subjected to judgmental eyes that were more likely to align them with grotesque realist images [of] the human body as multiple, bulging, over- or under-sized, protuberant and incomplete. The openings and orifices of this carnival body are emphasized, not its closure and finish. It is an image of impure corporeal bulk with its orifices ... yawning wide....[31]

Such language belongs to the dominant culture; carnival's big failing is not being able to get beyond its own complicity. Yet, Peter Stallybrass and Allon White take up this challenge in Bakhtinian thinking in their volume on *The Politics and Poetics of Transgression* in an effort to sidestep, if not reconcile, these dilemmas. To this end, they expand carnival, arguing that it encompasses not only the dichotomy of high/low, but also "as one instance of a generalized economy of transgression and of the recoding of high/low relations across the whole social structure."[32] This broadening out of Bakhtin's carnivalesque argument allows for multiple discourses, which will come into play in this study.

Other scholars on surveillance include Rachel Bowlby, who challenges Walter Benjamin's assessment of the 19th-century metropolis as not including a *flâneuse*. She proposes Virginia Woolf as the proper example of a woman who meets that definition; who walks in the public space unfettered, free to look at and engage in the visual pleasures of the city without any other definitive purpose. (Woolf herself creates such a character in *Mrs. Dalloway* (1925) who, beyond having the mission of wanting to "buy the flowers herself" for an upcoming evening gathering, spends the entire novel being just such a *flâneuse*).[33] Laura Mulvey first proposed man's exclusive surveillance of woman under the guise of the male gaze in narrative cinema, in which the woman exists only for her "looked-at-ness"; Mulvey argues that the passive woman in visual media produces in the male spectator both anxiety (as an image of castration) and pleasure (through the two avenues of escape, voyeurism and fetishism). While Mulvey herself later responded to her own critique as perhaps too rigid a dichotomy, Green argues that "what has remained persuasive is the notion that feminine spectatorship is a problem in popular culture and that femininity is aligned with a certain kind of visual pleasure."[34] What this study presents, then, in its consideration of these theoretical stances, is a conflation of those problems. Suffrage women use emblematic women, both actual and allegorical, to represent their desire for citizenship; yet, both they and their emblems are caught up in this narrative of visual pleasure and hence have to continually push against it and resist it at the same time as they promote the inspiring qualities that actual/active and allegorical/historical women possess.[35]

In terms of addressing suffrage artists' use of historical women as examples of leadership and strength, here with reference to Joan of Arc and Bodica, I employ poststructuralist discourse. In bringing such women's stories to light, as Joan Wallach Scott argues in relationship to the ideas of Judith Newton and Christine Stansell on social practices, such an approach

attribute[s] an indisputable authenticity to women's experience, [and it] ... establish[es] incontrovertibly women's identity as people with agency. It is also to universalize the identity of women and so to ground claims for the legitimacy of women's history in the shared experience of historians of women and those women whose stories they tell. In addition, it literally equates the personal with the political, for the lived experience of women is seen as leading directly to resistance to oppression, to feminism. Indeed, the possibility of politics is said to rest on, to follow from, a pre-existing women's experience.[36]

Framing Joan of Arc and Bodica in suffrage visual rhetoric in terms of their lived experiences not only proposes strong leadership examples but also addresses the central reason for the visual work: the desire for women's own voices as citizens and future leaders. Offering up Joan and Bodica shows that women in history did, indeed, exercise their own actions.

Organization of Book

The book conducts a thematic exploration of suffrage imagery that begins with a comparative analysis of women's lives in England and France in the 19th century and establishes the historical moment for feminist action as it is (or is not) reflected in a plethora of images of women in domestic settings. Chapter Two examines Joan of Arc as moral and spiritual leader, as well as historical precedent of military might as embodied in a transgressive woman. Chapter Three explores the significance of suffrage women's employment of historical women through their personification of Bodica, the ancient Celtic queen who so valiantly fought the Romans. It explores, in part, how her presence in suffrage imagery mirrors and reinforces Joan of Arc's role for suffrage women. Chapter Four examines images of Britannia, Liberty and Justice as the allegorical embodiments of nationalism and militancy, as well as their usage within the call for freedom and citizenship. The epilogue discusses women's protests in England, France and elsewhere from the late 19th century to the present in order to chart a dialogue about women's bodies entering the public sphere. It tackles the evolution of march imagery in terms of women's bodily language and their continued battle for bodily rights.

Background History on Suffrage Organizations and the Franchise

The fight for the vote in England was the work of several organizations. The NUWSS formed along constitutional lines and had been working towards suffrage since 1867; based in Manchester under the leadership of Lydia Becker, after her death the leadership eventually fell to Millicent Garrett Fawcett who was based in Cambridge and London. This group was also supportive of the WSPU during what is sometimes called "the honeymoon period" of 1906–12, after which the NUWSS distanced itself from the WSPU's militant tactics.[37] The WSPU was a militant group that had formed in Manchester in 1903 under the joint leadership of Emmeline Pankhurst and her daughter Christabel. The WSPU was not open to men (Frederick Pethick-Lawrence being the exception) but had a separate group, the Men's Political Union for Women's Enfranchisement (known as the MPU), which was also militant at times.

There were three splits from the WSPU before the First World War. The first, the WFL, formed in 1907 in order to create a more democratic leadership, led by Charlotte Despard and Teresa Billington-Greig. They claimed to be a militant society and while they never adopted the extreme tactics of the WSPU, many of them went to prison; they helped to organize the Women's Tax Resistance League and the 1911 census boycott. They made it clear that their militancy was aimed at the government but they condemned the later methods of the WSPU, which started with the window-smashing campaign. In their organ, *The Vote*, they announced their agendas which included not only the vote but also support of women's domestic and maternal roles, a view which became more complicated as the group became more progressive, arguing for choices for women.[38]

Another rupture came in 1912 when the WSPU leaders ejected Emmeline and Frederick Pethick-Lawrence, who then created the Votes for Women Fellowship, which aimed to promote the paper, *Votes for Women* and its policies rather than to be another militant organization. They had been its devoted editors under the auspices of the WSPU until that time. In 1914, they then joined the United Suffragists.

A further branching off from the WSPU came about because of Sylvia Pankhurst's battles with her WSPU relatives; she formed the East London Federation (ELF) of the Suffragettes in 1912 which fought for the rights of the woman worker.[39] It was initially under the umbrella of the WSPU, but in 1914 Sylvia's group, at the insistence of Christabel, completely separated from the WSPU. When Sylvia's group later became the Workers' Suffrage Federation, which did include men, there is a suggestion that the MPU merged with them.[40]

While middle- and upper-class women had the necessary leisure to devote to the movement in terms of volunteerism, that did not mean that working-class women were not present within the movement. Jane Marcus suggests that many feminist histories simply misread the WSPU as a middle-class organization; while Les Garner argues that "the militancy of the WSPU precluded the involvement of most working-class women, either individually or *en masse*," but, he admits, "militant tactics tied to a wider social movement would, in fact, have been far more effective."[41] On the other hand, Jill Liddington and Jill Norris look beyond the WSPU to note where there were exchanges between working-class women and other suffrage organizations.[42] Hays Harper suggests that the working woman's rights were well represented within the political agendas of British suffrage poster production.[43] Their lot also received hard-hitting protest within the political cartoons from the hand of A. Patriot within the pages of *The Vote*, for example; and Tickner gives considerable space to propagandistic imagery of the working woman.[44]

But nowhere was the intersection of classes and the worker more readily visible than, arguably, in The Pageant of Women's Trades and Professions held on April 27, 1909, organized by the NUWSS in conjunction with the Quinquennial Congress of the International Woman Suffrage Alliance in London. The pageant developed the self-presentation of women as workers[45]; the procession was powerful in its purpose of exhibiting which wage-earning women desired the franchise, one punctuated by their reception from the President, the American Carrie Chapman Catt, who declared upon their entrance to Albert Hall, "You are an argument."[46]

Perhaps more telling, and certainly one of the reasons why the binary presumption about class appears in the scholarly literature, is that Christabel and her sister Sylvia were frequently at odds over the representation of the working woman and her concerns within the movement. Christabel increasingly sought the support of middle- and upper-class women as members within the WSPU, claiming to Sylvia that suffrage was a women's issue.[47]

But we should not imagine that membership in individual groups embodied any kind of divide between the suffrage activists themselves. There were significant overlaps; many of them supported the work of all the groups and did not necessarily follow the dictates of their leaders too closely, often acting independently.[48] Further, there were numerous local chapters of each major group that operated under their own leadership. There were also subgroups of specific organizations that represented the interests of that particular group, such as the Actresses' Franchise League, some of whose members were in the WSPU and/or the NUWSS or in other groups, but who formed to promote women's enfranchisement through educational methods such as plays, literature, and lectures. Hence, many women were working towards suffrage both apart from and in conjunction with the larger umbrella groups.

Regardless of individual affiliations, all of the groups were united in pursuing the vote for women, and all of them would argue that the vote was a gateway to other rights for women; the various suffrage groups also promoted women's education and employment. Further, all of the groups would also, in various ways, address the necessity of citizenship and how they should embody good citizenship in order to earn the vote. It is important to an understanding of the context of suffrage imagery to recognize that their goals went beyond a struggle for the vote; the implication and symbolism of possessing the vote and hence citizenship is at the center of the visual discourse. As Tickner explains:

> The training and employment of women as artists, the division of labour in the home and at work, the place of women in the family, community, state and empire, the definition and regulation of female sexuality, women's special claims to moral virtue, the consequences of increased educational and employment opportunities for women...[49]

all contributed to the battle, and their collective hope was, that once they received the vote, they would then be in a position of power to help change women's circumstances.

What was harder to reconcile among the various voices of suffrage was the political arena. The NUWSS formed as a non-party group initially, while the WSPU originally aligned itself with the working classes. Yet, there has been much critique of these organizations as being too bourgeois, but many historians have been able to argue, through direct evidence, that these groups fought to be inclusive and represent the voices of women from all classes, as just discussed. Once the First World War started, however, the situation became more complex for all concerned. And that more multifaceted history is complicated by yet another system of fluidity among suffrage women: Their degree of devotion to socialism. Women's interest, influence and involvement in socialist groups went beyond those activities of ELF that Sylvia Pankhurst organized.[50]

In 1914, at the onset of the First World War, Garrett Fawcett took a pro-war stance which unsettled many NUWSS members and resulted in the resignation of the pacifist members of her NUWSS Executive Committee. While she had initially taken a pacifist stance at the onset of the war, Les Garner proposes why she changed her stance: To her critics she "could reply that any tinge of pacifism might endanger the essential success of the suffrage campaign" but he acknowledges her conflict in his claim that

> many women felt that suffragism was rooted in notions of democratic equality which argued that power was not, or should not be, based on physical force.... This essentially liberal position condemned the War as resulting from a world made by men and as contrary to true suffragist and democratic principles, and was a major force behind the demand for the NUWSS to campaign for peace and arbitration.[51]

But Garrett Fawcett was being diplomatic; the NUWSS did not abandon suffrage; as with its prior approach of working along constitutional lines, it still wished, in Garrett Fawcett's eyes, to be on the side of power in order to gain power.

Prior to this change in philosophy, there was a class shift within the NUWSS toward the Labour Party starting in 1909–12 which resulted in its creation of the Election Fighting Fund in 1912 to aid the Independent Labour Party (ILP). This revision in their focus came about because the NUWSS had pinned their hopes on a positive outcome from the Conciliation Bills of 1910 and 1911 but those did not materialize. Prime Minister Asquith then promised them a Reform Bill that would include a women's amendment but in the end the amendment was rebuked. Their frustration, as Garner argues, "convinced the national leadership of the need for a mass campaign and for a closer alliance with the

Labour movement."[52] This decision represented a major alteration in the NUWSS's philosophy since, previously, it had been non-party and had battled with the Labour Party over its ambivalent support of women's suffrage. In 1912, the NUWSS and the Labour Party groups merged in their philosophies, the Labour Party declaring that it would accept no bill that did not include women.

But the war and Garrett Fawcett's anti-pacifist stance changed all that since the NUWSS had to depart from the ILP because they were a pacifist group.[53] They initially desired to promote arbitration but that position soon gave way to pro–War agendas.[54] While the WSPU moved entirely away from women's suffrage, the NUWSS continued to fight for it, however. Sandra Stanley Holton has shown that, in fact, it was the work of the NUWSS, not the WSPU, which forced the hand of the government and insured women suffrage in 1918. Ironically, the NUWSS's gradual move to an alliance with the Labour Party aided them in this agitation and helped them gain government support. (Traditional arguments have included what feminists call "the gift argument," that is, that the government simply gave them the vote out of gratitude for their war work).[55] But the struggle was not over with the passing of the Representation of the People Act in 1918 as the NUWSS was not happy with the age restriction to women over 30; their continued demand for equal rights is reflected in their new title in 1919, the National Union of Societies for Equal Citizenship. Similarly, the WFL continued after the War in order to seek full equality for all women with men. They had to wait until 1928 for suffrage on equal footing with men.[56]

Like the NUWSS, the WSPU initially sought pacifism and arbitration rather than support of the war but that stance soon changed to one entirely of Chauvinism under Christabel's guidance. "The interests of women were submerged beneath the interests of the nation. *The Suffragette*, symbolically, Christabel replaced with *Britannia*. Their new zeal culminated in a 'Women's Procession' in July 1915 which they organized in conjunction with the Government to address a 'Woman's Right to Serve'" which David Mitchell characterizes as an attempt "to help Lloyd George to overcome trade union resistance to dilution and the employment of women."[57] How far the pendulum had swung for the WSPU who now put the franchise of soldiers and sailors ahead of their fight for women's suffrage.

But, in addition, in 1917 the WSPU folded, replacing itself with "The Woman's Party" for which Christabel Pankhurst announced a political party platform that combined a vehemently nationalistic foreign policy with a radical domestic one. Christabel then ran unsuccessfully on an anti–Bolshevik platform in 1918, after which the Woman's Party disbanded. With these events, militancy was dead.[58]

In a final assessment of the 1918 success for women's enfranchisement in England, Garner argues that the vote was not given to women based solely on their war efforts or the threat of renewed militancy but rather as a result of many factors.[59] The First World War itself removed some of the barriers that had been present previously, most important being its ejection of an "anti-suffrage" Prime Minister, an event which helped to raise awareness about universal enfranchisement, the women ensuring that any new measure must, this time, include women. Although it was a compromise at best, the restriction to women over 30 brought in more member votes from the Conservative Party than would have otherwise been in favor. However, what Garner does not stress is that the decision was based on the numbers of young men lost in the War, the Government fearing that same old argument, that women would take over the government by having the majority of the vote.[60]

But much had been gained beyond the franchise. For one, the voice of the working- class woman came to the forefront; for another, these suffrage groups had challenged traditional attitudes to women's abilities. The liberal feminist Winifred Holtby explained that the militant campaign had shaken up the taboos, suggesting instead that "[w]omen had accepted discipline, displayed capacity of organization, courage and tenacity. The very recklessness and extremism of militancy had shaken old certainties."[61] Garrett Fawcett in a reflective piece from 1927 argued that the passing of seven Acts between 1918 and 1919 was the direct result of the franchise victory. This legislation included protective laws on illegitimacy, midwifery and nursing, and improved laws for women who wanted to hold public offices. Beyond such measures, the decade following women's enfranchisement in England also saw enlargements in women's rights to property in Acts on Married Women's Property, Maintenance Orders, Infanticide (1920), Maintenance (1922), Divorce (1923), Guardianship of Infants and Pensions (both 1925), all for the purpose of improving women's lives.[62] Yet, ironically, these changes in the laws were largely aimed at women as mothers, wives or widows, Garner considering that this attitude was largely due to the shift back to a more conservative sexual division of labor which, more often than not, sought to force women out of the workforce and back into the home.[63] Thus, we could argue that some of the suffrage women's fears about positioning themselves as keepers of home and hearth, came full circle in the post–First World War period, our woman at the window who we meet in the first chapter, emancipated, but for what? All change is economically driven, the women going back to the home after the war as a direct reflection of the need for men to have jobs without competition. It is a history which repeats itself up to the present day.

In France, the progress of women's suffrage was much slower. I will use the French history of suffrage and its limited imagery as a way of illuminating and understanding the visual culture of the British women's movement. Both countries used allegorical and historical imagery to represent their causes; but Britain also maintained a significant dialogue with America as well as shared imagery and iconographic usage. Britain also kept strong communication internationally through the International Woman Suffrage Alliance, of which Garrett Fawcett was second Vice President. Affiliate societies existed in many countries around the world: Australia, Bulgaria, Canada, Denmark, Finland, Germany, Great Britain, Hungary, Italy, the Netherlands, Norway, Russia, South Africa, Sweden, Switzerland and the U.S., but not France. The French will appear here then mostly as contrast to the developments in England.

Considering that the suffrage campaign "was the first political agitation to organize the arts in its aid"[64] we will see here how it stands as example and visual dialogue with movements around the world. And yet, as art historians, we have not totally recorded its achievements and the messages of its art. It is my hope that this study contributes to the continued reappraisal both of these artistic expressions and their place in the propagandistic dialogue of a rich visual culture that continues, to this day, to inform us about struggles for equality and, specifically, women's rights to be persons in charge of their own bodies and lives.

One

Les Femmes Ennuyées
Bored Women in European Culture;
Presaging a Call to Action

"This world of simpletons, of mad, lazy and bored women."—Maxime Rude, *Confidences d'un journaliste* (Paris, 1876)

Hanging only a room apart at the *Musée d'Orsay* are two 19th-century paintings that, on first glance, might seem totally incongruous yet, on closer examination, reveal themselves to be two representations of the lives of French women in the 19th century. One, a cozy, domestic scene of Claude Monet's first wife, Camille, seated somewhat dejectedly on a couch, looking out of a window; the other, Henri Gervex's interpretation of the literary character Rolla, a man devastated by his own insatiable appetites, standing in front of an open Parisian window in a garret apartment of his prostitute seductress, Marie, while she lies in sexual abandon, completely naked, on a mussed-up bed (figs. 1 and 2).

When I first saw *Rolla* in the black and white pages of Linda Nochlin's *Realism*,[1] I thought, wow, how totally salacious it was, and I thought Rolla was the woman; I guess that was the feminist in me wanting her to be the center of the picture, which she clearly is, but not in an empowering way, rather in a destructive way. I thought the man must be totally in love with her since he, like us, cannot take his eyes off of her soft, pink, available body. But it is not so! The painting *is* about her powers of seduction, but it's more about her ability to ruin a weak man. He is at the window, its doors thrown open, his last gesture of despair before he takes his own life. The painting is based on an Alfred de Musset poem about Rolla's downward and destructive path.[2] Although the painting was accepted for the Salon of 1878, it was not exhibited because the jury considered it to be too immoral since it showed the aftermath of his sexual encounter with the prostitute Marie.

These paintings represent two extremes of 19th-century French culture that also mirror English constructs of womanhood, often referred to as the substance and the shadow. We find the respectable wife sequestered in her middle-class apartment, only able to glimpse the world through a window pane, while Gervex presents us with a morning-after scene of high contrast, no tidy interior but a garret bedroom with bedclothes significantly strewn, Marie's clothes thrown on the chair and floor in reckless abandon, along with Rolla's top hat. Her jewelry has been discarded haphazardly on the table; his cane pierces her corset in a mimicking of the sexual act, now over. Her pink garter lies carelessly on top of her undergarments, as if taken off in great haste. The

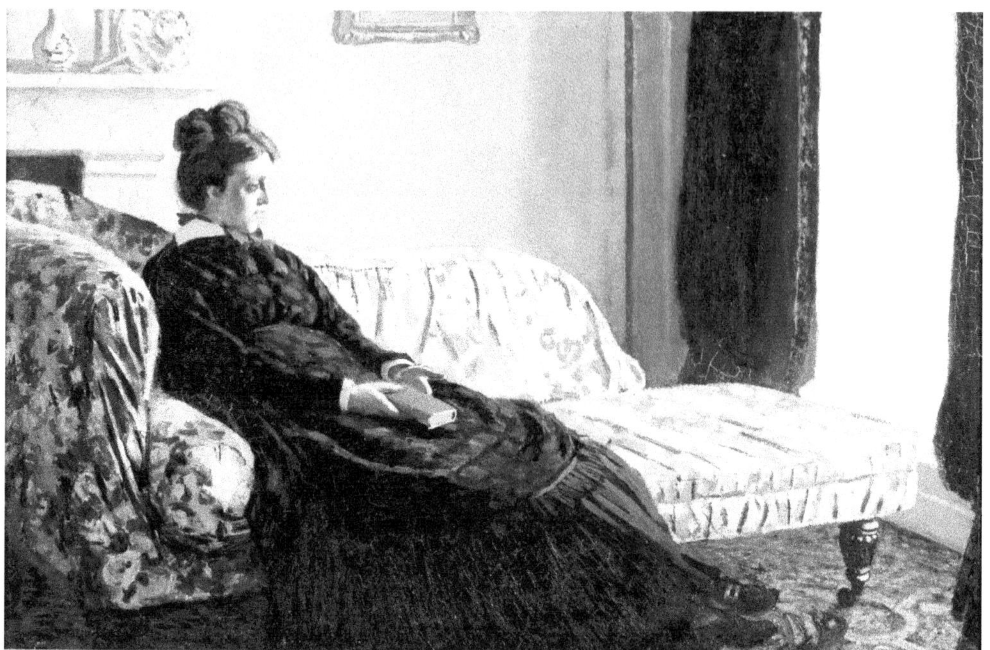

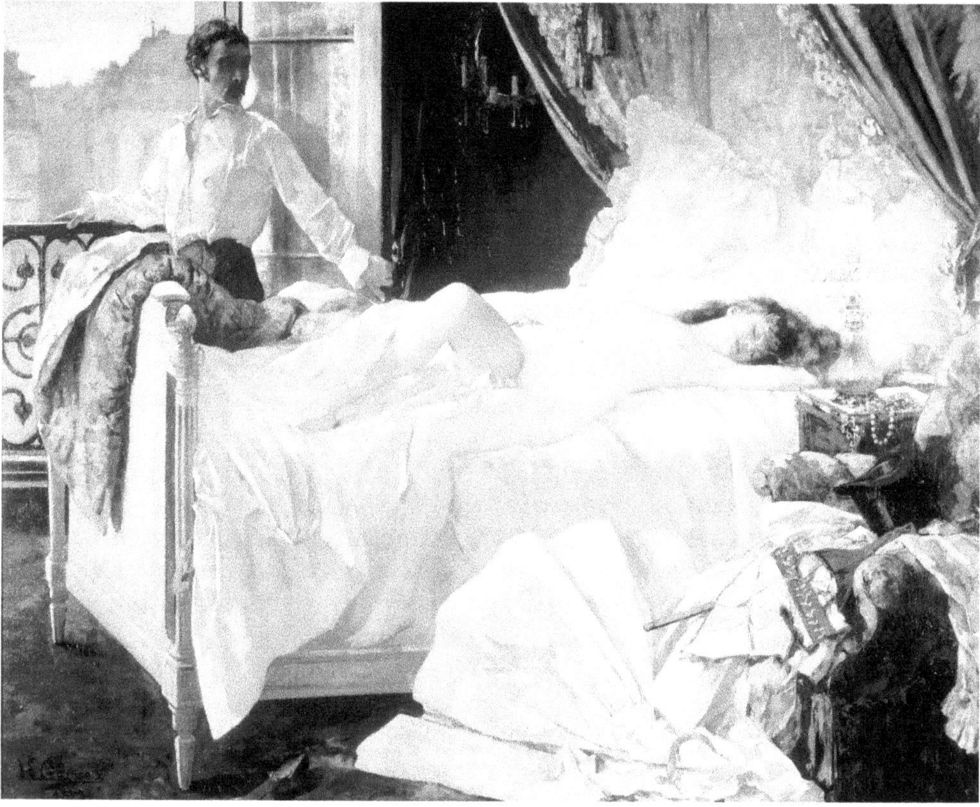

Top: Figure 1. Claude Monet (1840–1926), *Meditation: Madame Monet on a Sofa (Camille Doncieux [1847–1879])*, c. 1871. Oil on canvas. RF3665. Photo: Gerard Blot. Musée d'Orsay, Paris, France.© RNM-Grand Palais/Art Resource, NY. *Bottom:* Figure 2. Henri Gervex (1852–1929), *Rolla,* 1878. Oil on canvas. LUX1545. Photo: A. Danvers. On deposit with the Musée d'Orsay, Paris, France. Musée des Beaux-Arts, Bordeaux, France. © RMN-Grand Palais/Art Resource, NY.

anguished man, Rolla, stands at the open window, letting the sun in to light up Marie's beautiful, young body, her soft brown hair all disheveled. She begins to awaken under his intent gaze.

The irony of Camille's situation, next to Marie and Rolla's, is that she and Monet had their first child out of wedlock and did not marry until after his birth. In this painting, however, she is given the veneer of respectability whereas we are certain that Rolla's fate/Marie's fate, will not be so safe a one. One painting is about desire and the dangers of abandoning oneself to it, the other is the about the containment of that desire.

And yet, in both situations, what lies beyond the window encasement is a danger to both Camille and Marie. For them, the wide, wild world is a place where a woman, no matter her class standing, cannot tread with impunity. But there will be other choices for the generations that follow Camille and Marie; for women were on the march in both England and France to fight for women's rights both within the home and beyond it. Those battles to change laws would help poor Marie just as much as they would a middle-class woman like Camille.

In 19th-century Europe a recurrent theme in paintings and prints is that of *les femmes ennuyées*, or bored women, set within the proverbial interior, either gazing out of a window and/or being enclosed by it; my goal here is to relate such cultural production to social and political history in order to understand the predominance of this thematic occurrence within the context of the British construction of the "separate spheres" or "angel in the house," what the French called "*la femme au foyer*" (woman at the hearth). As Charles Rice explains, during the 19th-century

> the interior emerged in a domestic sense as a new *topos* of subjective interiority, and framed newly articulated and increasingly widespread desires for privacy and comfort, for the consolidation of specific gendered and familial arrangements that demonstrated acceptable norms, and for practices of self-representation in the context of domestic life.[3]

In this chapter, while examining the predominance of such domestic iconography, I focus on the strong march forward in British laws which, in their goals to protect women's personal safety and economic independence, began to free women from this private, and often suffocating, realm. In this context, I examine British women's ongoing agitation for women's rights, and its difference from women's experience in France, where such progress was much slower.[4] Karen Offen characterizes five developments in Europe that fueled feminist demands in the 19th-century: the rising literacy and burgeoning education of women; a phenomenon that was linked to increasing awareness of nationalism and population growth; the creation of an urbanized workforce (which happened earlier in England than in France); a rivalry between feminists and socialists that resulted in an increasing focus on labor rights as key to women's emancipation; and the resulting growth of nationally organized feminist movements.[5] Add to this grouping the fight for women's entrance to the medical profession and for meaningful employment; for control over child custody and property; as well as participation in local government, to obtain the big picture of how much work there was to do in order to turn women's life experiences into those of first-class citizens. The dialogue over the woman question was strongest in England and France by the late 1880s, as evidenced in Theodore Stanton and Frances Power Cobbe's 1884 volume, *The Woman Question in Europe: A Series of Original Essays.*[6] We can add to this polemic volume the evidence of the strain on women, best represented in Henrik Ibsen's character Nora from his play, *The Doll's House*, first performed in 1879 to much debate, due to Nora's abandonment of home, husband and children.[7] Offen argues that "with Nora's declaration of independence, a woman's individual search for her freedom and her right to happiness announced itself as a major theme in the debate on the woman question" throughout Europe.[8] Yet, in both England and France, there was a simultaneous insistence in systems of representation on the survival of the angel in the house/*la femme au foyer*, but she was not always content nor did women readily embrace her.

Nonetheless, in both England and France men wrote treatises to claim the angel as woman's key role, chief among them being the British John Ruskin's *Of Queen's Gardens* (1865) and the French Protestant pastor Adolphe Monod's *Woman: Her Mission and Life* (1848).[9] But, as I will argue, the imagery, such as the British artist George Elgar Hicks' satisfied and supportive wife, who also understands her duties as mother and daughter, in his triptych *Woman's Mission*, 1863 (Tate Gallery, London) vies with more ambivalent British representations of women in interiors, while French examples show women physically and psychologically isolated from their men, children and servants.[10] What do we make of such representations that, on the surface, seek to uphold traditional constructions of womanhood rather than to break them down?

Returning to Monet's *Meditation* (fig. 1), Camille is seated in a dejected posture suggestive of boredom or restlessness, her book lying idly in her lap, her countenance neither blank nor animated. Light comes in from the right through a lightly-curtained window, a familiar motif in 19th-century art, often including an open window, that art historians have considered in the context of humanity's yearning for nature, particularly in Romantic works of art, or of a middle-class coziness.[11] But often, as Elaine Shefer has suggested, such images address a young woman's hopes for future married bliss.[12] Shefer singles out John Everett Millais's *Mariana*, 1851 (fig. 3), based in part on Alfred, Lord Tennyson's poem of that title, as an example that disrupts these more sentimental narratives. She asserts that it depicts the poet Christina Rossetti, writhing in physical and emotional pain as she wrestles with her decision to reject the vain pleasures of the flesh.[13] But, this iconography is more complex than even she has indicated; why is Mariana/Rossetti confined to a domestic space at the same time that her psychological state seems to be one of longing, if not downright tension and boredom? Why is she so *ennuyée*, as the French would say?

Pamela Gerrish Nunn has argued that many representations of anxious Victorian marriages reflected the ongoing public dialogue about the difficult relations between men and women in a strictly patriarchal culture; and in France similar anxieties surfaced from the 1880s onward with the beginnings of agitation there for suffrage.[14] My focus differs; while I will examine some of these distressing images of what Nunn calls "trouble in paradise," I will do so as a way of elucidating representations of bored women, ones that embody the obverse of the angel. Such women's sexuality was firmly in check, but the strains and apprehensions bubbling underneath, reflected in the uneasy mood of the images, support the idea that these women's restlessness was real, that it presaged a desire to act, to move beyond the private interior. Such frictions relate to discourses on space and sexuality that operate to keep women within the respectability symbolized by the house itself, as Mark Wigley explains:

> The house can only operate … if the woman's sexuality, which threatens to pollute it … is contained
> within and by it. The convoluted spatiality of a violation of the house necessary to its integrity as
> such is dealt with by the complex social rituals around thresholds, rooms, streets, veils, beds, hygiene,

etc., that constitute the marriage ceremony. Only when these rituals domesticate the perceived threat to spatial integrity can the house literally provide the boundaries which control female sexuality. The house then assumes the role of the man's self-control. The virtuous woman becomes woman-plus-house, or, rather, woman-as-housed, such that her virtue cannot be separated from the physical space.[15]

Hence, the spate of imagery of women housed within interiors speaks directly to masculine control over their sexuality. It also relates to the history of privacy, one with which the 19th-century grappled, which constitutes, in part, the history of the control of the female body and its submission to rituals of cleanliness, both metaphorical and real: hygiene, order, discipline, all were exercised to ensure prohibitions.

Susan Sidlauskas examines the iconography of the interior more generally, asserting that interior images endorsed the

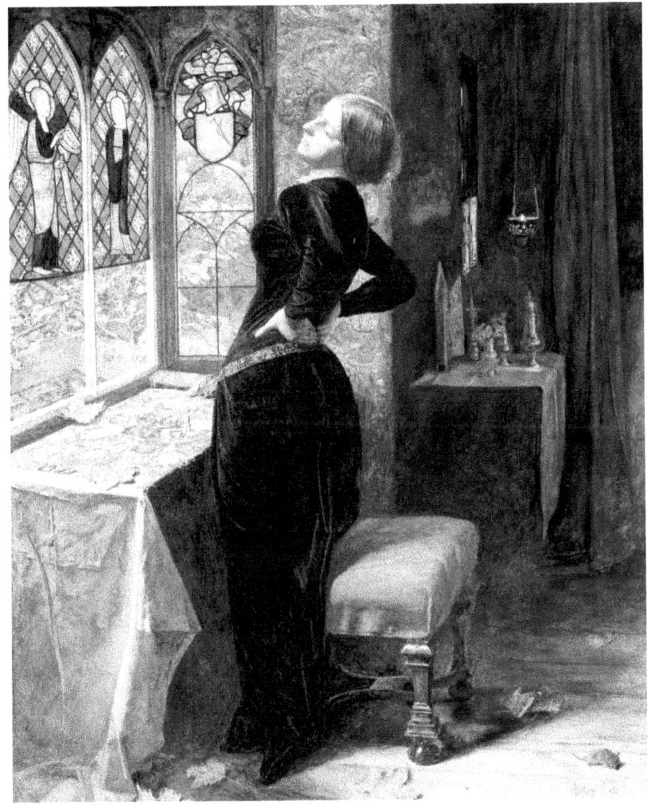

Figure 3. Sir John Everett Millais (1829–1896), *Mariana,* 1851. Oil on mahogany. Accepted by H M Government in lieu of tax and allocated to the Tate Gallery 1999. © Tate, London 2016.

instabilities that were the consequence of cultural change, mirroring critical shifts "from the private to the public, from the individual to the collective, from the everyday to the utopian."[16] I seek to explore here what role the imagery of the bored woman plays within such cultural change. At the same time, the fact that many of these women are depicted actively reading, or having just been reading, reflects constructions of traditional femininity, aligning such activity within the domestic environment "as both a space for quiet and an ideal sphere of female life."[17] I am more interested in what happens when she puts the book down, as Camille is doing in Monet's painting, leaving the world of the imagination and the traditional female realm behind to engage in the outside world. As she does so, she must contend with traditions of representation of the female subject that revolve around three themes, ones conflated in the woman at the window iconography: the family, both as a product of marriage and as an organizing cell of society; reproduction of the species; and property, with its counterparts, work and liberty.[18]

While two decades separate Monet and Millais's paintings (figs. 1 and 3), the emotions they emit, I contend, similarly dislocate the domestic environment, one that was recognized as being synonymous with bourgeois identity[19]; hence, this introductory chapter seeks to address why we see this dislodgment within an assiduous body of imagery that plants a woman firmly within an interior with the ability to glimpse the world outside only through a glass darkly. Do such images seek to enlighten us about how 19th-century women negotiated their gendered lives at a time of increasing agitation for women's rights?[20] Were their real lived experiences different from what the etiquette books told them it should be?[21] To answer these questions, I address the modern history of boredom within the context of women's burgeoning agency, changes in the laws governing their political and economic power, and moral and legal codes regulating their sexuality.

Challenging the Separate Spheres Ideology

Such iconography, through its containment of women in interior spaces, emblematizes the limits of women's personal and political power and effectively curtails their influence.[22] It mirrors the persistent lure of the separate spheres ideology in Europe through the early 1900s. Because a woman managed a ménage of servants, she was frequently at leisure, her state of inactivity an emblem of her husband's power in the public sphere. Morally superior to her often-wandering mate, yet physically and psychologically weaker, she could not safely or easily cross the threshold of home. To do so would incur considerable risk to her reputation.[23]

Scholarship in the past twenty years has successfully challenged this binary construction, acknowledging that we must look at the time period, in part, "in terms of a constant and persistent definition and re-definition of acceptable sexual behavior."[24] There was continual advocacy in three areas: work, education, and the law. Such dialogue was readily available in pictorial form to a gallery-going Victorian audience, such that by 1852, *The Spectator* had added a section on "Domestic Pictures" to its Royal Academy summer reviews.[25] Further, 19th-century authors, such as Harriet Martineau, herself a single woman, wrote as early as 1859, that not every woman could be supported by a husband, father or brother, forcing her to pursue employment. She stated that "the women of the United Kingdom have been led forth … into a life of labour and care, more strongly resembling that of men than either the men or women of old times could have anticipated."[26] And, as Donald E. Hall points out, Martineau's point of view reflected the general tenor of journalistic writing in England in the 1850s and 1860s. Members of the British feminist movement, such as Emily Davies, began to write in earnest about "the woman question" which sought to redress the role of women in terms of the need for education reform, opening up the professions, and suffrage, among other topics.[27] Hall characterizes this debate as one of strident protest against the status quo. Citing Martineau he says:

> Patriarchy is … decried, both [as] an oppressive and an overly simplistic theory, one that belies the fluid performances and changing "conditions of female life." Yet even as gender enactments continue to metamorphose, many discursive norms lag behind: "The need and the supply of female industry have gone on increasing, and latterly at an unparalleled rate, while our ideas, our language, and our arrangements have not altered in any corresponding degree." … Martineau speaks accurately about the generally conservative nature of laws and language, which failed … to reflect fully the fluidity of gender performances.[28]

Hence, part of the struggle we will see in imagery of women in interiors reflects this gap between actual experience and the cultural assumptions and practices that seemed to remain unmoved and unchanging. In her study of gendered spaces, Daphne Spain follows Pierre Bourdieu's argument that "the power of a dominant group lies in its ability to control constructions of reality that reinforce its own status so that subordinate groups accept the social order and their own place in it. The powerful cannot maintain their positions without the cooperation of the less powerful."[29] But we have plenty of evidence to the contrary; that women were not complacent acceptors of the status quo; that, literally, they were pushing at the barriers. Shefer gets under the skin of these assumptions by arguing that Millais's *Mariana* (fig. 3) portrays the real Christina Rossetti, who does not long for the status quo, but rather, rejects it. In viewing such images, we must keep in mind Martineau's clear vision, that circumstances of real, lived experience were, indeed, much more flowing than the cultural codes would have us believe.

Another such example is a controversial painting from 1861 titled *Women's Work: A Medley* (fig. 4) by the British artist Florence Claxton which creates a protest about the barriers to women's work.[30] It explicitly refers to a woman's boredom in a world in which men hold all the cards and set up all the barricades; the flagstones on the ground are carved with words, including one marked *ennui*. In addition, the slumped female figure on the right is unable to gain access to the medical profession (the medical man holds the keys) but the door is not solid; there are fissures and breakages that suggest she might break through this barrier. This vignette comments on women's real presence in the medical field by this date, two noted examples being the English-American trained in Paris, Elizabeth Blackwell who, in turn, inspired the first British doctor, Elizabeth Garrett. Such a painting was itself subject to critique, but one that suggested the incredible ambivalence

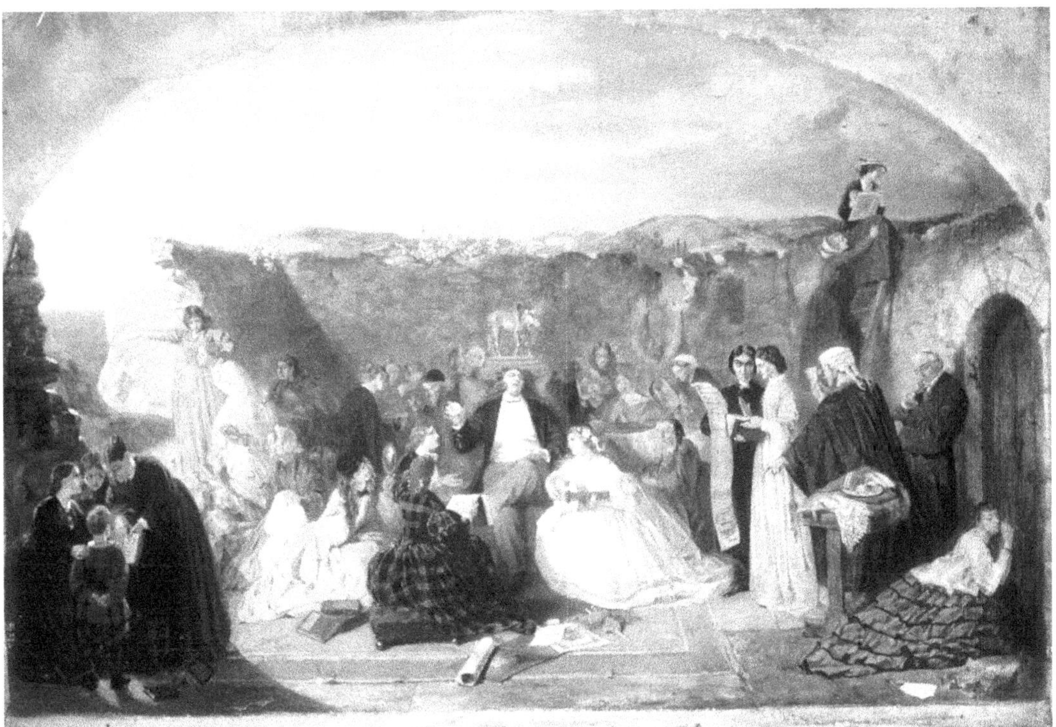

Figure 4. Florence Claxton (c. 1839–1879), *Women's Work: A Medley,* c. 1861. Oil on canvas, original now lost. Photograph courtesy of Sotheby's, London.

to women's entry into public fields as well as to what the culture considered to be acceptable avenues for women's work.[31] By 1861 the public debate about woman's proper realm was so overarching that Claxton's image was readily recognizable as being at the center of a dissenting debate. The British dialogue about women's proper place would not die down; it appeared in print, in cartoons, in feminist and more conservative publications alike, all of which acknowledged, even if they did not approve, of women's rights to education, meaningful work, legal reform and the vote.

Statistics in England reinforce Claxton's vision: There is a big shift between 1851 and 1901 in terms of changes in women's social and economic situation. The total number of women in the workforce almost doubled, the largest portion working in domestic service. In the professions (teaching, nursing, clerking) women's presence quadrupled between 1861 and 1901. However, the total number of unoccupied women, that is, the ones pictured in these interior scenes, also rose during this time, from 5,294,000 to 10,229,000, because of overall population growth.[32] With this increase being the case, it seems prudent to suggest that the artists involved in such depictions were literally reflecting the status quo; that is, an abundance of unemployed women in the middle-class sector who, despite improvements for women in terms of occupational opportunities, still remained at home. Perhaps this situation is one reason why, as art historians have pointed out, visual representations, despite dialogues about the slippage between feminine virtue and vice in the actual world,[33] continued to insist on clear distinctions between the angel/whore that reinforced the private/public dichotomy.[34]

The insistence on separate sphere ideology in the face of evidence to the contrary further suggests that the representation of bored women in interiors speaks on several levels at once that reveal a guarded ambivalence to change: Nostalgia for a picture that no longer mirrors reality and that never truly existed; a desire to maintain an uncomplicated, gendered world where everyone knows their place, more myth than fact; a resistance narrative such as we see emerging in Millais's *Mariana* and Monet's *Meditation*, one that uses the mood of boredom as protest; or backlash against women's increasing presence in the public arena. Nineteenth-century British women took their battle to the streets against economic inequity in the laws starting in the 1850s. But the dialogue had already begun in the period 1820 to 1848, in both England and France, among post-revolutionary social critics who were re-envisioning Enlightenment formulations in order to create a significant overhaul of relations between the sexes within the family and society[35]; women's rights were heavily debated in the major newspapers of both countries. Agitation for women's rights stemmed from women's experience in coming up against laws that did not protect them. Debates over marriage in England, for example, led to the 1857 Divorce Act, which the press and Parliament hotly debated and discussed for a decade before it finally passed. While in 1867 John Stuart Mill presented the first Women's Suffrage petition, the decade also witnessed the repressive Contagious Diseases Acts which sought to protect male military personnel from venereal diseases through inspection of female prostitutes. However, this system soon backfired, as the police indiscriminately harassed women on the streets of garrison towns and subjected them, as well as prostitutes, to debilitating and, often, life-threatening examinations. With protest by Josephine Butler and others, the Acts were repealed in 1886, a move forward that was made easier by other advances, such as the 1870 Married Women's Property Act which gave married women the right to their own earnings; and by 1884 they no longer had to stay in a marriage if they could prove a case of aggravated assault.

Early on, popular illustrations on women's suffrage showed a blatant counterattack to women's increasing visibility in the political realm, as evidenced by the commentary of John Tenniel's *Punch* cartoon, "An Ugly Rush," 1870 (fig. 5) which depicts women who enter the public field as aged, "ugly," and angry. Tenniel's point is that such women need the vote, or at least an education, since they do not possess the requisite beauty to lure a husband, an oft-repeated kind of censure in such caricatures. By contrast, he represents the typical Victorian beauty as a married woman (standing at

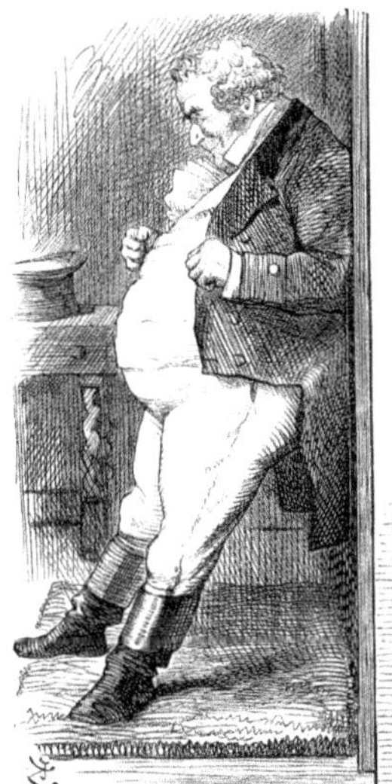
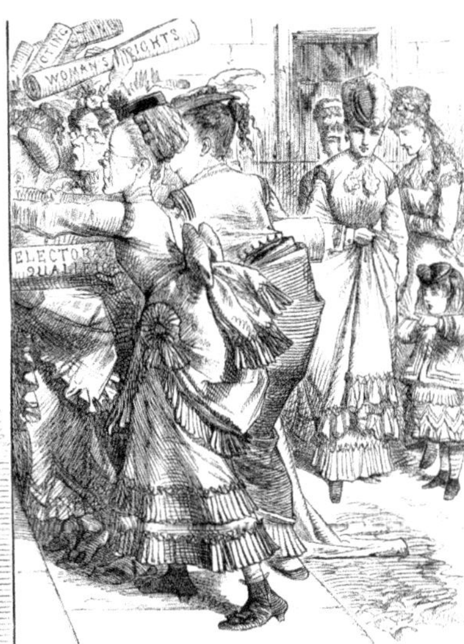

Figure 5. John Tenniel (1820–1914), "An Ugly Rush," *Punch* (1870). Reproduced with permission of Punch Ltd., www.punch.co.uk.

the right), who instructs her daughter that these "ugly" women represent an adverse example. They want an answer from "John Bull," symbol of English government, who has just rejected the Women's Vote Bill. This cartoon was one of many that addressed the issue of women in public who wanted the same rights as men, refusing to take them seriously and deflecting their purpose by keeping the focus on superficial issues of appearance, as well as on their transgression in terms of proper womanly behavior, the "ugly" of the title referring both to their physical selves and how they were acting outside the proper codes of conduct.

The ambivalence and threat to the status quo that seems present in this illustration and others of its ilk must be viewed in the context of other cultural examples that similarly attack this neat, binary construction. As Hall explains,

> one finds many remarkable disjunctions in the literature of the mid–Victorian era, between representations of powerful activity by women and surprisingly inadequate, debilitating commentary on that activity, between transgressive, paradigm-challenging behavior and the resilient, rigid paradigms into which it is nevertheless imperfectly placed and through which it is scathingly assessed.... [W]hat becomes readily apparent is that individuals are never simply trapped, bound and gagged, by discourse, that changing desires, varying economic necessities, and diversely disconcerting transgressive potentials operate as productive forces, ones that undermine simplistic, passé notions and binary designations.... [T]o undermine, to destabilize, is not, necessarily, to change radically. Oppressive discourses provide both a context and a filter for human actions that are simultaneously restraining and aggravating.[36]

Mariana (fig. 3), for example, seems to embrace both this sense of restraint and aggravation. Her back is stiff, as if she has been sitting for hours at her embroidery. She shifts, stands and stretches, looking out the window but with no hope of escape. Yet she appears to defy the outside world through her dejected posture.

Hall examines the gendered discourse of an 1859 essay for *Fraser's* on "A Fear for the Future," whose anonymous author bemoans "the days of romance" when women were preoccupied with the flights of fancy of the Romantic poets. The writer regrets that women have now given themselves over to the running of Committees and Associations, engaged themselves with the understanding of laws and hence have become "strong, sensible, and matter of fact ..."[37] As this writer's ideas suggest, the discourse revealed a real angst over a woman's place in public spaces and how such civic display could and would de-sex her. As Hall determines, such evidence shows us how this writer's "binarily constructed, fixed system of reference ... simply could not account for the complex ranges of social behaviors demonstrated by the women of the era; thus time and again, old gender discourses clash with fluid new performances and, at times, evoke a fearful admission of significant, even sensational, social change."[38] Like the Tenniel cartoon, this 1859 writer's attitude is indicative of a recurring reaction against forward-moving forces. Hence, we can expect to see a resistant narrative to such backlash in the images of women in interiors. They are *not* Martineau's single women of industry, for the most part, but married, middle-class, leisured women, the very ones with time on their hands to pursue education and to begin reforms. Their potential is ever-present in the images. Although the representations show women confined to interiors, in the real world many of them were increasingly trying to escape it or, at least, have a role both in and out of the home. But the act of desiring that escape places them outside the norm. Speaking of women writing autobiographies, for example, Jill Ker Conway says, "The mere act of sitting down to write an autobiography broke the code of female respectability, because doing so required a woman to believe that her direct experience, rather than her relationships with others, was what gave meaning to her life." It was a "conscious [act] of rebellion."[39] Some women are poised, such as Camille and Mariana, to commit just such an act. Gustave Flaubert's Emma Bovary, although she was ineffectual, would be one example of Carolyn Helibrun's similar claim that "some ... women unconsciously and indirectly take power over their lives by committing an 'outrageous act,' a social or sexual sin that frees them from the constraints of conventional society and its expectations...."[40] What I would like to suggest is that the upsurge of such imagery, coming as it does between 1850 and the early 1900s, reflects these ambivalent attitudes about women's increasing power in the public arena. It is no coincidence that we see these uneasy images at the same time that women in both England and France are helping to shape social policies through political and educational reform as well as in relation to suffrage and laws governing sexual disease.

What we need to realize is that this paradigm shift was one that took a single, isolated, disempowered woman and gave her the chance to work as part of a collective identity, an event which upset the system in place more than anything. Repeatedly, in the imagery and the debates over woman's place, there is a real concern to keep her separate from other women. Consider the importance of a collective gathering of women in France's history, in the example of the *petroleuses* of the Paris Commune of 1871, as just one example. Whether or not Parisian women on the barricades did set fire to Paris during the Commune, the cultural constructs blamed them, condemned them, sent them to prison and, in many cases, into exile.[41] A French woman had that memory fresh in her mind as an example of what the French government did to women who acted out. Then consider the implications of Annie Kenney's report on suffrage militancy in the early 20th century:

> The changed life into which most of us entered was a revolution in itself. No home-life, no one to
> say what we should do or what we should not do, no family ties; we were free and alone in a great

brilliant city, scores of young women scarcely out of their teens met together in a revolutionary movement, outlaws or breakers of laws, independent of everything and everybody, fearless and self-confident.[42]

In France, from the barricades to the *petroleuses* to the crowds of Emile Zola's novels, "the threat of the masses has been described in feminine terms," in the sense that, as Andreas Huyssen characterizes it, "the fear of the masses in this age of declining liberalism is always a fear of woman, a fear of nature out of control, a fear of the unconscious, of sexuality, of the loss of identity." Further, he asserts that mass culture and the masses are always gendered feminine while "high culture ... remains the privileged realm of male activities."[43]

How do we then contextualize this insistent imagery in light of these broad and sweeping changes in both countries? We must visualize how these women break free from their confines and relieve themselves of their *ennui*. As Emmeline Pethick-Lawrence explained of the British suffrage fight, "women of the upper, middle and working classes [realized] a new comradeship with each other. Neither class, nor wealth, nor education counted any more, only devotion to the common ideal. No longer did women feel loneliness or isolation or inhibition."[44]

The New Woman

Key for images of interiors, Peter Toohey contemplates that boredom is "a sign of worse things to follow unless there's a change in lifestyle."[45] It should provoke change, ironically, and should lead to a call for action. Inertia can only last so long. Toohey discusses cures for boredom: Music, exercise, and community. It is this last cure that seems to be the solution to these women's sense of emptiness and disgust—a move, a call to action, like that of the industrious, brave New Women in George Gissing's *Odd Women* (1893), one of many novels of the 1880s/1890s to explore changes in British law that allowed women more personal and economic freedoms. With more options, many women chose to live alone and to work; they were sometimes anti-marriage and often pro-suffrage and their new-found freedom was emblematized in the newest mode of transport, the bicycle. As New Women, they embraced educational reforms in the laws that began to liberate them from the choice of marriage versus starvation. Gissing's Rhoda Nunn and Mary Barfoot, as single women living together, run a small business, creating their own community of women and, while they are never bored, they still experience anguish over loss of love, loneliness, and ambivalent feelings regarding marriage that testify to an anxious debate over their potential sexual prowess.[46]

The dialogue over women's rights in France lagged behind that in England. French politicians were reluctant to change laws and wanted to continue to position women in the interior as its chief decoration. They operated under the Napoleonic Code; it essentially treated a woman as a minor, hence denying her rights of citizenship. She was to be ruled by a husband or, in the absence of marriage, by a male relative. She did not exist as a legal entity in her own right but rather came under the man's rule as coverture. Her role was restricted to the family yet she could not protect her children; all rights to children went to the father. Further, in cases of divorce, which was not liberalized until the 1880s, a husband could separate from his wife if she were adulterous but she could only separate from him if his mistress were living in the same domicile. While a woman could be imprisoned for adultery, the man only incurred a fine. Claire Goldberg Moses has argued that the chief reasons that French feminism, in its efforts to rectify the Code, lags behind its British counterpart is due to the continual upheaval of the political system in France from liberal to repressive, but also due to the cautious lessons of the French Revolution which meant that succeeding governments were reluctant to guarantee the rights of free expression, a disinclination which effectively delayed the development of a mass movement. And when we do find feminists at work, it is within the urban environment, particularly Paris, rather than in an organized and collective movement across the country as we find in England. One particular example of government repression was the official stance of the Second Empire, which prohibited open political debate at public meetings, a decree that shut down any attempt at feminist propaganda during its reign (1851–71).[47] Offen argues that the focus of feminist urgency shifted to England with the publication and wide circulation of John Stuart Mill's polemic *The Subjection of Women* (1869) as well as his vehement championing of women's rights in British Parliament in 1867 during the creation of the second Reform Bill, but, further, as mentioned earlier, by the suppression of radical feminist *petroleuses* who had been involved in the Paris Commune following the fall of the Second Empire which precipitated a bitterness towards French feminists under the newly formed Third Republic.[48] Offen suggests, further, that England was far ahead of everyone in Europe as early as the 1850s because they faced no revolution in 1848 as did the other European countries; as a result, women in England organized a lot earlier, Offen citing the key example of the formulation of the women-friendly National Association for the Promotion of Social Science (NAPSS) (1857) which snowballed into a number of women's organizations for the improvement of women's lives.[49] French feminists recognized and fumed over this French lag; in addition to issues already cited, Charles Sowerwine argues that it was due to the issues surrounding French Republicanism, while, in one study, Offen suggests that it was due to anti-feminist men.[50]

That said, the fits and starts of French politics in relation to a feminist movement finally began to gain some momentum under the Third Republic, during which time the Camille Sée Law gave women better access to education (1880) and the government liberalized the divorce laws with the passing of the Naquet Law (1884).[51] Despite these advances, however, republican discourse fought hard to maintain the association of woman with the domestic realm in order to exclude her from political suffrage.[52] In fact, this dialogue continued in the French press through the end of the century.[53] But French feminists themselves were divided on the issue of suffrage during the Third Republic, in their first French Congress for Women's Rights in 1878, striking it from the agenda which, some of them argued, would have put female votes in the hands of clericals and monarchists which would have jeopardized the goals of the Republic.[54]

Alongside this discourse was that of the New Woman; she began to appear in the French journals a little later than in England though, between 1889 and 1898. The chief French worry was that this New Woman would threaten "the essential divisions ordering bourgeois life: public from private, work from family, production from reproduction,"[55] just as she had already begun to do earlier in England. French feminists fought against a "prejudice of domesticism" among detractors, who sought to deny women a right to work outside the home,[56] hence, in part, why we see so much discomfort over this New Woman. In fact, the French perceived this New Woman as an import from the Anglo-American world, where women's rights were rapidly moving forward and where the press positioned the New Woman as the emblem of that change, no matter how inaccurate that reading was.[57] Yet, while the New Woman novel in England focused on a woman's emancipation based on these new laws, in France the New Woman novel emerged later (1894–1914) and it focused, more often than not, on issues of happiness in love.[58]

Some of the French feminists' demands were not nearly as radical as were those of the English or American feminists. Léon Richer and Marie Deraismes, supported the ideal of the mother-teacher (*mères educatrices* or *mères institutrices*). Together they were opposed to suffrage but, later, Deraismes moved towards suffrage, aligning her more with the radical feminist, Hubertine Auclert. Initially, the more conservative feminists had two major goals:

> [T]hey sought a broadly-based solidarity among women of different social classes, which entailed, to a large extent, a moralizing crusade by wealthy women to teach infant care to poor women and to aid widows, orphans, and prostitutes [and] they wanted to reform the Civil Code to give married women some control over family finance. The existing code relegated a married woman to the status of dependent minor, requiring that she give over to her husband all her financial resources.[59]

Hence, these women were working from within the home to improve their situation there, rather than emphasizing a desire to move into the public arena. Despite their more

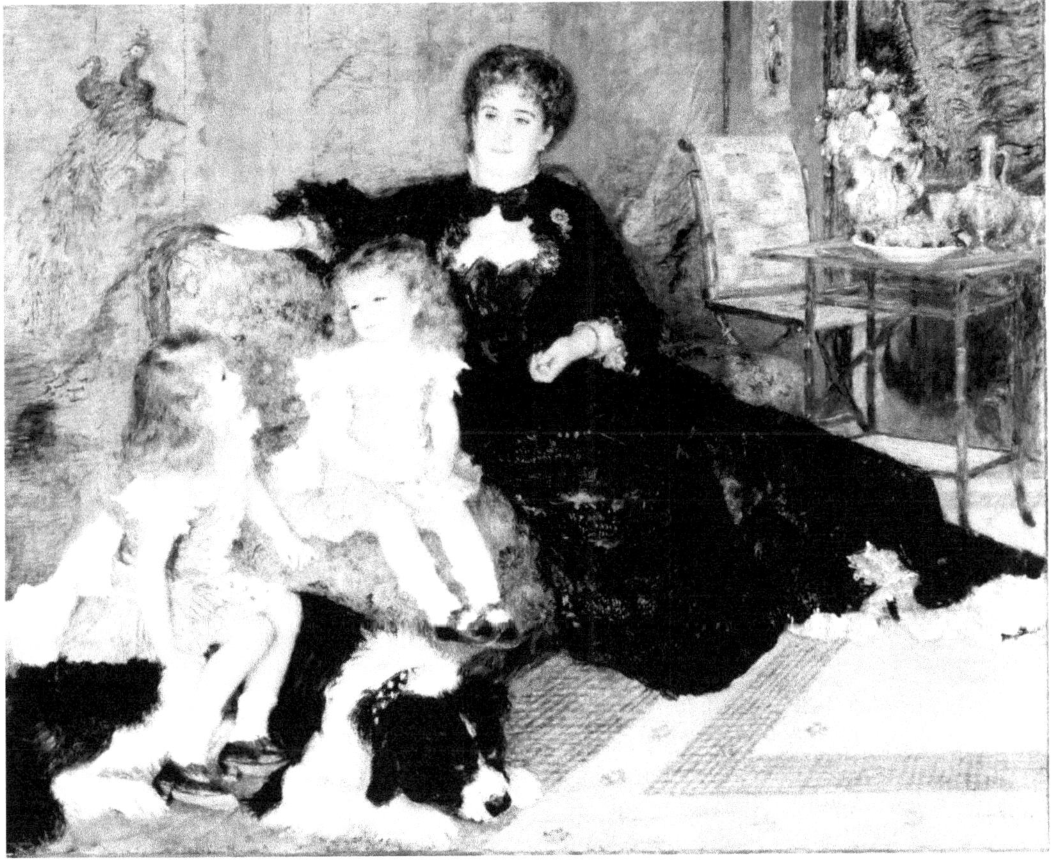

Figure 6. **Auguste Renoir (1841–1919),** *Madame Georges Charpentier (Marguerite-Louise Lemonnier, 1848–1904) and her Children, Georgette-Berthe (1872–1945) and Paul-Emile-Charles (1875–1895),* **1878. Oil on canvas. Metropolitan Museum of Art, NY. Catharine Lorillard Wolfe Collection, Wolfe Fund, 1907. Acc. No. 07.122.**

conservative goals, the French feminist movement became associated with the perceived transgressive demands of the amazonian New Woman.[60] Of course, French women's increasing access to education also fueled this threat; the French government wanted to wrest women's education from the Church but was only interested in educating them at the secondary school level. They insisted that women not be trained for professions but rather to situate themselves in the home. This stance was partly grounded in the fact that France was a Catholic country so the influence of Christianity there was stronger there than it was in England. The historian Adeline Daumard explains:

> The situation of women seemed hard to some of them, but it was accepted as an inevitable fact of the human condition. The influence of Christianity, as it was then understood, only reinforced this belief. Brought up to be married, locked within the confines of the family, not being permitted the collective responsibilities of civic life or even professional life, most women could have had only limited horizons.[61]

In this regard, Stephen Hause and Anne R. Kenney argue, based on statistics that granted women the vote in local elections around the world, that suffragism was thriving in Protestant countries by the turn of the century, whereas France was impeded by religious doctrine.[62] French women's struggles sat apposite to advances in Protestant countries "where individualism and the acceptance of individual rights grew naturally from a religious tradition that emphasized direct, individual access to the Bible, individual interpretation and investigation, and individual conscience as a guide to action."[63]

An even greater fear, however, was the implication of the declining birthrate in France in the 1890s in relation to the baby boom in Germany; French officials worried that there would not be enough conscripts for military service to match those in Germany, its chief enemy.[64] Even when French women did gain suffrage, the politicians still aired concerns for their reproductive role, instituting state-funded maternity care, among other benefits.[65] Simultaneously there was a debate about woman's potential power as mothers coming from the feminist groups; maternalist feminists in France and England argued for women's differences from men as being a chief reason to include them in the sociopolitical decision-making processes of their countries, an argument strengthened by increases in population and women's growing contributions to the economy.[66]

These circumstances present a picture of how and why women were being kept in the home in France in a way that could not exist in England. And we can expect works of art to reinforce this ideology or to comment on it; the Victorians in particular were accustomed to moralistic art that sought to improve the viewer or that protested against women's circumstances in heavily narrative dramas while French examples tended to be more understated, less about commentary than reportage.[67] French statistics bear out this idea; the percentage of women wage earners in France went from 23.7 in 1872 to 26.6 in 1891,[68] hardly a huge jump or a significant threat. And the occupational arenas where we find women working are not those of an educated, middle-class woman like the ones about whom the French are most concerned. Women's working populations dominated in the realms of personal and domestic service, textiles, apparel manufacturing, agriculture, and commerce, the largest percentage ironically being in personal and domestic service, that is, again in the home.[69] But, between 1866 and 1906, we witness a shift in France with a decline of women in domestic service whereas their numbers in banks and commercial establishments rose.[70] By comparison, statistics in England, discussed earlier, seem more acute and point to the fact that there is a bigger shift there than in France in terms of changes in women's social and economic situation.

That England and America were ahead of France in their activism is also evidenced in the fact that the French feminist writer, Leon Richer, modeled his own feminist society, the *Association pour les Droits des Femmes,* after the women's movement in those countries.[71] While French women did protest and agitate for changes to the laws as early as the 1860s, it is very telling that French women were not enfranchised until 1944, much later than most other countries in Europe and Scandinavia.[72] Such a history suggests that domestic life in England from 1860 onward was an ideology rather than a destiny for all women; in France, while women did fight for their own rights, they seemed to uphold the ideology as their destiny; that, or the cultural forces were too strong for them.[73]

In the context of the threat of the New Woman, a French woman artist who embraced a similar community in France to that in England, was Berthe Morisot. Katheleen Adler and Tamar Garb note that Morisot's letters are full of information about working with the Impressionist group on their exhibitions, something Morisot found very satisfying. She "hint[s] at the sense of community" she felt alongside her colleagues, one denied to her sister Edmé, formerly an artist but who gave it up when she married; she often lamented, in reading her sister's letters, how connected and lively Berthe's world was by comparison to her own.[74] While many of Morisot's images show bored, listless women in interiors (including her sister), her own circumstances suggest she moved more freely and, because she had a career and connections, she would never suffer from boredom. However, the images, such as Monet's of Camille, suggests a situation akin to what Toohey argues for the phenomenon of leisure time which was meant to be "impractical, amoral, pleasurable and sociable. What does all this have to do with boredom? It looks very much as if the current notion of leisure, because it's so tied in with work, is doomed to generate boredom." What might propel these women to leave the hearth and cross the threshold? Toohey explains that "boredom can encourage creativity. Boredom may drive thinkers and artists to question the accepted and to search for change."[75] Morisot was an instigator of that change, but many of her works still belong to this group of inactive women in interiors. Later I will discuss some of her ambivalence and how it relates to her imagery. Here it is important to note that her own world did not mirror the one she often chose to represent.

With regards to Morisot's situation, Ruth Iskin has taken on the challenge of finding the New Woman in French Impressionist works in particular. She concludes that we *do* see the New Woman in some of Cassatt's and Morisot's works and that, they themselves, as successful Parisian artists negotiating the public terrain, exemplify this New Woman. Thus, she, as with other scholars of the New Woman, see the real individual as much more multidimensional than the caricature would imply.[76] And, yet, Cassatt and Morisot were both cosseted, upper-class women with significant family and financial support; but Iskin observes of the French woman worker who she perceives as a New Woman: "While the work place for many women domestics was in a bourgeois household, for those women who worked in Parisian department stores, boutiques, cafés and café-concerts, the public spaces of consumption were increasingly a site of work."[77] But can we really call such women of the lower classes "New Women"? The term is invariably discussed in relation to a middle-class woman escaping the leisured prison to embrace the world, or an unmarried, educated woman who must make her own way. Some contemporary reports, in England, would say the shop woman was not of the middle classes; shop women, in particular, were only required to have an elementary school education. There is some slippage here, as Lee Holcombe explains, since shop assistants often believed themselves to be of middle-class respectability, but public opinion differed: "The upper and middle classes considered shop workers to be about on a level with the servant class, while the working classes sneered at their pretensions to respectability."[78] In some quarters, the consensus is that the New Woman would hardly be likely to be an entertainer or shop girl, but rather to choose meaningful work that would match her new education and her class standing. Such employed shop women co-existed with a burgeoning group of another kind of public woman in both England and France: Sidsel Maria Sondersgaard argues that, while women in France were becoming more visible in public by the 1870s, they were largely *"consumeuse"*; that is, fashionable women who knew where to shop for the best clothing and accessories. If they were anywhere in the French city, it was in pursuit of perfecting their beauty through such consumerism. While there are exceptions to this rule, the Parisians especially clung to this model of womanhood.[79] This view is explicitly spelled out in Emile Bayard's *L'Illustration* image of 1889, showing a fashionable *consumeuse* buying gloves, entitled *At the Bon Marché*. Such women interact with the shop girls and shop men behind the counter, the latter acting as a recognizable barrier

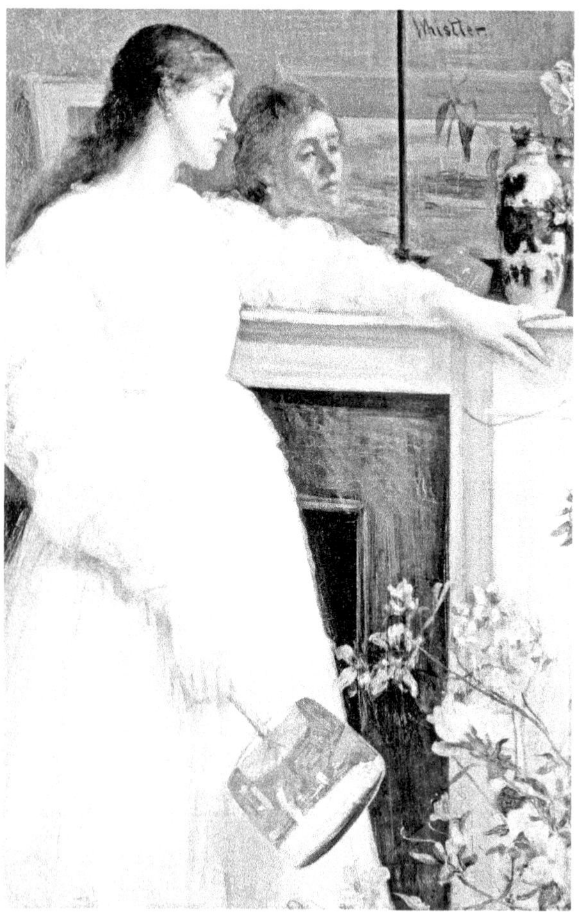

to their own consideration of such menial work. Yet this *consumeuse*, to whom I will return in the discussion of the urban environment, wielded considerable buying power and emblemized a shift away from domesticity in her increasing appearance within the shopping districts.[80]

Alongside this example of the wealthy woman who, even in public, reflected her husband's buying power, and the working woman, whether she be a shop girl, an industrial worker, or otherwise, there were French artists who wanted to maintain the status quo of the separate spheres and who evoked pronatalist sentiments. For example, Søndergaard examines Renoir's *Madame George Charpentier and her Children, Georgette-Berthe and Paul-Emile-Charles,* 1878 (fig. 6) as a pronatalist work that reinforced the necessity of woman as mother and wife rather than as individual. Here she is represented as both "the *grande dame* and the home's maternal center."[81] But the focus and attention that British and French culture pay to the New Woman provides evidence that both cultures were more concerned with controlling the middle-class woman than the lower-class one. A single, lower class woman

Figure 7. James McNeill Whistler (1834–1903), *Symphony in White No. 2: The Little White Girl,* 1864. Oil on canvas. Bequeathed by Arthur Studd 1919. ©Tate, London 2016.

worked, whether she was married or unmarried; the statistics quoted here bear this view out. Though her economic circumstances meant she had to work, her middle-class counterpart's position was otherwise; to work would be to bring shame to her bourgeois household. This position was further reinforced by the publications of Jules Simon, particularly his *L'Ouvrière (Woman Worker)*, in its fourth edition by 1862 and its seventh by 1872, due in part to the author's position as academic philosopher, moralist, liberal politician and future Prime Minister of the Third Republic. He expressed deep regret that the progress of industrialization interfered with the ideal of wife and mother.[82]

In this scenario, does the woman at the window look at the New Woman with trepidation? Jealousy? Envy? Is she destined to watch the world go by without a chance to participate in it? The attention given to the New Woman suggests a patriarchal nerve was struck hard. If the public could not control her burgeoning power, it could at least deflect it through caricature of her inappropriateness for marriage. Angelique Richardson and Chris Willis suggest that the stereotyping of the New Woman in this way acted as

> a strategy of control, aimed at containing the threat they posed to the status quo. The bicycling Amazon and ugly bluestocking of caricature were more immediately accessible and memorable figures than women concerned with social and political change, and thus were often used as a way of obscuring the latter's goals. Campaigners agitated on diverse and sometimes mutually contradictory reforms.... Journalistic exploitation of the more visual of these issues, such as rational dress, tended to downplay, or deny, the significance of more weighty issues.[83]

And, in this same way, perhaps the proliferation of imagery of women ensconced in interiors served to validate the status quo out of a fear of middle-class women's increasingly odd numbers (too many to pair off). The caricature of the New Woman responds to the accepted image of the appropriate woman in the private space, yet such a woman is often agitated, suggesting that she is closer to the New Woman and the possibility of greater freedoms the latter offers; both kinds of representations suggest an unease reflective of the fact that both the wearied woman and the New Woman are a threat to the establishment, no longer containable in an outmoded form.

The Monets in London

Claude Monet and his wife Camille lived in London from 1870 to 1871, during which time he painted *Meditation* (fig. 1). Monet may have been influenced (and Camille in turn) by their exposure to other expatriates in England at the time. John House has argued that the painting reflects Monet's visual and actual dialogue with the American expatriate James McNeill Whistler who, similarly, was doing paintings in which he encased his women in interior spaces with wistful expressions such as in *Symphony in White No. 2: The Little White Girl* of 1864 (fig. 7) or his more dejected *Symphony in White no. 3* of 1865–67 (fig. 8).[84]

Monet and Whistler's friendship began around 1865[85] so Monet may have known these works. Some scholars have seen Whistler's paintings as examples of pent up sexuality, ripe for the picking.[86] They could also represent a real sense of entrapment; the model in both scenes (she reclines in a resigned pose in no. 3) is Whistler's live-in mistress, Joanna ("Jo") Hiffernan, a woman who had already transgressed the respected barriers of female sexual propriety confined to marriage. In fact, *The Little White Girl* rings somewhat false in this context since she wears a gold wedding band. Aileen Tsui acknowledges

Whistler's often taunting behavior in giving his works aesthetic titles, ones readily absorbed by French audiences but which evoked different responses from British ones "playing upon mid–Victorian preoccupations with moralizing narratives about female sexuality."[87] But in either case, kept mistress or wife, she wears "a filmy, white at-home dress."[88] Hence, she is more suitably dressed for home, not the outside world, such a flimsy gown proving very inadequate for the dirty streets of London.

Could these works be cautionary tales to the men's respective partners? Do not cross my threshold for fear of indiscretion? Such works, coming at such a volatile time in women's political history, would seem to suggest not just reflections of the angel in the house (and Whistler's inversion of her) but rather of her demise. Hence, the reason we see images of women tied to the home in such seemingly suffocating images might be because they are nostalgic images, seeking to turn back time.[89] If we doubt that our artists Monet and Whistler were concerned with such struggles and such changes in women's lives, we need only look at Whistler's *Harmony in Green and Rose: The Music Room*, ca. 1860–61 (fig. 9) in which, even before he launches into his *White Girl* series, David Park Curry argues that he contemplates the changing roles of women in his life, contrasting his sister Deborah Haden, the "angel" reflected in the mirror above the hearth, with a more modern woman, Isabella Boott, in black riding attire, and against the more innocent young daughter, Annie, dressed in white and seated at a window "poised between convention and freedom."[90]

Further, he suggests that the awkwardness of the composition, the figures compressed in a confining space seemingly on top of each other, "reminds us that, for many, it was an awkward age: the artist's niece would grow up in a world of shifting values characterized by unprecedented social and economic change."[91] Such a reading suggests that Whistler was playing with irony in his title since the relationship between the three women, formally and psychologically, is anything but harmonious. This disjuncture is further made evident by the contrast between the interior in which we find these women. The music room, the title Whistler uses, refers both to the abstract arrangement of the color scheme and to the music room as a place of harmony, but it also underscores the obvious discord between the two women and the girl.

Yet this work implies more about a woman's uncomfortable situation in Victorian England: The formal compression of the work suggests the stifling lives of a mother and child as against that of this ominous intruder, dressed in black and carrying a riding whip whose point simultaneously pierces and bifurcates the book Annie is reading. Do we align Annie with Isabella and the outside world of possibility

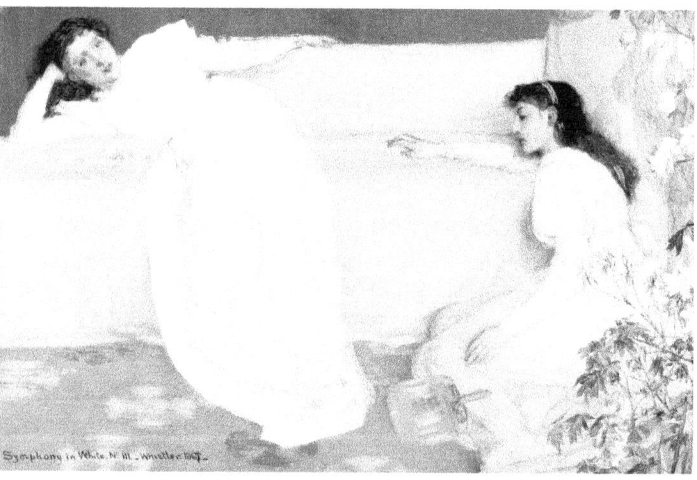

Figure 8. James McNeill Whistler (1834–1903), *Symphony in White No. 3,* 1865–67. Oil on canvas. The Barber Institute of Art, University of Birmingham. Acc. No. 39.29.

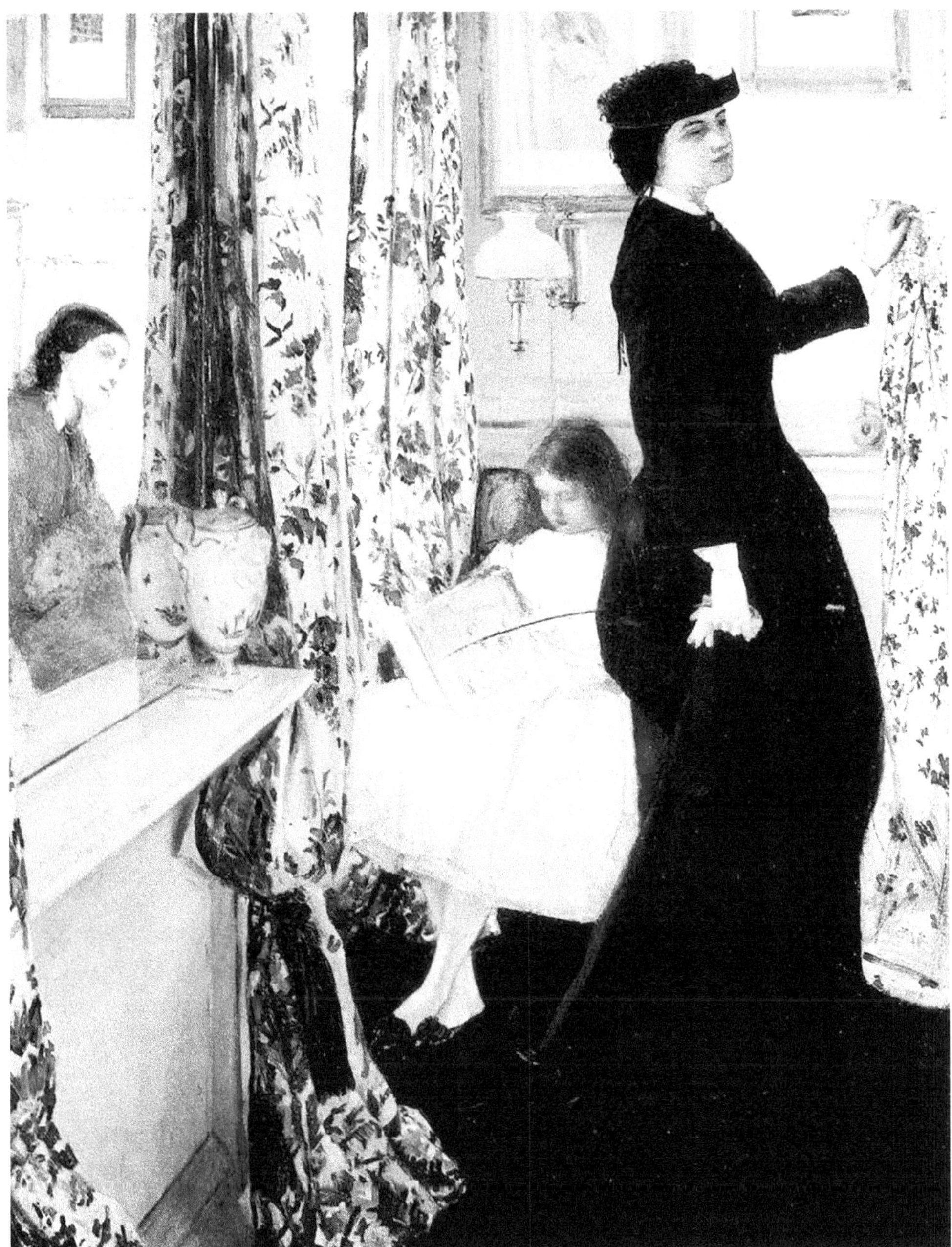

Figure 9. James McNeill Whistler (1834–1903), *Harmony in Green and Rose: The Music Room,* c. 1860–61. Oil on canvas. Freer Gallery of Art and Arthur M. Sackler Gallery, Smithsonian Institution, Washington, D.C.: Gift of Charles Lang Freer, F1917.234a-b.

and what it might offer this daughter who has her head in a book, itself a symbol of the wider world? Both of them are in the actual space of the picture while the mother appears only as a reflection. It remarks on those modern ambiguities and the paths available for young Annie. Is the mother's world fading away, or is Annie destined to repeat her mother's fate? While Whistler provides no space between Isabella and Annie, he presents a striking formal distinction between Annie's white dress and Isabella's dramatic black costume as if to suggest that the two worlds available to Annie are markedly contrasting.

We should connect the motif of this mantelpiece and its mirror in *Harmony* with that pictured in Whistler's *Symphony in White no. 2: The Little White Girl*. Like Deborah, Jo exists in a reflection; the mantle is a key symbol in the angel's arsenal of home comforts yet in both paintings Whistler suggests that it is a compromised location. Jo clings to this hearth, her melancholic face reflected back to her in the mirror above the mantle. She is waiting; is she waiting for change? Is she impatient because she is hemmed in by the dictates of men? Looking at the expressions on his women's faces in the two *Symphony* compositions, Whistler's women appear despondent if not suicidal. Do they desire to cross over? It is telling, in this context, that we find women in interiors not only isolated, but also sequestered from each other, few such images including more than one woman. When they do, as in Whistler's *Symphony in White No. 3* or *Harmony*, they are psychologically separated from each other.

Similarly, in Monet's portrait of Camille, we can see how he addresses such complexities that subvert the more traditional French codes. Writers up through the 1890s insisted that female portraits should be about a man's desire and should imply a male viewer and *his* sexuality[92]; we do not sense that exchange in Monet's portrait of Camille any more than we do in Whistler's white girls. The inner turmoil of Camille's experience, transposed from Paris from which she is temporarily exiled, to the flats of modern Kensington's artists' district of London, is not something that her husband can easily hide. She has to live by attitudes such as that of French art critic Théophile Thoré; writing in 1866 of Alfred Stevens' subjects of women in interiors, he claimed that they were no more than one more ornament in a well-appointed apartment: "They lead the lives of *'femme du qualité.'* Smelling flowers, examining knickknacks, putting on gloves or removing jewelry, reading or writing a note, growing impatient or dreaming—such is the existence of these beautiful women."[93] His observation about "growing impatient or dreaming," is symptomatic of Camille's malaise in the Monet London painting. Thoré is dismissive of this woman, but one look at Camille should make him do a double take. A woman's emancipation from hearth and home was on the horizon and Camille's dejected abandon of her book (seat of knowledge and emancipation) would seem to suggest the fruitlessness of a French woman longing for something the British women have almost within their grasp.[94]

But what of other European images, which are almost bone-chilling in their isolation of women,[95] such as Zacharie Astruc's 1886 *Parisian Interior* (location unknown) which shows a woman in a posture suggestive of strain, if not total apoplexy, as she writhes within a chair in her interior? Are they protest images about women's fate? Or are they about men's overarching concerns to keep women in their place? Or some ambivalent mixture that mirrors the mixed messages of the second half of the 19th-century about women's proper role in society?[96] Astruc's image is over determined in its positioning of the inactive woman who, while she wrestles with her confinement, is presented as yet another fixture in an over-decorated space. It is the European absence of narrative that creates her bored expression, although feminists would say she is full of narratives in her head. We should also consider, in this domestic context, the extreme importance the French placed on the home, although the Victorians were not immune to it either. As Sidlauskas explains, "Members of the bourgeois class were anxious to define both their new status and their newly conceptualized interior lives through an expressive, and legible, relation to their intimate surroundings."[97] But conversely, Iskin argues that women were increasingly visible in late 19th-century visual culture, such as posters, and that the Gouncourt Brothers bemoaned the real-life entrance of "women, children, households, and families" into the Parisian cafés as early as 1860.[98] That begs the question, though, of why we see such a persistent representation of isolated women in interiors up through the 1900s?

Images of men in interiors, such as Gustave Caillebotte's *Young Man at His* Window (fig. 10) gives precedent to the Parisian street and the man's confrontation with the outside, his posture with legs akimbo suggesting his command of what he surveys. Rodolphe Rapetti notes that Caillebotte reverses the usual motif in such works, focusing on "the transition from private to public space...." [99] Other artists who emulate Caillebotte such as the Norwegian Hans Heyerdahl in his *At the Window*, 1881 (National Museum of Art, Architecture and Design, Oslo) while imitating Caillebotte's use of the balcony railing, also suggests some of Cassatt's images of women on balconies. Like Cassatt's *Susan on the Balcony*, c. 1883 (Corcoran Gallery of Art, Washington, D.C.), for example, Heyerdahl shows a young woman confined within the interior space, dejected, holding a book in her lap as she daydreams, looking out over a city scene but unable to be a part of it.[100] What such examples suggest is the difference between the way the 19th century imagined its men and their prerogatives versus what those same men demanded from images of women. As Tamar Garb explains, based on the writings of the art critic Camille Mauclair as late as 1899:

> Whereas a portrait of a man was a psychological document through which the motivations and actions of the sitter were conveyed, his place in society stipulated, and his relationship to the broader culture communicated, a portrait of a woman was less a portrayal of an individual than a screen for the projected sensibilities and passions of the spectator.[101]

I contend that such French examples are not protest images about women's fate but rather seem to address men's overarching concerns to keep women in their place. I have suggested, also, that such images are nostalgic. It is clear that they respond to the hesitancy about women entering the public arena.

A Brief History of Boredom and Modernity

In this context, the word "boredom" came into use alongside of this disconcerted angel's appearance, Charles Dickens the first to address it in *Bleak House* (1852–53)[102]; his character Lady Dedlock suffers from it, but in her case it masks a dark, sexual past. Her boredom deflects a longing for a lost love; Patricia Meyer Spacks characterizes boredom in this context as suggesting "disruptions of desire: the inability to desire or to have desire fulfilled."[103] For Lady Dedlock, as with the representations of women in interiors, we witness what Haskell Bernstein means when he argues that boredom is that state of waiting for something exciting to happen.[104] Add to that Spacks' assessment of the treatment of boredom in 19th-century British male novels. We can group Dickens with her examination of other male novelists who "typically stress the direct connection between a decadent and corrupt society and the boredom of its participants."[105]

Spacks examines how this concern for a proper occupation for middle-class women

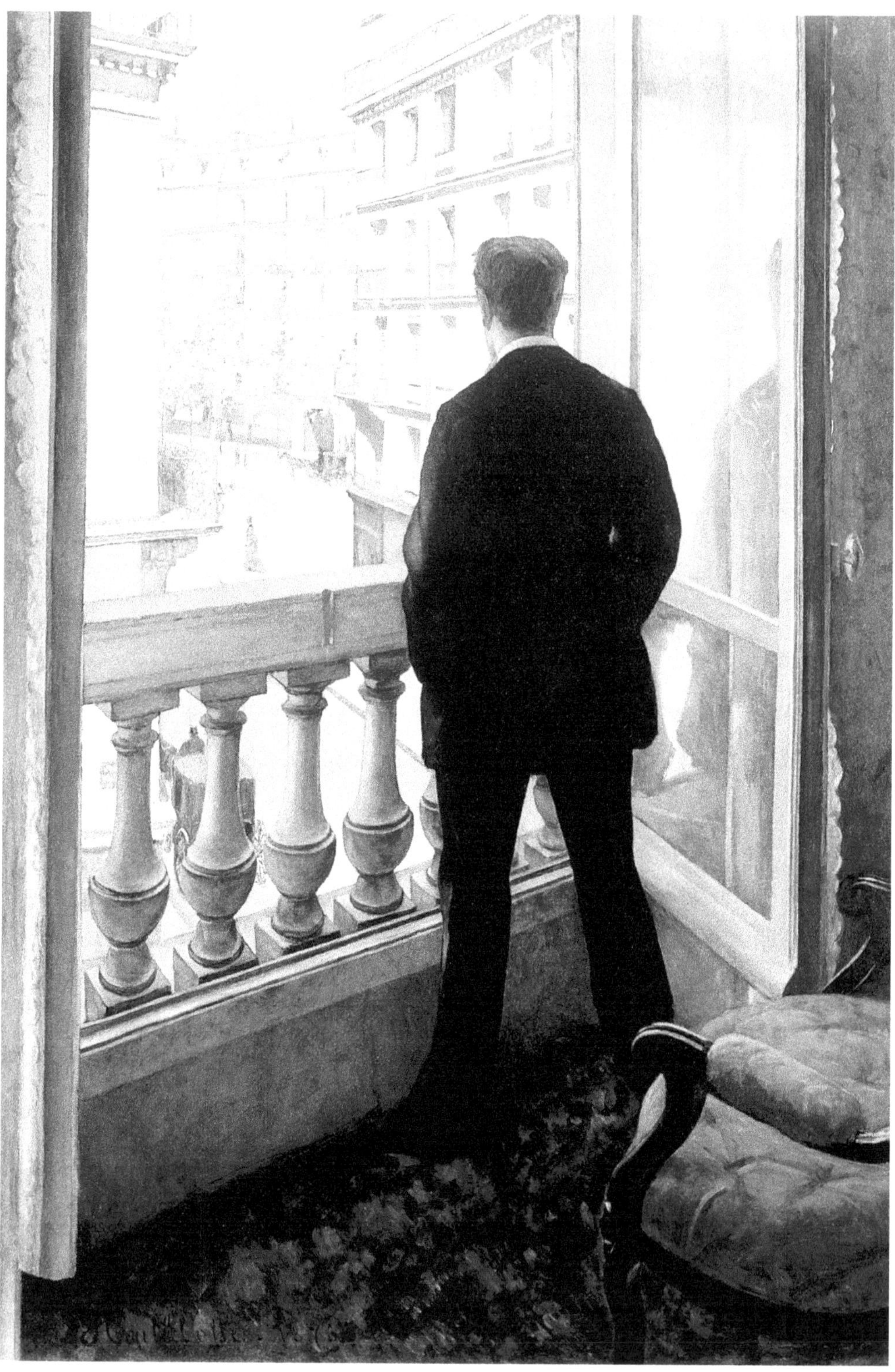

Figure 10. Gustave Caillebotte (1848–1894), *Young Man at His Window*, 1875. Oil on canvas. Private Collection/Bridgeman Images.

is also present in the works of Victorian women novelists who search, through their characters, for legitimate affronts to boredom such as some useful occupation. These novelists' concerns are similar to those of Sarah Stickney Ellis, who warns in her 1842 *Daughters of England*, of the need for middle-class women to have "wholesome and determined occupation."[106] Putting together the messages of male and female novelists of the time period, in order to dissipate boredom and the temptations that it portends, women must play an active part in their society. Hence, the representations here reflect that contemporary attitude; the visceral sense of listlessness, discomfort, and malaise were cultural markers that addressed the woman problem.

More complex readings of a 19th-century woman's boredom stem from Spacks' further observations that the state of boredom is both a blessing and a curse, an effect of the rise of modernity and individualism, a time during which leisure, particularly women's leisure and the pursuit of happiness, were considered a right and a responsibility.[107] Necessarily, then, a woman of leisure such as Camille Monet, was to accept boredom as her lot. Spacks asserts of this state of mind: "It implies an embracing sense of irritation and unease. It reflects a state of affairs in which the individual is assigned ever more importance and ever less power."[108] Hence, what the leisured woman gains in position and status, she loses in terms of her own agency. Yet, Spacks' examination of boredom's centrality to the lives of characters in Victorian novels is proof of boredom's tangible existence and of a cultural awareness of its limitations, ones similarly reflected in the imagery of women in interiors. We also find evidence of its existence in French 19th-century writings, a chief case in point being Flaubert's *Madame Bovary*. Ironically, her boredom was probably due, in part, to her overactive imagination, one she cultivated through reading. As Kathryn Brown explains:

> Giving its name to the disease, "Bovarysme," the model of reading in Flaubert's novel epitomized a pathological condition in which an individual's connection to reality was progressively and irrevocably diminished. Reading becomes the catalyst for self-abandon and erosion of the physical, emotional, and intellectual disciplines that sustained a woman's role in the domestic sphere.[109]

What made this motif of reading so threatening, was that it gave Madame Bovary a kind of female agency that was beyond the control of a desiring gaze.[110] Further, her reading of novels, poetry and newspapers not only contributed to her dissatisfaction with her lot, but also allowed her to participate vicariously in events and places beyond her narrowly circumscribed, provincial world.[111]

Like the fictional Madame Bovary, many French women were dissatisfied with their lot. One 19th-century administrative report from the French schools may serve as example. It explains that "the instructor [male] uses his wife as an associate. This helps her, giving her an interest both domestic and social and ... liberates her from that emptiness, that boredom, that need for distraction which torments so many women, even in the most humble ranks of society."[112] In fact, the woman at the window as a motif is closely paralleled by that of the woman reader; both respond to this issue of boredom, brought on by a lack of access to activity, intellectual or otherwise. As Kathryn Brown argues for the appearance of the representation of the woman reader, her "acquisition of literacy contributed to women's slow, but increasing, participation in public culture, facilitated women's self-expression as consumers and producers of cultural products, enhanced public demands for female suffrage, and spurred access to the professions."[113] Hence, we often see, as in the case of Camille, a bored woman with a book in her hands, suggesting that the world beyond that glass is available to her in print if not in real life. That said, the certain knowledge she gains from such reading contributes to her restlessness and longing. Camille does not make herself available to the male gaze; unlike some French paintings in which her reading is a pretext for the male viewer's delectation, signified by her downcast expression and often languorous pose,[114] Camille's pose is one of defiance, almost disgust. She shifts her gaze outward, not down, suggesting her contemplation of the outside world rather than the presumed male viewer.

Can Whistler's Jo and Monet's Camille be both bored *and* full of *ennui?* Spacks marks a distinction between the terms "boredom" and "*ennui*," believing that "*ennui* is closer to *acedia* … the ancient state of elevated melancholy" and hence distinct from "the ostensibly less important, less complex mental state of … the bored housewife. Historically, *ennui* was a condition in which its sufferers took a certain amount of pride" and some French artists even went so far as to determine that it was "an affectation of the British temperament that was calculated to hide strong emotion," a kind of "studied camouflage."[115] Certainly these women exhibit this "elevated melancholy" but would also be practiced in the art of "studied camouflage." Whether a British or French lady, they would have learned to control if not to hide their emotions. These women had so much potential; they sat or stood at a threshold that was both literal and symbolic, about to launch into a world where they would be, by the next century, on their way to the vote and hence real representation as citizens. The obvious misery of the women we meet in such paintings as *Meditation* speaks to what Toohey terms conventional definitions of boredom; the first being caught in circumstances that it is impossible to escape; the second belonging to the realm of repetitive activities, totally predictable and without excitement or variability.[116] Further, he acknowledges the existence of a kind of existential boredom. In this regard, David Londey encourages us to consider that boredom "might not exist at all. Better … to think of boredom as a grab bag of a term covering emotions such as frustration, surfeit, depression, disgust, indifference, apathy, and that feeling of being trapped or confined."[117] What unites Camille with Millais's Mariana and Whistler's women is a kind of world weariness that speaks to the above definitions, one borne of considerable frustration. The kind of "lambent tedium" that Guy de Maupassant's salon hostess and coquette, Madame de Burne experiences in *Alien Hearts* (1890) echoes Camille's disgust; casting aside her book with dismissive sideways glance suggests the same kind of angered dismissal of the world as Maupassant's madame who has to endure "long evenings with stifled yawns and heavy eyelids…."[118] Despite the years that separate Millais's painting from those of Monet and Whistler illustrated here, they all emit a dissatisfied mood, one reinforced by the rooms in which their women are constricted but to which they are not resigned; we sense their inner turmoil as a resistance narrative, both to their inability to escape and to the predictability of their circumstances.

As stated earlier, Spacks argues that boredom is a modern phenomenon, borne of leisure. Coupled in the 19th-century with the age of doubt and consequent growth in secularization, it created a rise of interest in inner experience as opposed to living one's life according to the dictates of a higher power.[119] Hence, we can position these *ennui* images in the context of a seismic shift that stressed considerable introspection. Monet, Millais and Whistler's interiors show such mediation (indeed, it is Monet's title), a feeling of isolation, even alienation, from both the interior environment and from the larger world, perhaps reflective then of this paradigm shift from the outward authority to a more personal one.

Burgeoning Sexuality; Boundaries Passed

In viewing these women's boredom as emblematic of a resistance narrative, we have to consider the certain knowledge that women were becoming a threat to men's professional monopoly, but further, that unmarried and married women, working women and women activists alike could not be respectably contained sexually. For example, Toohey asserts that "melancholy or existential boredom is a Gallic obsession" citing Flaubert's Madame Bovary as a chief sufferer who distracts herself with meaningless affairs.[120] How close is Madame Bovary to Millais's *Mariana*? Is she the obverse example? Shefer suggests Mariana portrays Christina Rossetti's rejection of vain pleasures of the flesh, while Madame Bovary throws herself headlong into them, seemingly without thinking, due to a sense of desperate boredom, loneliness, and a restless sexual appetite that her husband cannot satiate. An unnatural mother, a neglectful and unfaithful wife, she seeks excitement. It is not surprising that we find bored women in the visual and literary culture of the second half of the 19th-century since Europe was the key site for a fascination with such boredom at this time, borne out of the shift to the individual and his/her learning and experience of the eighteenth century.[121] Of Madame Bovary's resentment of this static state, Toohey argues, her "rule breaking is aimed at escape and the rules she broke were sexual."[122]

Although not nearly as heated as Madame Bovary's sexual awakening, a more conventional reading of Mariana than Shefer presents comes from its quotation from Shakespeare's *Measure for Measure*, Mariana's "dreariness" a response to her suitor's rejection

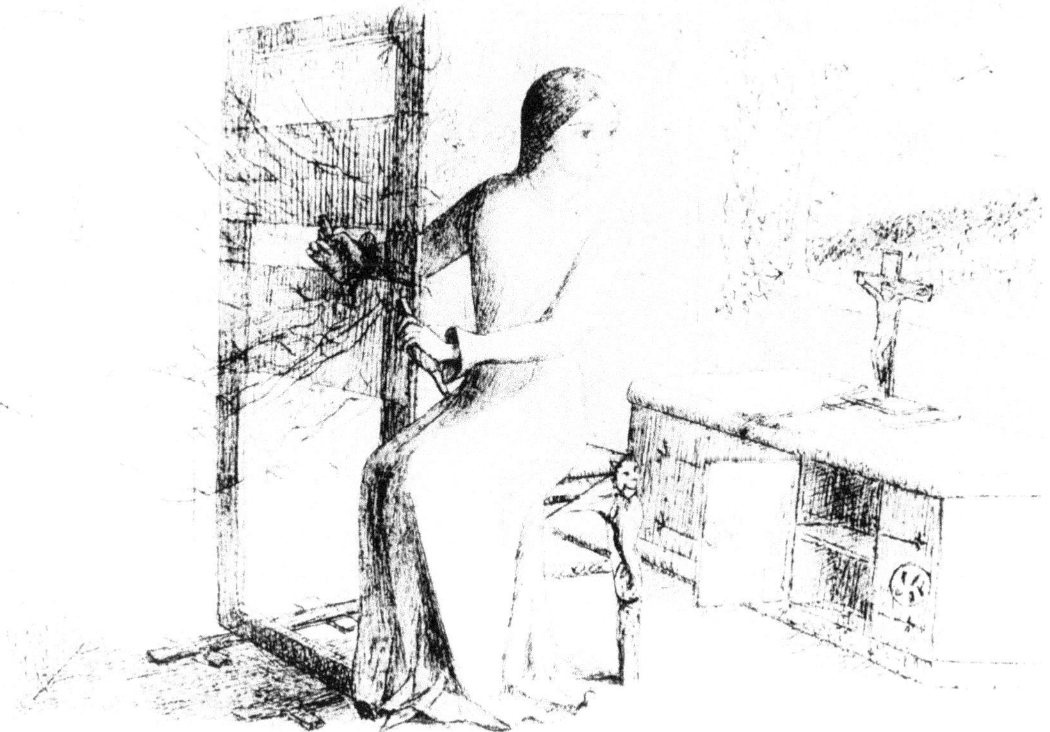

Figure 11. Elizabeth Siddal (1829–1862), *The Lady of Shalott*, 1853. Ink on paper. Private Collection. Photo © The Maas Gallery, London/Bridgeman Images.

because her dowry was lost in a shipwreck, suggesting her powerful sense of desire for reunification with her intended.[123] But that does not exclude Shefer's interpretation; in both cases she is left with no possibility of a world of love and sexuality. Instead her world becomes one of "baleful chronicity."[124] But at the heart of such women's experience, some psychoanalysts such as Otto Fenichel would argue, is an anger and hostility; instead of allowing such emotions to eat away at them, women deflect those emotions into the more banal state of boredom[125] which suggests a certain amount of agency. Although it seems more to our 21st-century eyes as a kind of passive-aggressive path, such action could be construed not only as a coping mechanism but also as a new system of self-control over one's sexuality, if not self-preservation. But the tensions these women reveal are indicators of changes on the other side of this cherished, protected threshold.

This moment, for both Jo and Camille, is reflective of the passive role of women and their angst over that passivity. Such imagery relates to that of Alfred, Lord Tennyson's poetic creation, the Lady of Shalott, who we see pictured in an 1853 drawing by Elizabeth Siddal (fig. 11) and in painted versions by William Holman Hunt, 1886–1905 (Wadsworth Atheneaum, Hartford, CT, and Manchester Art Gallery). These images show a woman imprisoned, chained to her embroidery frame, cursed to look at the world only through a reflection. In these renditions, the woman chooses to look out and, as she does so, her work (symbol of her domesticity) starts to loosen. Both images are sexually troubling, for the Lady's world is beginning to come undone due to her desire for Lancelot, who she sees in the mirror. These works take the images of Mariana, Camille and Jo a step further; beyond meditation to action, and hence suggest the fears of the Victorian era about how the social fabric will unravel if a woman forgets her place literally.[126] These works further suggest that, as Liana F. Piehler asserts of Augustus Egg's triptych *Past and Present* (1858) (Tate Gallery, London), "Neither the domestic space of the initial canvas nor the bleak promise of the outside world proves adequate. Once a transgressor, the woman has no place."[127] Hence, these images of the Lady of Shalott invert the Whistler paintings since they show that the woman looks at the world through the mirror, rather than passively allowing her-

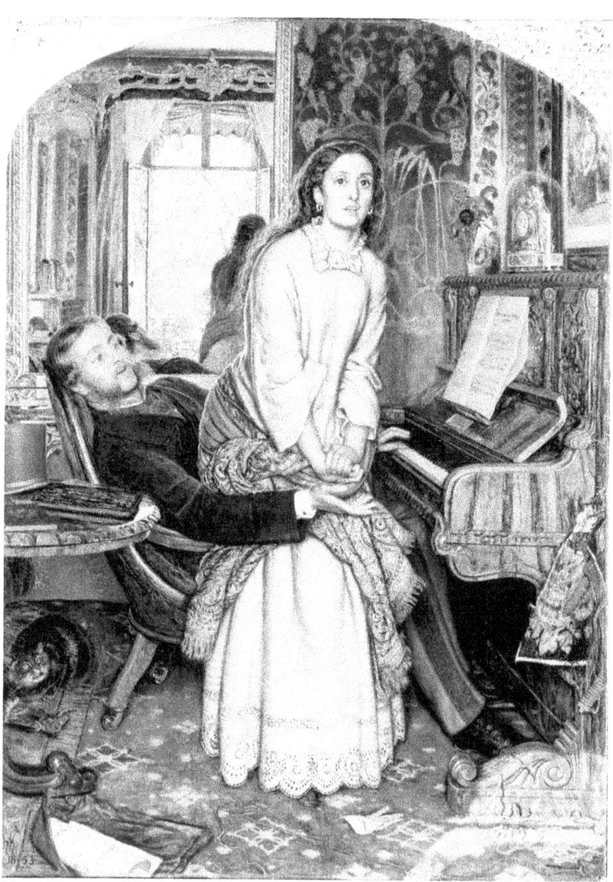

Figure 12. William Holman Hunt (1827–1910), *The Awakening Conscience*, 1853. Oil on canvas. Presented by Sir Colin and Lady Anderson through the Friends of the Tate Gallery 1976. © Tate, London 2016.

self to be the subject in the mirror's echo. Whistler's images, by contrast, show us the woman's likeness in the mirror; in the case of *Harmony in Green and Rose*, we see Whistler's sister only as a replication rather than as a flesh-and-blood self. Of Jo, even though Whistler pictures her, we see her reflection behind her in the mirror, suggesting that she is passive object rather than active self, unable to turn from her own likeness to engage the outside world.

But were these images of women in interiors meant only to confirm male desires to maintain the status quo, or reveal a nostalgia for a simpler time, or could they also absorb a woman's direct desire for change? Could such images, in fact, reveal an inversion, suggesting a woman's own desires? As Hilde Heynen explains about the relationship between modernity and domesticity: "To be modern thus means to participate in a quest for betterment of oneself and one's environment, leaving behind the certainties of the past. Inevitably, this journey results in the ambivalent experience of the gratifications

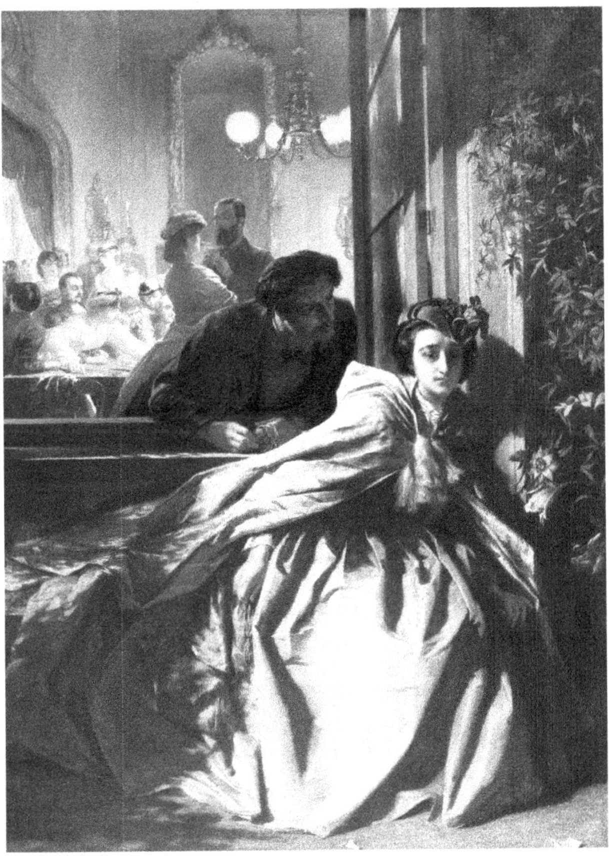

Figure 13. Alfred Elmore (1815–1881), *On the Brink*, c. 1864. Oil on canvas. Fitzwilliam Museum, The Friends of the Fitzwilliam Museum in memory of Dr. A.N.L. Munby, with a contribution from the Victoria and Albert Museum Grant-in-Aid. PD.108–1975. © The Fitzwilliam Museum, Cambridge.

of personal development on the one hand and nostalgia for what is irretrievably lost on the other."[128] The images I have discussed thus far reflect this irresolution, but it becomes even more clear in another grouping of Victorian paintings. While Shefer argues that Millais's *Mariana* (fig. 3) is unequivocally about Christina Rossetti's rejection of a sexual life for a pure state, other images might suggest the complication of that longing.

William Holman Hunt's *Awakening Conscience* of 1852 (fig. 12) depicts a young, kept woman coming to enlightenment about her position and her desire to be free from it; that is, to return to a purer state of innocent girlhood. Note here that she is *inside* the interior but it is a *false* one; replete with the "fatal newness" that critic John Ruskin associated with such clandestine sites,[129] it reeks of moral laxity. Yet here the open window suggests her crossing a threshold into a more morally upright life whereas the previous images I have discussed suggest that to cross that barrier is to risk transgression. This painting with its mirrored reflection of an innocent promise of a return of her reputation sits opposite the Lady of Shalott images; in those, the woman looks out to a world that will corrupt her whereas Hunt's kept woman seeks release from venality.

Another suspect interior appears in Alfred Elmore's *On the Brink* (fig. 13) in which a young woman who sits *outside* a window has just left the tables of a gambling den, a transgression in its own right for a respectable woman, obviously in despair at having lost her wager. But, worse, a man, still inside but leaning over the windowsill, beckons her back in, acknowledging that she has crossed the threshold and is hence fair game. Her visible distress could be due not only to her gambling losses, but also to her imminent loss of honor should she succumb to this man's offer (he's not a gentleman) to get her back in the game, if not *on* the game. Her physical self, outside the bounds of home and hearth, is in real danger.[130]

In these examples, the private/public discourse unites the angel/whore dichotomy but complicates that dialogue by suggesting the world beyond the false interior is safer than the world within. These paintings seem to comment on Heynen's observations that the world is fraught with regret for a lost past that does not sit comfortably with a desire for freedom, one which is complicated by a woman's understanding of the power of her own sexuality. A knotty precedent exists in a print by Philibert-Louis Debucourt, *The Casement Window*, 1791 (Bibliothèque Nationale de France, Paris). In the first state of the print, a young married woman reclines in the casement of an open window, separated from the exterior by only a bar, as she reads (in all irony) a new conduct manual, *The Art of Keeping Wives Faithful*; we view her from outside so we are privy to the advances of her lover in the bushes, who takes a note from her hand, unbeknownst to her elderly husband who has fallen asleep and who we glimpse in the interior. Debucourt produced this print at a time in France when the laws governing the Revolutionary family values that would form the Civic Code were coming into play. According to the new laws, it was no longer acceptable for women to engage in adulterous behavior; the change in laws concerning primogeniture to include all children of a marriage as opposed to the first-born son created a paradigm shift, which made adultery for women punishable. This topic was so fraught that Debucourt created a second state of his print for public consumption, in which he replaces the lover with the woman's children, converting it into a happy family scene.[131] That she is seated in the casement, and the window is open, suggests, like Elmore's painting, the dangers of such public exposure, ones which Debucourt had to dissipate.

Another aspect of this deconstruction of the private/public dichotomy comes from the work of Janet Wolff. Consider Degas's *In a Café*, or *Absinthe* (fig. 14) or Manet's *Plum Brandy*, c. 1877 (National Gallery of Art, Washington, D.C.). Both women are constrained by the barrier of a café table, and both show signs not of boredom but rather of physical and mental exhaustion and malaise, probably due to overwork and the unfulfilling, if not degrading, nature of that work, the very reason they are both imbibing. They are not candidates for what Wolff calls the woman *"flâneuse"* as I discussed in the introduction; Degas and Manet's women are no casual strollers; they do not provide evidence of a female counterpart to Charles Baudelaire's male *flâneur*, someone who was free to walk the city without purpose, anonymous, in search of the palpable pleasures of Paris. If anything, they are women who have been exhausted by serving men, whether it be as entertainers or as laundresses or milliners, their labor has served men either directly or indirectly. Hence why to Wolff, she was the *invisible flâneuse*; she did not exist. But Wolff has reconsidered her position in her more recent scholarship; a woman's invisibility is not, as she originally thought, due to the private sphere ideology but rather to the fact that women always move with purpose in the modern city rather than as idlers.[132]

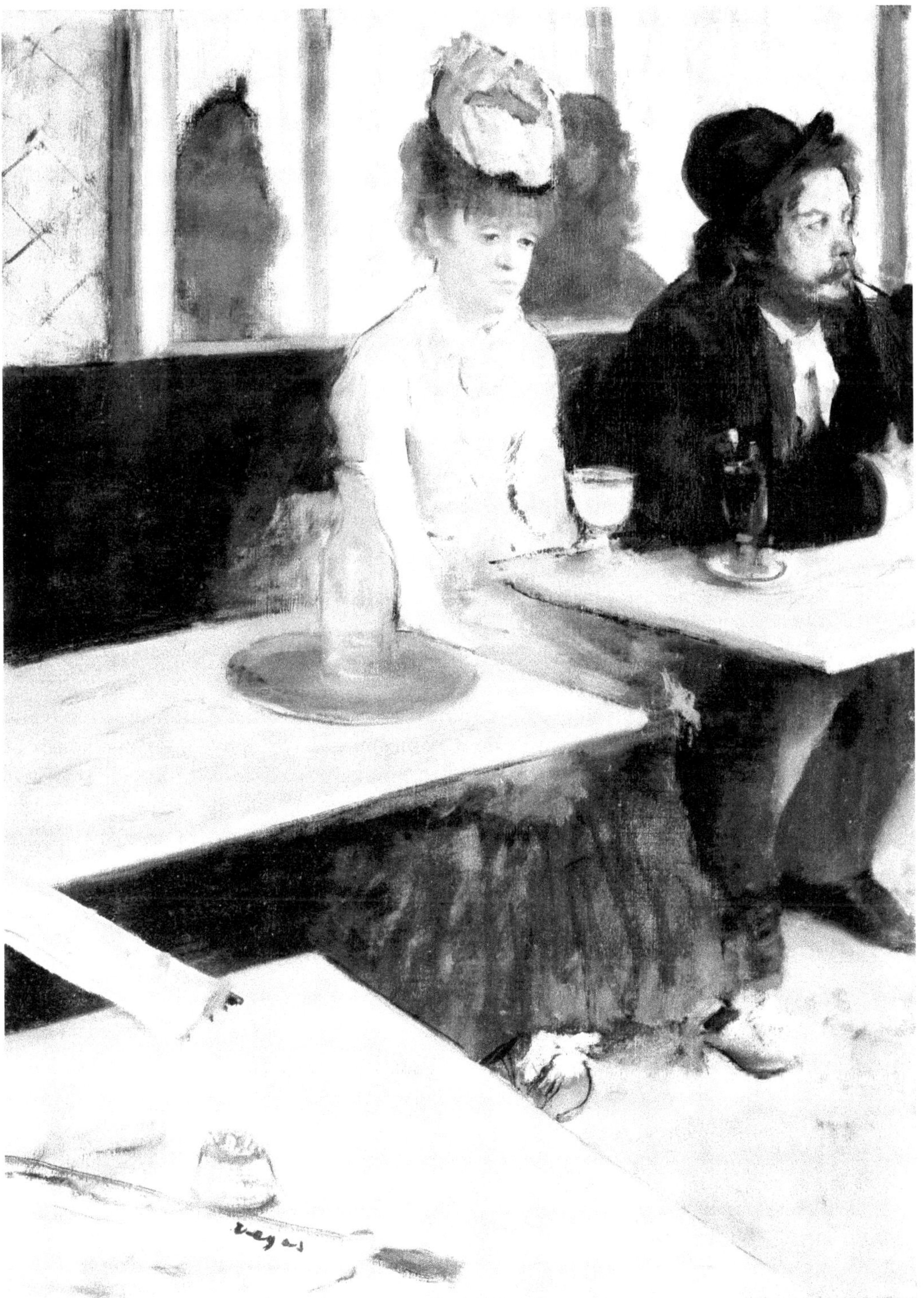

Figure 14. Edgar Degas (1834–1917), *In a Café,* or *Absinthe (Ellen Andrée and Marcellin Desboutin),* 1875–1876. Oil on canvas. RF1984. Photo: Martine Beck-Coppola. Musée d'Orsay, Paris, France. © RMN-Grand Palais/Art Resource, NY.

What I address in these images of women in interiors speaks to a revision in recent scholarship about the dissatisfaction with aspects of the separate sphere ideology and its inaccuracies—the statistics tell us that women were moving increasingly into the work force. Aruna D'Souza and Tom McDonough argue that:

> [I]f the workforce was becoming increasingly feminized, with the massive expansion of a tertiary sector of service labor, the culturally dominant representations of women were decidedly domestic, with a return to idealized images of homemakers and mothers. The city was again coded as a site of (white, masculine) pleasure, and hence as a potential threat to bourgeois femininity—even as lived experience provided examples of a tremendous variety of spatial practices across gender, classes and ethnicities.[133]

Wolff, in this same volume, says that the *flâneuse* is invisible because if she existed she would have to be aimless. She makes a new call:

> Instead of either bemoaning women's lack of access to *flâneuserie* and to the public sphere more generally, or taking to task theories of modernity and the city which privilege the male experience, we should adopt the rather different aim of exploring women's [and men's] actual lives in the modern city.[134]

The interior images here then speak to Norma Broude and Mary Garrard's similar suggestion that we need to examine

> the interplay between women's cultural assertion and the erasure or resistance that both followed and preceded it. We must rebalance the larger picture, describing a cultural dynamic that consisted not of men's cultural dominance and women's occasional achievements, but rather of a steady and ongoing participation of women in culture, as active agents at every level ... and as a conceptual force that *threatened a fragile and sometimes desperate masculine hegemony.* [italics mine][135]

Feminist scholars have been able to determine that those clear distinctions were, in fact, muddy at best.[136] Women gathered in their homes in order to move their dialogues to public spaces; this situation was especially true of the suffragists and educational reformers, Mary P. Ryan arguing that both spheres were "mere chimera."[137] Hence, we must examine these women not as research subjects but as potentially active agents, viewing their acts of boredom as conscious acts of defiance.

Traversing the Urban Environment

Camille's world, whether in London or in Paris, was one in which women increasingly participated as consumers beyond the home. With the birth of the department store and public transport, she became liberated from her previous immobilization, one characterized by the following constraints:

> [T]he law forbade a married woman to live where she pleased or to leave the country without her husband's consent. No woman, regardless of marital status, could attend political rallies, ... nor, according to a custom that constrained women journalists, could women sit in the press gallery of the Chamber of Deputies. Women could appear in public, although their numbers might be regulated in times of crisis, but in doing so they risked humiliation at the hands of the morals police (*police des moeurs*), the enforcement agency charged with supervising the laws regulating prostitution. They also encountered inconvenience in traveling about Paris, where municipal restrooms for men far outnumbered those for women.[138]

As discussed in the section on The New Woman, the department store became a site of urban convenience for the French woman that mitigated some of these restrictions and offered her some semblance of freedom. Yet, traversing the city was still a trepidatious affair. The urban bustle her London counterpart would have encountered is reflected in William Maw Egley's *Omnibus Life in London*, 1859 (fig. 15) in which passengers jostle each other for space, and unwanted glances, judging by the contemplation on the face of the young man with the phallic cane, will happen.

Does this image imply then that *if* a woman crosses her threshold that she, like Elmore's young woman, will find herself on the brink? On the brink of what? Of discovering her independence? Of discovering how much disquietude she will experience upon her return home? That she will be on the brink of succumbing to a man's attentions? As Heynen asserts, "The conceptualization itself of modernity as embodying the struggle for progress, rationality, and authenticity also bears gendered overtones. In as far as modernity means change and rupture, it seems to imply, necessarily, the leaving of home. A metaphorical 'homelessness' indeed is often considered the hallmark of modernity." Citing the writings of both Martin Heidegger and Theodor W. Adorno, she concludes that "modernity and dwelling are at odds and cannot be reconciled."[139] When women

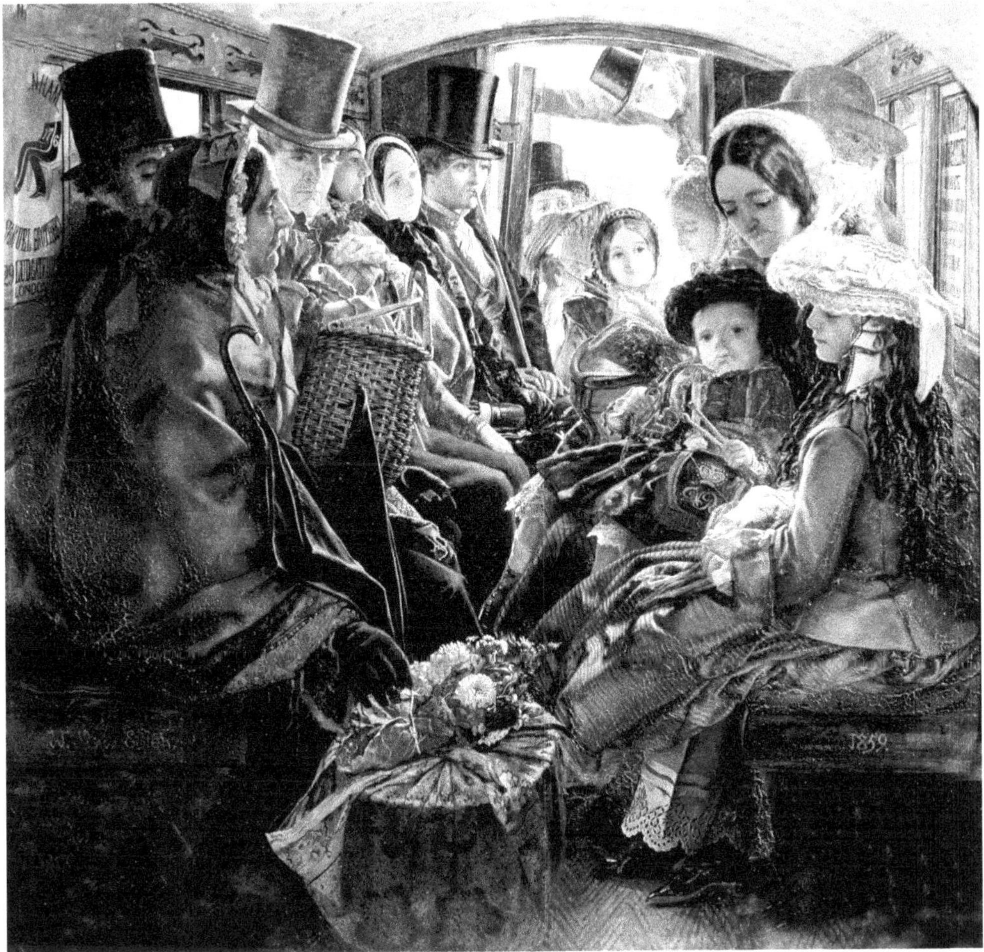

Figure 15. William Maw Egley (1826–1916), *Omnibus Life in London,* **1859. Bequeathed by Miss J.L.R. Blaker 1947. © Tate, London 2016.**

were no longer at home, it became difficult to identify them properly in terms of their class and respectability. Hence, the urban environment was an impersonal place that became a contested space where middle-class women, formerly tied to their homes, were in danger of being mistaken for disreputable types.[140] Women were able to leave the home because of such sophisticated transport modes around the urban city. In this context, Egley's painting implies the dangers of crossing the threshold and, like the Hunt and Elmore paintings (figs. 12 and 13) seems heavily imbricated with a desire to act out. I argue that it is because of the continuing changes in laws that addressed women's rights that we see a "threshold as possibility for change" kind of intent in such British images.

Compare Egley's *Omnibus* with Cassatt's *In the Omnibus* print of Paris (fig. 16). Although Cassatt's French women are in a public transport vehicle, they are as enclosed and encased as Camille is in her London living room both formally and in terms of their quiet family grouping. Egley's painting implies the dangers of crossing the threshold while Cassatt's echoes the same containment of Camille in her interior. In Hollis Clayson's study of Impressionist interiors,[141] she discusses Camille as one of many "threshold" pictures, but does that threshold imply possibility? Camille is visibly perturbed, but Cassatt's madame with her servant and child, while wistful in her glance askance, is formally tied

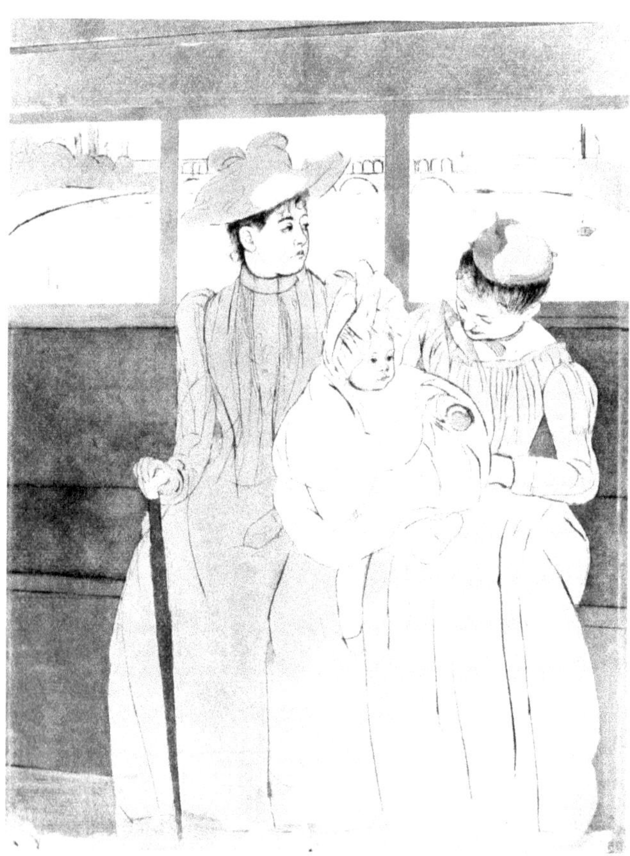

to an interior space even though she traverses modern Paris. The British images, by contrast, begin to embrace transgression. We have seen this action in Elmore's *On the Brink*, and the results of such acting out in Hunt's *Awakening Conscience*. Because the women's movement starts much earlier in England than in France we see more imagery of the threshold as demarcating a possibility for change than in the French examples which are more constrained because women's political agitation was not as visible or volatile.

As Griselda Pollock writes of the omnibus as modern site, "Like the balcony and the theatre, it represented a hybrid space of seeing and being seen—a public space where people of several classes and both sexes are thrown into confusing proximity and socially unregulated situations."[142] Nonetheless, Pollock reads the Cassatt print as a representation of confinement punctuated by class, claiming that it "is not an interior scene, but even outside the home,

Figure 16. Mary Cassatt (1844–1926), *In the Omnibus,* c. 1891. Soft-ground etching, drypoint, and aquatint. 1943.3.2764. Courtesy National Gallery of Art, Washington, D.C., Rosenwald Collection.

women occupied the spaces of bourgeois family, which, of course, was always permeated by 'an outside' in the person of servants,"[143] such that it expresses the classed experience that confines the mother to home and binds the servant to her, a continuation of the angel in the house ideology transferred to "this simple juxtaposition of modern, classed femininities in public space."[144] Considering Egley's painting alongside Cassatt's print, we see that both images embrace the dialogue about domesticity of the time. As Heynen suggests:

> Since the home is associated with women and femininity, the metaphor of homelessness reinforces the identification of modernity with masculinity. It seems as if the vicissitudes of modernity are cast into a scenario which ascribes the active and generative roles to the masculine qualities of reason, dominance, and courage, while leaving the more passive and resistant roles to the feminine capacities of nurturing and caring. Agency, consequently, is most of all located with predominantly male heroes venturing out to conquer the unknown, whereas it is generally the role of women to embody modernity's 'other' tradition, continuity, home. This scenario is, to a large extent, also the script of modernism.[145]

But what happens in the modern era as well is that certain women desire to cross that threshold and hence shake the foundations of home and hearth in an effort to escape cultural restrictions. While many of them went out in public as consumers, many of them also left the home to work.

Kate Krueger Henderson explores the possibilities of such transgression in the modern London metropolis via omnibus in Evelyn Sharp's New Woman story, "In Dull Brown," in which she discusses the experience of Jean Moreen, modern schoolteacher who arrives at work by omnibus.[146] Like Egley's painting, the story explores her direct engagement with the gaze and conversation of a gentleman stranger on the omnibus. We see Egley's passengers face each other in a long row, a spatial arrangement which meant women needed "to learn how and when to look,"[147] so that they were both commanding surveyors of the scene, and knowing objects of the male gaze. Unlike the young woman in Egley's image, however, Jean "chooses to look" and because she does so, she "becomes the principal voyeur of this public space."[148] In the modern city, the individual has to learn to behave anonymously, avoiding the gaze of others so as not to engage or excite contact with strangers. Henderson argues that Jean defies that rule, "deliberately countering the privatization of the space of the omnibus through her own aggressive spectatorship."[149] Clayson, in observations on Cassatt's *Omnibus*, suggests the madame's "oblique glance instances her desire for engagement with the city both geographically and temporally 'beyond the tram'" but "is cut off from the metropolis proper while confined to the bus with the child and servant."[150] Unlike Jean, she cannot step outside the boundaries of the home, even in public. Because of Jean's boldness and because of her unusual dress "in dull brown," the stranger gentleman mistakes her for a shop girl and hence assumes she is sexually experienced and available.[151] It only transpires that she is *not available* when she declares that she is a schoolteacher and hence of middle-class respectability. Like Cassatt's print, then, the story invokes anxieties over mistaken identities of class as well as sexuality. In a reversal of Cassatt's print, however, in the story Jean rejects the domestic hearth, a place where she eventually finds the stranger, now known to her as Tom Unwin, in conversation of a domestic kind with her younger sister Nancy. Tom had been awaiting her arrival but she rejects him, and, telling for this study, rejects the domestic scene itself.

Henderson argues that because Jean is a New Woman who, like others, has struck out on her own in the modern city, she embraces the empowerment and freedom she feels in the public space but, ironically, it is a space and a position that has effectively sealed off domestic possibilities.[152] She cannot re-cross the threshold to the comforts of home any more than Camille can cross over into the urban spaces of London without risk; the situation suggests that the Victorians were beginning to recognize that the angel in the house ideology was not redeemable in light of women's move forward into the political and sexual arena.

Camille's bored moment suggests she is on the edge, on the verge, but contained by French policy. The critic Camille Mauclair, while writing of representations of women

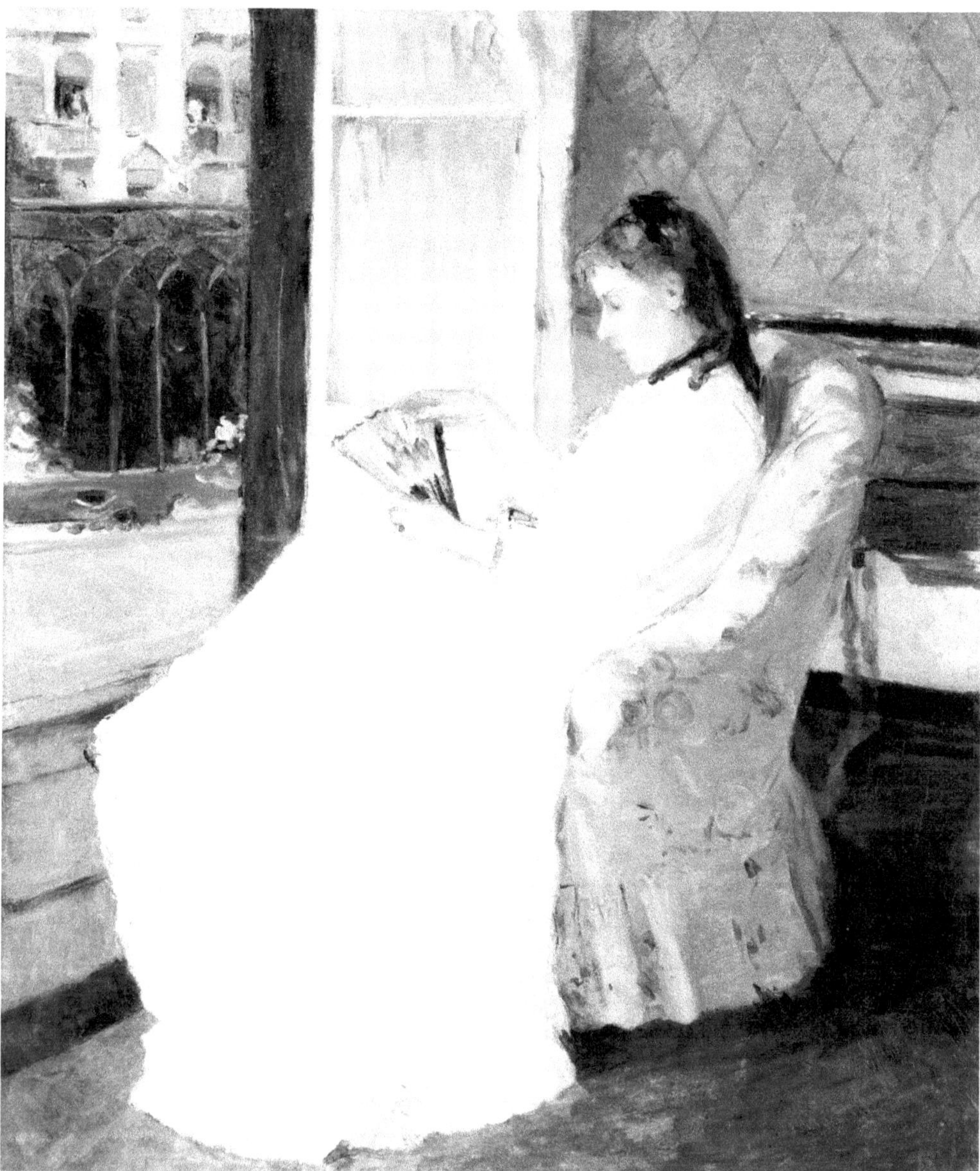

Figure 17. Berthe Morisot (1841–1895), *The Artist's Sister at a Window*, 1869. Oil on canvas. 1970.17.47. Courtesy National Gallery of Art, Washington, D.C., Ailsa Mellon Bruce Collection.

as objects of desire, also articulates a new conception of the new woman. Writing in 1899, he speculates that "a woman's portrait will cease to be a *tableau,* and will become an intimate, analytical, and ideational document."[153] Thus does Camille sit outside the typical portrayal and is on the threshold of change long before her French compatriots. Similarly poignant, but largely traditional in its approach, is Berthe Morisot's *The Artist's Sister at a Window,* 1869 (fig. 17) which depicts Edmé Pontillon, newly married and ensconced in her seaside home of Lorient. Her sense of dejection and unease matches that of Camille; she has had to give up and hence denounce the exterior world, which she had experienced as a painter alongside her sister. She is reduced to a model and is not even reading but focused on holding a fan which, as Clayson suggests, she looks at determinedly,[154] presumably so that she does not set her sights on the exterior tangibly present just beyond the open French doors. Anne Higonnet suggests, "Behind Morisot's women's reserve we sense a life all the more intense because it is withheld."[155] Yet, I would argue that her position, while more complex than that of women in other French paintings, does not match the despair and disgust of Camille or the actual transgressions we see women commit in Victorian paintings on this same theme.

Morisot's own situation suggests she was fully aware of the contradictions of a woman's existence. She was subject to sexist reviews by the 19th-century press who viewed her as "an intuitive, unreflective artist, living out her natural femininity through her painting," but, her letters evidence that we cannot sustain this view of her. They also suggest that we cannot call her a true feminist in the sense that she would challenge the status quo; she is ambivalent and often reluctant to move beyond her prescribed role. Adler and Garb argue that "today's feminist art historians" cannot embrace her "in the role of lofty female ancestor, politicized by her gender and willing to confront the institutional sexism of her time."[156] Adler and Garb note that Morisot remained aloof from the *Union des Femmes Artistes* who formed to protest exclusionary male agendas of the Salon system and she did not exhibit with them in their regular *Salon des Femmes* either. They argue, however, that "[t]his does not mean that she was unaware of the debates around women's position, or the restrictions, social and psychic, which were placed on women's lives, but that her responses are not unified and worked out. They are often confused, ambiguous, and tellingly self-denigrating."[157] For example, in an oft-quoted passage from a letter to Edmé in which she tries to comfort her sister over her choice to leave painting behind for the roles of wife and mother, Morisot is dismissive of painting: "Do not grieve about painting. I do not think it is worth a single regret." But she later apologizes for her "lamentation," attributing it to a low moment she has had while recovering from an eye injury.[158] Yet the barriers were real. The Morisot sisters' first teacher, Guichard, realizing their great talent, told their mother that

> they will become painters. Do you realize what this means? In the upper-class milieu to which you belong, this will be revolutionary, I might almost say catastrophic. Are you sure that you will not come to curse the day when art, having gained admission to your home, now so respectable and peaceful, will become the sole arbiter of the fate of two of your children?[159]

Morisot was trapped, as she literally is in Manet's first painting to include her as a model, *The Balcony* (fig. 18). It suggests the real barriers she faced as not only a woman artist, but also one from the upper classes. She struggles, like every woman who faces work with seriousness, with self-doubt. After her sister's marriage, she writes to her: "[T]his painting, this work that you mourn for, is the cause of many griefs and many troubles.

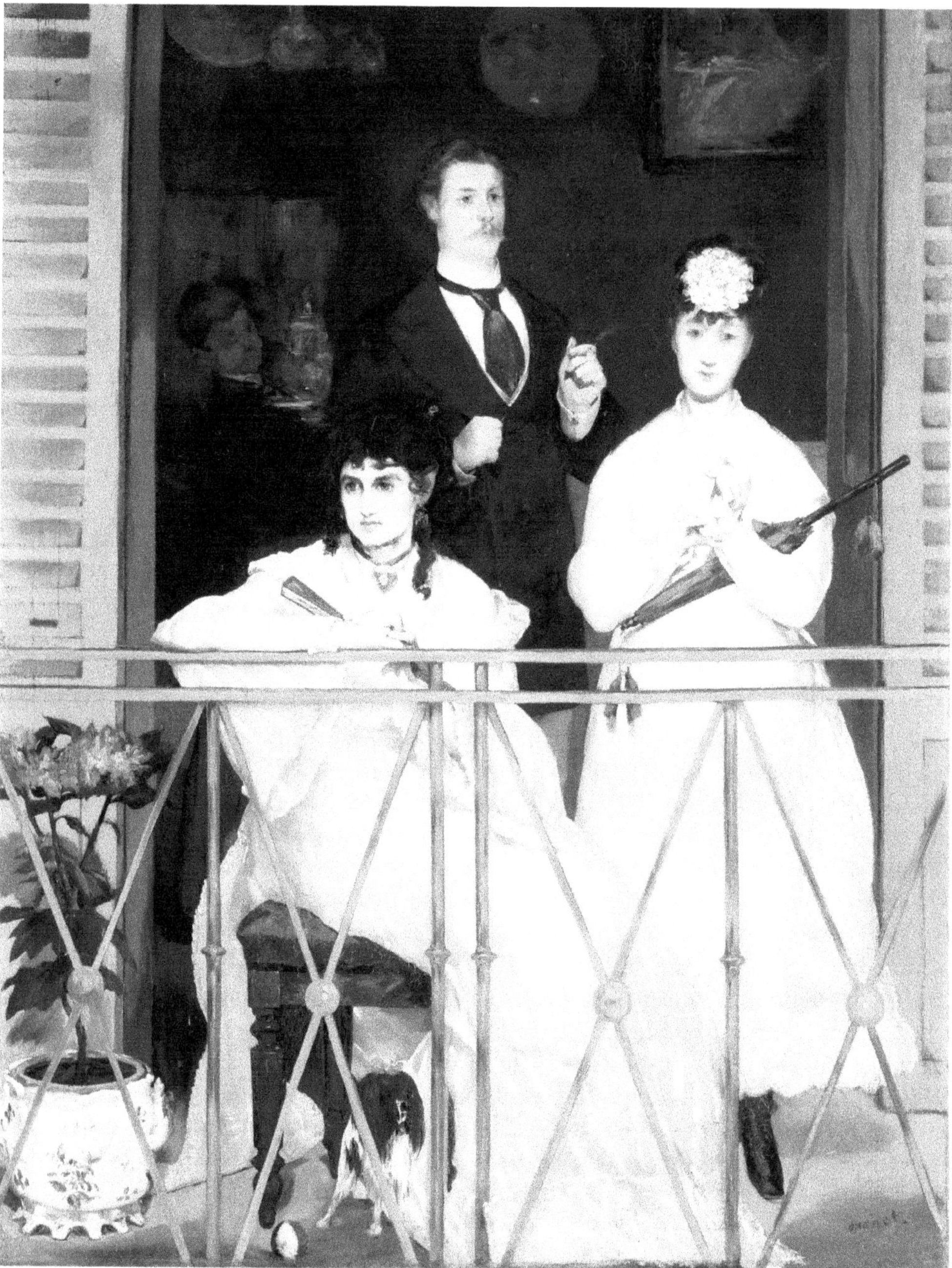

Figure 18. Edouard Manet (1832–1883), *The Balcony,* 1869. Oil on canvas. RF2772. Photo: Hervé Lewandowski. Musée d'Orsay, Paris, France. © RMN-Grand Palais/Art Resource, NY.

You know it as well as I do, and yet…. You are already lamenting that which was depressing you only a little while ago." She later cautions: "Do not revile your fate. Remember that it is sad to be alone; despite anything that may be said or done, a woman has an immense need of affection. For her to withdraw into herself is to attempt the impossible."[160]

This letter reveals Morisot to be a complex, modern woman, struggling with a desire for work and love. And *The Balcony* complicates her representation. Upon seeing it at the Salon in 1869, the year she wrote this lament to her sister, she says: "I am more strange than ugly. It seems that the epithet of *femme fatale* has been circulating among the curious …."[161] The epithet was due more to her dark-eyed good looks than to Manet's treatment of her. The passage of the pot of flowers at the left corner of the painting vies with her for beauty and prominence within the composition. She, like it, is a "still life," young, as yet unmarried, carefully secluded behind the barrier of the balcony. As in her own correspondence and the ambivalence of her high position (literally in the painting but also in terms of her class standing) she needed chaperoning and protection. She bought into it, berating Manet at the 1869 Salon for not acting the proper part of chaperone when she was accosted and, in her view, dragged off for a private conversation by the artist Puvis de Chavannes. She wrote to her sister: "I did not think it proper to walk around all alone."[162]

Why the difference? How much of it is due to the fact that the Victorians liked their moral tales and narratives in text and in imagery, and how much to the more prominent discourse in England on women's increasing rights? We are hard-pressed to find a moral narrative or political statement in the works of the Impressionists or other French artists that can vie with Elmore's *On the Brink* or the other troubling British images I have illustrated, with few exceptions.[163] The weightiness of the *Meditation* narrative, though, could be due to Monet's encounter with other artists in England who were working on narrative-driven subjects for the British art market.[164]

Similarly complex is Caillebotte's *Interior with Woman at the Window*, 1880 (fig. 19) in which a bourgeois woman is encased in her home, through formal elements of a balcony on the exterior and a framing through gauzed curtains on the interior. While some scholars have seen this work only as "an image of conjugal boredom," or of a woman's typical nosy behavior,[165] they miss the fact that she engages the woman opposite, whose position mirrors her own. Could this image be an instance of women conspiring, of women in need of uniting to fight for their rights to the space beyond their respective windows? Or is it a case of the potential damage of women's idle gossip? French moralists of the day warned against letting women congregate in groups where they could indulge in such behavior, which might incite them to "dangerous romantic reverie."[166] It is telling, in this context, that we find women in interiors not only isolated, but also isolated from each other, just as in the earlier Whistler images. But, we start to see a shift in such imagery starting in the 1880s, which attests to women's sense of community and purpose beyond the domestic realm. This is true in the paintings of the artist, Marie-Louise-Catherine Breslau, such as her *Les amies (Friends)*, 1881 (Museum of Art and History, Geneva), in which Breslau shows herself painting a female companion who is seated at a table, while another female friend at the table takes notes in a bound book and seems to be sharing information with the other two. The scene is made into a comfortable domestic setting, rather than a stifling one, by their engaged presence and by a little white dog who sits on the same table, suggestive of their domestic indulgence. Similarly compelling is Breslau's *Les amies (contrejour) (Friends [Twilight])*, 1888 (Kunstmuseum, Bern) in which one woman, resting with her back to the window, leans forward to hear the words of a second woman who is reading from an open book. They are silhouetted against the waning sunlight through the window behind them. Such works, by a woman artist, suggest a resistance to Mauclair's construction, as Garb explains:

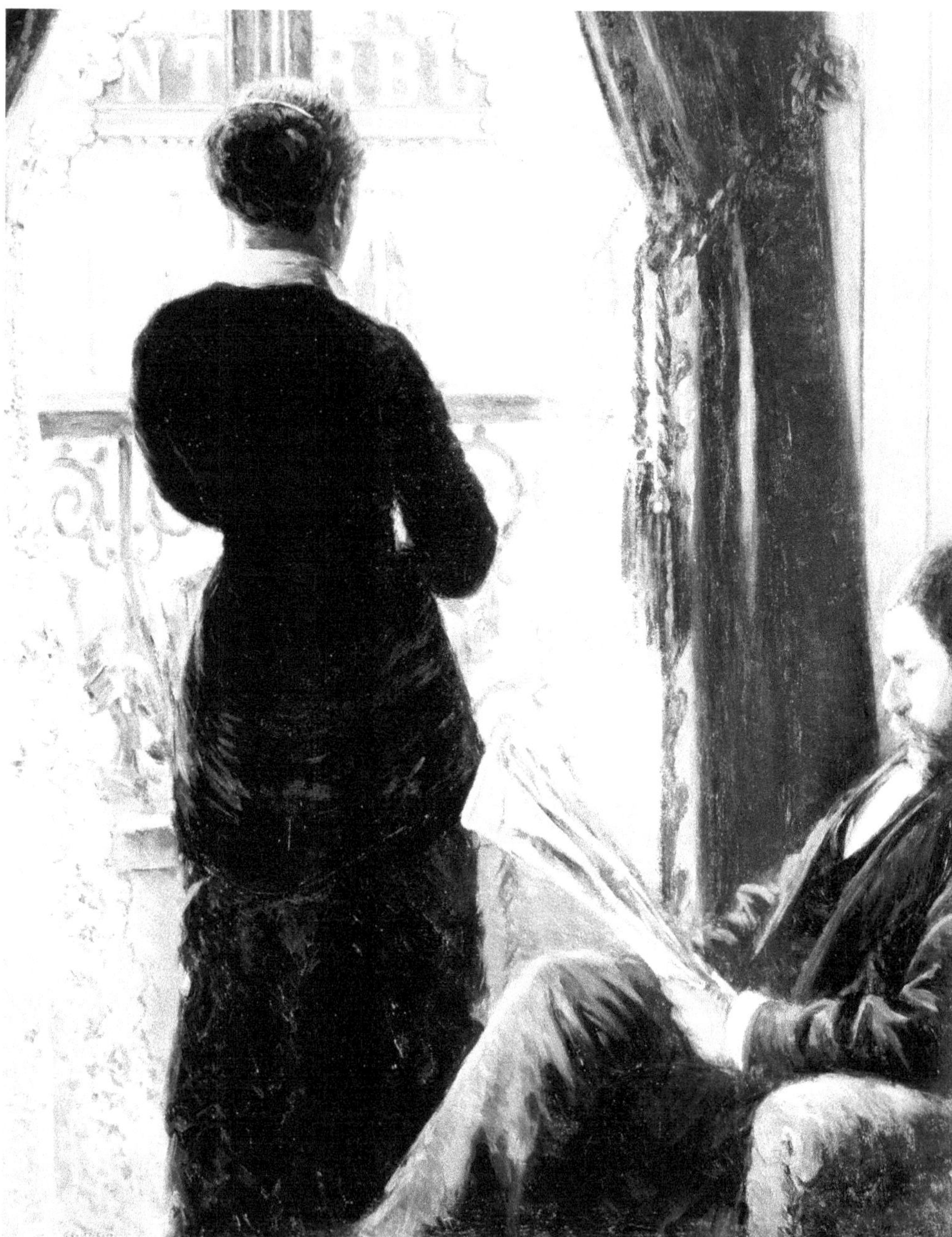

Figure 19. Gustave Caillebotte (1848–1894), *Interior with Woman at the Window*, 1880. Private Collection. Scala/White Images/Art Resource, NY.

Women's traditional role, as objects to be adorned, surfaces to be painted and embellished, whether in the flesh or on canvas, according to the dictates of style and fashion, had made them, ... a tabula rasa onto which an infinite number of dreams could be projected. Such a construction of femininity was incompatible with the image of forthright professionals taking the brush into their own hands.[167]

Conversely, in her painting *At Home or Intimacy*, 1885 (fig. 20), Breslau shows a mother and daughter contained in a domestic interior, still, quiet, yet the daughter working at her embroidery appears decidedly agitated, as if contemplating that her own fate will be the same as that of her mother. Garb has given a different reading of the painting, considering it to belong to a new vision of the new woman, of "contented women ruminating in their interiors ... of a satisfied sorority of high-minded women ..."[168] whereas when we consider this painting in comparison with the Siddal drawing and Hunt painting, we catch a glimpse of something much more unsettling taking place in the interior. In the agitations of women suffragists, what the public feared most were women in numbers. The potential of women's anxiety for equal rights in the public realm is palpable in such images. Yet, unlike the Victorian images, there is no moral here about a fall. It is kept at bay unlike in the Victorian images.

I have shown that the traditional image of the angel in the house does not exist in these images of bored, restless women in interiors; they suggest, instead, the complexities of women's real lives during a century of rapid change in women's rights and in women's access to the public space. While such a state of distress exists in the Victorian images and in Monet's portrait of Camille, other French examples are devoid of narrative. I conclude with one more set of images to emphasize the ways these images address boredom

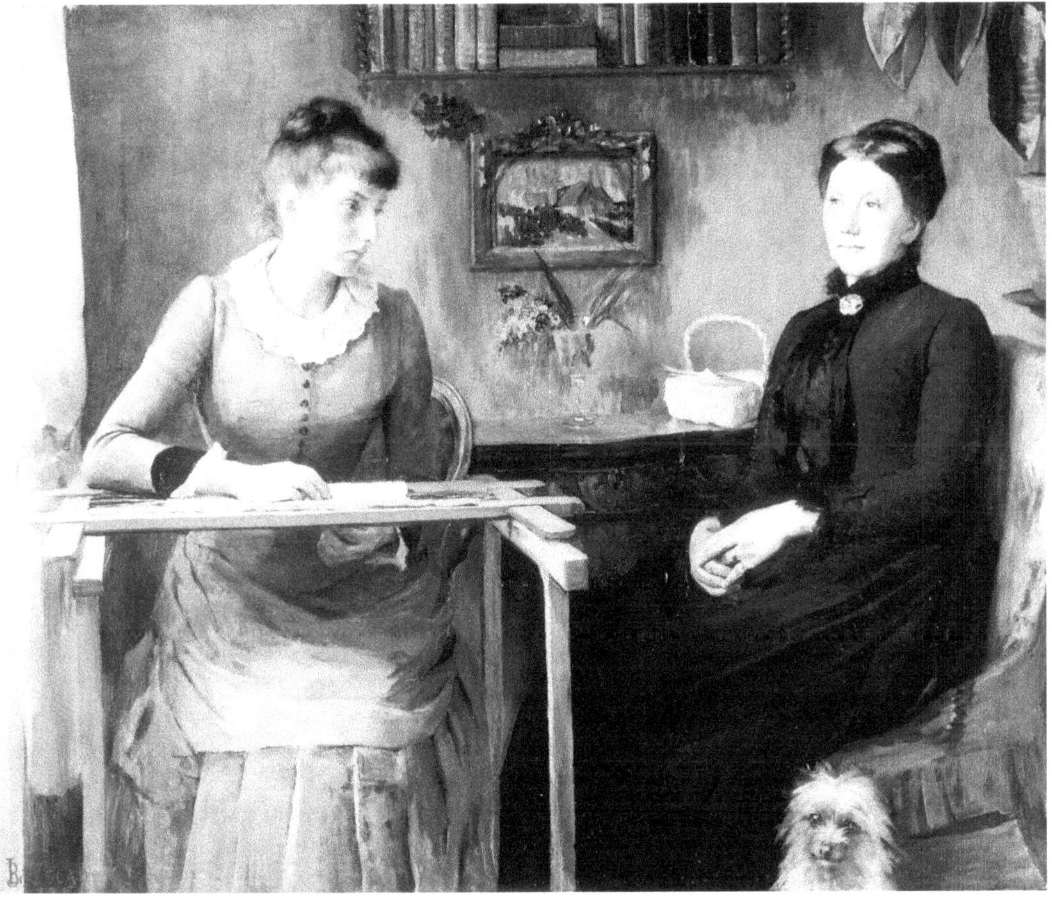

Figure 20. Marie-Louise-Catherine Breslau (1856–1929), *At Home, or, Intimacy (Mother and Sister of the Artist)*, 1885. Oil on canvas. RF 1980–76. Photo: Jean-Pierre Lagiewski. Musée d'Orsay, Paris, France. © RMN-Grand Palais/Art Resource, NY.

as a protest, redressed in each woman's burgeoning sexuality as emblematic of her desire for exposure to a wider world.

James Collinson's *To Let*, c. 1855–60 (fig. 21) ostensibly shows a landlady at a window, about to let a room to an observed potential tenant; subliminally, or perhaps not so subtly it suggests that she, too, is "to let" and hence represents another inversion painting like Hunt's *Awakening Conscience* or the equally compelling *Thoughts of the Past* by John Roddam Spencer Stanhope (fig. 22), another Pre-Raphaelite artist concerned with modern morality plays. Here the entrapment is due to the prostitute's sexual transgressions; contrast it with Camille and you have two equally dissatisfied women, the prostitute nostalgic about her unstained past when she was young and innocent (as opposed to uncovering a dark past), the other without a past or a present or a future, but stagnant, trapped, just like her wayward sister whose curtains, however, are frayed and damaged, like her own reputation.

These examples address the Victorian culture's trepidation over a woman's sexuality head on, suggesting an ongoing ambivalence and commentary on women's proper place, while the French just skirt around it, with some exceptions as I have discussed here. Monet was clearly trying to address a British market and a British taste for narrative in the Camille painting, which we can not only document but can also deduce from the narrative title: *Meditation*. Monet was adept at reducing his wife to a fashion plate emblem of French modernity, mirrored in his technique, as Søndergaard discusses of his *Camille*, 1866 (Kunsthalle Bremen), an example of such "aesthetic spectacle."[169] We cannot say the same of his London portrait of Camille; gone is the superficiality of exhibition. Instead we're invited into her "meditation" on larger concerns. One other example reinforces the difference. In Monet's painting of Camille from c. 1868–70, *The Red Kerchief: Portrait of Mme Monet* (Cleveland Museum of Art) he positions Camille *outside* while he is inside, looking out at her through the French windows. It is an inversion painting like Elmore's *On the Brink* yet there is no narrative tension here; he has merely caught her momentarily looking his way as she takes the air in the winter garden.

If these examples suggest an ongoing ambivalence and commentary on women's proper place, would we not expect early 20th-century imagery to begin to show the resolution of that dilemma the closer we get to suffrage? As we get nearer to the vote in England, do works become more retrograde or more liberal? Or do we see a continuation of

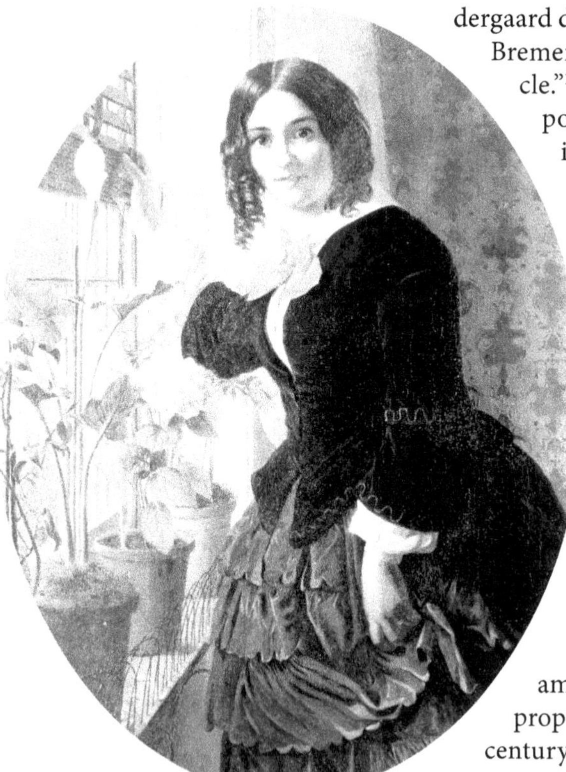

Figure 21. James Collinson (1825–1881), *To Let*, c. 1855–60. Oil on canvas. The Henry P. McIlhenny Collection in memory of Frances P. McIlhenny, 1986. Philadelphia Museum of Art, 1986-26-274.

the tensions we now realize are apparent in our 19th-century images? Kenneth McConkey, in his essay on Edwardian interiors, sees a real shift in power dynamics. He states that in the Edwardian period

> private space became public. Mass literacy and the thirst for images, supported by the proliferation of illustrated newspapers, catered to public curiosity as never before…. Paintings of interiors … were subject to a new kind of scrutiny. Although, at one level, artists reported on what they found, they were fundamentally responding to rooms which reinforced notions of identity, class, culture and taste….[170]

William Orpen's *A Window in London Street*, 1901 (fig. 23) and others shows this conversion. McConkey explains: "The consciousness of the world outside, one that is at once inviting and dangerous, dominates…. Orpen['s] … composition."[171] As the title suggests, the focus has transferred from the interior to the street itself; that is, what is beyond the window. The woman presses on the windowsill, anticipatory of a world outside the interior space. Such imagery suggests a huge leap forward; the woman is not bored, but rather expectant, having moved from a state of inertia to anticipation of action. The largesse of the window in Orpen's painting suggests the myriad possibilities now open to this woman of the Edwardian age, ones for which her Victorian predecessors fought so hard. Yet it remains a quiet interior.

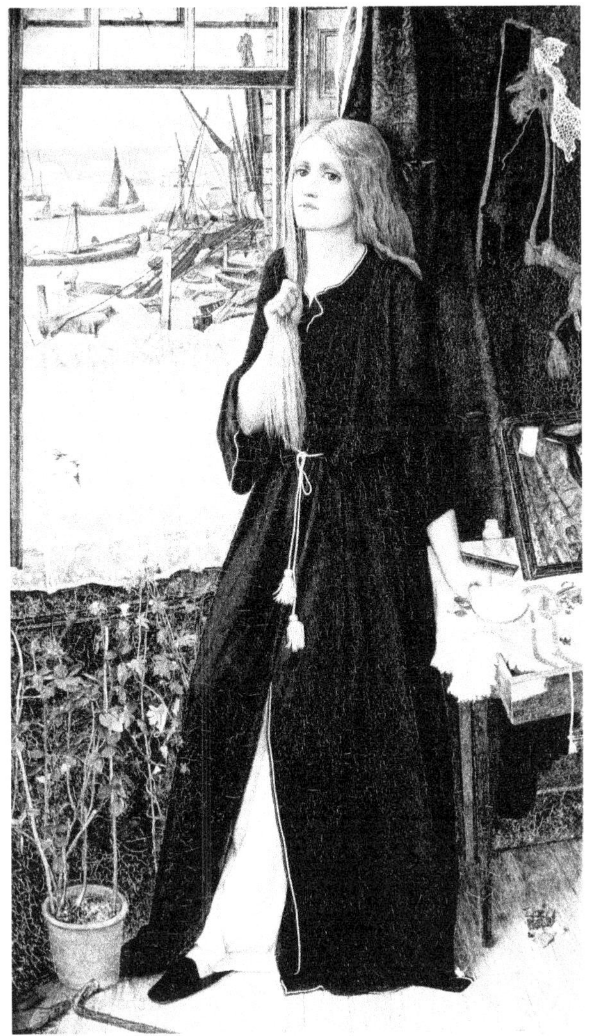

Figure 22. John Roddam Spencer Stanhope (1829–1908), *Thoughts of the Past,* **1858–59. Presented by Mrs. F. Evans 1918. © Tate, London 2016.**

A virile, passionate disruption of that interior quiet happens when we contemplate Orpen's *Night (No. 2)*, 1907 (fig. 24). No longer do we see Mariana awaiting an absent, cruel lover or considering a life of abstinence; rather we see a passionate embrace unprecedented in English art. The woman's open pose and eager encirclement of her lover suggest a physical abandon unavailable to her Victorian counterparts, one wrought by the larger world open to the Edwardians. While her sexuality is contained within the interior, the open show of not only affection but also desire proclaims a visceral identity shift.[172]

Contrast a French painting by Denis Etcheverry, *Vertige (Temptation)*, 1903 (Musée Carnavalet, Paris) in which we see a dialogue with Orpen's couple in *Night (No. 2)*, who engage in the same abandoned embrace, but they are not alone. They are at a party, one just visible behind a curtain, suggesting that if they were discovered, there would be scandal for this couple. The painting reveals the couple in formal attire in an antechamber of a ball, the woman reclining on a sofa, the man leaning over her and kissing her. They are overcome with desire and caught by the artist in a clandestine, illicit tryst. Although contained in an interior, in a secluded space, the painting offers up nothing but disruption whereas the English example is safely contained within middle-class marital bliss. In France our bored woman is not far from Emma Bovary; suffrage for her is still 40 years away, suggesting that her "way out" like Emma's was through a new love and by using her sexuality to gain it. In England, with suffrage only a decade away and women increasingly entering the wider world, the intensity of this moment suggests women's move into man's arms and his world.

In both countries, however, the imagery reflects the modern ambivalence of living in a world where the rules were no longer clear-cut; such bold works reflect the fact that the gender rules and roles had broken down. The modern world that was ushered in by the Industrial Revolution gave birth not just to the leisured woman, more fiction than fact, but also to the independent, educated woman with political representation and sexual desires, at least in England. The fact that French women had to wait until 1945 to achieve such representation is perhaps the reason why we do not see the kind of bold acts in French painting of the early 20th century that we see in Orpen's Edwardian examples.[173] But, even within the suffrage debates, the separate spheres were still central. The most radical of British suffrage journals, *The Freewoman*, for example, gives a nod to the debate even while it attempts to break free from it in the words of Caroline Boord: "Anyone who talks of Women's sphere is not truly 'Feminist' ... the Freewoman wants no ready sphere ... the Freewoman wants the whole round earth to choose from.... [I]t is a retrogressive idea to call any particular sphere or work 'Women's.' We do not know what women's work will be, we only know what it has been."[174] The voices of this journal saw all of women's "natural" roles as suspect: maternal, domestic, sexual, all needed to be re-examined in light of women's continued oppression. What she offers in this state-

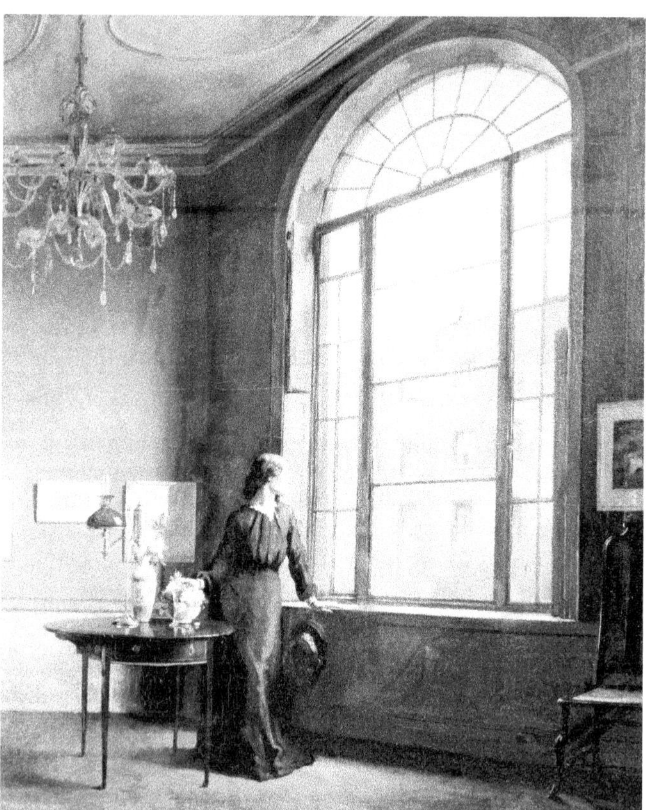

Figure 23. Sir William Orpen (1878–1931), *A Window in London Street*, 1901. National Gallery of Ireland Collection NGI.1978. Photograph courtesy of the National Gallery of Ireland.

ment is a way forward, an opening out of a woman's place.

A woman's lack of political representation is reflected in an illustration by William Hatherell from an American article in *Harper's New Monthly Magazine*, entitled "The Ladies in the Windows of the Inn." In this article, Richard Harding Davis reported on a general election in England in 1893, during which, in the region of Midlothian, a group of 300 Radical and Conservative men threatened to riot. The women are not among the throngs but rather "in the window of the inn [becoming] anxious."[175] In this illustration then the two worlds of political engagement and a woman's place in relationship to it are brought together in actuality as well as symbolically. The two women in the window look out at the action hesitantly. The inn stands in for the domestic interior, protecting them from the fray beyond the window, yet they look out now, suggesting their interest

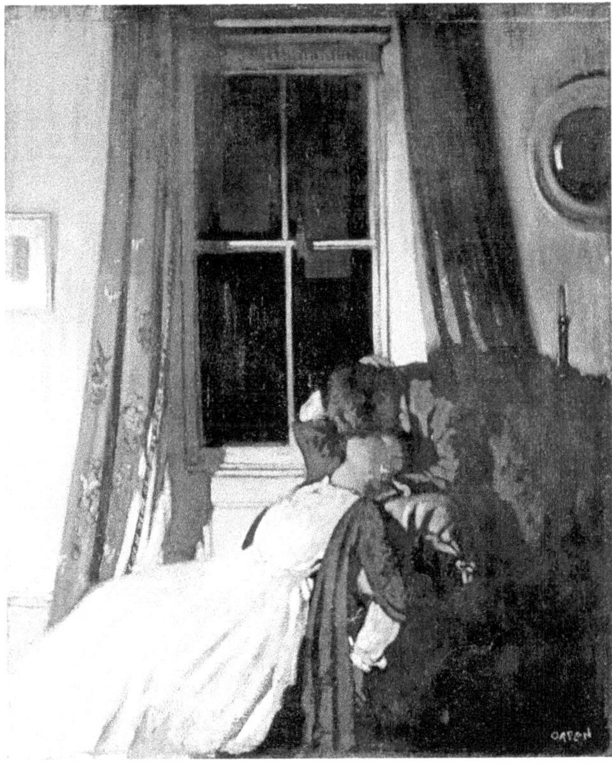

Figure 24. Sir William Orpen (1878–1931), *Night (No. 2)*, 1907. Oil on canvas, 76.5 x 64.0 cm. National Gallery of Victoria, Melbourne, Felton Bequest, 1929 (4237–3).

and desire for change. Further, the fact that we find them at an inn rather than sequestered in a home interior suggests that they have moved beyond this limiting realm in terms of their physical presence.

In contrast to this representation of a woman's lack of engagement, part of the attraction of the suffrage movement itself, in England, was its insistence on commitment to a collective body; a woman was no longer isolated in private; she moved into public spaces *en masse*. Olive Schreiner in *Woman and Labor* (1911), for example, argues, for each woman in the movement "the abiding consciousness of an end to be attained, reaching beyond her personal life and individual interests ... [to bind] with the common bond of an impersonal enthusiasm into one solid body."[176] Characterizing this philosophy of the greater good within feminist polemics, Mary Jean Corbett explains:

> ... for women who have so long been consigned to the personal, the private, and the familial, the opportunity to live for something other than that must have been a heady experience.
>
> While put to a new political use, this ethic of personal renunciation is continuous with some aspects of the Victorian ideology of femininity.... Victorian women's claims to autonomy had always been rejected on the basis of their prescribed part as the servants of others' needs and aims. And even independent women were used to defining themselves in terms of self-sacrifice and self-abnegation.[177]

Hence, we see women move, literally, to the other side of the window and do violence to it. Examining this issue of the bravery such an act took, as well as the ways she had to force herself to step outside her feminine self (and the private environment that identified her as such), Margaret Haig (later Viscountess Rhondda), a wealthy daughter of a mine-owning Member of Parliament, opined: "It required an almost unbelievable effort of will before a woman brought up with all the inhibitions of the decent Victorian 'lady' could bring herself to throw stones through a street window. The women who did it broke more than windows with the stones; they broke the crust and conventions of a whole era."[178] The major newspapers covered this event in March 1912 at which a reported 150 suffragettes smashed window fronts with stones and toffee hammers all over the West End of London in protest over the government's continued unwillingness to grant them citizenship. The aggressive activity necessary for such an act created a shift in women's body language within the suffrage movement, a topic to which I will return in the epilogue. The threat of women in numbers was one issue but the threat of women in numbers with hammers ready to do violence created a major paradigm shift in the public imagination.[179]

At the same time, as Erika Rappaport argues, the window-smashing campaign emblemized the ways that women's emancipation from the home and the availability of consumer pleasures had both merged and remained antagonistic.[180] Women were moving into the public sphere not just as campaigners but also as consumers of goods, the latter role upholding their key place as guardian of the hearth at the same time that it was physically liberating them from the home. But we continue to see friction in representing women's place within Edwardian culture and in French culture. Rappaport explains that "[f]eminists and entrepreneurs had argued … that public women were not necessarily immoral or fallen. They had created similar female public spaces and had used the media to promote those spaces." But "neither feminist nor entrepreneurial discourse wholly overturned traditional notions of femininity. Indeed, 20th-century marketers increasingly promoted the ideal of a modernized housewife who cheerfully consumed goods to improve the domestic haven."[181] The Goncourt Brothers discussed this concept of consumerism, Edmond creating the term "bricobracomania" to describe what he saw as a "disease" of the 1880s. As Pamela Todd explains, for him, "it linked to the emptiness, the loneliness of the human heart in the new industrial society and its modern cities…. [H]e believed that the men and women of this fast-paced modern age were plugging their *ennui* and anxiety with possessions…."[182] Thus, the window-smashing of the suffragettes was doubly prophetic; on the one hand, it signaled the path away from boredom to action, the actual destruction of the window as alleviating the barrier to change; on the other, it signaled a commentary on woman's efforts to assuage boredom through more conventional and acceptable means. Women smashed windows not only of commercial businesses, but also of government offices. Martha Vicinus argues that "[b]reaking windows also served the important purpose of demonstrating the weakness of established institutions…. [T]he barrier between the inside (the government offices) and the outside (the women refused entry) was metaphorically destroyed, leaving a gaping hole (or boarded window) to remind others of women's position."[183] Yet, the fact that artists depict women in interiors with varying degrees of ambivalence about the politics of that glass window speaks to the real struggles of women in public, trying to negotiate the modern world; no longer bored, but beginning to engage.

By 1917, this crust had definitely burst. Our omnibus images resurface in the context of women's suffrage, echoing the radical freedom of the young Jean Moreen in Sharp's story. For one, suffrage women volunteered on "Votes for Women" omnibuses covered with the WSPU colors of purple, white and green on notices announcing suffrage meetings (fig. 25) which they drove around the West End. A *Punch* cartoon of 4 April 1917 (fig. 26) references both this suffrage activity and new forms of employment for women; here a woman conductor makes "The Catch of the Season." In April 1915 the Glasgow Corporation had hired the first women tram conductors so it is fitting that a woman employee is pulling the Prime Minister Asquith onto the Suffrage bus as she says: "Come along, Sir, Better late than never." Asquith had finally renounced his hostility to the women's movement in England in 1917, which resulted in the 1918 Representation of the People Act, that gave 8.5 million women over the age of thirty the vote.[184]

The image was reproduced in *The Vote,* the organ of the WFL as its cover for April 13, 1917, acknowledging suffrage women's awareness of this dialogue. While Cassatt's bourgeois French woman

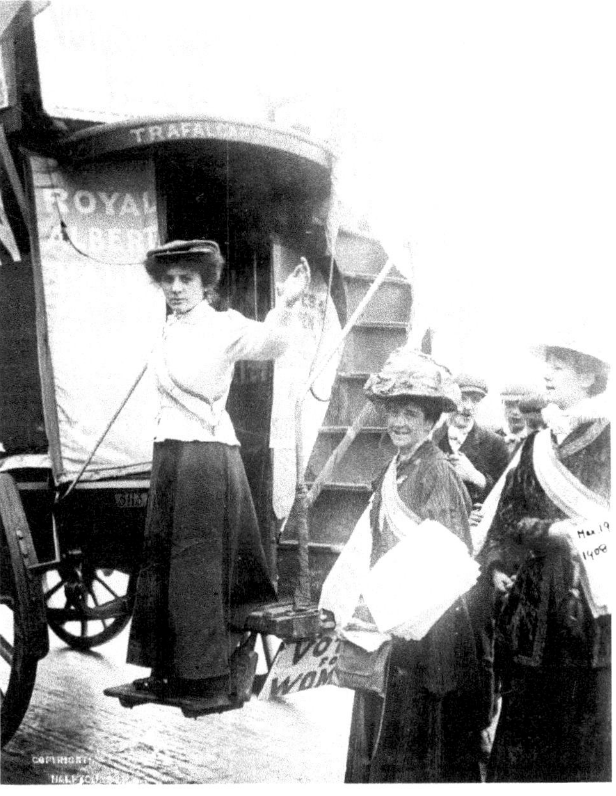

Figure 25. *"Votes for Women" Omnibus,* 1908. **Museum of London, 50.82/1559.**

was left to catch a brief glimpse of life outside the home on the French omnibus, the British images suggests that the woman had finally crossed the threshold of home and hearth and entered the world to make a difference.

This phenomenon of bored women was not, however, restricted to 19th-century Europe. With the publication of Simone de Beauvoir's *The Second Sex* (1949; published in the U.S. in English in 1953) and Betty Friedan's more widely circulated assessment of the lives of middle-class white women in *The Feminine Mystique* (1963), we witness important catalysts for the women's movement of the 1960s. Both books address women's oppression in the industrialized West in the same ways I have discussed them here; yet, as with the 19th-century experience, the 20th-century one reflects a "profound dissonance" between ideology and fact. While female labor numbers increase from 1850 to 1990, men's numbers experience a slight decline.[185] Yet, the evidence in both de Beauvoir and Friedan's texts suggest a tangible malaise among women, ones who see themselves as slaves to the home and family. Friedan characterizes women who succumb to the feminine mystique as being like these 19th-century women: empty, hypnotized, bored. And it should not be lost on us that the book that really launched the feminist bomb on the world to announce women's widespread misery was by a French woman, writing in 1949, soon after women had finally been granted suffrage in France.

We must reflect on the similarity of pressures within mid–20th century British and French cultures, adjusting to the demands of post–Second World War America and

Europe, where women were ushered *back* into the home with alacrity. Women's discontent was palpable, a constant topic for discussion in American women's magazine of the era of 1945–1965. As Eva Moskowitz asserts, "They documented on an unprecedented scale the difficulty women had in finding satisfaction in their homes and personal lives" and paved the way for Friedan's message.[186] The pervasiveness of women's displeasure with the domestic realm suggests that these women's experiences as represented in the visual evidence was in fact a real struggle, despite the disparity between the numbers of women involved in the labor movement versus those confined to the domestic interior. Such discontent erupted into the women's movement of the 1960s and Friedan's formation of the National Organization of Women (significantly abbreviated as NOW to imply its urgency).[187] An extreme example of continuity comes in the SCUM Manifesto (Society for Cutting Up Men) of Valerie Solanas who conflates issues of boredom with extreme politics when she says: "Life in this society being, at best, an utter bore and no aspect of society being at all relevant to women, there remains to civic-minded, responsible, thrill-seeking females only to overthrow the government, eliminate the money system, institute complete automation, and destroy the male sex."[188] I will return to the second-wave women's movement in the epilogue but here it is important to keep in mind the link we witness between the *ennuyée* of 19th-century, middle-class women and that of their mid-20th-century counterparts.

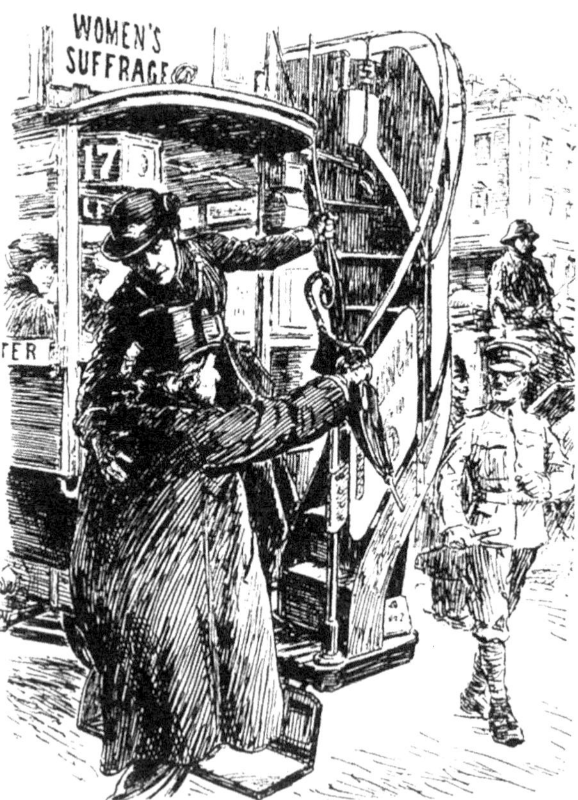

Figure 26. "The Catch of the Season," *Punch* (1917). Reproduced with permission of Punch Ltd., www.punch.co.uk.

What I have argued here and what propels this book is the false opposition between housewife and feminism. These 19th-century women, emblematized in Monet's portrait of the discontented Camille, needed to break free from that interior if they were going to embrace their rights as citizens. As Jennifer Scanlon characterizes Friedan's call, "Friedan set up the opposition between feminist and housewife, arguing as vociferously as anyone that the public world, the male world, the work of paid rather than unpaid work, trumped women's work in the home to such a degree that little further discussion of domestic life's ups and downs was warranted."[189] While the situation and its history is much more nuanced than this simple opposition would suggest, it sits as the foundation of the motivation for women to act. Yet, we must also acknowledge that both within Victorian/Edwardian dialogues and arguments for liberation, and those of the 1960s, there is a continued tension between the domestic realm and the public one, motivating many advocates to insist on a woman's continued presence in the home. Further, as symbolized by the differing approaches of Friedan and the advocate for single women, Helen Gurley Brown, part of this debate concerns the role of a woman's sexuality within the political debate, one which many identify as a distinction between second-wave feminism (Friedan) and third-wave feminism (Brown). Some critics argue that a woman's political liberation is directly aligned with her sexual appetite.[190] Consider the debates here over the woman who moves beyond the window; the danger is not just that she will be liberated from the home, but also that she will become sexually liberated and available. Often, she is in a liminal space, neither in the interior nor outside, awaiting liberation but one based not only on laws that offer her access to the outside world, but also on the promise of sexual freedom. And while for Friedan the women's movement was often about moving women into the working world, it was coupled with a woman's sexual exploration. I will explore such motivations and dialogues further in the subsequent chapters, concluding with an epilogue that brings us back to the relationship between women's bodies of the 19th-century and today, as they leave the interior and negotiate the city.

But I would like to end on this note: That a real desire to break free of Victorian conventions was at the root of suffrage rhetoric is evident in the words on a banner that Mary Lowndes created for the East Anglian branch of the NUWSS demonstration on 13 June 1908. In it she transposed the words of Pope Gregory, commenting on the maltreatment of Anglo-Saxon boys in a Roman slave market as *"Non Angli sed Angeli"* (not English but Angels) such that the banner motto read: *"Non Angeli sed Angli,"* which translates symbolically as "Not Angels but Citizens."[191]

Two

"Not Only Perfect Patriot but Perfect Woman"

The Evocation of Joan of Arc in Suffrage England

In a letter to her aunt, dated August 15, 1893, some fifteen years before she joined the WSPU, Lady Constance Lytton summed up both the conundrum and challenge of women's issues that would become central to the debate for the enfranchisement of women:

> On the subject of the Women's Movement, I hardly know what I agree with. I get so angry with the old-fashioned man's woman, and so furious with the advanced woman who goes in for women's superiority over men, so enraged with the people who demand equality for men and women, not in the sense of justice and fairness, but meaning sameness, which I think wildly impossible and unnatural for such differently constitutional beings. My all-round rage with these makes me too giddy to form sound opinions of my own.[1]

Despite her protestations, she very clearly laid out the various strands of the woman argument as they existed in 1893 and which have continued to be central to women's politics, both inside and outside of the academy, ever since. With this characterization in mind, I present a caveat in terms of Joan of Arc imagery within the movement: it is multivalent, fluid, and often contradictory, Lytton's exasperation mirroring my own in terms of coming to grips with Joan's presence and importance for both conservative and radical groups of feminists. But, as the Marxist philosopher V. N. Volosinov has argued, it is because of the aptitude "of any powerful sign to carry different meanings, which makes for its 'vitality and dynamism and the capacity for further development.'"[2]

At the center of the activities of the British suffrage movements of the early 20th-century was a public expression of such multivalent meanings on feminist thought, sexuality, and the body. These multiple discourses were reflected in the visual culture the suffragists created, particularly with regards to the bodily evocation of Joan of Arc as symbol of the struggle for the vote (fig. 27); she represented feminist action, femininity, citizenship, and a gendered, sexual positioning.

Hence, this chapter examines the ways the NUWSS dialogue intersects with and diverges from that of the WSPU (and, to a lesser extent, the WFL). The visual rhetoric each group employs relies on their respective political tactics: The militant WSPU, who, while they espoused public action in the streets, often through violent methods, simultaneously led a platform calling for celibacy, abstinence, and virginity as feminist statements of women's difference from men; the NUWSS asked its members to be respectable, would-be citizens, checking their sexuality in order to be taken seriously by the electorate; and the WFL whose members, like those of the WSPU, realized that any protest, even without violence, would involve the risk of imprisonment. Like their WSPU sisters, they often went to jail but they particularly embraced "political passive resistance."[3]

This is the first art historical analysis of how the NUWSS used Joan imagery, both alongside of, and in response to, changes within the strategic events of the WSPU and WFL. Its focus is three threads of inquiry: moral purity arguments, warrior symbolism, and transgressive, gendered behavior. It analyzes how suffrage women employed Joan of Arc imagery to create resistance narratives to prevailing ideologies of womanhood, ones which empowered them in their cause for women's emancipa-

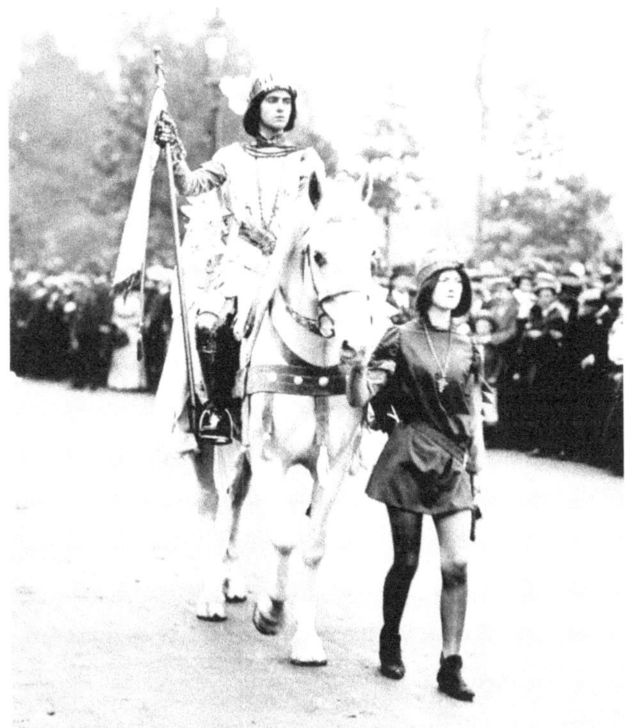

Figure 27. *Miss Joan Annan Bryce as Joan of Arc, 17 June 1911, Women's Coronation Procession.* **London, England. Museum of London.**

tion.[4] Linda Gordon finds it pointless to discuss the suppression of women "unless it is integrated with discussions of the resistance, compromises, and ambiguities with which women actually negotiated relations between the sexes."[5] Such a stance is important in terms of addressing the nuances of the debates on sexuality and moral purity that were central to the groups' representations of Joan which, while its aim was the vote, targeted larger issues of hegemonic patriarchal structures.

To give a clear picture of the impact of Joan imagery in Edwardian England, the study also gives a comparator examination of the representations of Joan in France, in order to address the myriad ways that her life acted as inspiration for various political groups. Following Nora Heimann's lead in her study of Joan imagery in France (1700–1855), I posit that not only was Joan exploited by various groups on the political spectrum, but also that the response to a particular icon like Joan has everything to do with who absorbs the image (what we call reception theory).[6]

In the current literature, Lisa Tickner is our key scholar of suffrage imagery, but her study focuses on militancy and spectacle rather than on such historical representations. Rosemary Betterton examines the stereotypical images of the suffragettes alongside images of Joan within the militant suffragette campaign, focusing on the militant debates such images raise about the inherent conflicts and dichotomous constructions between tradition (read: femininity) and modernity (read: feminism).[7] A new analysis of Joan imagery calls for a more multilayered approach than either Tickner or Betterton could cover in their respective studies.

Iconography

There is a long history of cultures using Joan's image to meet the needs of their respective causes. This phenomenon is historically marked, belonging to the language of iconography. An anonymous writer (1909) for the NUWSS was certainly aware of such visual language and its purpose, calling in its official organ, the *Common Cause*, for "agitation by symbol," because of its "object-lessons, by signs and emblems and pictures, by procession, and many other visible and audible displays." In this context, Joan is a complex character who offers herself up in a number of guises: as warrior; as Christian martyr; as celibate woman; as gender transgressor; as symbol of divine right, among many others. She is represented not only in public pageant as participant (fig. 27), but also through her own banner (fig. 28), this one created by Barbara Forbes of the Artists' Suffrage League for the NUWSS; it shows a field of cream with blue lettering and a *fleur-de-lis* design; above is a crown over crossed swords and a riband that carries the characterization of Joan as: "*Sans Peur et Sans Reproche*" (Without fear and above reproach), hence conflating her example of celibacy and warrior spirit.

The motto of the militant women of the WSPU—"Deeds not Words"—was one of combat, tapping into Joan's warrior spirit: they took the expression from the radical Percy Bysshe Shelley, such a choice reflective of their sense of belonging to a larger, continuous history of resistance.[8] The WSPU understood what Marina Warner argues, that Joan is a preeminent heroine "because she belongs to the sphere of action" rather than contemplation and, further, that "she is anomalous in our culture" because she is "a woman renowned for doing something on her own...."[9] In the WSPU organ, *The Suffragette*, an anonymous writer (1913) summed up this incongruity by using the phrase "not only perfect

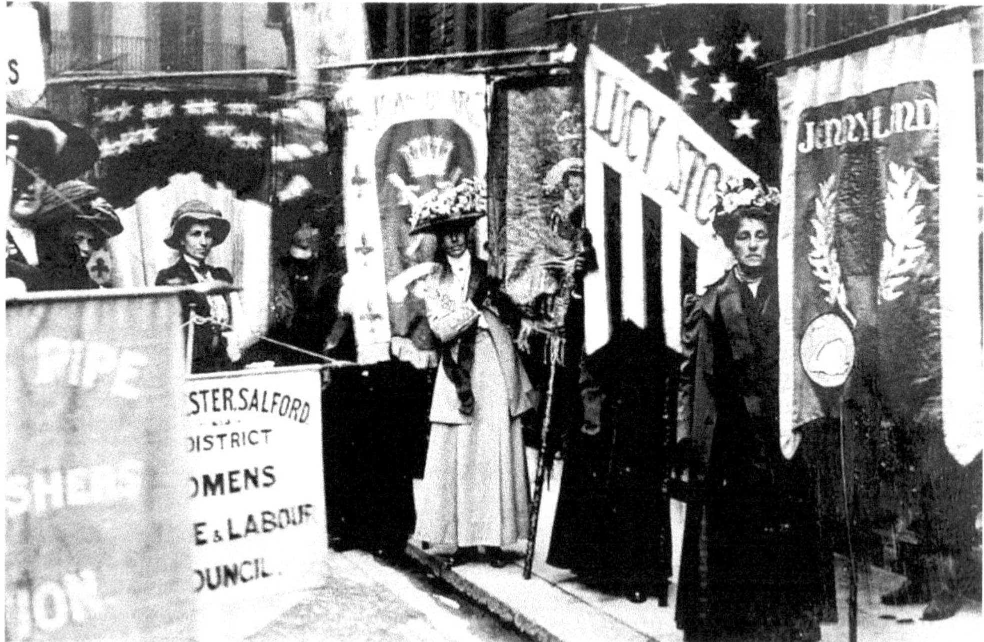

Figure 28. *Joan of Arc Banner, by Barbara Forbes (c. 1871–1946), included in NUWSS Procession,* 12 June 1908. Women's Library, London.

patriot but perfect woman" to describe Joan of Arc. By 1913 such an evocation was far from unusual; Joan had achieved beatification from the Catholic Church in 1909. She would receive sainthood status much later, however, in 1920. But suffrage women took her on as their matron saint by 1908.

Within suffrage imagery and spectacles, Joan covers a myriad of representations which encompass, broadly, Maurice Agulhon's argument for three kinds of representation within revolutionary moments: the woman fighter, the woman standard-bearer, and the woman who was a live allegory, in this latter case speaking to her "live" appearance in pageants and protests.[10] Specifically, we see Joan stand in for (1) sexual purity and sexual freedom; in which Joan acts as the pure, virginal, perfect woman, as part of the sexual purity campaigns of the NUWSS and the WSPU, so that we see Joan as impermeable and celibate in her armor (fig. 29); or, as in *The Suffragette* 1913 image "The Forces of Evil Denouncing the Bearers of Light" we see Joan with a white shield marked "Purity" and a WSPU belt around her armor, warding off the beast of "indecency" which "the press" is corralling, but also instigating (fig. 30); (2) Joan as leader, offering both an example of strength and inspiration, partly through her role as matron saint of militant suffragettes, evoked frequently in her presence at the head of their elegant processions (fig. 27); (3) Joan as warrior, fighting for the cause of women's freedom, frequently dressed in armor on a white charger at the head of their processions (fig. 27); or in press imagery, such as the WSPU image of her on the front page of the first installment of *The Suffragette*, entitled "The Day of the Lord" (fig. 31).

In such images we often see a conflation of Joan and Justice; in Figure 31 Joan carries a sword marked with the phrase "Votes for Women," while "Equality" is literally on the horizon of the globe on which she marches while wielding a flaming torch of Justice.[11] Joan as Justice also exists as in Hilda Dallas's poster for the WSPU (illustrated and discussed in Chapter Four); and (4) Joan as a transgender warrior as in "The Forces of Evil Denouncing the Bearers of Light" (fig. 30). In such examples, her nationalism is often meant to evoke that of St. George, patron saint of England.

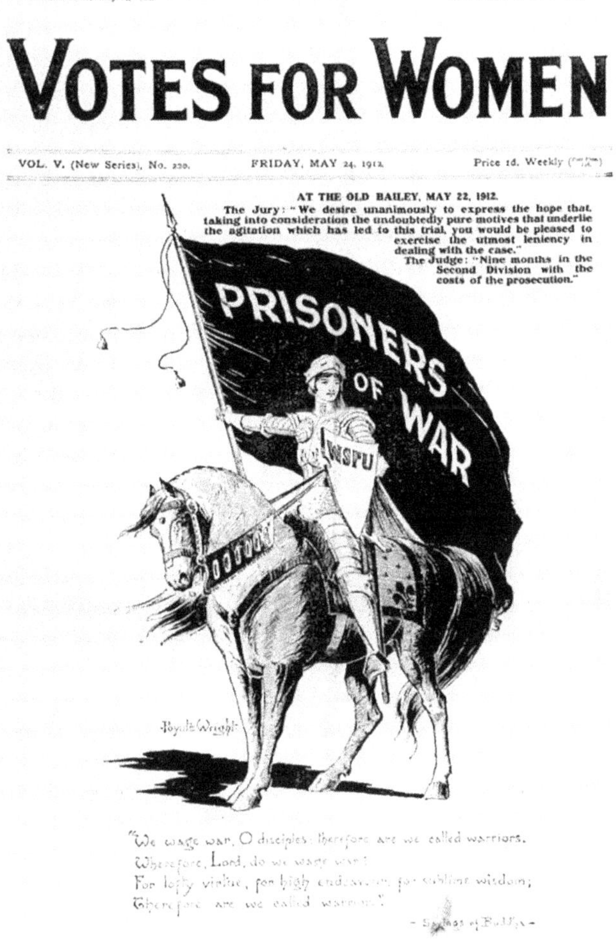

Figure 29. Poyntz Wright (active 1912), "Prisoners of War," from *Votes for Women* (24 May 1912). Museum of London.

Leadership and Moral Purity

Tickner and Betterton both argue that the suffragettes use Joan as a symbol of moral purity, virtue, and femininity specifically to counter the prevailing press stereotype of the frenzied, suffrage woman (figs. 32 and 33) as an ugly, emotionally out-of-control harridan akin to the psychologically deranged "hysteric" who, according to 19th-century medical theories, suffers from lack of sexual stimulation.[12] Tickner and Betterton both avow that Joan embodies this campaign for sexual purity[13] but, we can take that argument further: It is a fight couched in terms of resistance to male authority in women's search for a sexual self-identity.

In terms of the NUWSS approach, Barbara Caine sees the "impossibility for Garrett Fawcett of connecting her national political activities, including her campaign to have women included within the state, with her whole analysis of sexual politics. Experienced as she was at dealing with the world of national politics, she could not make comprehensible within [that] framework … her concern about the oppression and exploitation of women."[14]

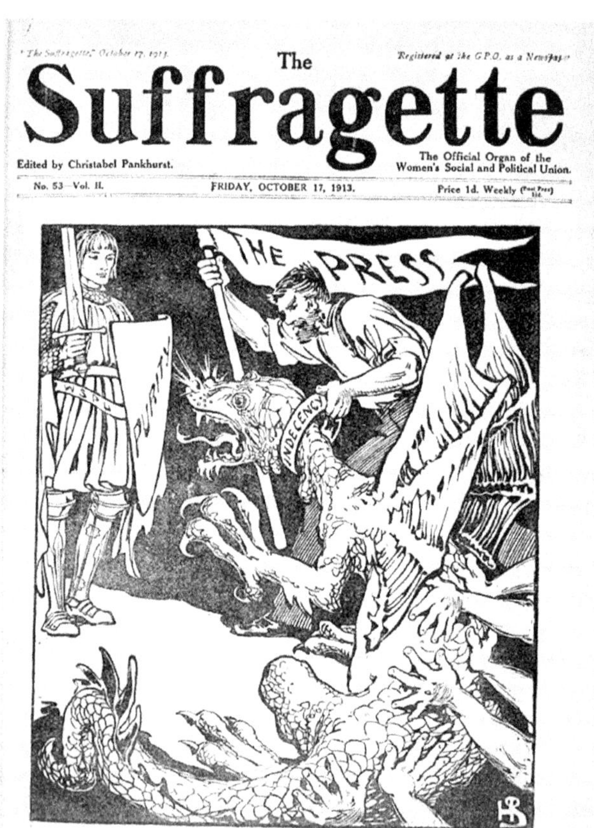

Figure 30. Hilda Dallas (1878–1958), "The Forces of Evil Denouncing the Bearers of Light," from *The Suffragette* (17 October 1913). Museum of London.

Caine's analysis would have been better had she couched it in terms of feminist theory and practice rather than feminist biography. She seems to be discussing the difference between victim feminism of the second wave [Garrett Fawcett's preoccupation with women's exploitation in and out of marriage] versus empowerment feminism of the third [women's claim to the vote] but she is writing in 1992, before the third wave issues of authorization had really come into discourse. From a 21st-century standpoint, it seems that Garrett Fawcett was engaged in all the issues that affected women and for which activism still happens. It could be argued, then, that Garrett Fawcett was ahead of her times in her sensitivity to all sides of the issue regarding women's oppression.[15] Yet, within the narrow vision of the press we have images like the following: Bernard Partridge's *Punch* 1906 cartoon, "The Shrieking Sister" (fig. 33).

I have contended elsewhere that Partridge juxtaposes Garrett Fawcett herself, the rational, "sensible" leader of the conservative

NUWSS, with her hysterical "sister" of the WSPU. The content of the commentary is one that both groups employ; the virago is not a true representation of individual suffrage women within either group and, as Garrett Fawcett says here, does not help the cause![16] Her lack of viability is palpable in John Hassall's ironically titled *A Perfect Woman* (fig. 32) where he marries the hysteric stereotype to the suffragist.

How could imagery of Joan displace such damaging representations in this struggle? As Michelle Cliff suggests, "This cycle of women's voices bursting forth only to be interrupted and silenced is women's tradition."[17] Just as Joan's victories on behalf of her King, Charles VII, suffered mutation and distortion in the voices of her tormentors, ending in her silence through death, so we see suffragists suffer similar silencing in the press imagery. Unearthing strong women in history like Joan to support their cause and their collective voices was a necessary evocation if they were to succeed at separating themselves from patriarchy's view of them as second-class citizens. They weren't going to take opposition lightly and would fight back, their resistance mirroring that of Joan.

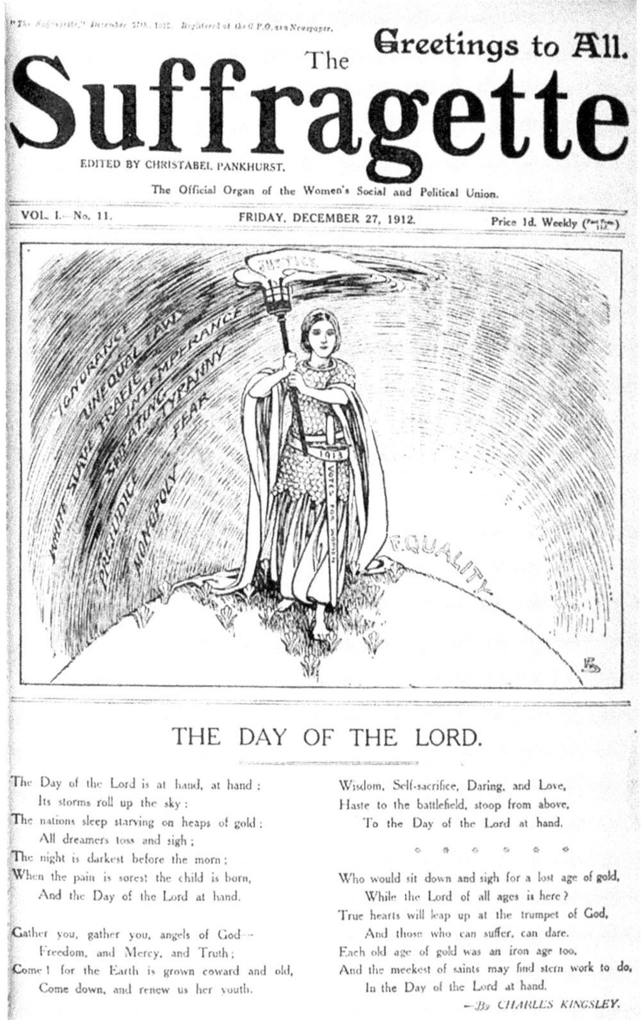

Figure 31. "The Day of the Lord," from *The Suffragette* (27 December 1912). Museum of London.

In light of this desire for their own lived experiences, Joan of Arc becomes a symbol of leadership for Garrett Fawcett and the guiding light of the WSPU, Christabel Pankhurst. Ann Oakley even declares that Garrett Fawcett "was ... like Joan of Arc 'born' to, or for, her particular struggle...."[18] Similarly, in visual form, a suffragette postcard of Christabel (fig. 34) conflates Christabel with Joan, embedding her in stained glass. The glass is marred with blemishes that are an obvious reference to the window-smashing activities of the militant suffragettes, but Betterton argues that these cracks signify "the wounds that, like stigmata, she must bear in the Cause."[19] Betterton also suggests that the cracks could represent attacks she was receiving from anti-suffragists and from former WSPU members who did not support her perceived extremist views on social purity, the cracks in the window embodying the threats to her own body within the political fray.[20] For example, in Christabel's publication, *The Great Scourge*, a collection of her articles she originally published in *The Suffragette* in 1913 on the topic of the threat of venereal disease to women, she advocates against marriage because of men's infection of innocent women as a result of their own uncontrolled vices, a serious cause of women's ill health. The "cure" became her rallying cry: "Votes for Women and Chastity for Men."[21] Implicit in the WSPU rhetoric is a protection of women's bodies that mirrored Joan's own position. Militant women had faced many public indignities at the hands of men; first being arrested for interrupting meetings, in attempts to present their case in the House of Commons they were met with fierce violence at the hands of the police and men in the crowds. Martha Vicinus argues that this "pawing and pushing by men whenever the suffragettes entered any public space frightened and angered women, leaving them eager for Christabel's message, 'Votes for Women and Chastity for Men.' For the militants men seemed to control the streets, the courts, and the prisons; they readily linked sexual impurity to the enforcement of woman's economic, political, and marital enslavement."[22] More recently, both Linda Martz and June Purvis have pointed out that Christabel's publication coincided with the instance of the worst treatment of women in prison, through forcible feeding, and also coincided with new laws governing both such hunger striking and the White Slave Trade that were meant to protect women but which, in fact, did not.[23]

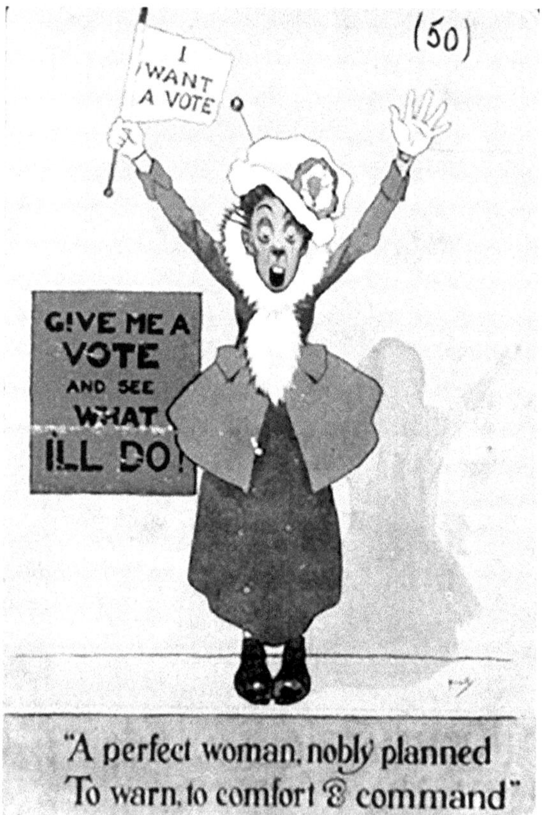

Figure 32. John Hassall (1868–1948), *A Perfect Woman*. Anti-suffragette postcard. 1912. Women's Library, London.

In both instances here, the rhetoric equates the leaders with Joan as martyred saints responding to a calling. In *The Great Scourge* Christabel warns women against the dangers of marriage and assures her readers that "large numbers of women were refusing it," even going so far as to determine, through statistical analysis, that "[m]an is not the 'lord of creation,' but the exterminator of the species." She puts forward that the "injuries of women in the sex relationship were … the main reason and basis of militancy."[24] But her sister, Sylvia Pankhurst, misrepresents her in her own assessment of the suffrage movement by implying that Christabel saw women as superior beings:

[F]rom the columns of *The Suffragette* the deduction was clear: women were purer, nobler and more courageous, men were an inferior body, greatly in need of purification; the WSPU being the chosen instrument capable of administering the purge. Masses of women, especially of the middle class, were affected by this attitude, even though they remained outside the ranks of the Union.[25]

In fact, Sylvia sells her sister short. As Elisabeth Sarah has argued, *The Great Scourge* was the most cogent expression of the subordination of women; Susan Kingsley Kent specifically positions Christabel's discourse as anathema to the separate spheres construction; and Margaret Jackson sees it as a call for "female sexual autonomy."[26] But, in another sense, Christabel was honoring women's existence on a higher spiritual plain than that of men, a topic that inflects the WSPU's usage of Joan as it does that of the NUWSS. And just how wide was Christabel's call from the pages of *The Great Scourge* that allowed her to influence women's attitudes? Who was Christabel's audience then? The majority of suffragettes appear to have been either single or widowed rather than married, a number that grew with the increasing militancy of the group.[27] June Purvis argues that what Christabel was presenting was, in fact, an alternative way of living for women; that marriage was not necessarily their destiny but rather that they could live useful (and safe) lives apart from men, a topic that many historians have ignored, while focusing on the prevalence of discussion of venereal disease and avoidance of marriage.[28] Purvis further points out that Christabel was an experienced strategist, capable of rallying her troops, who "deliberately linked suffrage and sexuality as a way of motivating her followers, increasingly young single women, into militant action against their enemy, men." Purvis also discusses the views of Jane Marcus who asserts that Christabel was responding from the position of her disillusionment with male-centered politics and so she chose "to excite sex hatred in the same way that her earlier friends on the left excited class hatred, as a spur to revolutionary violence."[29]

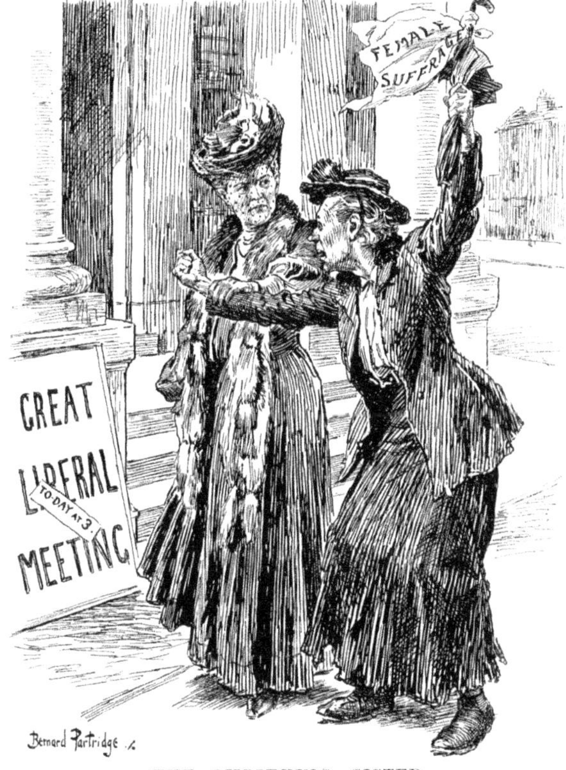

THE SHRIEKING SISTER.

The Sensible Woman. *"YOU HELP OUR CAUSE? WHY, YOU'RE ITS WORST ENEMY!"*

Figure 33. Sir John Bernard Partridge (1861–1945), "The Shrieking Sister," *Punch* (1906). Reproduced with permission of Punch Ltd. www.punch.co.uk.

Equally controversial, Garrett Fawcett was initially ambivalent about the social purity mission of the late 19th-century, as embodied in the Contagious Diseases Acts, which were in place to keep prostitutes free of disease, with Josephine Butler as the chief campaigner against its methods and motivations. Constables could pull women off the streets for inspection to make sure they did not have disease or, if they exhibited any type of vaginal discharge, send them to Lock Hospitals for treatment. Such acts resulted in a form of rape, a rank violation with the speculum. Butler fought successfully to repeal the Acts because of the dangers they imposed to women. Garrett Fawcett initially felt "it was mistaken tactics to confuse the suffrage campaign with the explosive issue of sexual exploitation." But by the mid–1880s she had changed her tune because "the suffragist case" was "in parliamentary eclipse and child prostitution" was "sensationally presented to a shocked middle-class public by W. T. Stead's lurid revelations in the *Pall Mall Gazette*."[30] She began to embrace the stance of moral purity as Christabel was later to do and it serves as one reason she promotes Joan as an example to emulate. This view is nowhere more clear than in her 1905 publication, *Five Famous Women*, in which she devotes a chapter to Joan of Arc, emphasizing that Joan remained impervious to evil, living in the world "without acquiring any of its impurities."[31] Fawcett stresses, above all, the significance of Joan's virginity, discussing the record of Joan's trial, when university authorities consulted the archbishop who determined that "God had many times revealed to a virgin what he had hidden from men.... Moreover, the devil was held to be incapable of making a compact with a virgin."[32] Fawcett asserts of Joan, an attitude Christabel later echoes, that she had "within her the pure fire of self-devotion to a noble cause which enable[d] her to keep herself unspotted from the world."[33] The record of Joan's trial was published in English for the first time in 1902, so it is fair to assume that this publication served as a new source of inspiration for suffrage women like Garrett Fawcett who themselves wanted to put forth a pure example of womanhood, unspotted by taint or scandal.

Thus, a woman, unsullied by men, became the most appropriate matron saint of suffrage. It should be noted, however, that while Garrett Fawcett promotes Joan as pure example, the NUWSS executive board did not support such frank writings on venereal disease. An important case in point was the contentious publication by one of her national executive board members, Louisa Martindale, medical doctor. The resulting 1908 pamphlet, *Under the Surface*, was, according to Purvis, "the first feminist tract devoted solely to venereal disease," written at the request of the NUWSS; in it Martindale outlined the horrible effects of the disease, linking it to prostitution and hence to the demand for the vote in order to make women economically independent from men. But the other NUWSS executive board members considered the publication too controversial and Martindale ended up publishing it herself, yet, it was "considered so shocking that it was debated in the House of Commons—and denounced as obscene. It resulted in adverse publicity for the group."[34] Hence,

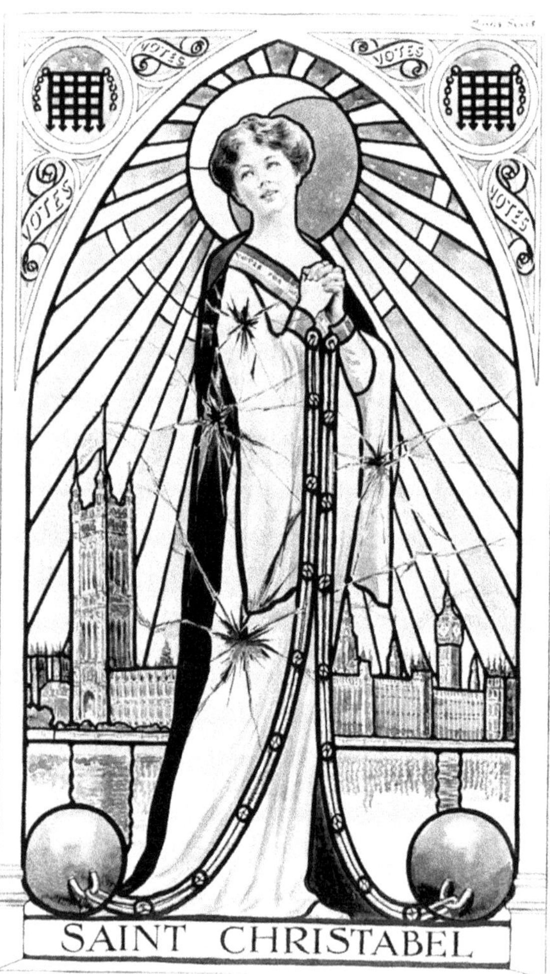

Figure 34. Charles R. Sykes (1878–1950), "Proposed Suffrage Martyrs' Memorial" from *The Bystander* (20 March 1912). Republished as "Saint Christabel" in *Votes for Women*, 1912. Museum of London.

we need to consider degrees of discourse and steps the NUWSS took to reach the moment of the 1908 publication with regards to the moral purity campaign.

Behind Garrett Fawcett's 1905 celebration of Joan lay her efforts in the 1890s to disassociate suffrage women from the extreme representations of the New Woman. Sally Ledger attests that it was difficult to unravel a single definition of this New Woman's behavior: Views were mixed even among 19th-century feminists as to whom the New Woman was, as discussed in Chapter One; Sarah Grand, who coined the term, saw the New Woman's concerns as those of motherhood and sexual purity while Mona Caird argued that the New Woman attacked motherhood and Grant Allan championed a New Woman's espousal of free love, while "the constitutional feminists of the late 19th-century saw themselves neither as campaigners against motherhood nor as sexual radicals, but as supporters of female suffrage."[35] What rankled Garrett Fawcett most was the connection of the fight for women's rights with the New Woman's ideas of free love and sexual freedom. The suffrage groups sought to distance themselves from the press representations of the New Woman who rode a bicycle and spoke openly and critically about the institution of marriage while promoting free love relationships. In a famous rebuttal to Grant Allen's novel *The Woman Who Did* (1895) Garrett Fawcett calls him an enemy who "claims to link together the claim of women to citizenship and social and industrial independence with attacks upon marriage and the family."[36] Free love, that is, love without the bonds of marriage, would not protect young women from contagion any better than marriage with an unchaste partner would. And, if a man were willing to engage in a free relationship, the assumption these women made was that he was already tainted and experienced, hence creating the possibility of exposure to sexual disease for any woman with whom he had intercourse. Garrett Fawcett and Christabel would have both remarked that it was better to remain chaste and focused on the cause than to become caught up in such a dangerous and immoral situation.

This guise of purity is embedded in histories of Joan such as that of the Jesuit priest at the court of Louis XIII, René de Cériziers, who claimed Joan as a prototype of "wronged innocence." He spread the legend that if any man looked on her with impure thoughts, he would be struck impotent forever.[37] Similarly, our suffrage women, in Christabel's eyes, would be saved from "wronged innocence" if they chose to remain celibate. In this regard Garrett Fawcett was infamous for making examples of men who seduced women.[38] Hence, this representation of Joan as simultaneously untouchable and provocative, is transferred to commentary on suffrage women; as Joseph Kestner has shown, the surging forces of suffrage could instill fear in men, as evidenced in many late 19th-century paintings that depict powerful women luring men to their doom such as Edward Burne-Jones's *Depths of the Sea*, 1887 (Fogg Art Museum, Harvard University) in which a bewitching mermaid with a determinedly seductive gaze, paralyzes a young man by embracing him, dragging him down to her underwater lair. Warner summarizes the historical writings on Joan: she is at once the beautiful, seductive maiden, in full command of her sexual power, yet she "annuls the usual consequences of those characteristics, remaining in the virginal state of prepubescence."[39] Is it any wonder then that suffrage women wore white, symbol of purity and innocence, and, further, that while they were seductive in their collective beauty in pageants and portraits, they were doubly strong for resisting the temptations of the flesh?

While Garrett Fawcett promoted sexual purity and respectability for women, she did not enforce the kind of extremism that Christabel has been accused of in subsequent readings of *The Great Scourge*, which began with her sister, Sylvia's, analysis. Instead Garrett Fawcett said:

> I never believe in the possibility of a sex war. Nature has seen after that; as long as mothers have sons and fathers, daughters there can never be a sex war. What draws men and women together is stronger than the brutality and tyranny which drives them apart.[40]

She believed that votes for women and feminism would benefit everyone. She said, "This is what we meant when we called our paper the *Common Cause*. [Suffrage] was the cause of men, women, and children. We believe that men cannot be truly free so long as women are held in political subjection."[41] Her approach was much more moderate than Christabel's position in *The Great Scourge*. Jane Marcus sees Christabel's stance as a "deliberate political choice to exacerbate *difference*, to conduct the suffragette movement as a sex-war against the enemy, men." Further, she defends Christabel's motives by saying she was "[d]eliberately fanning the flames of sex hatred [as] an exercise in sexual politics like modern feminism's campaign for abortion rights. It was a political choice to champion the 'wrongs' issue rather than the 'rights' issue—venereal disease rather than birth control." Put more bluntly, she concludes that "she hoped to freeze and frighten and symbolically castrate the enemy with her armed-virgin, Joan-of-Arc posture, whose sword would surgically un-womb the diseased venereal State."[42] Christabel's attitude has been viewed as extremist, David Mitchell, Christabel's unsympathetic biographer, seeing it echoed in Valerie Solanas's SCUM Manifesto, which Susan Douglas also views as similarly over-the-top.[43] Yet, Solanas's words mirror the dialogue on hysteric/ activism which we will see throughout this study, particularly her desire to "destroy the male sex."[44] Like Christabel's own manifesto, it was not very popular with feminists in general, but it gets at the sources of power then as now that stand in the way of women moving forward.

The Great Scourge's message met with some opprobrium among Christabel's contemporaries, particularly the left-wing, free-love feminist Rebecca West, who urged Christabel to reject what she saw as her puritanism because it would "set back the medical treatment of syphilis by renewing moral disdain for the victims."[45] She specifically exhorts Christabel to cease what West perceived as her hate campaign as it would, in West's eyes, destroy the suffrage movement. West's view is echoed in a political cartoon by Mabel Lucie

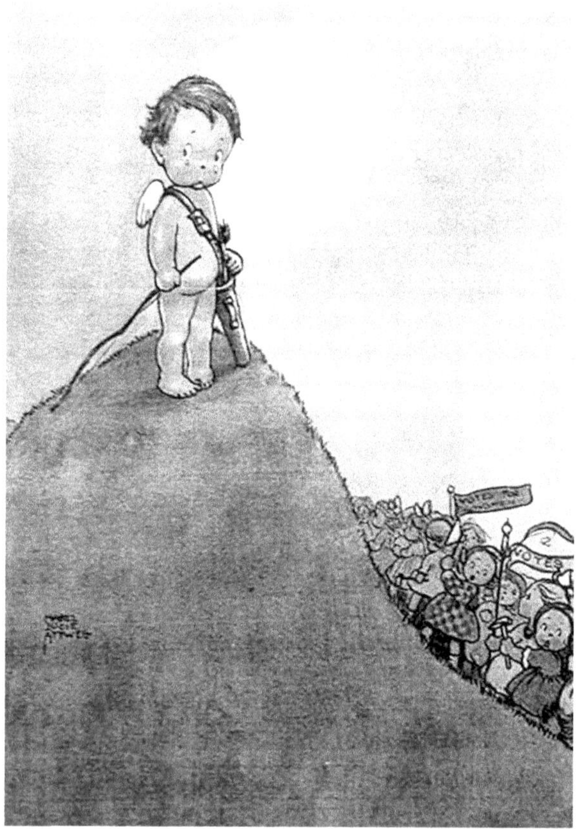

Figure 35. Mabel Lucie Attwell (1879–1964), "Oh Christabel!" *The Tatler*, 1912.

Attwell, "Oh Christabel!" in which a weeping Cupid stands on a hill with his bow withdrawn while below him is a throng of young girls demanding the vote for women (fig. 35). The editorial note below the image when published in *The Tatler* declares "Cupid out of work." But Christabel was arguing for equal standards of purity before marriage.[46] This discourse continues to inflect views of feminists today and it has become a convenient way for men, then as now, to simply dismiss women's call for change as nothing more than a male-bashing campaign. To take such a stance is not to be a listening ear but rather a patriarchal, dismissive voice, as is Mitchell when he says: "Demonstrations against the exploitation of women as 'sexual objects' (Playboy Clubs, Miss World Contests, strip joints, girlie magazines) are in direct line of descent from Christabel's Moral Crusade." As Purvis notes of such statements, many male historians have not "engage[d] with the discourse of sexual subjection in Christabel's writings, on the grounds that those suffragists who agreed with her were only a small minority of the total."[47] Marginalization and sexual exploitation go hand in hand, that's part of Christabel's point; if women had the vote, then they would be in a position to help both themselves as a marginalized group and these other sectors who were subject to exploitation. Mitchell really hit the nail on the head even though he was trying to be trivializing. The world is still ruled by men whose privilege is both to maintain and partake in the double moral standard.

Yet, according to some reads of Christabel's position, her moral crusade was quite conservative. Les Garner, for one, argues that "[i]t reflected Victorian attitudes to sex and the uncertainties about the sexual drive of men. Sex was sinful and its only legitimate purpose was procreation…. If men found restraint difficult they should exercise self discipline and control aided, if need be, by drugs." Further, he asserts, she included no arguments on a woman's right to sexual desire or need of it, nor anything about contraception.[48] Writing in 1998, in assessing the historiography on this topic up to that point, Lesley A. Hall argues that at the time there was a more nuanced debate going on rather than "two beleaguered opposing camps" of social purity and sex reform.[49]

In this regard, it can also be argued that these women worked against prevailing Victorian attitudes about women, as described by Mary Poovey, who explains that within liberal, bourgeois ideology, women were seen as "sexualized, susceptible and fallen," hence they were in need of control by men, an image "that provided a defensible explanation for inequality. If women were governed not by reason (like men), but by something else, then they could hardly be expected (or allowed) to participate in the economic and political fray."[50] The efforts of the suffrage women as outlined here would seem to be working against that damaging construct, allowing women to take their sexuality into their own hands, to conquer the baser elements, and to turn that construct around, arguing that men were in need of a serious check rather than the women. Thus, Joan, a woman unblemished, became the matron saint of suffrage and we find her characteristics of moral purity embodied in the leaders themselves.[51]

Joan as Warrior

We see differences in how each group manipulates Joan's image. For Garrett Fawcett, she represented something pure and above reproach, perhaps mirroring women's own desires to be able, ironically, to stand outside their sex, purely spiritual, in their quest for the vote. For the WSPU however, as Christabel states in *The Suffragette* in 1913 by which time militancy had reached fever pitch: "Joan of Arc is the militant wom[en's] ideal. They feel the closest kinship with her and in every word and in every act of hers they recognize the same spirit as that which strengthens them to risk their liberty and endure torture for the sake of freedom."[52] The suffragette was necessarily a female fighter; her identity "was one built around a feminine heroic, and a rhetoric of female rebellion…,"[53] hence why Joan, like other symbolic, historic heroines, takes pride of place as her spiritual leader. According to Christabel, "militancy is the highest virtue" because it does not tolerate evil but rather works to eradicate it.[54] In this sense, Joan is both the virtuous example and the warrior who fights the evil.

If we agree with Brian Harrison in his characterization of WSPU militancy, we can see that they, like the NUWSS, sought to operate on a spiritual plain:

> Militant companionship is consolidated by commitment to a faith. The suffragette movement's appeal required response to a "call" at least as compelling as that of any religious obligation…. [I]n the secularizing society of Edwardian Britain, feminism resembled Socialism and imperialism in attracting intense dedication from people whose conversion-experience would earlier have taken religious rather than secular form. The greater the self-sacrifice demanded, the greater the need for an elevated, and perhaps politically impractical, ideal to make it all seem worthwhile. Even a feminist so rationalistic and non-militant as Mrs. Fawcett assigned the cause the place in her life that religion had occupied in her mother's.[55]

Other suffrage women echoed these sentiments of spiritual quest, one which, I argue, aligned them with Joan's own sacrifice through divine inspiration.[56] Similarly, Cheryl R. Jorgensen-Earp talks about the transfiguring sword, not as a weapon for actual battle but as embodying the sword of the spirit, the militant women's spirit being indomitable and the government unable to break it.[57]

So, is it possible to conflate this ideal of pure womanhood existing on a spiritual plain with Joan as warrior? In a book on royal imagery I have shown that cultures create female royalty because they need examples of pure, young women to represent moral purity, women who, for example, can tame the wild beasts that they ride in barrel races as Wyoming Rodeo Queens (fig. 36) during the annual "Jubilee" celebration of statehood.[58] Wyoming, like other U.S. states, constructs such homespun royalty to keep at bay those wilder, unruly, pre-statehood days. These Rodeo Queens are not that different from Joan, in full armor, astride her famed white horse (fig. 29). The horse, in traditional iconography, represents the unruly passions. Joan astride her steed, or a rodeo queen perfectly coiffed and sitting her Western quarter horse, signifies a woman's moral superiority to the baser instincts, the very ones that Garrett Fawcett and Christabel were trying to combat.

This comparison is more apt than you might at first suspect since Wyoming was the first place to grant women the vote, in 1869 while it was still a Territory, such that this image of the Rodeo Queen and her court literally embodies women as equal citizens with men. In fact, Fawcett used the case of enfranchised Wyoming women repeatedly in her arguments for suffrage in England.[59]

Pure woman and warrior combined reflect Betterton's characterization of a "sealed and resistant body of suffrage," that "signifies *self*-possession rather than male ownership, command over the passions and pride in female resistance," for WSPU militants.[60] Further reflecting such images as "Prisoners of War" (fig. 29), Agulhon calls such public processional presentation a "live allegory," noting two instances during the French Revolution when a woman took up a pose of Liberty; and another woman who mounted on horseback

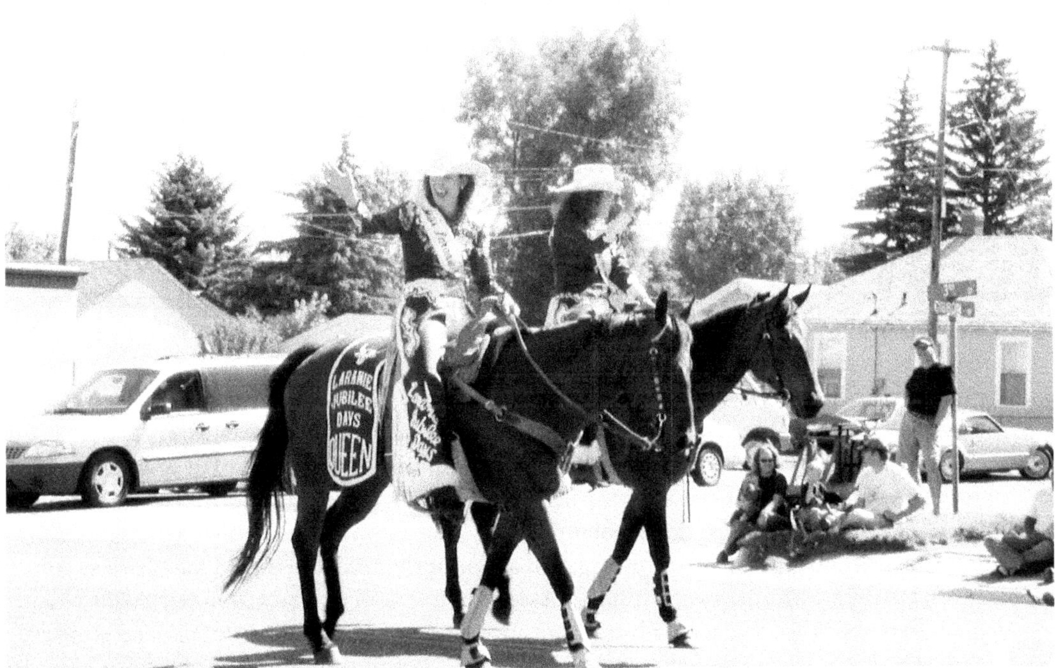

Figure 36. *Jubilee Days Rodeo Queen,* Laramie, Wyoming. 2003. Author's photograph.

with a red flag, and was able to get soldiers to follow her. Agulhon exclaims, "Goddesses … were inevitable in these solemn, theatrical, and at the same time ritualistic, ceremonies. Somehow or other they always appeared on the scene; or if they failed to, they were conjured up."[61] Hence, the necessity of such a symbol is ingrained on such occasions.

Further, Christabel called Joan "our patron saint," claiming her as the archetypal militant warrior and an example for the militant suffragettes in the most heated part of their history: 1909–14. As Tickner observes in her analysis of Christabel's famed essay on Joan in *The Suffragette,* "Joan served the millennial zeal of the WSPU, and also its increasing antipathy to men (neither of which the [NUWSS] could understand)."[62] One of the key WSPU members, Emmeline Pethick-Lawrence, even hailed Christabel herself as "maiden warrior."[63] In another instance, Christabel told a meeting with regards to the WSPU stance on militancy, that the Reform Bills had been won "by hard fighting, and they could have been got in no other way."[64] Her stance here mirrors one of her mother's speeches, given in New York in 1913. Entitled "Why We Are Militant," Emmeline Pankhurst called upon the men in the room, saying: "You know perfectly well that there never was a thing worth having that was not worth fighting for." Further, in her discussion of militant tactics, she asserted that "nothing ever has been got out of the British Parliament without something very nearly approaching a revolution. You need something dynamic in order to force legislation through the House of Commons," before admitting that "the extension of the franchise to the men of my country have been preceded by very great violence, by something like a revolution, by something like a civil war."[65] Although she does not invoke Joan, her fighting spirit and its rhetoric is at the forefront of her speech, as is her strategic appeal to a country whose own freedoms have come from both revolution and civil war. It is in this context that Jorgensen-Earp positions the WSPU as legitimate fighters in a just war rather than as criminals, the very protest women voiced when in prison: "Through this relatively minor image of the suffragette as a prisoner of war, union members sought the legitimacy for their actions that would come, in part, if they were officially recognized as political prisoners."[66]

Christabel incited defiance rather than persuasion, at times, in her rhetoric. Harrison categorizes her strategy as involving "projecting women into what were then seen as male roles, creating a gallery of heroines selected for emulating male feats, and relishing the delectable revelation of male stupidity provided by flat-footed detectives," evidence found in a series of articles on warrior women in *Votes for Women* in 1911.[67] In this instance, the WSPU was at odds with the NUWSS, the former trumping "female superiority over men even in the male spheres of war and politics" while the latter continued to support a platform of shared humanity between the sexes.[68]

And yet, the WSPU and the NUWSS shared many views on the significance of Joan as warrior, which coincided with their use of her as moral exemplar. Garrett Fawcett stated, in her study of Joan, for example, that beyond the obvious reason of Joan dressing in armor because it was necessary for battle, was a more important one: "That armour was a real protection to her which she would never willingly relinquish as long as she had to live without the companionship of women in the midst of a wild and lawless soldiery."[69] Further, Garrett Fawcett implied it was not to protect herself from her own sexual desires that she wore the armor but rather to keep men at bay. Christabel used similar arguments in her slogan and clarion call: "Votes for Women and Chastity for Men." Further, Garrett Fawcett argues that Joan possessed "inborn military instinct, which com-

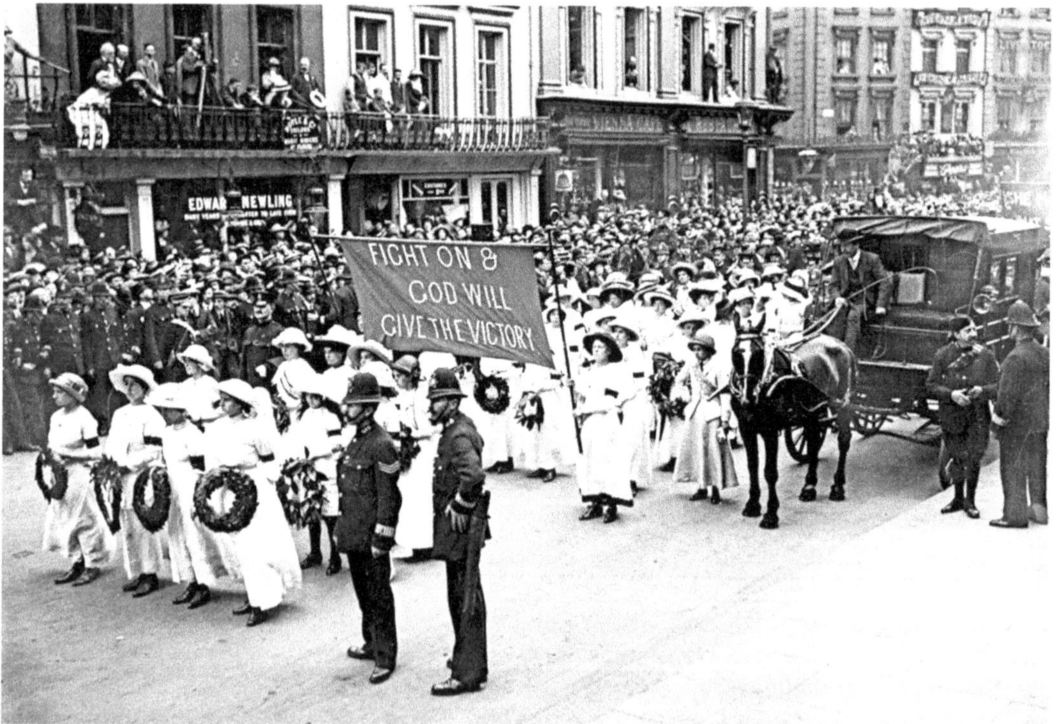

Figure 37. *Emily Wilding Davison Funeral Procession*, 1913. Includes banner that reads: "Fight on and God will give the victory." Museum of London.

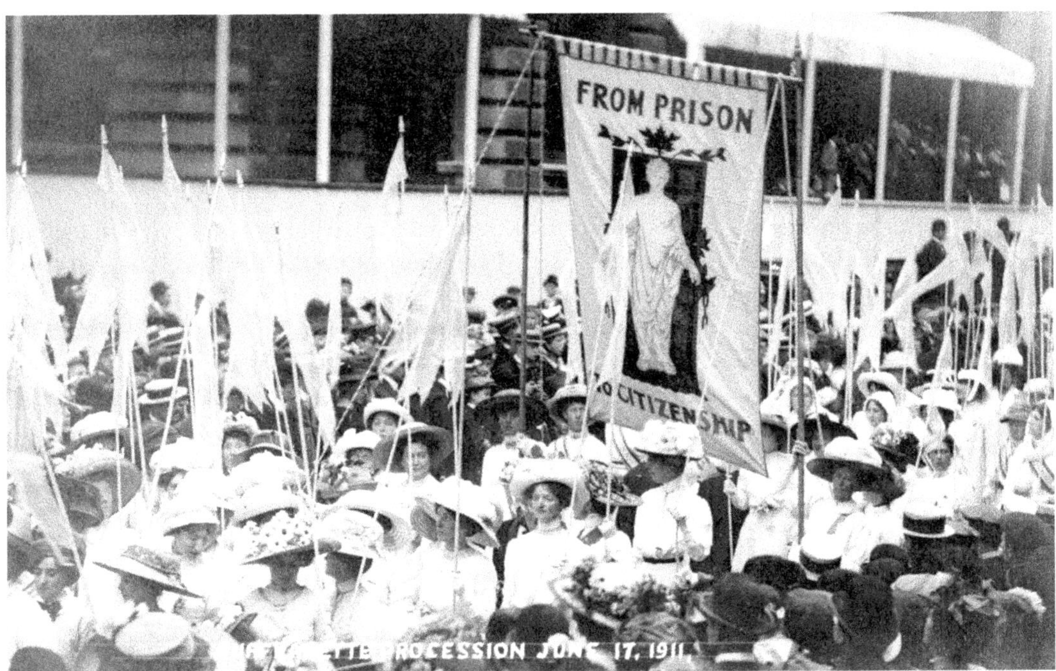

Figure 38. *From Prison to Citizenship,* banner design by Laurence Housman (1865–1959). June 1911, London, England. Museum of London.

manded the respect of the men-at-arms," and "she had absolute sincerity as well as common sense and ready wit, and was wholly womanly in the use of her tongue. Thus she had the man's weapon, the sword, as well as the woman's weapon, the tongue."[70] Hence, in this statement and its sentiment, Garrett Fawcett conflated the metaphorical muscle of the WSPU ("deeds") with the power of women's voices ("words"), the respective approaches of the two groups. For Christabel, as Jorgensen-Earp characterizes her rhetoric on Joan, she was a real, historic woman who was a militant, hence she provided a true example of militancy as "not unwomanly."[71]

The visual rhetoric of women's marches also evokes the warrior element (figs. 37 and 38). First the WSPU then the NUWSS started to employ color-coded sashes to embody ideals of the cause. The purple, white, and green of the WSPU, according to Emmeline Pethick-Lawrence, represented dignity, purity and hope respectively.[72] The NUWSS then adopted the colors of red, green and white (red and white initially) not only to distinguish themselves from the WSPU, but also to align their philosophy with that of the nationalism of the Italian Garibaldi whom they greatly admired. The WFL took the colors of green, white and gold. Apart from this symbolism which embodied the ideals of the cause, we must remark on the association of the sash with that of military men in uniform, as well as the formation of the marches themselves in organization of rank and file with accompanying banners.[73]

Further, like the military men, the women of these groups dressed in a kind of uniform, the white dress, which showed them to be unified not only visually but also in terms of their singular vision for the cause at hand. Like the military men, whose rank and position the public could easily identify by their uniforms, so too could the public easily identify suffrage women by their white dresses and sashes.

Joan, like her suffrage sisters, took on male armor to protect herself from the advances of men or, in the case of the suffrage woman, from the jeers and chants of men. The suffrage women's over-feminized dress could be seen, like Joan's armor, as a shield. This idea is reemphasized in the numerous militant images of women with shields in suffrage imagery; whether she is Justice, Bodica, or Britannia herself, she is usually carrying a shield and is armored. Further, we see a specific conflation of shield/purity in *The Suffragette* image of "The Forces of Evil Denouncing the Bearers of Light" (fig. 30) in which Joan carries a white shield marked "Purity" as she battles the dual beasts of the "the Press" and "Indecency." In each case, the women are maintaining a pattern of resistance to male authority, a topic to which I return below.

Cicely Hamilton, who had been a member of the NUWSS, then the WSPU, said, there "may have been some connection between this 'dressiness' and the combative impulse, since soldiers, all the world over, are inclined to be fussy about their personal appearance."[74] In one sense, this makes them akin to Joan herself, who by all reports wore special white armor.[75] In this vain, Vicinus argues that

> the militants turned this [spiritual] superiority into a shield, protecting them as they entered public space, and into a weapon, altering public opinion as they asserted their rightful freedom. Freed from self-doubt and traditional inhibitions, the militants felt an inner freedom that sustained them like an "angel of destiny."[76]

This view is reflected in the appearance of Joan of Arc, embodied by Miss Elsie Howie, in the suffragette procession for the WSPU mass meeting in honor of Emmeline Pethick-Lawrence's release from Holloway Gaol. Clad in shining armor and riding a white horse she stands with a banner in the *Daily Mirror* photograph that records the event: "This afternoon a suffragette procession will form up at the Marble Arch, and march to the Aldwych Theatre, where a public meeting will be held. The picture shows Miss Elise Howey [*sic*], who will march in the procession as Joan of Arc."[77] Thus, suffrage women had Joan as their visible leader, one whose warrior attitude they emulated both in their honoring of her at the start of such processions, and in their own form of presentation within the marches.

Transgender Representation and Resistance Narratives

As Elaine Showalter explains, initially suffrage women sought the vote for single women: "While married women seemed to be excluded from enfranchisement by the common law doctrine of coverture, adult single women, it could be argued, needed to vote since they were legally unrepresented."[78] For them and, later, for married women, Susan K. Kent argues that the vote "became both the symbol of the free, sexually autonomous woman and the means by which the goals of a feminist sexual culture were to be attained."[79] As discussed earlier, some suffrage women were anxious about the appearance of the New Woman in the 1880s and 1890s, a situation due to her alliance with "a new political and sexual group, not just an absence or cipher in the social body, but a constituency with potential opportunities, powers, and rights."[80] But it was more complex a case than these scholars imply. Using Joan as inspiration could suggest that you sought to live outside your body—its urgings and sexual appeal—reaching an ascetic domain as did Joan. Alternately, what should a "sexually autonomous woman" look like and what, exactly, were the goals of this "feminist sexual culture"? I would argue, in this path of resistance, that women sought out Joan as a spiritual guide. As Purvis points out, Christabel's stance on women's ability to rise above the physical abuse of their bodies in a spiritual context, has only just begun to receive attention from feminist historians, yet it is a central component of their representation of Joan.[81] In their endeavor to rise above the average woman, these activists often denied their own sexuality *or* they overplayed their femininity card, *or* they tried to achieve some respectable representation in between those extremes in order to present a serious, sober, professional self. This complex situation does not mean, however, that they did not have sexual lives; the sex writers of the 1890s began to explore the damage of the call for celibacy for women versus their need for sexual gratification as being equivalent to that of men.[82] Lesley A. Hall shows that suffrage women from all groups debated, embraced and alternately changed their opinions in a fluid manner regarding such sexual politics in the writings of the period.[83] But there were certainly competing discourses on this issue, Showalter pointing out, for example, that many women were raised to believe that women were superior to men because they were perceived to be passionless and more spiritual, a stance reinforced by the social purity campaigns of the 1880s which "left women traumatized by their discoveries of abusive male sexuality."[84] British society thus aligned suffrage women with the Virtues as the suffrage leaders had done with Joan, the Virtues belonging to "the world of ideas, where sex has no place."[85] We have threads of this dialogue in both the NUWSS and in the WSPU so we need to identify how the leaders used Joan in this capacity versus how individual women in the movement might have perceived her.

Like an angel, asexual, Joan rose above the skirmish in the same way as did the suffrage women. We see them, in their processions of the early 20th-century, impeccably dressed in clean white gowns, with well kempt hair under elaborate hats and bodies in check, such as in the NUWSS Demonstration of 13 June 1908 when 30,000 suffrage supporters marched through the streets. This event launched a new phase of mass suffrage campaigns; one woman carried a Joan of Arc banner that read: "Sans Peur et sans reproche" ("Without fear and above reproach"), thus aligning their well-kempt, respectable appearance with Joan's own philosophy: courageous and pure. The most famous example of Joan's presence is in the image with which I opened from the Women's Coronation Procession in 1911, held in London (fig. 27), which included both the NUWSS and the WSPU contingencies. These processions demonstrate Joan's importance as symbolic and actual leader; tying women to their own history, one they had to invent to counter patriarchal exclusion of women's lives, thus showing them creating a resistant narrative. That this is the case is punctuated by Tickner's observation that they "produced a pageant to rival the official Coronation procession, to question their exclusion from it and also the values on which it was based."[86]

Similarly, in the WSPU funeral for Emily Wilding Davison in 1913, who had made the ultimate sacrifice by throwing herself under the King's horse at the Derby races, the banner above the women's heads quotes Joan's words: "Fight on and God will Give the Victory" (fig. 37).[87] Joan uttered this cry when Charles II sent her to Poitiers so that the university officials could cross-examine her. They wanted some miraculous sign of her divine commission. She replied:

> I have not come to Poitiers to give signs or to work miracles. My sign will be to raise the siege of Orléans. Let them give me men-at-arms, few or many, and I will go.... The men must fight; it is God who gives the victory.[88]

The figure that led this solemn funeral procession was dressed in white, holding a large gold cross; the press at the time identified her as Joan of Arc. The banner with Joan's words was the first banner in the procession. Tickner says that this last great procession was "a way of assimilating the associations of Joan of Arc into the imagery of a guerilla campaign."[89] Similarly, in her assessment of the 1911 publication *The Suffragette*, which set down the history of the WSPU to date, Kathryn Dodd states that they struggled with the "problem of representation," suggested in clear terms in Emmeline Pankhurst's "Preface" to the history

> where she talked of the experience of militant feminism in terms of "the joy of battle, the exaltation that comes of sacrifice of self for great objects and the prophetic vision that assures us of the certain triumph of this 20th-century fight for human emancipation." Here is suggested the combination of womanly strength in battle and womanly spirituality … [which is] the dominant representation of the "militant woman" within the WSPU from 1911.[90]

If we doubt the tone of noble self-sacrifice is purposeful, akin to Joan's experience in battle and then in prison, we need only examine the rhetoric of articles from the WSPU's *Votes for Women*. In the December 1907 issue, for example, remembering my argument that suffrage women made use of Joan to counter the image of the unhappy, unmarried, old dried-up spinster, Mary Phillips contrasted this stereotype with her experience of the typical suffragist. She described the stereotype as a

> [g]aunt, unprepossessing female of uncertain age, with a raucous voice, and a truculent demeanor, who invariably seems to wear elastic-sided boots, and to carry a big "grampy" umbrella, which she uses as occasion demands to brandish ferociously by way of emphasizing her arguments, or to belabour any unfortunate member of the opposite sex who happens to displease her…. [Contrast her with the true suffragist who is] fighting in a high and noble cause, not for herself, but for others—for her sisters, on whom the burden of life rests heavily, and for all the men and women who will live after her.[91]

Even though Phillips was writing about the typical WSPU militant, Garrett Fawcett kept this article in her personal papers, indicating that she was aware of this representation of self-sacrifice.[92]

Vicinus discusses this self-sacrifice among the militant women, arguing that

> they believed that they had to be willing, like soldiers, to sacrifice themselves even unto death…. [T]he emphasis upon spirituality provided both a rationale and a means. If men confused the spiritual beauty of women with their physical bodies, women tended to the opposite extreme, confusing bodily sacrifice with spiritual ascension. The suffragettes believed that only by giving their bodies—the physical self—to the cause would they win the necessary spiritual victory that would enable them to enter the male political world.[93]

In this endeavor, Joan stood as the important example.

While Joan's imagery does allow for the sealed, secure and safe virginal example for suffrage women, such imagery also allows for sexual deviance: Joan was a cross-dresser. Michel Foucault reminds us that by trying to repress sexuality, the Victorians actually allowed for competing discourses on sexuality.[94] The celebration of Joan in masculine dress is just one way that we see this kind of resistance. As Tickner argues, Joan was a figure the militants could manipulate because she did not represent any one virtue:

> In her virginity, transvestism and military vigilance she subverted the order of femininity, but she was something other than a masquerade. She was and was not a woman. She transcended the limitations of her sex and yet it was from the position of femininity—however unorthodox—that she posed a challenge to the English and to men.

Hence, Tickner further argues, her appeal lay in the fact that she was neither "the domestic feminine ideal nor … its obverse, the hysterical fanatic."[95] However, Showalter attests that Joan was an especially significant figure for single women; she belonged to a cause rather than to any one man.[96] Although Leslie Feinberg and Nora Heimann argue that Joan was persecuted because she refused to put off male clothing, the transcripts suggest she was also tricked, her female clothing taken away from her such that she had no choice but to put on the male attire that remained in her cell.[97] Others argue that she put male clothing on to discourage the attentions of her jailors, while others have interpreted the transcripts of the condemnation trial as being more about her insistence on hearing the voices that told her to attack the English; she could put women's clothing on again but she could not deny her voices again, as she had originally done in a moment of weakness.[98] That does not negate the fact that, as Feinberg proves, Joan's persecution was grounded in a history of the suppression of cross-gender behavior.[99] In this sense, she acts as an important predecessor for the suffrage women who, by simply taking to the streets, were literally crossing similar barriers.

Feinberg defines Joan as a "transgender warrior"; yet she does not define transgender for Joan as strictly the case of "someone who lives full time in the gender opposite to [his/her] anatomy," but rather as one of many "courageous trans-warriors of every sex and gender—those who led battles and rebellions throughout history and those who today muster the courage to battle for their identities and for their very lives."[100] Just as Joan wore male armor, crossing both gender and class barriers, men and women in history often cross-dressed to rise up against rural and urban disturbances such as the case of enclosure in late eighteenth-century England. Cross-dressing was a sign of serious subversion since cross-dressing had been forbidden by the church because of its ties to pagan rites; yet, in many local rebellions, men dressed as women as a very symbol of their transgressions.[101] Hence, this over-attention on Joan's part to male attire could be, in part, a symbol of rebellion, one that the suffrage women definitely took up in their imagery of this cross-dresser who, in turn, gave them liberty to overemphasize their femininity. Criticized as being over-masculine, as in the case of the stereotypical images (figs. 32 and 33), they dressed in over-feminized attire as a resistance not only to that stereotype but also as a symbol of their own rebellion against patriarchal ideologies from which they were trying to break away.

Warner argues that through Joan's transvestism

> she abrogated the destiny of womankind. She could thereby transcend her sex; she could set herself apart and usurp the privileges of the male and his claims to superiority. At the same time, by never pretending to be other than a woman and a maid, she was usurping a man's function but shaking off the trammels of his sex altogether to occupy a different, third order, neither male nor female, but unearthly, like the angels whose company she loved.[102]

Like Joan, many of the suffrage women were adamant about their sexual freedoms independent of men and their influence. In this regard, Joan's transvestism "contravened the destined subordination of her sex when she wore men's clothing" according to Warner.[103]

Harrison uses the language of inversion in his discussion of WSPU militancy, a language that we can align with this theme of resistance and transgression. For him, the deviancy comes from the militant stance: "The militant gradually comes to repudiate society's values, and creates an alternative set of standards and criteria for status." He argues that this position was partly symbolized by the system of honors and awards that the WSPU gave its members who served prison time.[104] Susan Schibanoff offers a similar read, arguing that the most disturbing question Joan's cross dressing posed to her cohorts and judges alike was not who she was, or what her gender was, but what gender itself was, specifically the male gender—what constituted it, what menaced it, what preserved it, and what relationship it bore to biological sex.[105]

Her cross dressing was a menace to men and manhood in general, a threat to the status quo. While the NUWSS supported the rewards of sexual purity, they would not have embraced sexual transgression. Garrett Fawcett fired her NUWSS secretary, Elizabeth (Emmy) Wolstenholme, because she was living openly with a man without benefit of marriage. Ironically, Wolstenholme defended herself by saying she did not want to marry because she wanted to maintain her independent identity.[106] Christabel encouraged the WSPU women to be more radical in their sexual attitudes and take on Joan to help them create their own resistant narratives, as Wolstenholme did in her response to Garrett Fawcett. *The Suffragette* employs this rhetoric in "Both Irrepressible" from 23 May 1913. A fashionably dressed woman is selling copies of *The Suffragette*, the implication being that the woman will resist complacency and *The Suffragette* is her vehicle of defiant expression. If we read third-wave feminism as a moment when we can embrace gender and power, NOT conformity and repression, then we can begin to discuss these images of Joan in terms of how they empower such an "irrepressible" woman. Sophia Phoca and Rebecca Wright define the post-feminist (a term many feminists use interchangeably with the third wave) as "tough, sexy, and irreverent."[107] While this definition may seem far from Joan the impermeable, virgin warrior, when we look at the images of suffrage women, we gain a sense of their incredible toughness, marching in the streets, not to mention their ability to withstand the tortures of forced-feeding in prison, a topic to which I will return shortly. It's not impossible to argue that, as with "Both Irrepressible," they conflate Betterton's dichotomy, discussed earlier, the images revealing that the women embrace feminism (empowerment) and femininity (maintaining an attractive but safe allure). Then as now, women are searching for ideologies that allow them to express their sexual identities.[108] The second wave has taught us that in order to be taken seriously, women needed to deny their femininity and make themselves over in the image of men (a gross oversimplification but one aspect of the movement nonetheless) such that it became hard to distinguish between heterosexual women and sexually transgressive women. The third wave takes that notion head on, challenging the idea that women had to deny their own sexuality in order to be taken seriously. Why *should* women deny their own attractiveness in order to be taken seriously?

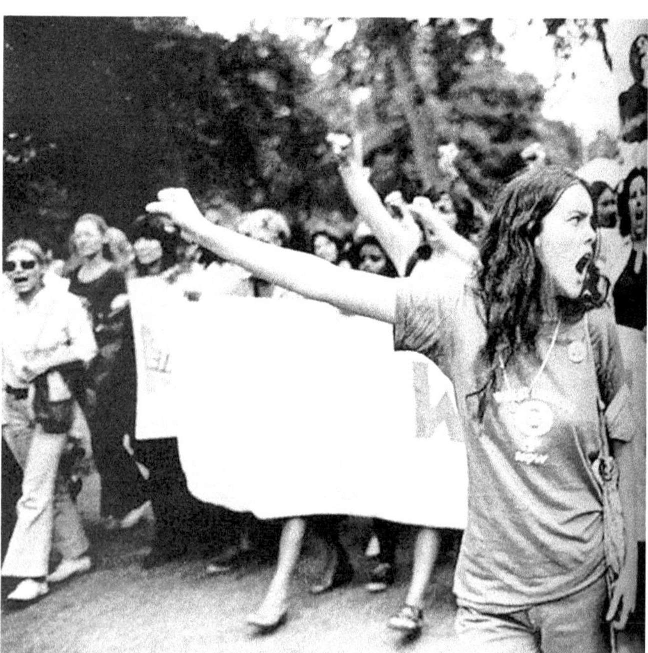

Figure 39. *NOW March* 1970s. Author's collection.

A case in point: Look at the images of suffrage processions (figs. 37 and 38) and contrast them with those of the second wave marches, such as this NOW photograph (fig. 39). There's a kind of hyper sense of femininity, almost a camping of it, in the suffrage marches in contrast to the hyper sense of denial of femininity in the 1960s/1970s marches. When Joan dressed like a man, Warner, writing in 1981, declared that it defied men and rendered

> them useless; on the social level, it affirm[ed] male supremacy, by needing to borrow its appurtenances to assert personal needs and desires. Copycat fashion today from executive suits to the workers' look ... are an equivalent. They announce that women can do men's work, are as good as men, are up to men of every station; but men remain the touchstone and equality a process of imitation.[109]

Both first-wave groups were united, however, by the idea of female experience and identity as separate from that of men. The contrast we see then between the suffrage women of the first wave and the 1960s/1970s feminists rests on sexual difference. Emmeline Pankhurst "refused to concede that women had to become like men to be worthy of the vote: stylish dressing accentuated difference."[110] For example, the NOW march women are vocally engaged and physically strident, whereas the suffrage women are silent and in control of their emotions in the earlier photographs. In the NOW March, the women speak out freely, stepping outside the feminine construct to voice their anger; their tactics are the opposite of our suffrage women who maintain bodies of feminine deference rather than imitating gestures and voices of male power.[111] That the suffrage women were very cognizant of the necessity of this female presentation is evident in earlier discussions of the New Woman such as an 1895 letter from *The Woman's Signal*, in which its author condemned "the 'Manly' New Woman of Mr. Punch" as repugnant because she "seeks to be an imitation of man in every aspect," whereas the "real New Woman" (who we are meant to read as the feminist who wants the vote) "is pre-eminently womanly and desires to remain so. She prefers the society of her own sex to that of men, and is, as a rule, popular among women—which I think you will admit is a very good test of her womanliness."[112]

This resistant narrative is reinscribed on the suffragette in the pages of *Votes for Women* (1907). In response to an attack on suffrage women as masculine put forth by the Anti-Suffrage Society (with the unfortunate acronym ASS that the WSPU exploited to full advantage!) the WSPU imposed the stance that "[t]he suffragette is essentially a feminine woman, with the full feminine grace and charm, and with the full feminine courtesy of manner."[113] These first-wave representations reflect Vicinus's thinking on the militant suffragettes. United with this emphasis on femininity were larger issues:

> Freedom was personal and psychological, reinforcing a sense of woman's spiritual leadership. The very vagueness of the word meant that it could be evoked repeatedly by leaders of every stripe. For some women, it meant simply the vote, but for most it meant casting off the old ways and entering public space without fear. Since so many middle- and upper-class women had never participated in public political activities simple actions such as chalking the pavements to announce a meeting or selling *Votes for Women* felt liberating. Indeed, freedom of movement came to symbolize the wider freedoms that women were seeking through the vote. The refusal of this freedom by the government, by crowds of men at rallies, or by the doctors who forcibly fed the prisoners reinforced the belief that only spiritual superiority would conquer.[114]

Cicely Hamilton, marching in the NUWSS 1908 parade (she was then aligned with them but soon came into the Pankhursts' fold) articulated this new-found sexual freedom, this resistant narrative. Writing to the *Daily Mail*, she said:

> A new force is making its mark upon the history of the race, the force of a womanhood conscious of its own individuality, conscious of latent capacities and eager, fiercely eager, to develop them—a womanhood that declines to see life henceforth only through the eyes of men, and will take upon its own soul the responsibility for its own actions.[115]

Tickner argues of Hamilton's revelation that "[i]n struggling to change their political circumstances, women were also changing themselves."[116] Public cognizance that women were promoting transformation but also altering themselves, insisting that they be represented by their own life experiences and circumstances,[117] is evident in S. Bulan's 1911 review of a production of Henrik Ibsen's *Doll's House*, for *Votes for Women*. The author comments on a change of reaction to the work whereas ten years previously it had been seen as scandalous:

> [I]t is we who are changed. We see the play in the light which the Votes for Women Movement has put into our souls. It stands out clear and precious and by the same light we know it represents but one of many situations which will be illuminated as the light spreads through the world. It is not only we who realize this; it is so patent that even the critic of a Liberal paper sees it.

Bulan then cites the similar opinion of the *Daily Chronicle* critic which suggests how widespread this shift in attitude had become by 1911. Further, Bulan expresses the dilemma of the feminist heroine of the play, Nora Helmer, who had "to play down to her husband's conception of her, which meant hiding her true self under deceit" and the incredible burden that was for her, ending with her declaration to be a human being in her own right, which brought cheers from the audience.[118]

In their quest for change, the WSPU embraced an increasing militancy, seeking to mitigate critique by using the admirable image of Joan as personal inspiration. The *Votes for Women* 1912 image of Joan, with her banner of "Prisoners of War" (fig. 29) reinforces Will Dyson's independent image "An Interlude," which addresses the subject of a militant protester, put away in Holloway Prison (fig. 40).[119] Members of the WSPU and the WFL went to prison as political prisoners, but prison officials treated them as common criminals. Women started going on hunger strike as early as 1909 to protest this disregard for justice. Marion Wallace Dunlop was the first to do so when she was arrested for stamping the Bill of Rights on St. Stephen's Hall. She requested

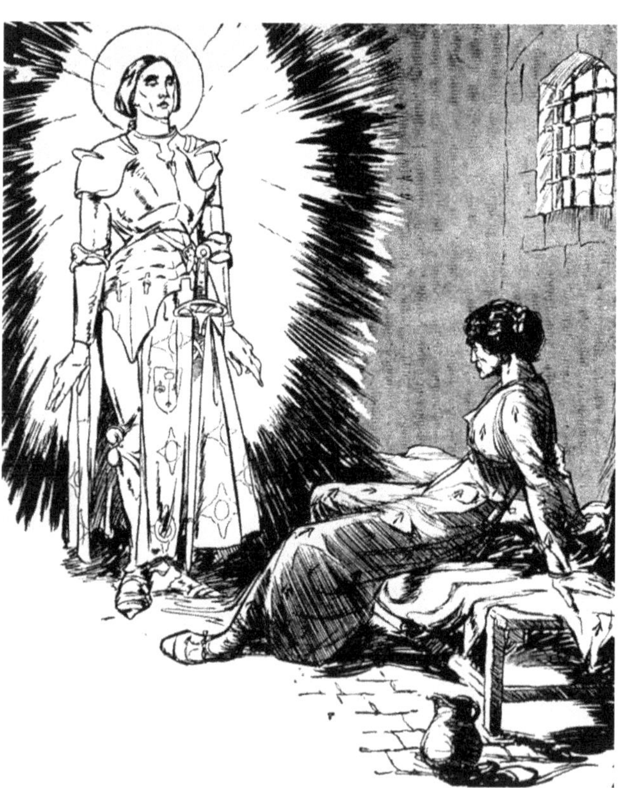

Figure 40. Will Dyson (1880–1938), "An Interlude" from *The Suffragette* (7 November 1913). Originally published in *Daily Herald*. Museum of London.

the privileges of political prisoner since she was engaged in a political war; these included first-division status, the ability to correspond, retain civilian clothing, and freedom from the rule of silence. But her protests were in vain. While she was not forcibly fed, other women who began hunger strikes were. Vicinus explains:

> [F]orcible feeding was used against hunger strikers, despite widespread public protest. In response, Winston Churchill formulated rule 243a, granting special privileges to prisoners of good character but without admitting the political nature of the women's protest. His temporary concessions lasted for a little over a year, when a recurrence of hunger strikes led to the renewal of forcible feeding, accompanied by more public protests.[120]

These actions then forced the government to launch the "Cat and Mouse Act" in April 1913, which let women out of prison to recover from hunger strikes, but would re-imprison them upon recovery. The suffragettes used the prisoners as a key piece in their arsenal against the government, staging parades and breakfasts for the released prisoners, creating medals for them, publishing photographs of them in prison, and simulating prison life at suffrage fairs, among other activities.

Barbara Green characterizes this new dramatic advertisement of prison struggles as a destruction of the earlier spectacular activism and its representation: "The disintegration of the female body in prison dramatized the disintegration of both the dream of citizenship and the fantasy of equal participation in a traditional public sphere won through the pleasing performances of the ornamental feminist body."[121] But there was no going back. Christabel claimed Dyson's image for the WSPU when she republished it on *The Suffragette* cover of 7 November 1913 with Joan's words beneath: "Fight on, God will give the victory." Betterton interprets this image as one that involves the prisoner's self-identification with Joan:

> The figure of Joan is erect and radiant and that of the prisoner slumped but both appear equally androgynous in their physiognomy and unswerving in their determination. The impregnability of Joan's female body, encased in armour like a corset, is in striking contrast to the open pose of the suffragist—only her tense arms reveal her will to resist. While there may have been only one Saint Joan, each and every suffrage prisoner was her own "Joan of Arc," carrying within her the model of female resistance to oppression. It was in this context that the sealed body of the suffragist took on more than purely allegorical significance.

In this self-identification, Betterton views both women in Dyson's cartoon as androgynous. But, even in armor, Joan possesses an hour-glass figure (and Betterton herself equates it with a woman's corset in its similar containment of her form). The "open pose" of the suffrage prisoner actually indicates partly surprise and shock, and partly trust in the vision before her, if not an outright sexual frankness.

Betterton stresses that "[w]omen's means to power lay, initially at least, in the exercise of control over their own bodies," but such a stance, I contend, included control over how they experienced their own sexuality. Perhaps this is to impose a third-wave feminist argument onto a first-wave agenda, but this prisoner in her conjured-up vision of Joan would seem to celebrate femaleness and female power as much as it does a spiritual experience. Like Joan in her armor, such ideologies work to delude men into thinking that they're in charge. A dual dialogue is in place for both the suffrage women that this cartoon in particular exposes. There's something wrong-thinking in continually asking women, in Betterton's words, for the sake of "[m]ental and bodily resistance to external pressure" and as "an important source of strength and new-found self-identity for militant women" to repress their sexual power and hence achieve something above Victorian respectability which simply encased a woman's sexual activity as reproductivity within marriage.[122] Joan's choice words underneath Dyson's cartoon reinforce such male oppression: "[Y]our English had a way with them in dealing with women!"

For the purposes of arguing that the prisoner is in control of her sexuality, we might want to make that case for sexual openness, but the compelling dialogue in representation among militants and non-militants alike involved an overemphasis on femininity to counter the masculinized shrieking sister. In this regard, I compare it with Gianlorenzo Bernini's famous *Ecstasy of St. Teresa*, 1647–52 (Cornaro Chapel, Santa Maria della Vittoria, Rome) based on the saint's own writings which are heavily impacted with the sexual rhetoric of ecstasy. The prisoner's open pose echoes that of St. Teresa, shock and compliance conflated.

The context of Dyson's cartoon is also important. Such "prisoners of war" as they began to be called in the press, were real female heroines. In 1909 the Asquith Government introduced forced feeding as a way of repressing militant suffrage hunger strikes rather than properly treating the women.[123] Suffrage women of the WSPU and WFL fought back, both during the actual feedings and in imagery, such as in the cover image for the first installment of *The Suffragette*, showing a minuscule Joan of Arc standing on a rock marked "militancy" with a sling shot, readying to throw it at the triple-headed "Coalition Government" over a sea of "broken pledges" (fig. 41). Her enemy wears a sword marked "Forcible Feeding." The illustration creates Joan, in part, as the Biblical David, a smaller force whose sling-shot brought down the enemy giant Goliath; it was a case of the underdog taking on the big dogs. The image reflects the historical moment in 1912, when the suffrage women suffered the defeat of the Coalition Bill, and the absence of a general election, such that these real prisoners became one of the focal points of the WSPU propaganda against the

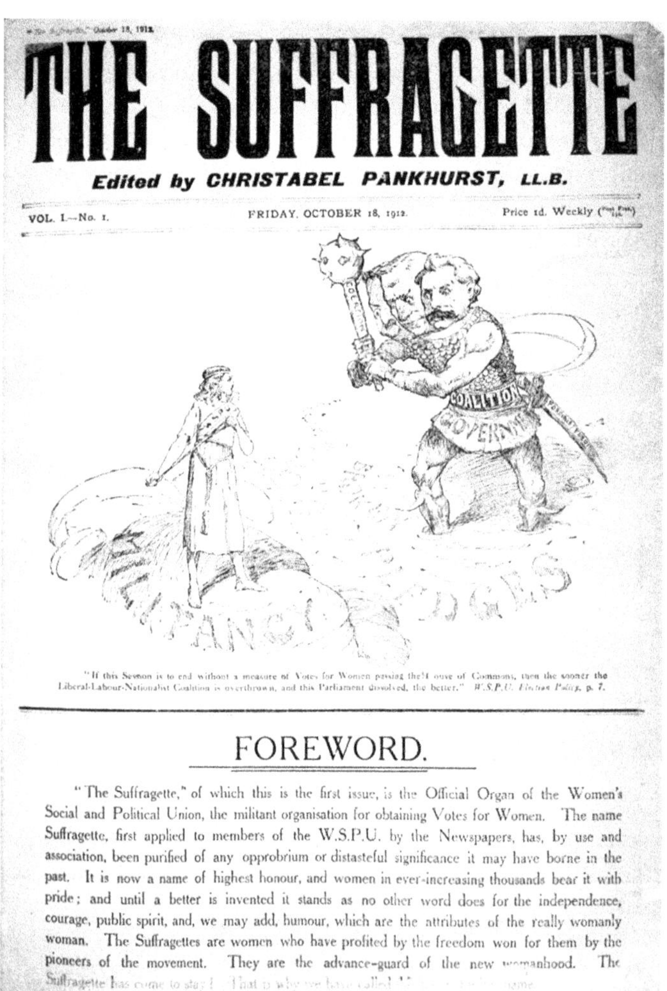

Figure 41. **"Militancy, Broken Pledges, and Coalition Government."** *Cover image of first installment of The Suffragette* **(18 October 1912). Museum of London.**

government. Due to the Government's failure to meet their demands, the suffragettes began their violent activities with stone throwing *en masse*, such that Joan is not just embattled here, but aggressively involved in hurling a similar direct assault against the enemy government; hence, she stands in for them in this illustration, mirroring their activities and their stance.

It is at this juncture that the NUWSS could no longer support the tactics of the WSPU. While they were initially sympathetic to the imprisonments, even going so far as to host the first celebratory breakfast for the released prisoners, Garrett Fawcett not only distanced her group from them based on their escalating violent actions, but, as she expressed to the hunger strikers:

> The objection which I feel to your voluntary starvation plan is that all the inconvenience and suffering it would cause would fall on suffragists and their families, and that it would not inconvenience the Government in the slightest degree. I can in my mind's eye see Mr. Asquith chuckling at the thought of the suffrage ranks being depleted by the suicide of whatever number of women decided to adopt your plan.[124]

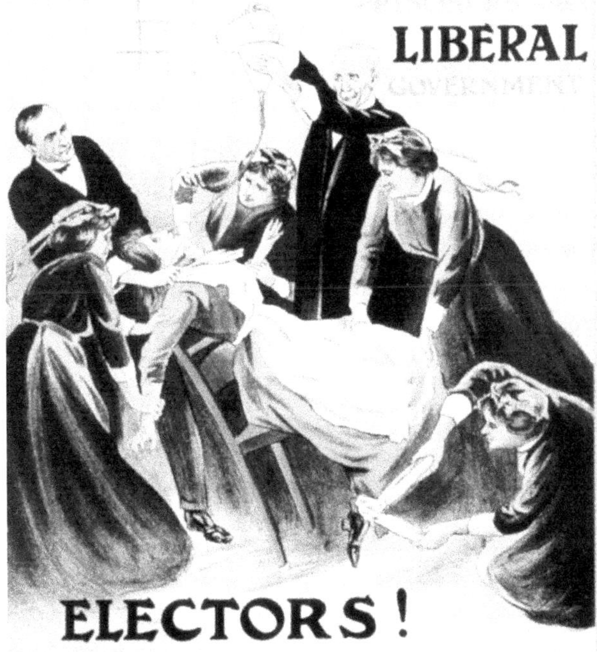

Figure 42. A. Patriot (Alfred Pearce) (1855–1933), *The Modern Inquisition Poster,* 1910. Museum of London.

She was questioning both their tactics and the results they would achieve. Her arguments for a pacifist approach, rejected both their outwardly violent acts and the violence that their actions brought upon them in prison. Yet, they did not heed her advice. One significant WSPU protest image in this continued resistance is the *Modern Inquisition* poster, which first appeared as the cover image of *Votes for Women* in 1910 (fig. 42). Hunger strikers, as this illustration indicates, were subjected to a rank violation of their orifices in an effort to force feed them, according to many excruciating self reports.[125] As Purvis argues:

> In a women's political movement where heterosexuality was openly criticized and sexual purity a strong theme, such atrocities were viewed with horror. The fact that the majority of suffragettes were single, some being lesbians and others celibate, must have intensified reactions.[126]

No wonder they evoked Joan, for pure strength of character. During a hunger strike, Mary Richardson (who would later become famous for attacking Velazquez's *Rokeby Venus*), wrote a note to Kitty Marion, a fellow WSPU member in prison, on lavatory paper, saying,

"Certainly you get to know yourself physically and mentally in prison and I suppose if we were true philosophers we would be glad of this. I have been thinking of Joan of Arc.... How marvelous she was so alone, with vile men night and day so tormented."[127]

John Mercer characterizes the WSPU resistance posters as instances when the WSPU chose to discredit the Liberal Government: "Common perceptions of the militant campaign were overturned in these images, with the suffragette placed as a victim, and the guilt over campaign violence shifted to the Liberal Government" whereas the other suffrage groups tended to create more general allegorical posters to justify their right to the vote.[128] He sees this poster and others like it as examples of WSPU aggression used to undermine "the government at decisive times in the campaign."[129]

But some historians think images like the *Modern Inquisition* poster do not go far enough. Caroline J. Howlett, for example, suggests that it falls short because it shows her with the tube going through her nose rather than her mouth, "in an attempt to avoid the connotation of silencing and of oral rape." Further, she sums up the dilemma of the prison imagery, finding that written accounts are more impacting, an argument with which many suffrage visual historians disagree. However, Howlett seems on point in concluding: "Such an image of a woman being forcibly fed, regardless of its producer's intention, could equally be read as a horrific indictment of a misogynist culture in which women's bodies are violated or as a pleasing reassurance that, in spite of women's rebelliousness, men still have them under complete control."[130] Showalter would agree with this assessment within the clinical context of feminism and hysteria when she argues that the

representation of the forcible feeding of suffragettes in the press, with a struggling woman held down by nurses while an elegantly dressed male doctor assaults her with funnels and tubes, echoes the sexual iconography of Charcot's hysterics, and anticipates the clinical photographs of electric-shock treatment in the 20th-century.[131]

Hence, she moves this dialogue into one of a conflation of hysteria with frustrated sexuality, one of the arguments that was used against giving women the vote.

Compare the posture of the woman in *Modern Inquisition* (fig. 42) with that of the woman in Dyson's Holloway cell (fig. 40); perhaps Dyson is indicating to us that this prisoner has already suffered the degradation in question, her open pose reflecting her exhausted dejection over some kind of forcible feeding that mirrors the pose of a woman after a rape, humiliated, yet resistant. Betterton draws the parallel between this kind of violation and that of the "surgical rape" which took place under earlier acts of the British state, the Contagious Diseases Acts of the 1870s and 1880s.[132] As discussed earlier, the fight to repeal these Acts was the very campaign that propelled Garrett Fawcett to change her mind about throwing in her lot with the moral purity cause.

But such imagery highlights the larger dilemma of breaking down our traditional dichotomy of oversexed, dangerous women who sucked away all of men's energies versus the totally de-sexed shrieking sister (figs. 32 and 33). While the former, in Joseph Kestner's argumentation, appeared in England as well as all over Europe as counterattack and backlash to the women's movement, the latter was her counterpart, equally damaging. Betterton suggests, as have other feminist scholars, that "both sexual *and* non-sexual femininity was represented as sharing the same structure of deviance which could be ultimately located in the dysfunctioning of the female sexual body." The problem as she sees it in suffrage imagery, is "to steer a course between the Scylla of disordered feminine sexuality and the Charybdis of refusing to admit any sexuality to women at all."[133] If, as Betterton asserts, forced feeding "like rape, replaces an act of love with an assertion of power"[134] then perhaps the suffrage prisoner regains a belief in love through the vision of Joan herself, a love of self so necessary after such a debasement as she would have encountered in prison.

Such a reading reflects Foucault's history of the disciplined subject, formed by institutions of surveillance and management like the prison. In *Discipline and Punish* he examines the ways that prisons and the judicial system develop a docile body.[135] Going back to the introduction, Marion's belief that all eyes were upon her was probably apt in this kind of theoretical framework; the Panopticon is ever-present and actively at work in Marion's street experience as it was embodied in the behavior of men on the street. How much truer this was then, of women in prison, under constant observation and subjection to brutality. As Green argues, however, while Foucault "could describe the containment of rebellious femininity, [his theories] cannot make sense of feminist rebellion. Foucault's description of discipline cannot explain the deliberate *reproduction* of the prison in countless narratives of imprisonment…." She concludes that Foucault could not make sense of the active rebellion from within the prison that appears in such confessions, acting as they do as both narratives of obedient docility and as a protest of such docility in narrating women's experiences of such subjection to authority.[136]

However, I keep coming back to Foucault's observation of the Panopticon in which he concludes "visibility is a trap." To me, this expression sums up Marion's street experience *and* that of the women in prison: exposure and vulnerability are both at play, along with powerlessness. While the women, as Green asserts, did indeed revolt through their hunger strikes and in their physical battles during the forced feeding, they were in such a position because they were visible symbols of women's acting out. As Foucault elucidates: "The major effect of the Panopticon is to induce in the inmate a state of conscious and permanent visibility that assures the automatic functioning of power." Further, he argues, as with Marion's experience of internalizing the male gaze on the streets of Piccadilly,

> that the perfection of power should tend to render its actual exercise unnecessary; that this architectural apparatus should be a machine for creating and sustaining a power relation independent of the person who exercises it; in short, that the inmates should be caught up in a power situation of which they are themselves the bearers.[137]

Of course, in this context, the Panopticon is a metaphor for patriarchal power and its ability to make women police their own bodies.

Dyson's image and the *Modern Inquisition* poster both speak to the Panopticon's dissemination of its power model "throughout the whole social body" into a "disciplinary society," such that we witness doctors' surveillance of women's bodies as the women balk at a society that does not see fit to grant them citizenship. Hence, they are like Joan in the tower. Foucault characterizes the 19th-century prison as a site of the "deprivation of liberty." For the suffrage women, this was a double blow; arrested for protesting their lack of liberty under the law, they were imprisoned like citizens (which they were not) and then, treated as common criminals (which they were not). Further, the 19th-century prison, according to Foucault, was a place that called for the reformative transformation of individuals[138]; herein lay suffrage women's greatest transgression perhaps, since they were repeat offenders, ignoring the lessons that being imprisoned was supposed to entail.

Further, the Dyson image might be implicating the kind of transgressive sexuality for the women in question that Purvis articulates above and that Green postulates for the textual, confessional responses. Betterton recognizes and documents lesbian relationships between women suffragists, presenting them as examples of sexual behavior that do not conform to "the model of respectable marriage or single-minded chastity so publicly embraced by the leadership."[139] But she does not see that the Dyson image might be implicating that kind of transgressive sexuality for the woman in question. Joan could be seen here as an emblem of love for women exclusively, creating just one example, not of docile compliance under the Panopticon, but rather of a Foucaultian competing discourse. In this sense, it would also reflect Barbara Caine's observation of Mary Wollstonecraft, that a key part of a feminist undercurrent came from Wollstonecraft's "refusal to comply with existing social and sexual mores."[140] WSPU member Frederick Pethick-Lawrence noted the female camaraderie and unconventional behavior of women in the movement: "[M]any of the women, to my surprise at the time, were singularly debonair and gay ... they had broken down life-long inhibitions and already achieved a freedom that they had never before known."[141] Similarly, relationships between women, even innocent ones, were seen as a threat, as in Lena Connell's double portrait of Edith Craig and Cicely Hamilton, c. 1909 (Museum of London). Connell presents them as a talented working team, young women in their fashionable attire, Edith the spitting image of her mother, the actress Ellen Terry, in her own youth, as she was depicted in G.F. Watts' early painted portraits; Cicely, ever the actress, looking admiringly at Edy. The double portrait commemorated their professional partnership in the theatre, this taken a year before their great joint feat, the theatrical production of *A Pageant of Great Women*, which included Joan of Arc. Connell's picture captures their intensity, youth and enthusiastic energy for the cause through their productions of the Actresses' Franchise League. Such images can be seen to combat, in a new way, the dilemma many suffrage women faced in terms of representation between the feminist, activist assertion and a more modest, feminine compliance. Val Williams characterizes this double portrait, published as a postcard, as a portrait of two women "united in comradeship and thought. Such directed picturing in the service of a feminist cause was an important development within women's photography, and indicated just how effectively studio portraiture could be used in this context."[142] Such propagandistic portraiture offered a way of fighting the popular press image of the single woman who, like her predecessor the New Woman, was represented as a conflation of "elements of the lesbian, the angular spinster, and the hysterical feminist."[143]

Thus, Connell's representation asks us to redefine a woman's sexuality and her sense of self-identity; in light of her new-found activism, she does not have to model conformity to maintain her integrity, and she is in charge of her self-identity. She does not have to model compliance to maintain respectability. As Williams states, "The Suffragettes, with their acute consciousness of the effectiveness of dramatic publicity, produced postcards and badges illustrated by photographs made by studio portraitists who supported the cause. For the first time, women controlled and directed their own image in the cause of politics."[144] That would seem to be yet another message of the Dyson cartoon. Beaten down and drawn, humiliated, and fatigued, she is still defiant, strong, and determined. She is more connected to our third-wave feminists than we might at first have believed possible. After all, then as now, women desire their own sexual freedoms. In light of this information, the Dyson cartoon could be depicting Joan as an inspiration for sisterhood in a sexually transgressive sense, just as Joan embodied resistance and transgression in her armor. Like Green's assessment of women's prison narratives, the imagery suggests resistance within performative docility.

But such transgression also implies a need to act out against the authorities; fear mingled with pleasure, Sylvia Pankhurst recalling her sister's triumph at speaking out at the seminal election meeting, a gratification at disruption, one echoed by Mary Richardson, the suffragette who slashed the *Rokeby Venus*, and who later explained: "In a sense I was glad to hit back, to hit out at anything if I could in some way express my detestation of all the filthy remarks I had had to listen to."[145] In this regard, the Foucaultian concept of discipline and punishment often met with defiance, not acceptance.

Joan and Suffrage Theatre

Another aspect of the production of Joan's image took place in suffrage theatre. Joan of Arc is one of many historical women that activist women recreated to represent challenging (yet appealing) women to the public eye. Joan was one such example of heroic womanhood celebrated within Cicely Hamilton's play *A Pageant of Great Women* which Edith Craig produced first at the Scala Theatre in London, opening the same year as the first hunger strike campaign, 1909. It was the joint work of two different suffrage organizations: the Women Writers' Suffrage League (WWSL) and the Actresses' Franchise League (AFL). Cicely Hamilton founded the former group with Bessie Hatton to produce suffrage texts such as plays, novels and biographies. The AFL sought to turn speeches and pamphlets into dramatic form. And both groups were neutral, neither militant nor constitutionalist. Hence, as Green explains, they encouraged debate and dialogue across different feminist groups.[146]

But, as Katharine Cockin points out, Hamilton staged the majority of the Pageant productions all over the country for the WFL; further, Cockin asserts that Hamilton initially created the Pageant for the WFL, with only two productions for the WSPU, one in Bristol in 1910 and the other in Liverpool in 1912. I make this point because Cockin then uses the play to interpret WSPU representations of women in its "normalization of militancy through civic pride and national heroism," largely ignoring the lion's share role of the WFL in disseminating the play widely across England and in creating the large historical pageant of inspirational great women. Further, she gives no militant role to the WFL when, in fact, we know that although they split from the WSPU in 1907, they often went to prison alongside their WSPU cohorts for passive resistance.[147] For example, in speaking of the Heroic Women group and Warrior Women group (Joan leading the latter group) she asserts that if a speech had been given to Joan it "may have rendered the play less amenable to some audiences, such as the Women's Freedom League (WFL), for whom militancy was an unacceptable political strategy."[148] On the contrary, militancy was a part of their mission and the use of Joan in this context was then certainly purposeful. Her stance mirrors the relative lack of attention that suffrage scholars have given to the WFL[149]; but their inclusion and use of Joan within the play is telling of their militancy, not their lack of it. Further, they staged their own pageants, as in a photograph within the Women's Library collection (fig. 43) which shows an unknown actress dressed as Joan of Arc as part of the Edinburgh Women's Freedom League Pageant of Women Through the Ages which, according to notes attached to the image, was written by Helen McLachlan, Assistant Secretary of the WFL branch in Edinburgh and was performed on the steps of Donaldson's Hospital for the Deaf and Dumb.[150]

Cockin asserts, "In Hamilton's manuscript ... the stage directions indicate that Joan of Arc chased a tearful Prejudice off stage; in which case, the warrior most closely associated with the WSPU concluded the play visually on stage by performing an act of enforcement, all of which is implicitly endorsed by Justice."[151] Yet, this inclusion of Joan in a play written, by Cockin's own admission, for the WFL, would seem to foreground Joan for the WFL, not the WSPU. While Cockin asserts that the productions coincided with the increasing militancy of the WSPU,[152] they also coincided with the militant struggles of the WFL who participated in two highly publicized public protests in 1908, the "grille protest" in the Houses of Parliament and in 1909 "The Siege of Westminster," the latter the sensational occasion that saw WFL Australian member Muriel Matters flying over Westminster in an airship to deliver leaflets explaining the protest.[153]

And Joan's presence speaks to the larger significance of the non-partisan production itself which I have already shown did not exist along any suffrage group lines nor any political lines. Yet, the play speaks to suffrage militancy. I prefer not to align militancy solely with the WSPU, Joan's inclusion in this play for the WFL speaking to the need for greater largesse of consideration of the broad-ranging initiatives among many suffrage groups. As Laura E. Nym Mayhall argues:

> Suffragette militancy enacted the radical idea that citizens had the right to resist tyrannical authority; militancy's implementation became a contest over the uses and utility of physical force in negotiating with the state. Thus, suffragette militancy was performative and spectacular but not only and even primarily because it exhibited women's bodies in pain. Suffragettes utilized a range of strategies, gendered in complex and sometimes contradictory ways, designed to highlight what they saw as the arbitrary and historically anomalous exclusion of women from the constitution.[154]

The play was one such strategy, both "performative" and "spectacular" to address Joan's importance for such militancy. Further, what better way to highlight women's exclusion than to call upon powerful women in history who represented concepts of leadership and governance as well as militant bravery. The exclusion of the NUWSS from sponsorship of this pageant may have partly to do with their political stance which was to assert women's rights to citizenship through non-militant tactics, while the WSPU and WFL asserted their rights to resist the government and its laws until it recognized them as citizens. Thus, we can view the pageant as a resistant appeal with Joan representing one of its heroic, defiant examples.

Imagine the impact of fifty women on stage, a visual body of evidence, of women's greatness: Local women suffragists took part in the play, along with well-known act-

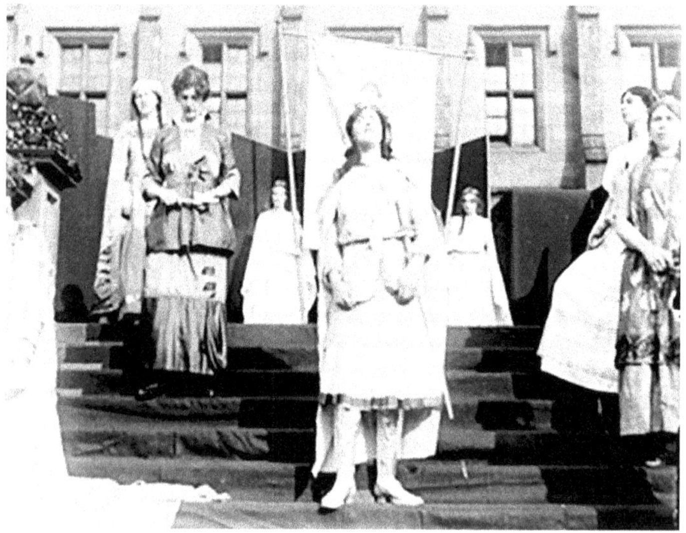

Figure 43. D. H. Munro, *Joan of Arc, Edinburgh Women's Freedom League Pageant of Women Through the Ages*, c. 1908–10. Women's Library, London.

resses such as Ellen Terry, and, in certain stagings, well-known activists participated. They took on the roles of great women of the past who appeared, silently, on stage in groups: the saintly women; the rulers; the learned women; the artists; the heroic women; followed by Joan's group, the warrior women. They created a silent chorus for the debate on women's enfranchisement between Woman and Prejudice, a debate presided over by Justice. The play was shown all over England between 1909 and 1912.

Green problematizes the characters' silence, however, in this critique:

> Like suffrage processions, the *Pageant of Great Women* visibly demonstrated the difficulties of this sort of political activism, for not only did play and pageant link feminism to state ritual by connecting civic participation to the elaborate display of exemplary and exceptional subjects, but they also revealed how that exemplarity, for woman, was often tied to her status as visual object to be seen rather than viable subject to be heard and reckoned with.[155]

Yet, silence itself is a strong form of protest, a topic to which I return in the epilogue.

The Unraveling of an Ideal Is Politically Marked

In 1908 Caroline Watts created the poster *Bugler Girl* for the Artists' Suffrage League of the NUWSS (fig. 44). Using this image as her focus, Tickner argues that the NUWSS tried to distance itself from associations with the WSPU once the latter group increased its violent attacks in 1912.

While Watts created the poster to drum up enthusiasm for the 1908 NUWSS suffrage procession, by 1913, when the WSPU had become more significantly militant, the bugler girl had become "a controversial image" for the NUWSS.[156] In their efforts to distance themselves from the violence of the WSPU, the NUWSS started to make compromises in their representations. In the *Common Cause*, they explained:

> Our Bugler Girl carries her bugle and her banner; her sword is sheathed by her side; it is there, but not drawn, and if it were drawn, it would not be the sword of the flesh, but of the spirit. For ours is not a warfare against men, but against evil; a war in which women and men fight together.... We are militant in the sense that the Christian Church is militant.... We are in arms against wrong, but we inflict none. The great adventure to which we are called is ... not to overcome evil with evil, however heroically undertaken, but to overcome evil with good. It is the supreme adventure, and to it we summon all who care for the things of the spirit, all who welcome hardship and suffering in the great

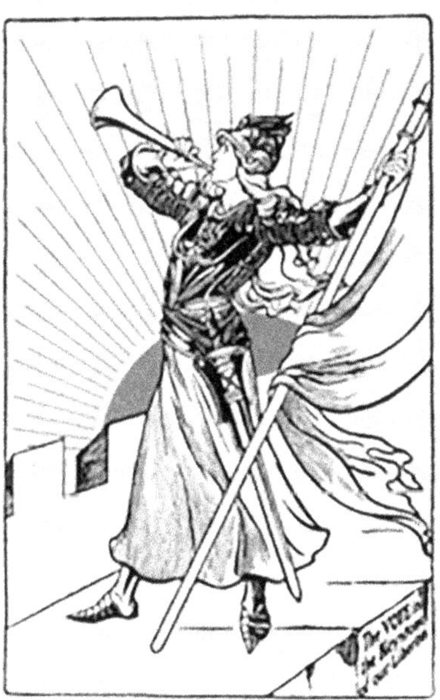

Figure 44. Caroline Watts (1868–1919), *Bugler Girl*, 1908. Women's Library, London.

hope that by suffering themselves, they may shorten and lighten the sufferings of others, all who refuse to be sheltered and protected and happy while their sisters are exploited and enslaved.[157]

Tickner argues that with this stance, the NUWSS asserted its own rights to "heroism and sanctified suffering" which were not, in their eyes, "the exclusive province of the WSPU." While she maintains that the NUWSS "had a greater stake in 'womanliness' than the militants," at the same time "they could not afford to seem feeble or servile as they struggled to maintain their identification with the campaign in the face of WSPU notoriety."[158] The *Bugler Girl* also appeared in *Common Cause* in 1913 with a flag of wisdom and below it the words: "Better Wisdom than weapons of war,"[159] which could be construed as a direct affront to the militants while, at the same time, using Joan as their image of wisdom suggesting that they evoked her for entirely different purposes than did the WSPU and WFL at this point in the fight.

With the onset of the First World War, as discussed in the introduction, the suffrage women had to regroup and retool. The WSPU's shift in stance to extreme nationalism is best represented in terms of their changing imagery of Joan of Arc. Once the "Famous Militant" on the cover of *The Suffragette* in May 1913, she became "The Great Patriot" by May 14, 1915, by which time the heading for the journal declared "For King, For Country, For Freedom." Underneath this latter image was a reprint of Christabel Pankhurst's assessment of Joan's importance from the May 9 issue of *The Suffragette*:

> Joan of Arc lives on still as the glory and inspiration of France. To British women also she has left a great inheritance. She has taught them the loveliness of simplicity, purity, courage and militancy. Joan of Arc belongs to France but she belongs also to the womanhood of the whole world, and the women of our country are one with the men and women of France in adoring her memory.[160]

It is telling that in this 1915 image the WSPU uses Ingres's painting *Joan of Arc at the Coronation of Charles VII*, 1854 (Louvre, Paris) in a propagandistic moment, aligning themselves with the French views of nationalism and patriotism. Such imagery summoned Joan to demonstrate the WSPU's alignment not only with British patriotism but also as ally to France. Many were taken aback, in fact, by the radical shift in WSPU politics to a zealous jingoism, which is reflected in these examples in their embrasure of Joan as patriot.

As Betterton points out, any cooptation of Joan would be fraught with inconsistencies: "The adoption of Joan, a pre-democratic feudal figure, as a model for women's claim to democratic rights was always bound to be contradictory. By 1914, Joan herself had been taken up as a symbol by the extreme right wing in France...."[161] Yet, she had already been used much earlier by the French Right, following the Franco-Prussian War and the Commune, in order to "restore national identity and pride" essentially creating Joan as their national patron saint.[162] But political representations continued, such as in popular images during the First World War showing the French using Joan as nationalistic inspiration to soldiers on the field.[163]

In her study of Joan of Arc imagery between 1700 and 1855, Heimann examines the visual and textual representations of Joan in France. She notes the consistent misrepresentation of her in terms of a lack of historical accuracy but notes, in this context, that the French public did not have access to documents about her inquisition and imprisonment until the 1840s.[164] The historical record shows that she did, indeed, wear her hair short like a man and put on male attire, at the behest of God's will that she do so. In her study, Heimann details how Joan, at the hands of the French, began as a "relatively minor provincial heroine," but was soon transformed into an internationally notorious figure of satire in Voltaire's hands. During the next one hundred and fifty years of French history, through the ravages of civil war and social upheaval, the collapse of the first Republic and Empire, and the rise and fall of the Bourbon Restoration and the July Monarchy, Joan of Arc emerged as a powerful, protean figure, able to embody a vast (even contradictory) range of qualities. By the close of the July Monarchy in the mid–19th-century, her posthumous persona fully emerges as a modern icon of nationalist unity, martial strength, female fortitude, and, above all, fervent piety.[165]

The French used Joan in multifarious ways to meet the needs of individual governments, just as we have seen the suffragists use her image to meet their various purposes. During the Commune, anti–Commune writers and political artists positioned Joan in opposition to the *Communardes*, targeting her virginity versus their proposed looseness of morals, just as one example of ways her representation was co-opted for political purposes.[166] But, beyond that usage, Heimann articulates that it was "her gender, her femininity, and her virginity" which remained "an ongoing concern" in the rhetoric. These kinds of apprehensions, while not tied to the French feminist movement, certainly offer a parallel situation to the ways the suffragists later utilized Joan's image, Heimann argues:

> For Voltaire, Joan of Arc's sexual life was a vehicle of social and political critique, as the epic preservation of her virginity provided the means for illustrating the hypocrisy and corruption of the monarchy and the Catholic Church during the ancient regime in France. During the Revolution, the Consulate, and the Empire, Joan of Arc's feminine gender made her an apt allegorical figure, able to evoke a new personification of Republican national identity and martial resolve.[167]

Like Voltaire, the British suffragists celebrated Joan's virginity within the context of male hypocrisy; as in the later governments, they turned her into an allegorical figure of "martial resolve" as an example of both how to fight and the strength necessary to carry out the battle.

Heimann characterizes subsequent French representations, specifically raised in Ingres's painting that the WSPU reproduced in 1915 as discussed earlier, saying "Joan of Arc was reborn as a historical incarnation of France's heroic virtue."[168] In this context, the representation is aligned with the British suffragists' manipulation of her as heroine to women, but note too that in the shift from Joan as warrior to the Ingres image reproduced in *The Suffragette*, she moves from battlefield to the right side of the law, from militant to patriot. The fact that Ingres's image is reproduced in *The Suffragette* is just one example of the British suffragists' cognizance of French visual representations of Joan.

In an exhibition catalogue focused on the late 19th-century cycle of prints on Joan's life by Louis-Maurice Boutet de Monvel, Heimann observes that he is one of the first artists to depict Joan in all her historical accuracy, based on contemporary accounts of her appearance.[169] But Ingres's *Joan of Arc at the Coronation of Charles VII* preceded his cycle; Ingres's painting exhibits not only Joan as heroine, but also Joan as spiritual inspiration in all of her historic detail. Jules Bastien-Lepage follows suit in his mesmerizing *Joan of Arc Listening to the Angels*, 1879 (Metropolitan Museum of Art, New York). She is standing in her father's garden, transfixed by the voices whose apparitions we see but she does not. Heimann argues that Bastien-Lepage's image depicts "her compelling virtue" which "is implied by her unaffected beauty, humble industry (signaled by the spinning wheel), and saintly sources of inspiration…."[170]

These are a few of the accurate representations of Joan in the latter half of the 19th-century in France. What is more perplexing, apart from the way she is taken up by so many dissimilar voices for propagandistic and inspirational purposes, is her absence from French suffrage imagery (of which there is only a smattering in comparison to the campaign in England and America). It would seem to be more appropriate to discuss the ways her imagery comes into play in America where Joan is readily taken up by U.S. suffrage groups, a move partly due to such American women as Alice Paul having spent time with the militant suffragettes in London.

But I am more fascinated with trying to determine the link, or lack of one, between British and French political propaganda as it continues or dissipates the dialogue begun in Chapter One on the French lag. In this context, Karen Offen shows that when the *Union Française pour le Suffrage des Femmes (UFSF)* formed in 1909 to spearhead the drive for French women's suffrage, they purposefully took a stance akin to that of the NUWSS rather than the WSPU, particularly disavowing militant tactics. Except for Madeleine Pelletier and Hubertine Auclert, most French advocates "insisted that French women could—and must—obtain the vote and eligibility to run for office by 'ladylike' means."[171] Yet, with a few exceptions they did not employ Joan as inspiration; she was a vehicle for nationalism, taken up most specifically by the editors of the journal *Action Française* who used her image in the cause of restoring monarchical authority through rebellious activism, the opposite of the various women's suffrage groups' purpose in France.[172]

Few groups in France, until the 20th century, actually argued for women's suffrage. Auclert through the vehicle of her newspaper *La Citoyenne (The Citizen)*, called for women's suffrage as a question of justice, purposefully naming her newspaper to reflect a call for women's rights to citizenship, long denied them. Her path was a lonely and frustrating one, for she had few followers.[173] And there was no push for the franchise among other feminist groups, with one exception. The French woman, Marie Maugeret, and her Catholic feminist group were the ones to rally beneath Joan of Arc's banner through the founding of a Joan of Arc Congress within the Joan of Arc Federation group. They opposed the burgeoning large *Conseil National des Femmes Françaises (CNFF)*, a branch of the international movement for women through the International Council of Women, the latter of which still was not targeting suffrage as a demand. At the 1906 third Congress, Maugeret managed to get a motion to endorse women's franchise, but it was quickly squelched at the next Congress.

It was not until 1914 that we see the *CNFF* numbering 100,000 members, but, as with England, any plans they might have had were cut short by preoccupations with the war effort. James McMillan even suggests, as was the case in England, that the example of the WSPU's radicalism was seen as excessive and French women shied away from it, being fearful of identifying with radical politics openly.[174]

Back in London, once the violence on the part of the British militants began to increase, suffrage women experienced mounting tensions. In 1914 Christabel overstepped her bounds by claiming that Garrett Fawcett and the suffragists had no right to use Joan's image because they had denounced the WSPU's militant tactics.[175] Such a charge reinforces that, for the WSPU, militancy was uppermost in their minds in their representations of Joan, a stance that they used to recruit women to their side. But no one group had monopoly over Joan's image and what it could convey. Garrett Fawcett remained undaunted by Christabel's threats; even taking over the militant image itself (rethinking, then, the implications of the *Bugler Girl*). She continued to authorize Joan imagery for the NUWSS; witness a 1918 *Punch* publication, "At Last" (fig. 45), showing Joan's victory at Orléans as an emblem of the final victory: women's enfranchisement in England. Here Joan has replaced her "Prisoners of War" banner with one that reads "Women's Franchise." Garrett Fawcett, in turn, used this cartoon as the frontispiece to her 1920 history of this victory.[176] In fact, she even used militant language in her dedicatory preface to this volume: "I wish to dedicate this little book to the thousands of faithful friends and gallant comrades whose unwearied work, steadfastly maintained through many years, made women's suffrage in Great Britain no longer a dream but a reality."[177] In addition, the WFL reproduced it on the February 1, 1918, cover of its press organ *The Vote.*

Standing against it, however, was the continuing struggle over the proper representation of women's citizenship. "The Shrieking Sister" (fig. 33) represented the rhetorical battle between the constitutional suffragist Garrett Fawcett and her seemingly out-of-control militant counterpart Christabel. As the first press image of the militant, this cartoon embodied the entrenched battle that lay ahead, yet each group had a right to

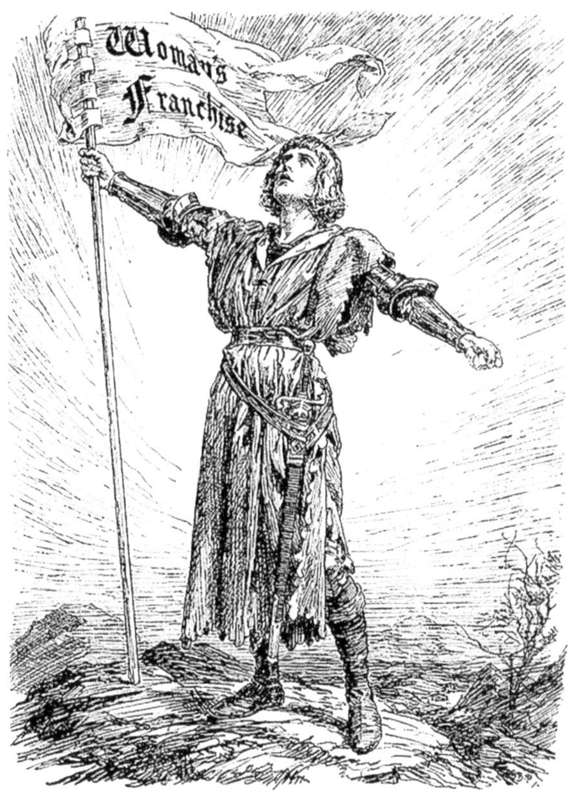

AT LAST

Figure 45. Sir John Bernard Partridge (1861–1945), "At Last," *Punch* (1918). Women's Library, London.

privilege Joan of Arc in its collective cause for the vote and in its efforts to stage a feminist plea, one that it literally embodied. Each group had equal access to Joan of Arc for this collective purpose. Each group exercised its own version of moral purity, using Joan as exemplar. While the WSPU chose Joan as radical example of their strength and will, their right to citizenship was marked by transgressing the culture's codes of sexuality and how it was expressed in the body. The WFL took a tack of dramatic disseminations of her historical importance in their production of Hamilton's *Pageant*, while the NUWSS used the body as the site of struggle, but more often than not chose to suppress notions of deviant sexuality in favor of reinforcing codes of respectability. Each group used Joan's image to forward its beliefs on moral purity, the role of the warrior, and disruptive sexual behavior, creating resistant narratives. The groups were bound together in making history through their move into the public arena, and Joan, a woman who chose her own noncompliant narrative, was central to the success of their activism and their collective search for self-identity. In March 1918, the Artists Suffrage League decorated the Queen's Hall, London, for the NUWSS victory celebration for women's enfranchisement. Included in the display was Mary Lowndes' ASL banner which included its motto, "Alliance not Defiance," an apt summing up of the efforts of all suffrage groups to reach this momentous event.

Joan's legacy in England represents just one example of Joan's easy cooptation by different groups. The British organization, St. Joan's Social and Political Alliance, invited all Catholic women "interested in Equal Franchise and Social and Political questions," and it welcomed men associates, but it, like other associations, did not include campaign imagery, beyond including images of the fighters themselves.[178] Perhaps this instance represents an apt transition; while Joan was still their inspiration, they were on their way to full citizenship, individuals in their own right, and Joan's example fueled their fight.

Three

Bodica

Patriotic Woman Leader,
Mother and Resistant Warrior
for British Women's Suffrage

Sir Julius Vogel, New Zealand Member of the House of Representatives and an early proponent for New Zealand women's suffrage, gave a speech in 1887 in which he defended women's suitability for the vote by invoking historical women leaders, stating that "from the very first Queen, Boadicea—'the British warrior-Queen'—down to Victoria, the Queens of England have been among the best rulers of the country. If women have been allowed to enjoy the rights of sovereignty, they ought to share in the general government of the country."[1] A similar positioning in advocating for the elevation of women's status, this one by culling warrior women examples from history, comes from a haberdasher known as "La femme Monic" in a 1793 speech she delivered to the Parisian Society of Revolutionary Republican Women in which she proclaimed of female warriors:

> What do all these examples prove, if not that women can form battalions, command armies, battle and conquer as well as men? … If women are suited for combat, they are no less suited for government. How many of them have governed with glory![2]

Joan Wallach Scott's characterization of this speech demonstrates one approach the suffrage women took in using Bodica as an inspirational example: "If women's subordination—past and present—was secured at least in part by their invisibility, then emancipation might be advanced by making them visible in narratives of social struggle and political achievement."[3] Motivations for securing a place in making decisions about government led suffrage women to gather such examples of strong women leaders and warriors from history in order to write themselves into history.

This chapter will use a theoretical framing of history and memory; and the gaps that lie between them. When suffrage women took up Bodica as historical example, they had to contend with competing histories and memories of her reputation. She was a fiery, red-headed, ferocious leader, but also an avenging mother. In terms of addressing the possibility of such disturbing accounts of Bodica as have come down to us, Bodica is far from the pristine, virginal Joan of Arc. She offers up a number of contending narratives to memorialize that express the suffrage vision of both militants and constitutionalists. Like Joan, Bodica was a real, historical militant leader. Unlike Joan, most importantly for suffrage visual rhetoric, she was not a virgin but a mother, representative both of Briton as motherland and as an example of British motherhood. Women suffragists took up Joan as warrior example and matron saint, as discussed in Chapter Two. But scholars have not examined Bodica within the suffrage visual culture; although Marguerite Johnson, as a Classicist, has positioned Bodica in suffrage rhetoric through the lens of dramaturgical theory, exploring issues of ancient pageantry and ritual.[4] Here, for the first time, I examine her role as historical Queen leader, protective mother/land, and resistant warrior example. Emblematic not only of warfare but also of nation,[5] she echoes Joan and Britannia, hence I position this discourse between the chapters I devote to each of them.

We have mistakenly called this ancient Queen "Boadicea," due to an error of a Latin scribe; she is properly called Bodica from the Celtic word "bouda" meaning "Victory," but during the Victorian and Edwardian periods she was known by Boadicea.

As first Queen of England, Bodica was the Celtic Queen to King Prasutagas of the Iceni people who resided in what is present-day Norfolk during the first century CE. When he died, he willed his land to his two daughters but the Romans did not honor his will, instead accessing his land and making the Iceni their slaves. In CE 60 the Iceni joined forces with a neighboring tribe, the Trinovates, to revolt against the Romans, electing Bodica as their leader. But the Roman army eventually defeated them, Bodica fighting from her chariot alongside her daughters, whose previous brutal violation at the hands of Roman soldiers only fueled the determined Queen further. In the end, Roman historian Tacitus (CE 56–117) says she poisoned herself to avoid the shame of imprisonment, while her other historical recorder, Dio Cassius (CE 150–235) states that she died shortly after the final battle from an illness. Her legacy was well-established by the time the Edwardian suffrage women took her up as a historical example; she had been reinvented from Elizabethan times forward, in plays, poems, historical accounts and public monuments.

In terms of establishing Bodica as a historical leader precedent, Eileen Yeo explains of the suffrage women:

> Such women who wished to communicate with and persuade often doubtful and hostile groups would not, on the whole, invent brand new identities for themselves. In fact, few historical men and women, no matter how daring, have ever created immaculately new revolutionary identities.[6]

In this context, Yeo cites Karl Marx's assertion that there is a paradox "of how revolutionaries take on identities from the past to dignify their cause, adopting 'names, battle cries and costumes in order to present the new scene of world history in this time-honoured disguise and this borrowed language.'"[7] Yet this "borrowed language" is ancestral and the suffrage women's choices of historical precedents were purposeful in terms of which women they felt would help present them in the best possible light. More problematically, these suffrage women were also addressing the issues and critiques that they faced in a patriarchal culture that, while it honored motherhood, dishonored women who acted outside of that role; unsettling accounts of Bodica were heavily at play. Bodica's importance, then, stems from her representation being both a conflated and often contradictory one: like the suffrage leaders Millicent Garrett Fawcett and Emmeline Pankhurst, she was a leader, mother, and warrior for the cause of saving Britain. Like Charlotte Despard, she was also an honorary mother, Despard, after her husband's death devoting herself to improving the lives of girls and boys, as well as being a poor law guardian and a continual fighter for the improvement of women's lives.[8]

In this context, suffrage women resurrected Bodica visually, in part, as a response to important recent statues of her erected by and for the British people. For example, many of the commemorative images of Bodica that the suffrage ateliers and political cartoonists created were based on the Thomas Thornycroft 1902 bronze sculpture of her in her chariot with her daughters (fig. 46); funds for the bronze were raised through the London County Council. Prince Albert had initially encouraged Thornycroft's project, but upon his death in 1861 the work existed only in plaster form, not yet cast in bronze. Thomas Thornycroft's son, John, spearheaded the funding campaign.

A. Patriot (Alfred Pearce) did a cartoon version of the sculpture for *Votes for Women* in its opening page for November 18, 1910 (fig. 47), attesting to Bodica's importance for the WSPU, as does an Emmeline Pankhurst portrait by Elliott and Fry published as a postcard by J. Beagles & Co., Ltd., c. 1909 (Private Collection) in which she wears a Bodica brooch based on the sculpture itself.[9] For Britain in general, as for suffrage women, she stands as a cultural, iconic leader, mother, and warrior, a symbol of strength and resistance to an occupying power; these roles would seem to be conflicting, but they honor this assessment of the way history not only remembers, but also investigates ideal heroines. For example, Samantha Freénée-Hutchins argues that during the Victorian period Bodica represented maternal imperialism, in part because she had so much in common with Queen Victoria. Beyond sharing the same name (Bodica means Victory in Celtic) "both were mothers and both were widows. The political advantages of a policy of maternal imperialism were enormous since it somehow justified Britain's imperialism whilst the prophetic myth of the immortal Bodica added a heroic lustre to Britain's expansionist programme."[10] Richard Hingley and Christina Unwin similarly argue that the statue was meant to represent British imperialism in the form of Bodica as "a patriot, woman and mother, seeking to avenge political, sexual and familial wrongs."[11]

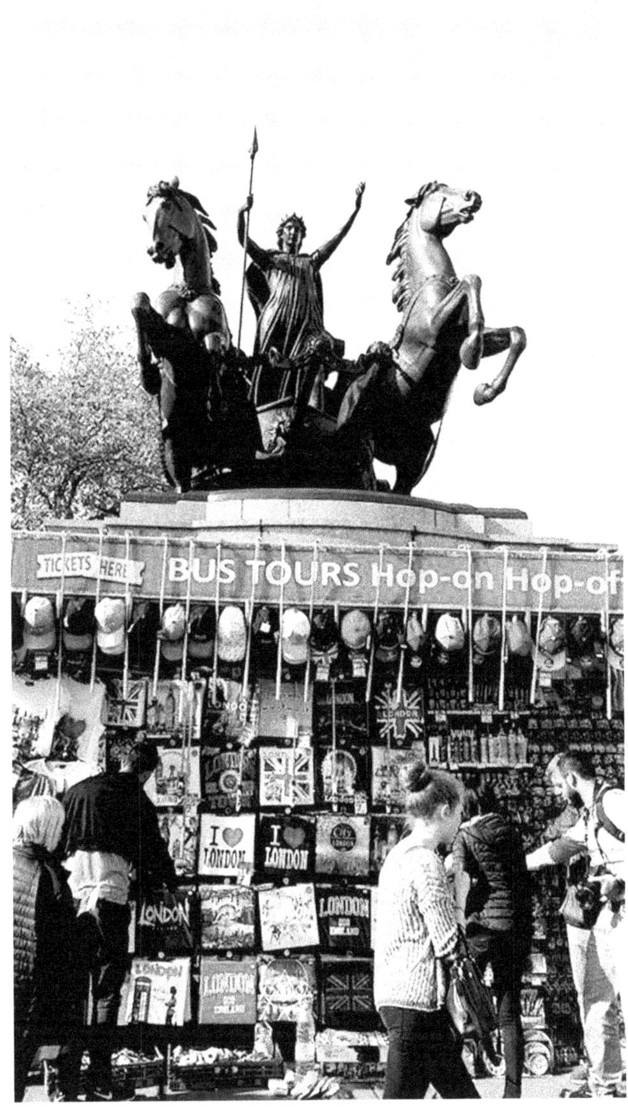

Figure 46. Thomas Thornycroft (1814–1885), *Bodica in Her Chariot with Daughters, in situ, opposite Houses of Parliament on Victoria Embankment at Westminster Bridge.* 1902, bronze. Author's photograph, 2016.

It is fitting, then, that we find Bodica facing the Houses of Parliament at Victoria Embankment, while on the other side of Parliament we find The Emmeline and Christabel Pankhurst Memorial at the entrance to Victoria Tower Gardens, providing a visible and symbolic framing to the British Government of the importance of women's rule throughout history. While Bodica commands her chariot, Emmeline is positioned as if addressing an audience; both are engaged in battle.[12] It is further impacting to realize competing narratives at work: Memorializing a historical woman as warrior (Bodica) and as speaker and leader (Pankhurst), shows both statues responding to the ideas set down in the campaigning leaflet that former suffrage women distributed to raise funds for the Pankhurst memorial:

> A statue is the recognized form of tribute paid to historic personalities, the highest and most lasting honour that humanity has ever been able to pay to those who have rendered great services to civilization. As in ancient days, so now, men commemorate their heroes and liberators by erecting statues. Shall not women claim equal honour for her who led them to victory?[13]

In this way, they acknowledge the ideals both Bodica and Pankhurst represent for them as leaders, while bringing a woman into the historical record visibly, which Wallach Scott argues above is central to feminist historical discourse.

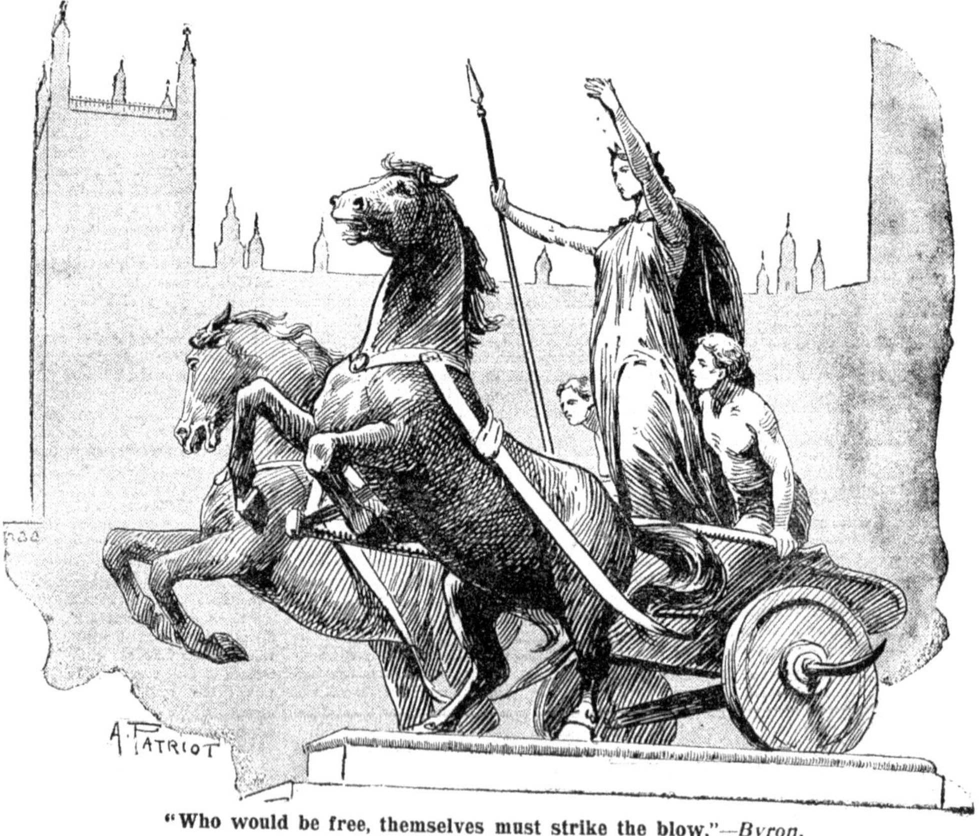

Figure 47. A. Patriot (Alfred Pearce) (1855–1933), Cartoon version of Thomas Thornycroft sculpture for WSPU from *Votes for Women* (18 November 1910). Includes Byron inscription: "Who would be free, themselves must strike the blow."

Patriotism and Bodica's Role as Leader

The NUWSS suffrage women honored Bodica with her own banner which the Artists' Suffrage League created for the NUWSS procession of 1908 (fig. 48). For the WFL and WSPU, Cicely Hamilton included Bodica in *A Pageant of Great Women* of 1909–1910. Further, she was a prominent presence in suffrage processions as an actual persona, just as with Joan of Arc, here represented in her chariot (fig. 49) in the Pageant of Queens of the Historical Pageant section during the Women's Coronation Procession of 1911. According to Maud Arncliffe-Sennett, who received such a memento at an annual meeting of the NUWSS, the organization gifted emblematic pictures that represented Queen Bodica in her chariot, waving a flag inscribed "Votes for Women."[14] She refers to T. Blake Wirgman's drawing which quotes directly from the Thornycroft sculpture (Women's Library, London School of Economics).

These propagandistic exercises reflect continual feminist work to resurrect women's foremothers. Within the Arts and Crafts Movement, for example, there are significant images of historical women that predict suffrage material culture, including Alexander Fisher's 1898 *La Rose Mystica* enamel on copper which depicts Bodica being inspired by rose thorns to attach blades to her chariot wheels before she meets the Roman invaders. Fisher's student, Geraldine Carr, beat into the metal surround the image of Bodica in her chariot.[15] Honoring Bodica is part of a pattern of remembering historical women amongst feminist artists, one which continues in Judy Chicago's *Dinner Party,* 1974–1979, that includes a setting at the table for Bodica (Brooklyn Museum, New York).

Within the Edwardian suffrage visual rhetoric, artists specifically positioned Bodica as the first in a long line of strong, respected women rulers. For example, A. Patriot produced an illustration for the *Votes for Women* cover in September 1910 that links the Queens of England and points to the absurdity of denying women voting rights (fig. 50).

Titled "Anti-Suffragisms Illustrated III. Men will never be ruled by women," at left is Bodica in her chariot, giving the call to charge, while, at center, Queen Victoria sits on her throne, receiving homage from members of her colonies. At right, Queen Elizabeth I is seated on horseback holding a scepter and making a gesture of leadership; behind her are ships which reference her navy's great defeat of the Spanish Armada. Like the other Queens, Bodica was not an allegorical figure but rather an actual historical leader of her

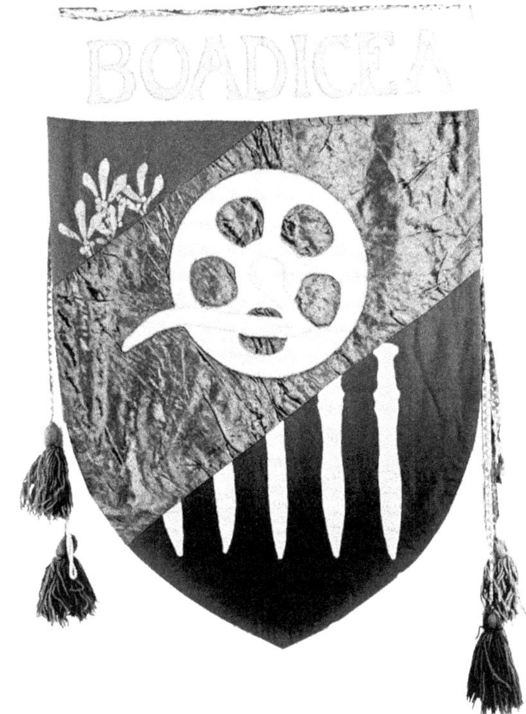

Figure 48. Artists' Suffrage League, *Bodica Banner for NUWSS Procession,* 1908. Probably designed by Mary Lowndes (1857–1929). **Women's Library, London.**

people. The title thus suggests the hubris of men who think they have never been ruled by women. This view is punctuated by the dialogue that follows the cartoon on the next few pages, which includes a section on "Men and Militant Methods," that focuses on each of these women's roles as ruthless rulers who used militant schemes: "Men, however much they may criticize the methods of the Suffragettes, are quick to sympathise with members of their own sex who, with far less justification, resort to similar methods."[16] This commentary appears in the WSPU journal, its members very aware of the barbs it is throwing while referencing its own leftist methods which the Pankhursts had learned in their radical social circles in Manchester.[17] Thus, this commentary sets up a critique of those who have tried to undo the historical work of these brave leaders and to question them within the context of appropriate womanly behavior; hence it offers up just one account of British patriotism and its complexities rather than offering a straightforward narrative.

Yet, one thrust of Bodica's representation and the rhetoric surrounding it was her historical precedent. As such, in relation to the Bodica banner (fig. 48), Tickner has argued that all suffrage banners had the express purpose of celebrating women's history as they focused on "a sense of shared identity and imbued it with political significance," further arguing that

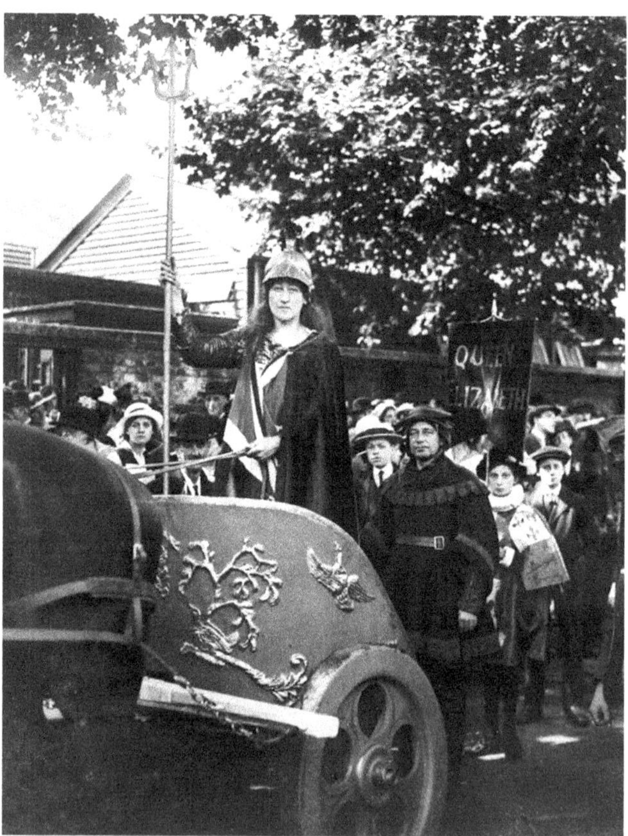

[i]n so far as they made reference to the past it was as part of a political strategy for the present; and in so far as they mobilised women's traditional needlework skills—so much a part of the contemporary feminist stereotype as to be almost a secondary sexual characteristic—it was to challenge the terms of that femininity in a collective political enterprise.[18]

This acknowledgment of historical feminist artistic practices is one which Judy Chicago duly understood and repeated in her team's careful research of needlework methods that were historically accurate and implemented in the place setting of each woman honored in her *Dinner Party*, women speaking with women's tongues and in women's language.

The suffrage groups were able to unearth strong women in history to support their cause and their collective voices. This kind of evocation was necessary if they were to succeed at separating themselves from patriarchy's view of them as second-class citizens.

Figure 49. *Bodica in her Chariot in the Famous Women Pageant of the WSPU-Organized Women's Coronation Procession,* 17 June 1911. Museum of London.

ANTI-SUFFRAGISMS ILLUSTRATED.

III.—Men will never be ruled by women.

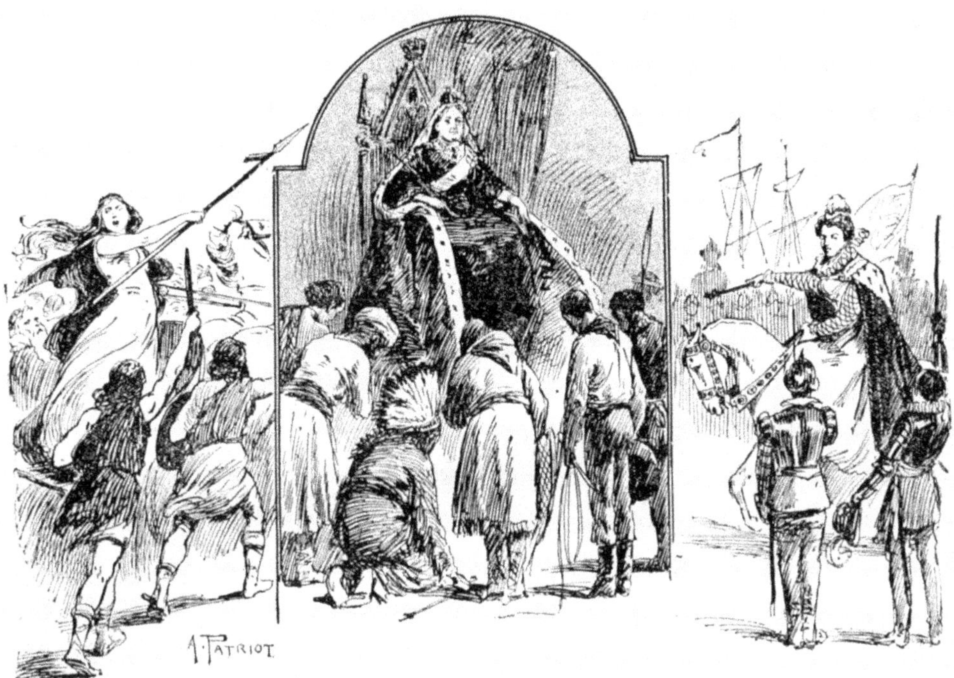

Figure 50. A. Patriot (Alfred Pearce) (1855–1933), "Anti-Suffragisms Illustrated. III. Men will never be ruled by women." Cover of *Votes for Women* (September 1910).

They weren't going to take opposition lightly and would fight back. As Ellen Carol Dubois explains, once they chose this rebellious path:

> It is not simply that women must start from the beginning; they must first unlearn what a patriarchal society has taught them about themselves. Having been initiated into a male-dominated society they have been well instructed in the art of woman-devaluation, and if they have learnt their lessons well women will have emerged with their confidence undermined, their assurance dissolved and their sense of self debased. It is from this position that they must start to reject the prevailing wisdom and begin afresh to construct the meanings which are consistent with their own experience.[19]

One of the ways in which the historical women and suffrage women were brought together is in a powerful page from the *Illustrated London News* entitled "The Woman Militant: Leaders of the Suffragist Procession and Their Symbolic Banners Commemorating Great Women of all Ages" (fig. 51) which illustrates the Artists' Suffrage League's twenty-three historical banners for the NUWSS, including the one of Bodica, which are intermingled with photographic portraits of women leaders of the 1908 NUWSS procession who are identified by name below each of their portraits. Visually, the audience could make the connection between women leaders of past and present.

A notice from the NUWSS of a "Press Reports of the Banners" includes an excerpt from the *Sunday London Times* which revivifies the connection between traditional women's work with a call for liberty and representations of womanhood:

The new banners of the movement are wonderful.... Many of these emblems of woman's demand for liberty were exceedingly artistic, and put to shame those painfully gaudy devices which are used to emblazon the aims of fellowship merely masculine. Many of the banners were designed to celebrate the memory of the great women of all ages, from Vashti, Boadicea, and Joan of Arc down to Mrs. Browning, George Eliot, and Queen Victoria. It was an attempt to represent pictorially the Valhalla of Womanhood.... As the procession moved away it presented a vista made up of wonderful colours, and it reminded one somehow of a picturesquely clad medieval army, marching out with waving gonfalons to certain victory.[20]

These banners appeared in exhibition displays to help raise funds for the cause; in suffrage shop windows; in parades as organizational rallying points; as informative and educational media for suffrage goals; and as identifiers of collective group values. Further, they appeared at bazaars and as backdrops for speakers at meetings. In each context, they united, in their form and content, women's work and women's history, honoring women of spiritual, moral, and intellectual purpose and yet they also belonged to a tradition of radical protest, preceded as they were by Trade Union banners, a topic I address in the epilogue.[21]

Bodica as historical leadership figure (fig. 49) appeared in the Famous Women Pageant of the Women's Coronation Procession of 1911. According to the WSPU *Official Programme of the Women's Coronation Procession*, this pageant was meant to represent "the great political power held by women in the past history of these Isles, the last vestige of which was lost with the vote in 1832 when the Reform Bill was passed."[22] Tickner's interpretation of this kind of representation suggests that it was

a reasonable attempt to establish that different forms of power had existed before the bourgeois revolutions, and women's gender and social standing had determined their rights and capacities in the feudal and early modern period in complex ways. The important point was to drive a wedge, by whatever means, into that cluster of beliefs which made women's exclusion from political citizenship a *natural* consequence of their feminine gender.[23]

The fact that the suffrage organizers used the title of "pageant" for this particular historical grouping is significant since they created their marches as true spectacles. A visible presence was their goal,

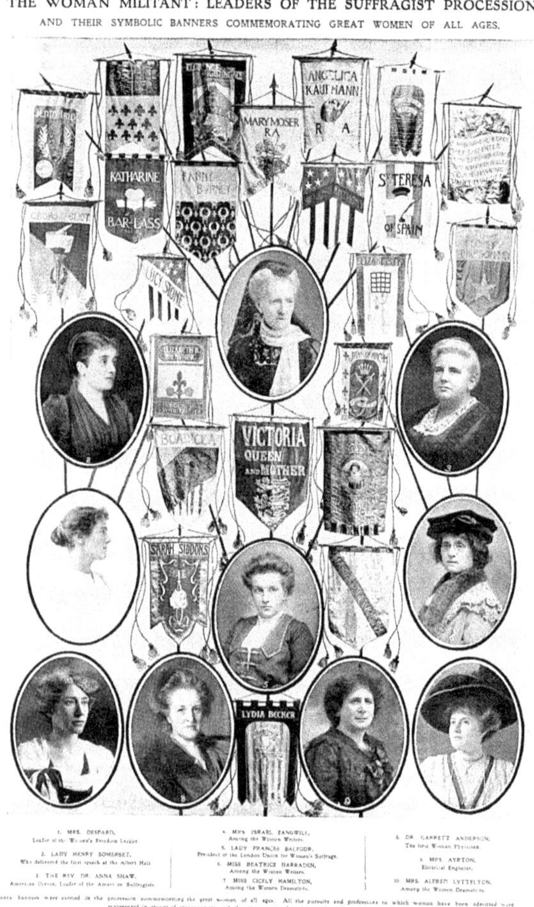

Figure 51. "The Woman Militant: Leaders of the Suffragist Procession and Their Symbolic Banners Commemorating Great Women of All Ages." *For NUWSS Demonstration,* 13 June 1908. Banners designed by Artists' Suffrage League. From *Illustrated London News* (20 June 1908). Photograph courtesy of Mary Evans Picture Library, London.

but to have a pageant of great women at the center of any march showed that they were tied to a history of women, using the pageant form as a way to educate their audience about women's real, documentable, historical placement as a solid argument for citizenship.

Challenging the Hysterical Stereotype: Bodica as Mother/land

In a pamphlet by the Brighton Society of the NUWSS regarding the creation of the Bodica banner (fig. 48), they refer to her in her typically-represented stance of commanding her chariot with her daughters at her side as "this heroic figure of woman, mother, and ruler" who "represents a type of the 'eternal feminine'—the guardian of the hearth, the avenger of its wrongs upon the defacer and despoiler."[24] Hence, she offers up an example of leadership, but specifically couched within a mother's fierce defense of her home and her children, a fitting example for suffrage women who argued, repeatedly, that they were not trying to wreck domestic arrangements but rather improve them. This concept and the critique of it in Edwardian culture survives in Tracey Chevalier's historical novel set in the Edwardian period, *Falling Angels* (2001) in which one wife and mother neglects her daughter, home, hearth and husband to join the suffrage movement. Chevalier positions her in direct opposition to the dutiful mother and wife of a neighboring family, who is still firmly rooted in Victorian traditions, and who represents the dialogue of anti-suffrage rhetoric.

In this context, Bodica imagery offers up a defense to the anti-mother rhetoric of the Anti-Suffrage leagues. For example, Harold Bird's poster published for an anti-suffrage meeting of the National League for Opposing Women's Suffrage depicts a woman with a sign that reads "No Votes. Thank You." Below it is written "The Appeal of Womanhood" (fig. 52). Behind her and in direct opposition to her feminine representation in a long flowing gown, is the hysterical agitator, wielding an ax and a hammer, symbolically outside of the bounds of respectable womanhood in her awkward running stance. Her appearance in these anti-suffrage propaganda images acts as

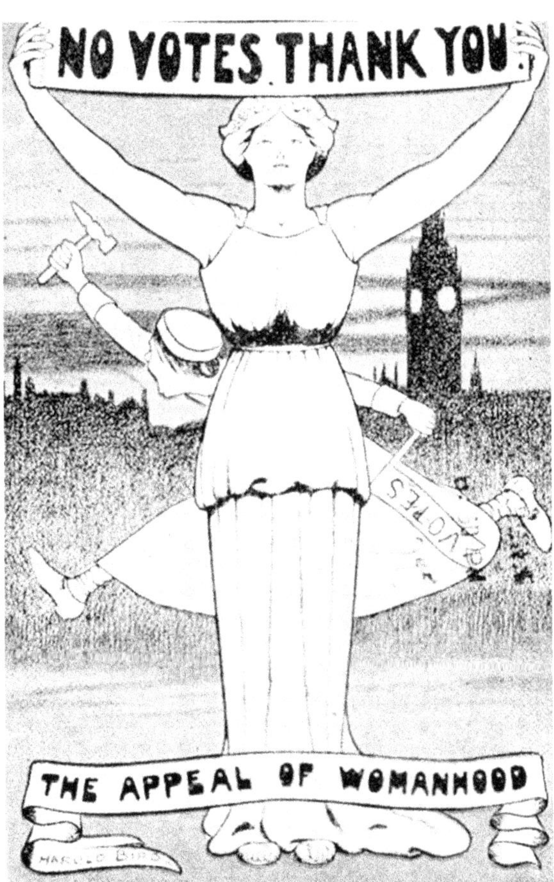

Figure 52. Harold Bird (active 1912), *No Votes, Thank You; The Appeal of Womanhood,* postcard for National League for Opposing Women's Suffrage, 1912. Author's collection.

counter balance to the ideal of womanhood; in other such images, she is often represented as a mother neglecting her domestic duties. The WSPU and WFL specifically fought back at such imagery with a quotation of the Bird illustration; in Louise Jacobs' Suffrage Atelier rebuttal, advertised in *The Vote* in 1912, the same woman holds a banner that reads: "We want the vote to stop the white slave traffic, sweated labour, and to save the children" while below it repeats "The Appeal of Womanhood" (fig. 53).

Behind her stands not the ax-wielding hysteric but rather a true cross-section of women who need the vote: mothers, laundresses, prostitutes, and factory workers. Behind them to one side is a silhouette of factory chimneys, on the other a silhouette of the Houses of Parliament. The women here are not one type, but rather individuals whose body postures are bent and weary, as if weighed down not only by their daily labors, but also by the desires that the slogan itself requests. Published as both a postcard and a poster, the atelier created it for the WFL Edinburgh to London March for the Brown Women of 1912, so named for the brown coats they wore on their march, during which they gathered signatures on a petition for women's rights. This image anticipates the work of Julia Kristeva, specifically her "Stabat Mater" essay; just as she positions the Virgin Mary as the *stabat mater dolorosa* (literally translated as "Stood the Mother, full of grief"),[25] we can reflect on Bodica's role as a mother who grieves for her daughters' violation and seeks to protect them from further harm, a sentiment we can extend to her people as represented in Jacobs' image.

One additional poster by John Hassall for the National League for Opposing Women's Suffrage entitled *A Suffragette's Home*, 1912 (Bodleian Library, John Johnson Collection) protests against the campaigning mother, positioning her as a neglectful wife and mother, whose family suffers from her absence. In the image, the children's socks go undarned, the lamp oil is depleted, children and husband go without dinner and are starving, both physically and emotionally, because the keeper of the hearth has vacated, leaving no warmth or comfort for her household.

As discussed in Chapter One, there was a strong pronatalist movement in France after the Franco-Prussian War that kept French women at home. The anti-suffrage rhetoric in Edwardian England would seem to echo that movement in its desire to keep women within the private sphere. The economic shift brought on by the Industrial Revolution, accom-

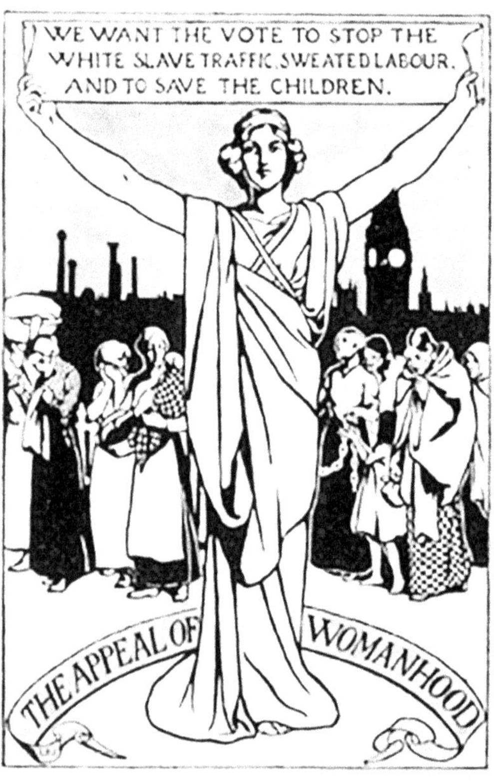

Figure 53. Louise R. Jacobs (active 1910–1938), *The Appeal of Womanhood,* designed as poster and postcard by Suffrage Atelier for WFL and WSPU, advertised in *The Vote* (6 July 1912). Women's Library, London.

panied by the writings of Jean Jacques Rousseau, created mothering duties as the natural purview of women. Yet, this suffrage positioning of Bodica in relation to women's primary role as mothers would seem to suggest that the suffrage women share the same values on motherhood with the antis; that is, that their presence in the home is vital. The two need not conflict. Neither is the conjuring of Bodica as mother/land example the first instance of mothering rhetoric within women's reforms. As Tickner observes:

> The participation of women in a range of reforming movements in the 19th-century was made to derive its legitimacy from motherhood. Josephine Butler went into rescue work as a mother to save daughters. Mrs. Pankhurst was introduced to a Presbyterian congregation in Chicago on Mother's Day as "one of the great Mothers of the World".... Mrs. Fawcett argued that women's suffrage was needed "because we want the home and the domestic side of things to be more fully represented in politics" and the WSPU claimed to fight for "conditions which will not block the mainsprings of good motherhood and crush the life out of it."[26]

As discussed in the introduction, once women achieved at least the partial vote, they were able to make improvements in the laws to protect women in the home and at work. While the anti-suffrage press fought to position suffrage women and domestic women in a battle, that stance did not reflect reality. Further, while many women in the movement were single, many more were wives and mothers. Reconsider Bodica in Thornycroft's sculpture (fig. 46) in this regard. She stands erect, arms raised, protecting her daughters and her people; her daughters crouch behind her, honoring her shelter and her fierce power as shielding mother. Further, as if in answer to this damaging separation of the domestic woman from the woman activist, the Suffrage Atelier published for the WSPU and WFL *Polling Station*, c. 1912, which includes the mother and child alongside not laboring women this time, but rather professional women, including a college graduate (perhaps Garrett Fawcett herself), a nurse, a mayor (this could have been Elizabeth Garrett Anderson, once retired from her career as medical doctor, as first woman mayor in England, in the Garrett childhood town of Aldeburgh) and a woman in legal robes (Christabel Pankhurst was one such; women could take law degrees but not practice until 1919). Also present are a woman artist, journalist, and factory inspector. All of them are being denied entrance to the polling station while men of every rank and profession, from farmworkers to aristocrats, gain ready entrance.

This image of the *Polling Station* can be buttressed by the symbolism of The Pageant of Women's Trades and Professions, held in London on 27 April 1909 which included representatives from countries around the world, France conspicuous by its absence. Organized by the International Woman Suffrage Alliance with Carrie Chapman Catt as President and Garrett Fawcett as second Vice-President, the London Society was in charge of the pageant as part of the Quinquennial Congress. Tickner argues that the pageant "developed the self-presentation of women as workers, in determinant social and historical conditions, rather than as members of a conglomerate and domestic 'womanliness.'"[27] In this context, this pageant's goals were multifold: to show the breadth of suffrage women across classes and occupations; that the vote would be a means to help working women with employment and, in the sweated industries, with working conditions; and to demonstrate the numbers of middle-class women who wanted to work as well as the vast numbers of working-class women who had no choice but to work.[28] In positioning Bodica as emblem of mother/land and nation, suffrage artists declared that she represented all such working women as an example of a strong mother who was protecting not only her children, but also, by extension, the children of the nation. Her position at the entrance to the Houses of Parliament, arms raised, facing Big Ben, and the suffrage reiteration of that image in political cartoons and memorial imagery alike, suggests such a safeguard for the nation. Further, as discussed earlier, the government buildings are propped up by two women leaders, yet they are both mothers, both fighters for women's rights, as if to suggest that Britain owes its very existence to mothering women's forces.

The styles the atelier artists used within their production of motherhood propaganda varied according to their training, talent and intent. Many images of motherhood and womanhood use the beatific woman of Pre-Raphaelite imagery, or the more formalized beautiful female with long tresses of the Art Nouveau and Arts and Crafts Movement, as in Jacobs' *The Appeal of Womanhood* (fig. 53). Paula Hays Harper is critical of this kind of representation, a critique that this chapter challenges:

> It was a style generally considered unsuitable for political posters and rarely used in the World War I posters. But the Pre-Raphaelite and art nouveau styles have this advantage: they romanticize women. They are "feminine" styles not created by women but carrying connotations of what constitutes femininity from a masculine point of view.[29]

The suffrage imagery in this chapter, both of Bodica and the broader representations of motherhood, can be contextualized in terms of the need for a positive female example, one tied to the groups' desires to present a respectable image of femininity. Hays Harper comes closer to a nuanced reading when she says: "The posters ... visually illustrate the dilemma of the suffragists, who wanted political power and freedom from an oppressive social status but hesitated to part with their traditional sexual identity (even though it was one that had been defined by men), perhaps for fear of being left sexless."[30] In the images in this chapter, suffrage women used their femininity as a weapon to help them gain the vote.

But, Hays Harper insists that we see only this kind of feminine representation rather than any more direct kind of attack when, in fact, such works themselves offer a critique of patriarchal culture and what it lacks. Further, she posits that "this acceptance of a language of form from within the conventional vocabulary may have reflected the reluctance or inability of the suffragists to take up a political position that would place them in direct opposition to the social status quo."[31] It is possible to subvert from within. The NUWSS certainly used this method in their non-party, non-violent, constitutionalist approach to the campaign. Yet, like Hays Harper, Tickner argues that women trained in the traditions of the Arts and Crafts and Art Nouveau at the end of the 19th century "still lacked the cultural power to shape the world to their own image."[32] I argue here that embracing Bodica as a historical example of motherhood, one reiterated in atelier posters, periodicals and postcards, was one way such artists both began to reclaim their own history and to develop an iconography of their own making.

That said, there are, however, myriad examples in the posters, postcards and other print ephemera that utilize a more direct mode of representation with bold, crude lettering and a more realistic style. In Jacobs' poster, for example, she brings both styles together, evoking the feminine beauty alongside coarser lettering that aligned the women's cause with not only the womanly woman of the hearth but also political propaganda of the street.

Another side of Bodica's mothering role in conjunction with this feminizing dialogue can be seen in T. Blake Wirgman's cartoon based on Thornycroft's statue, in which the artist has added two vignettes of mothers, one a Madonna and child image, the other showing mother and child reading together. Hence Wirgman offers up not only the feminine, protective mother but also the feminine, educating mother. Sharon Macdonald argues that in their distribution of this image to WSPU released prisoners at a celebratory dinner, that Fawcett and the NUWSS were trying to convey a gentler approach for the militants: She argues that, apart from the additions of the two motherhood cameos, "the female figures in the chariot itself are not so wild as Thornycroft's originals, and Boadicea's spear is transformed into a banner reading 'Votes for Women.' In Boadicea's other hand are scales of justice, and an angel presents her with a laurel crown (a symbol of victory)."[33] While Macdonald might be responding to this stylistic and representational conundrum of powerful AND feminine women, an echo of the dilemma of the multiple narratives that Bodica represents, perhaps here she is also referencing the philosophy that all suffrage leaders had originally taken up, one in which, according to Wallach Scott:

> The woman as mother is the antithesis of the female public speaker. While the orator wrestles with her inappropriate masculinity, the mother embodies acceptable femininity, fulfilling as she does her designated reproductive role. Despite its apparent endorsement of normative gender relations, maternity has sometimes served to consolidate feminist identification.[34]

Such a characterization was at the center of representational dialogue for suffrage women. But Bodica, even in this Wirgman image, is multifaceted: she is Justice and Victory, making a plea for the vote, yet she is also mother *and* leader. Wallach Scott contextualizes such representation in saying, "Appealing to prevailing ideas of maternity, often in contexts of pronatalist political pressure [as we have seen with French women], feminists have argued that mothers deserve rights because they guarantee the future of the race or the nation or the species."[35] This observation reinforces the symbolic power of Thornycroft's statue and Wirgman's somewhat softened interpretation simultaneously. In England, as in France, the power of maternity was often invoked. Wallach Scott discusses the French delegate Maria Verone who called for unity at the International Council of Women held in Rome in May 1914, when she appealed "to all women of all nations, who suffer childbirth with the same pain and who, when their sons die in war, shed the same tears."[36] Although feminists are divided on the efficacy of creating motherhood as a collective identity, motherhood remains at the center of the Edwardian suffrage debate. Wirgman's inclusion of the two vignettes and suffrage women's use of it offers us proof of just one of their strategies to offer up women as respectable, as educators of children, and as keepers of the hearth who deserve the vote.

In punctuation of this positioning of Bodica as mother/land/nation, in 1928, once women had won complete suffrage victory in Britain, Edith How-Martyn had the idea to commemorate the militant leaders in an annual Suffragette Lecture. In Geraldine Lennox's 1931 Suffragette Lecture entitled "The Suffragette Spirit," she speaks of Bodica's leadership example:

> Tacitus records that under the leadership of Boadicea the Britons all rose to arms and he gives a report of her speech on the eve of battle in which she was defeated. She had already driven Catus over the sea, been victorious against another general. Subdued Colonia, sacked Verulam, and was marching on London. Her army built an entrenched camp near what is now called Islington and addressing it she called on them "to witness that it was usual for the Britons to war under the conduct of women, but on that occasion," she said, "she entered the field not as one descended from ancestors so illustrious to recover her kingdom and her treasure, but as one of the humblest among them, to take vengeance for liberty extinguished, her own body lacerated with stripes and the chastity of her daughters defiled ... they would see that in that battle they must conquer or perish. Such was the resolve of a woman; the men might live if they pleased and be the slaves of the Romans."[37]

In this context, Lennox combines Bodica's role as mother with that of her protection of the land itself. Although Bodica was ultimately defeated, suffrage women used her representation to reflect their concern for the security of the daughters of England who themselves were emblematic of a non-colonized body.

Bodica as Resistant Warrior

In her speech, Lennox also conflates Bodica's position as mother with that of resistant warrior; Lennox recognized her downfall as the event against which Edwardian suffragists were fighting, in her closing remarks:

> The defeat of Boadicea rang the death-knell of the freedom of British womanhood and of the spirit of British manhood. Under the Romans the British wife was no longer the brave help-meet, counselor and inspirer of the British man. Roman customs completed what the Roman arms and Roman laws had begun and the spirit of British womanhood was crushed.[38]

Tickner has argued that the image of the militant woman amongst the WSPU stemmed from iconography of a long tradition, including that of Bodica, and the militant woman "claimed her 'womanliness' from … female heroism in history, allegory and myth."[39] Hence, as with Joan, Bodica is held up as an example who is both strong and competent, yet has not forsaken her feminine appearance. Just as her femininity is a representation that suffrage artists invoke for propagandistic purposes in her role as mother, so it exists in her representation as warrior. The militant woman's role, according to Tickner, was

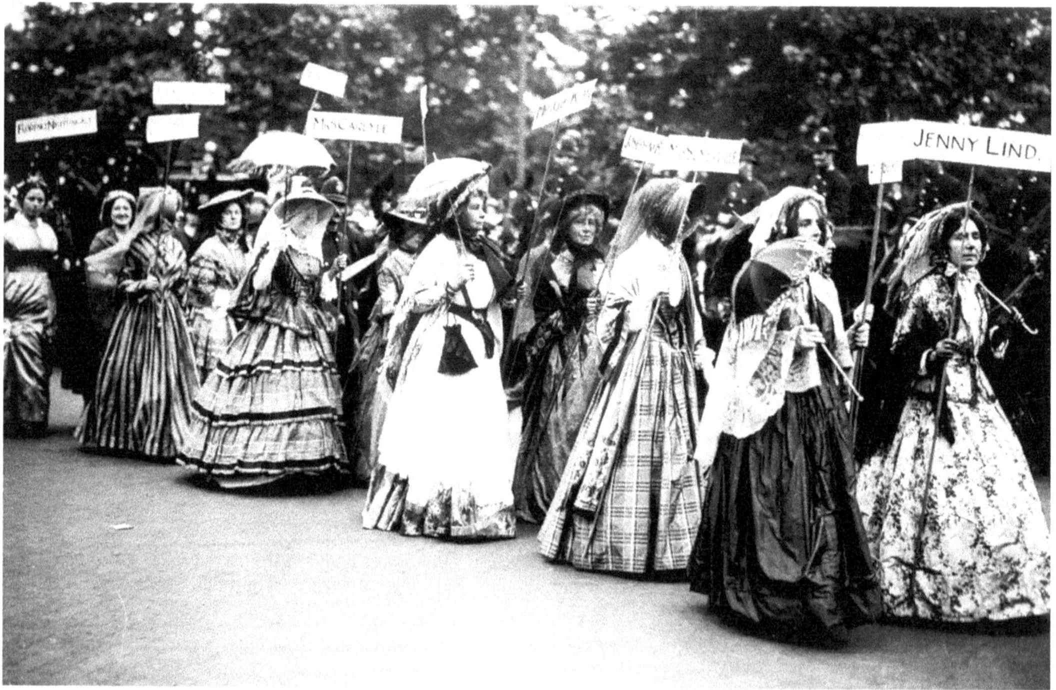

Figure 54. *Famous Women Pageant of the WSPU-Organized Women's Coronation Procession,* 17 June 1911. Museum of London.

to throw over individual acts of violence the mantle of Boadicea or Joan of Arc; in the face of accusations of hysteria, criminality and incompetence … to assert the possibility of a collective political struggle by women, for their own emancipation and against all that was venal and bumbling in the world.[40]

This attitude is evident in the inclusion of Bodica in her chariot at the Women's Coronation Procession (fig. 49), part of a large group of the Famous Women Pageant (fig. 54). But suffrage women were summoning such imagery long before they became militant in their own actions. It seems that Bodica was representative of women's desire for a ruling role and hence their place in governance, at least until 1912 when the WSPU turned to more direct militant tactics. At that point, they could invoke Bodica in terms of her historical precedent of seeking social justice through battle as a result of violation, in the same way they embraced violent action as a response to their own imprisonment and torture.

Macdonald differentiates the ways that militant and constitutionalist suffragists employed Bodica's representation. For the militants, she uses the example of Dora Montefiore who wrote about a WSPU meeting held under Thornycroft's statue (fig. 46). She "saw Boadicea in her chariot as advancing threateningly on the Houses of Parliament," and said 'she was therefore a symbol of the attitude of us militant women.'"[41]

Similarly, for the WFL, within *A Pageant of Great Women*, Hamilton includes Bodica alongside Joan of Arc in the Warrior Section rather than in the Heroic or Ruler section. In the London Scala Theatre staging in 1909, by one report, "She presented a robust figure with a long flowing cloak of many colours, with a garland in her hair and a spear in her right hand to emphasize her military role…."[42] As she enters, the character of "Woman" proclaims: "Oh, look on her who stood, a Briton in arms/ And spat defiance at the hosts of Rome!" She follows on the heels of Joan who "Woman" pronounces "Brave saint, pure soldier, lily of God and France/Whose soul fled hence on wings of pain, of fire!"[43] Yet Hamilton seems to have construed this warrior designation broadly and metaphorically in some cases; for example, she includes Florence Nightingale in this same grouping.

Nevertheless, Hamilton's characterization of Bodica alongside of Joan in the pageant suggests her role as one of resistance to the patriarchal order. She was doing battle with her oppressors in the same way that Joan did so in prison, similarly fighting for her own life. The fact that both were defeated does not dull their symbolic power for suffrage women. As Katherine Cockin has argued of Hamilton's pageant performance, for example, it evoked militancy within a historical narrative that was tied directly to nationalism, such that it regularized "the idea of women's achievements" and "militancy as national heroism."[44] Fighting rhetoric and imagery were central to Bodica's persona as they were for Joan.

This sentiment is clear in A. Patriot's *Votes for Women* illustration of the Bodica statue at Parliament (fig. 47); underneath the image are the words of Lord Byron: "Who would be free themselves must strike the blow," a stance that positions Bodica as an impervious warrior fighting for freedom. A similar opposition to authority exists in A. Patriot's "Fighting the Spirit" for *Votes for Women* (fig. 55), in which McKenna of the Home Office threatens Bodica (here represented by Thornycroft's statue) by telling her he will exterminate her "unwomanly descendants," yet she replies, "My poor little official, give it up! You can't fight the Spirit with weapons like yours!" and underneath there is an editorial comment that suggests Bodica and her ilk are winning the battle: "He has been giving it up ever since." His donkey's rump is branded with "Liberal Government," while he holds a Liberal Whip, his shield reads "Official Lies," his staff says "Prison Regulations" and his sword reads "Forcible Feeding." Dressed as a knight in armor, he is at war with Bodica's defiant descendants. This cartoon illustrates that Joan was not the only warrior that the WSPU invoked in their call for equality and freedom from prison constraints.

This fighting spirit rhetoric also exists in Lennox's speech from 1931, mentioned earlier, which positions Bodica's defeat in relation to the suffragettes' unflagging spirit:

> There is no more touching picture in the history of our country than this of the forces of oppression and lust—the spirit of Nero himself, who was then Emperor—pitted against this woman, who as patriot, mother, and as individual fought in defence of country, home, and honour and failed. Here I feel was the first known record of that spirit we are dealing with to-night.[45]

Suffrage women used actual emblematic women to represent their desire for citizenship; yet, both they and their symbols were caught up in a narrative of visual pleasure and hence they had to push continually against it and resist it at the same time as they promoted the inspiring qualities that actual/active women possessed. In Lennox's speech, she deflects such a narrative of visual pleasure entirely, focusing instead on the attributes

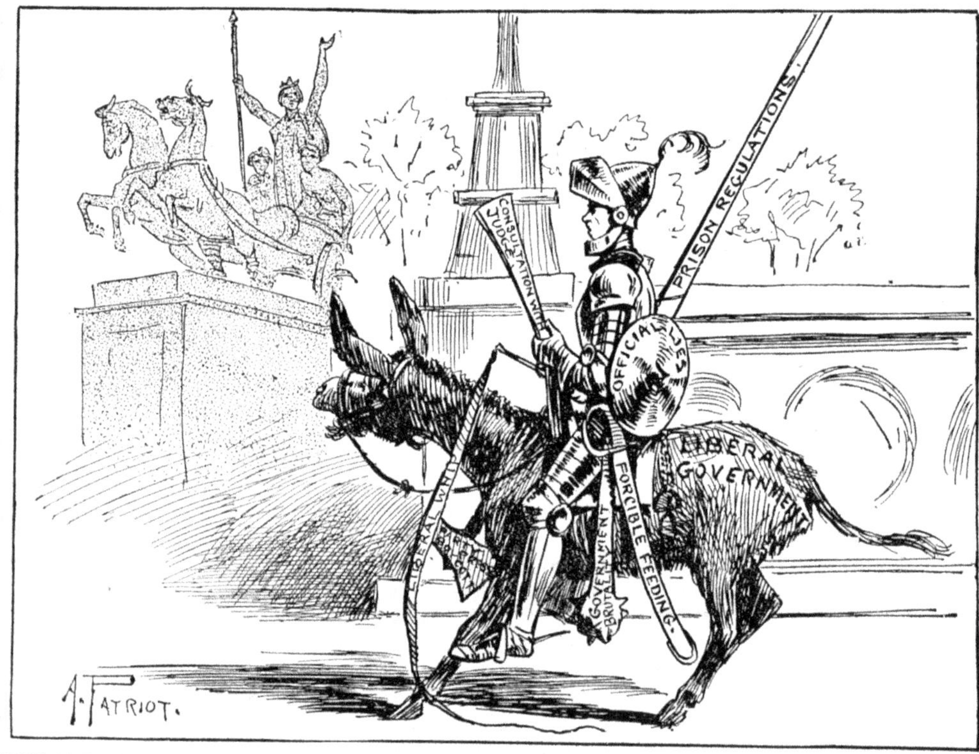

BRAVE McK.NNA OF THE HOME OFFICE: Hail, Boadicea! I hie me in hot haste to His Majesty's Gaols to exterminate therein thine unwomanly descendants!
BOADICEA: My poor little official, give it up! You can't fight the Spirit with weapons like yours!
(He has been giving it up ever since.)

Figure 55. A. Patriot (Alfred Pearce) (1855–1933), "Fighting the Spirit," from *Votes for Women* (June 1912).

that made Bodica such a significant model for suffrage women: determination, strength, absolute resistance, alongside the courage to protect her daughters and, more symbolically, the daughters of England. It was these same attributes that made her readily available to Christabel Pankhurst when, on June 22, 1917, she put Thornycroft's statue of Bodica on the front page of *Britannia*, usurping Bodica's other roles but keeping her role as resistant warrior for the war cause, claiming her "For King, For Country, For Freedom," the rallying cry of the newly reformulated WSPU journal for wartime.[46]

Four

Allegory in Suffrage Propaganda
Britannia, Liberty and Justice

Because of women's marginality in patriarchal cultures, Judith Walkowitz argues that they often become the markers of meaning rather than the creators of it.[1] Hence they are available for co-optation and can carry a multitude of messages that can often be conflicting. In addition, as Lisa Tickner asserts, "for the same reason they can come to symbolise in the abstract that from which they are excluded in the concrete (Justice is a woman, though women may not practice law)."[2] Marina Warner would agree with Tickner and Walkowitz when she suggests, "Often the recognition of a difference between the symbolic order, inhabited by ideal, allegorical figures, and the actual order, of judges, statesmen, soldiers, philosophers, inventors, depends on the unlikelihood of women practicing the concepts they represent."[3] Or, in the case of suffrage women's struggle, whether or not the culture allows them to practice such concepts. Gay L. Gullickson similarly argues:

> The effectiveness of the female allegorical figures depended on gender conventions or stereotypes (positive and negative) and the exclusion of human women from the traits they embodied, conventions and exclusions that would have made it difficult for male figures to convey the same message even if the gender of abstract nouns had been masculine.[4]

The challenge, then, for suffrage art—here in the form of Britannia, Liberty, and Justice—was how to "reinhabit the empty body of female allegory, to reclaim its meanings on behalf of the female sex."[5] We have already witnessed this struggle with a historical woman as mother in the figure of Bodica.

What we see in images here are the allegorical Britannia, Liberty, and Justice, sometimes alone, sometimes in concert with real women. Tickner suggests that such representations are one way to solve the problematics of how the allegorical female is not always a "suitable representation of the generality of women."[6] Thus, I will argue in this chapter that suffrage allegory invokes a long tradition of exchange through the symbolic form of the female figure. Such allegory maintains an open declamatory speech, yet it also contains layers of meaning. Speaking more generally, Warner argues that "a symbolized female presence both gives and takes value and meaning in relation to actual women, and contains the potential for affirmation not only of women themselves but of the general good they might represent and in which as half of humanity they are deeply implicated."[7] The suffrage artists' goal was to persuade their audience of just such a stance through an eloquent kind of visual speech.

To buttress the opinions of contemporary scholars, the WFL suffragist Maud Arncliffe-

Sennett collected suffrage allegorical imagery in her scrapbook. On one page, she proclaimed in heavy black ink, "More Allegories!!! They label Woman—Liberty, Justice, Humanity and rob her of every power or share in these abstract names." On another page she pens, "Please note that in all the Allegories the woman is omnipotent and politically imposing—in Real Life—she is politically helpless and impotent."[8] But that would seem to be exactly the point of the propaganda: To offer up images of strong, determined ideals that, should women be successful in their suffrage quest, they can readily embody themselves. The culture's continual denial of women's access to those powers fuels the battle itself.

Britannia

In the case of Britannia, suffrage visual rhetoric had the desired results of order and inclusion, representing this invulnerable epitome of the nation most often as a warrior with helmet, trident (given to her by Poseidon), and shield, as protector of her people. Viewing Britannia's first appearance in suffrage imagery, A. Patriot's "Never put off til to-morrow!" from *Votes for Women* (fig. 56), allows us to acknowledge this warrior stance. As Warner argues:

> The examples of personification which still surround us, like Britannia, often return directly to Athena; she provides the original standard measure, as it were … that is kept in the vault of memory and to which all later measures are apt to conform. If we are to understand the origins and the continuing significance of such signs in our daily lives, it is essential to look at her nature and her character, as transmitted to us through the Greek texts in which she appears as a protagonist, a dominating force and the arbiter of an ideal order.[9]

In Patriot's image, Britannia emulates these traits of Athena, as she attempts to right the wrong order of Prime Minister Asquith, so that she can set him on the proper path to women's emancipation rather than his "denial of liberal principles." To continue on his current path, she argues through her emphatic gesture, is to invite disaster, represented in the image by the downed bridge

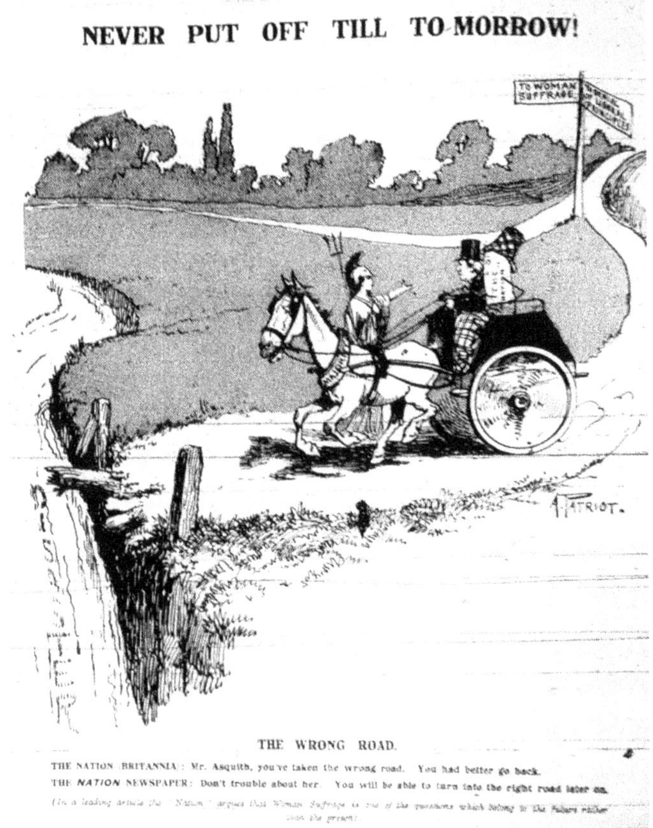

Figure 56. A. Patriot (Alfred Pearce) (1855–1933), "Never put off til to-morrow!" Britannia's first appearance in suffrage visual rhetoric, from *Votes for Women* (August 13, 1909).

over turbulent waters that Asquith will find before him should he continue to progress in this perilous direction.

Patriot depicts Britannia in her warrior garb which both makes her strong and impermeable to man. In this context, Warner observes that

> Britannia, like Justice, often wears warrior armor to demonstrate her struggle for the forces of good against the forces of evil.... Her armour ... shows her allegiance lies with the fathers; it masculinizes her. But the armour does something else, related to both these themes: it renders her a watertight, strong container.... It helps to abolish the ascribed nature of womanly bodies, and confirms an irreversible virginity. The armour inverts the sign of the woman's body so that it can properly represent virtues or ideals; it emphasizes that a leaky vessel has turned into a sound vessel.[10]

And in this way, while she wishes to enforce ideals that will aid women, she is separated from them through this kind of protection, much in the same way we saw this protection of the real-life Joan of Arc's purity.

At a suffrage meeting held by the Suffrage Atelier presided over by Laurence Housman, he discussed the subject of "Art and National Movements." In determining the importance of symbolism, he noted that

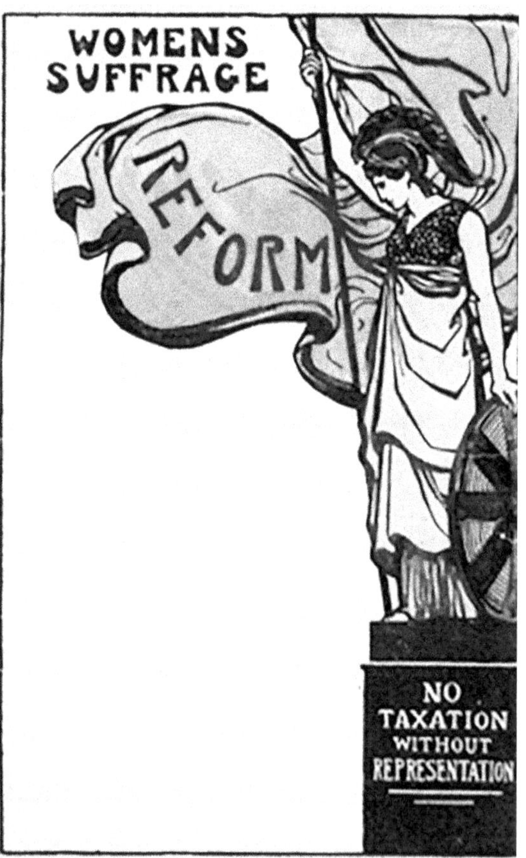

Figure 57. *Women's suffrage reform poster showing Britannia as woman warrior in Greek helmet and toga, standing on plinth that reads "No Taxation without Representation."* **Women's Library, London.**

when a small war was the subject of cartoons in *Punch*, England was represented by John Bull, but when a really national crisis intervened the national spirit was symbolized by Britannia, the woman.[11]

We see direct evidence of this observation in a poster/pamphlet for the WFL protesting "No Taxation without Representation" (fig. 57) where Britannia in her battle dress stands on a plinth above the protest statement. Many versions of this poster have survived. The Women's Tax Resistance League used it to voice their resistance to being included in the census; their motto was "No Vote, No Tax" and this motto appears on other versions of the poster alongside Britannia's image.

This sister organization to the WFL began its work in 1909, as a conscious act of civil disobedience. In addition to census evasion, Elizabeth Crawford explains that "[u]ntil the outbreak of war it was by a refusal to pay a variety of taxes and, after 1910, the dues under the Insurance Act, with the attendant publicity, that WFL members were most 'militant.'"[12] Hence, it is fitting that the warrior Britannia graces their propaganda posters.

Another "national crisis" was the torture of suffrage women in prison through forced feeding. *The Suffragette* cartoon entitled "Forcible Feeding" (fig. 58) shows Britannia revealing the true state of the torture at Holloway Prison: The death of the tortured woman which emulates the real, lived experiences of many women prisoners. But national crises also change; *Votes for Women* shifted its focus during World War I, using Britannia as the centerpiece of its "War Paper for Women" in A. Patriot's "A Vote—For the Child's Sake." The cause for all women is at the center of Britannia's protest here; shown crying, she holds a list of complaints about the increase of infant mortality during wartime, positioning the vote for women as one necessary defense against such outcomes. Hence, here, as in images of Bodica, Britannia symbolizes sympathy of and for the mother; she is mother Britain, distraught at not being able to fully protect her people.

Similarly, under wartime, Christabel Pankhurst renamed *The Suffragette*, calling it *Britannia*, in order to emphasize the national spirit of patriotism and nationalism that Britannia now represented. While Patriot's image for *Votes for Women* maintained a fight for the vote amongst the United Suffragists, the WSPU reinvented its goals at the start of World War I, choosing to serve the war cause rather than suffrage. It claimed a pro-war line and denounced pacifists, while favoring women's labor as a means to free men for military service. Thus, other groups were aligned for a continued fight for suffrage, while the WSPU changed its focus and never returned to the suffrage cause, using its newly-named *Britannia* journal, instead, as the voice of the Woman's Party.

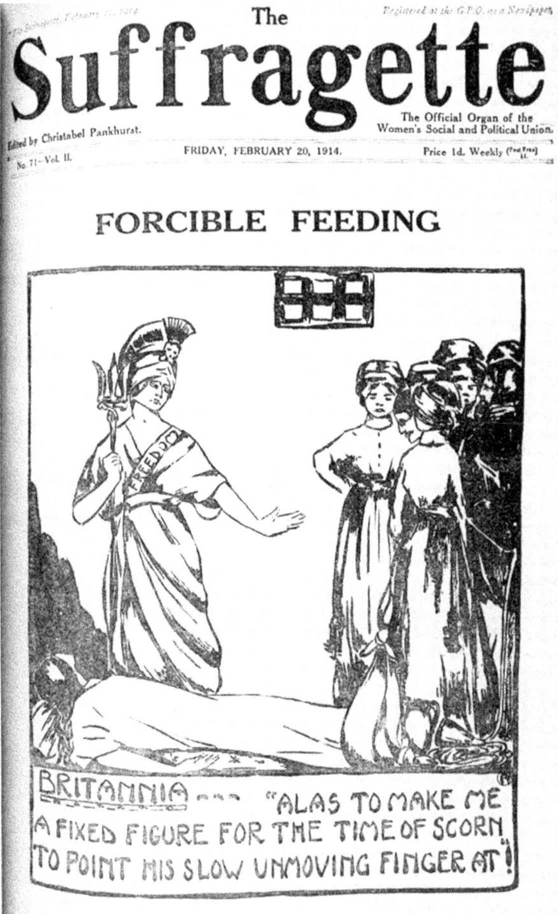

Figure 58. "Forcible Feeding," shows Britannia revealing forced feeding at Holloway Prison from *The Suffragette* (Feb. 20, 1914 cover).

Such a shifting of priorities shows that Britannia could be put to many uses and confirms just how accurate (and broad-reaching) Housman's comments were. In each of these images (figs. 57–59) Britannia represents a kind of female figure who "radiated power when real women were presumed, or forced, to be powerless; [she] represented governments that excluded women from full citizenship; [she] embodied attributes that were thought to reside more fully, if not entirely, in men than in women."[13] This representation is brought home to us in the Australian banner that shows Britannia as mother country, wearing her helmet and white gown and holding her trident, while she is being supported by Australia, whose women already had the vote. Set against a stunning green background, its statement proclaims in gold lettering: "Trust the Women Mother, As I Have Done" (Parliament House, Canberra). Created by Dora Meeson, an artist in the Artists' Suffrage League (later Dora Meeson Coats) in London, Australian women carried the banner in the 1911 Coronation Procession; their grouping included wives of the Australian Prime Minister and Premiers, as well as important activists such as Vida Goldstein.[14] Thus, Meeson represents the two groups, Mother Country and enfranchised colonies, on the banner, that was then carried by those enfranchised women colonists in a procession that argued the plea of full citizenship for the mother country.

The Suffrage Atelier certainly embraced Housman's argument of Britannia as exemplary of national crisis, producing *The Anti-Suffrage Society as Portrait Painter* (fig. 59) which, beyond giving the antis the tongue-in-cheek acronym of A.S.S., further punctuates the notion by depicting the anti as an actual ass with a palette and brushes. As it sits on a stool, it gestures to Britannia, recognizable by her warrior helmet and Union Jack skirt. She looks at the ass's portrait of her that is entitled "Britannia unsexed," showing her with a scroll that reads "vote" with a woman on it running, in typical hysterical fashion, uncontrolled, uncontained, and unkempt. She wears the requisite high boots and has hiked up her skirts, a gesture meant to show her lack of propriety; she screams violently, her lack of control echoed in her messy hair which streams out behind her. The implication here, as with many anti images, is that any woman who receives the vote will become masculine and lose all of her femininity. This idea comes out of the mouth of the A.S.S. who says: "This, my dear Mrs. Britannia, is a true and authentic portrait of yourself if ever you get the vote." The Suffrage Atelier mocks such a charge by imaging Britannia as being on the side of the vote. The ass speaks for itself in this regard. Further, the image exemplifies the dilemma the artists faced when using Britannia as their representative; in this instance, they show her as a feminine example, in striking contrast to the stereotypical representation of the hysterical suffragette. The image acknowledges the binary of representation of either feminine or masculine; either docile, compliant woman in no need of the vote or out-of-control, masculinized protester. To bring the example of Britannia, as calm figure and witness to such absurd arguments creates a strong counter-argument for equal representation.

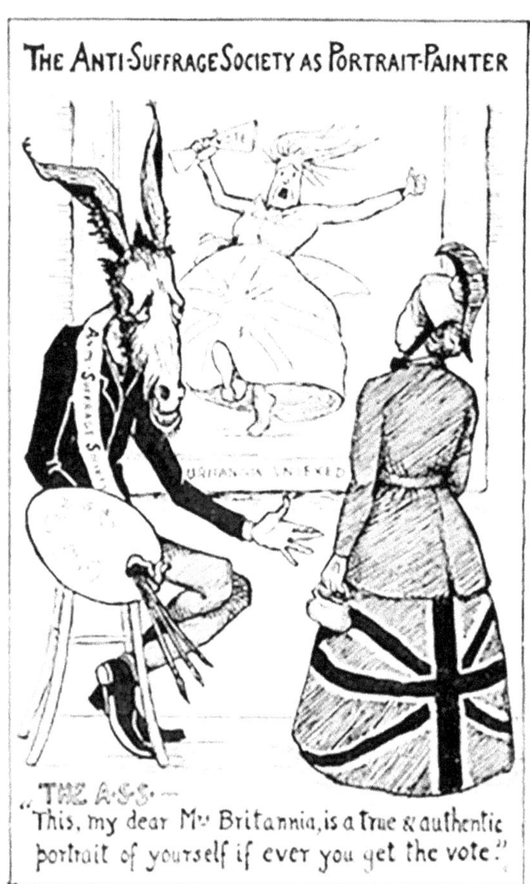

Figure 59. Suffrage Atelier, *The Anti-Suffrage Society as Portrait Painter,* published by Suffrage Atelier for WFL. Women's Library, London.

Britannia and Liberty

In many images Britannia argues for freedom for women through the vote, hence images of her often conflate ideals of Britannia as nation with Liberty as the ideology of that nation. We see it in the "Forcible Feeding" image of Britannia protesting the treatment of prisoners (fig. 58) in which she wears a sash, but it is not simply a suffrage sash; emblazoned on it is "Freedom." In Patriot's "Bond and Free" cartoon from *Votes for Women* (fig. 60) he depicts Australia and New Zealand, the British colonies in which certain women are already enfranchised. Ironically, they plead for their Commonwealth sisters, England represented by Britannia with her Union Jack shield and warrior helmet; with Canada behind her designated by the maple leaf on her shield, her women only receiving enfranchisement slowly, province by province, between 1916 and 1940; and next to Britannia, perhaps Patriot depicts the Cape Colony which did not enfranchise its women until 1930 under the Union of South Africa. The latter three representatives are shown in chains while New Zealand and Australia gesture freely in protest before King Edward VII and Queen Alexandra, exclaiming "Our women are enfranchised citizens. We claim the same freedom for the women of our Mother Country and of our Sister Colonies."

While this image brings the physical representation of Britannia together with the concept of Liberty, an engaging visual mingling of Britannia and Liberty occurs in Hilda Dallas's cover of *The Suffragette* in 1913, depicting Britannia leading women from every class forward as one of them carries a banner that reads "Votes" (fig. 61). Britannia gestures them onward and in this way emulates Eugene Delacroix's famous example of *Liberty Leading the People*, 1830 (The Louvre, Paris) in which Liberty similarly leads the way to freedom. In Dallas's image, we see women clustered behind Britannia in a long line that leads into the distance across a bridge while in the upper right-hand corner we see a vignette of the Houses of Parliament, to indicate where they are headed to protest their cause. While the women are numerous, Britannia is shown above them and larger than them, as the key conceptual focus. In images in which she has her arms raised such as this one, we are witnessing a gesture that goes back to the Romans where the outstretched arm establishes authority and identifies a military leader oftentimes.[15] But here Dallas unites her image with that of Liberty's inspirational directional force forward; the way to freedom is through the fracas, not around it.

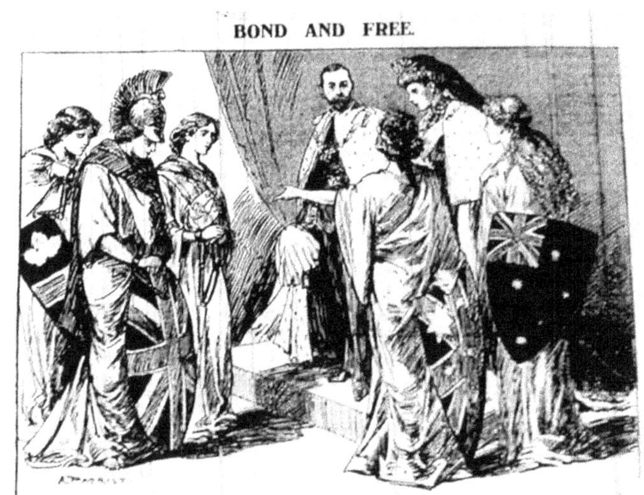

Figure 60. A. Patriot (Alfred Pearce) (1855–1933), "Bond and Free," from *Votes for Women* (May 27, 1910).

Liberty

Like images of Britannia, those of Liberty within the suffrage campaigning show her fighting a battle. In Hilda Dallas's compelling "March on, March on, Face to the Dawn—The Dawn of Liberty!" we see Liberty dressed in long flowing robes, desperately seeking to escape the clamor and uproar of men as she struggles to stride ever forward (fig. 62). In this cover image for *The Suffragette* in March 1913, like other representations of Liberty, such as Bartholdi's *Statue of Liberty*, she "gluts the eye with a sense of power, springing from the sensation of seeing the future."[16] Warner, in making this comment, speaks specifically of Bartholdi's statue in New York harbor, but we can extrapolate such commentary to Dallas's Liberty as she too looks to the future; she is battling to get free literally from male bondage, implying the future liberty of women is at stake.

It is no mistake that we see the attributes of Britannia and Liberty come together in suffrage visual rhetoric in England. They have a precedent in the French examples of the 19th-century, a period during which artists were struggling to create the image of France as Marianne, an image that absorbed, as Gullickson argues, the attributes of Liberty herself. Appearing

> among counter-revolutionaries as a symbol of what was wrong with the republic (rule by commoners), Marianne, a girl of common origins, gradually became the positive embodiment of the republic from which, had she been an actual woman, she would have been politically excluded.[17]

Thus, as with our other allegorical representations, what she symbolized was often at odds with the actual experiences of women of the time. Of the conflation of Liberty and

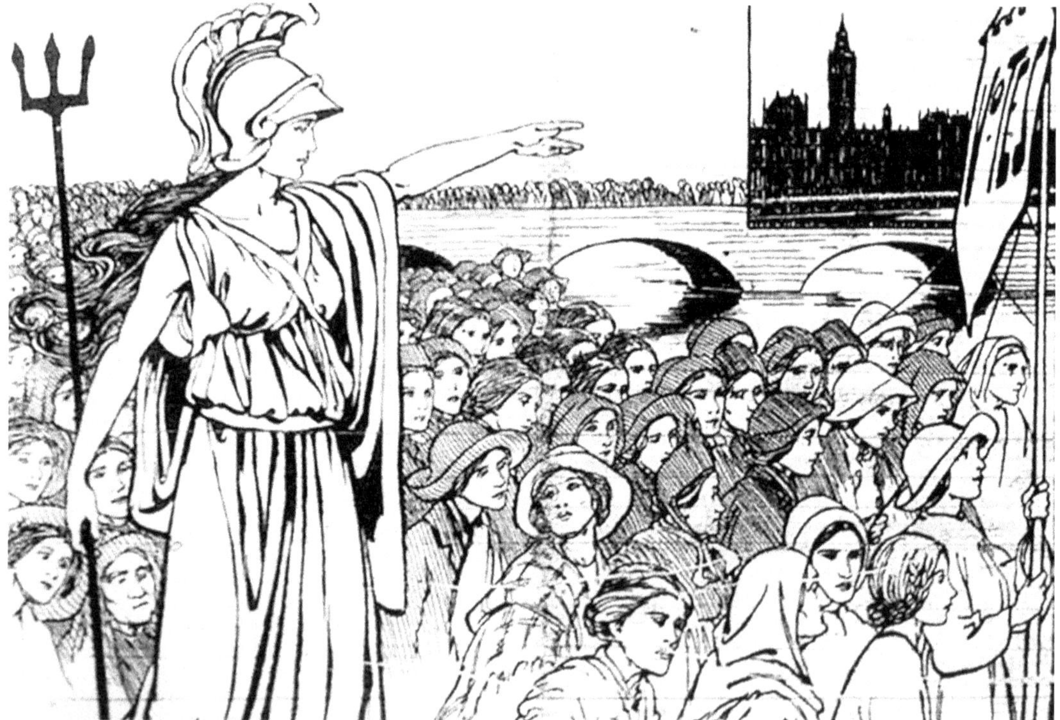

Figure 61. Hilda Dallas (1878–1958), "1913," from *The Suffragette* (1913 cover).

Marianne, Gullickson gives this description based on her reading of Delacroix's *Liberty Leading the People* mentioned earlier:

> This powerful goddess, clad in the garb of the working class and baring her right breast ... is linked representationally to the Greek Amazons and the Virgin Mary.... Well-equipped with the symbols of freedom and revolution—a Phrygian cap on her head, the French tricolor flag (in this case, a symbol of the republic, although it was also used by both French empires) in one hand and a flintlock in the other, she strives radiantly forward.[18]

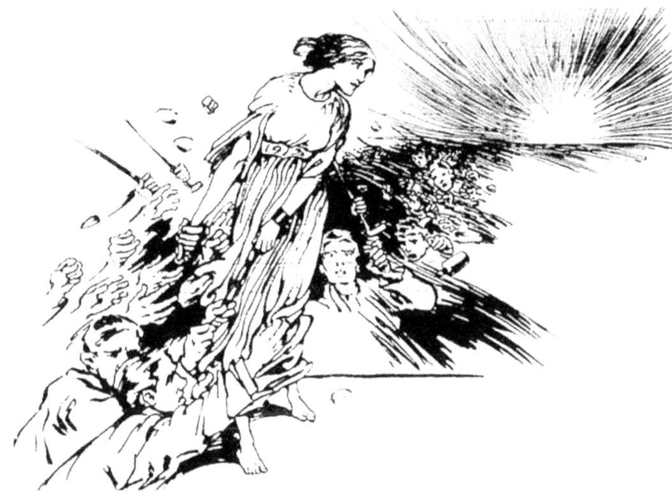

Figure 62. Hilda Dallas (1878–1958), "March on, March on, Face to the Dawn—The Dawn of Liberty!" from *The Suffragette* (March 7, 1913).

In her characterization of Catholic France aligned with the power of the Greek Amazons and revolution, she presents an almost mirror imaging of Britannia and Liberty in England. While not represented as the virginal Lady of Grace, England being largely Protestant, Britannia and Liberty, in concert or singly, similarly call for revolution. Maurice Agulhon argues that custom creates such allegories but they are not fixed; rather "they may in their turn be replaced by new customs born of revolutions."[19] In the English examples for women's suffrage, Liberty is stripped bare save for a gown. She does not wear the attributes of her French counterpart although she retains the gestures of leadership. And, of course, inevitably such ideologies meet with resistance, witness this image entitled "Liberty Constrained" from the London newspaper *The Herald* which Maud Arncliffe-Sennett saved in her scrapbook as an especially apt example of Liberty's power and its limits (fig. 63).[20] Under the image the text reads: "Madam Freedom! Would you have an English Prime Minister break his pledge?" indicating that his political machinations have led him far from embracing the cause of liberty for women in England in 1916, referring to an "Asquith Pledge" written on the knife with which he is about to slit Liberty's throat. This image is by far the most impacting and violent one of Liberty in British suffrage visual rhetoric, Liberty being not only "constrained" but also facing death. It suggests the ongoing battle of the remaining suffrage force of the NUWSS and WFL to push forward with the argument for women's suffrage during wartime, a very unpopular movement forward, one which Asquith was trying to stop entirely. Contrary to the French examples that Agulhon studies, however, the English Liberty while she shows signs of struggle, does not act out. Agulhon, in studying French examples of Liberty, by contrast, suggests that

> two images of Liberty are discernible. One is young, active, with a short dress.... The other ... is completely draped in a classical style. She looks more solemn and her posture is more calm; sometimes she is seated.... [T]he wavering of political imagery between the notion of popular, dynamic, even vehement struggle and one of serene power established in the wake of victory ... is something that dates from the Revolution itself.[21]

Yet, in the British examples here, Liberty is not "serene" but rather in turmoil, not free to express herself in the same revolutionary fashion as the young, active French example.

Agulhon does suggest, however, that in the case of popular revolt, we might find, "an image of vehemence," in posture "always standing and sometimes on the march," "hair floating free," with an uncovered bosom.[22] This description is acted out in the Dallas image of Liberty (fig. 62). Although she is chained, her hair is unkempt due to the struggle she is having with the overwhelming audience of male rabble rousers; her expression is not compliant but defiant and she is not static, but rather lunges forward away from the angry crowd. While in *The Herald* image (fig. 63) she is restrained, we, as audience, are vehement on her behalf. Hence, the elements of Agulhon's popular revolt are present; they are befitting of the state of the battle for suffrage among its activists.

Justice

Brian Harrison, in his analysis of WSPU militancy, asks, "But surely it is impertinent to inquire into the militant's inspiration, for does it not originate in awareness of injustice? True—women's suffering—wife-beating, prostitution, poverty, ignorance, unemployment, indignities of every kind—often features in feminist rhetoric, …" He then admits that inspiration cannot lie solely here since both militants and non-militants suffered such ill-treatment.[23] Yet, justice is at the center of all the groups' motivation, so it is fitting that I end with allegorical images of her that attest to the supreme reason for the long suffrage battle.

If we needed any better example of the value of Justice for suffrage women, we need only look at Hilda Dallas's *Joan of Arc as Justice* (fig. 64) which the WSPU disseminated as a postcard and poster to advertise *The Suffragette* journal but, overarchingly, to demonstrate both that Joan was their militant example and that her goal was justice. Like Britannia, she wears armor, both as Joan and to honor the allegorical rhetoric of Justice, who is often depicted as a medieval warrior. Here Justice has taken on emblems particular to the WSPU. In other images of her within the suffrage visual rhetoric, she speaks to an alter-

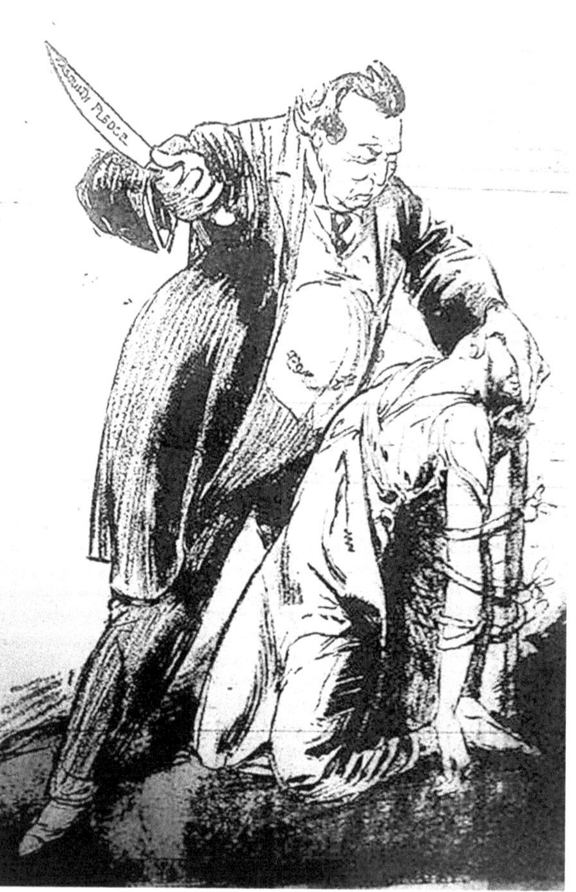

Figure 63. "Liberty Constrained" from *The Herald* (January 8, 1916 cover).

native iconographic tradition. As an ideology, justice is paired with "reason, fairness, righteousness, and wisdom. Justice is served in the process of decision making and the act of judgment.... [J]ustice has a positive connotation because a correct decision determines the 'just' punishment or reward."[24] Particularly pertinent to the suffrage cause, "justice protects against oppression and warfare and ensures harmony, tranquility, and prosperity."[25] In terms of her physical representation, by the Baroque period she held the attributes of the sword and scales, and was shown blindfolded to indicate her impartiality as judge. In Cesare Ripa's *Iconologia*, Justice wears a crown and is dressed in white. The sword is of particular importance for her role in suffrage propaganda and battle: "to avenge crime and wrongdoing."[26] Further, as Warner explains, Justice's sword represents "the ability of humanity to judge between one thing and another, to part right from wrong, truth from falsehood, yes from no; ... It was a cipher of a basic aspect of judgement, the drawing of distinctions."[27]

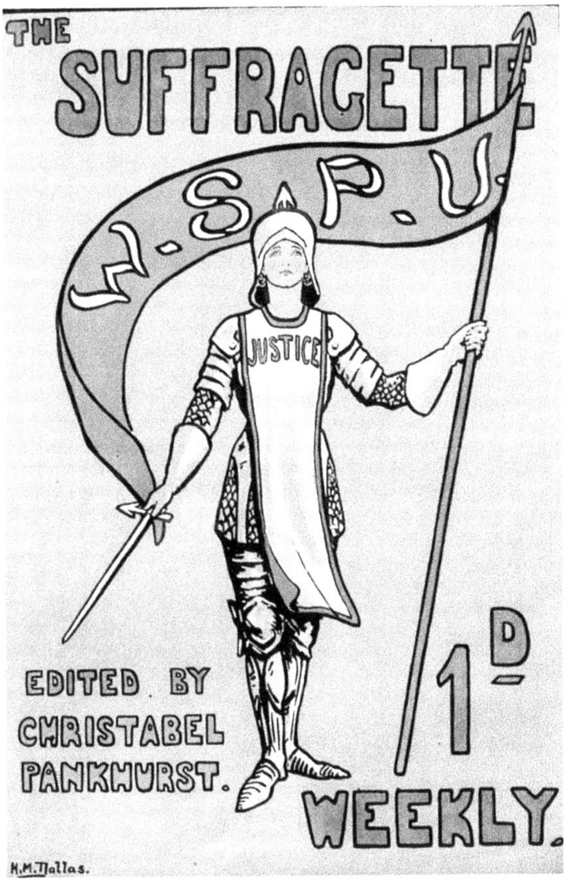

However, by the Baroque period, according to Ripa, "the allegorical figure of Justice no longer appears involved

Figure 64. Hilda Dallas (1878–1958), *Joan of Arc as Justice*, disseminated as WSPU postcard and poster. Advertises *The Suffragette*. Women's Library, London.

with the determination or punitive process.... Justice [is] empowered less and Judgment and Punishment" become "her authoritative masculine counterparts."[28] Hence, in some of the suffrage imagery we will see her powers being thwarted, her protests going unheard. However, she never becomes an object of sexual scrutiny, rather, she maintains her place as the most important of the Virtues.[29]

A typical suffrage representation of Justice in this regard is an image from *The Suffragette* titled "Justice—Another Wronged Woman" (fig. 65). She does not wear armor here as in the medieval warrior presentation of Dallas's *Joan*, but rather the white regal gown. She has been doing battle and has lost, symbolized by her being in chains; she has been rendered vulnerable by her association with the suffrage cause. She holds her large sword defiantly, as well as her scales, and looks disdainfully at her prosecutor who is simply called "The Leader," a not-so-subtle reference to Prime Minister Asquith who continued to deny women the vote. She asks to be released "from tasks that are an outrage to my name!" suggesting that the British government has not treated women fairly, or righteously, with reason or with wisdom. He accuses her, in turn, of not being impartial (an important attribute of Justice) but rather in taking the side of the suffrage women, indicated to us by a poster on the wall behind his head that makes a reference to the Cat and Mouse Act, in relation to a "released suffragette" who has been "re-arrested." The title, "Justice—Another Wronged Woman," suggests that the WSPU see Justice as being aligned with their side and their cause rather than with the government that refuses to honor them. She is here both to note and protect suffrage women from oppression (one attribute of Justice), yet she is kept from her goal, chained, her power literally curtailed and kept in the pocket of the Prime Minister.

Justice, as a concept, is evoked in many suffrage processions. In the Women's Library, there is a photograph, for example, of WSPU women in a 1910 parade holding placards that simply say "Justice" on them.[30] Similarly, in Cicely Hamilton and Edith Craig's *Pageant of Great Women*, Justice presides. At the very beginning of the play "To her enters Woman, pursued by Prejudice. She kneels at the feet of Justice."[31] The voice at the end of the play is that of Woman, responding to the support and good will of Justice while Prejudice "slinks away." Justice herself is pursued by Prejudice in the Artists' Suffrage League poster, probably designed by Mary Lowndes, *Justice at the Reins of a Chariot with White Horse being Pursued by Prejudice at Reins of a Black Horse* (fig. 66). This representation speaks to Ripa's characterization of Justice as not possessing the original powers of her post; while she maintains the protest, she is hotly chased in an unfair battle, the force of good hounded by the force of evil. Yet, Prejudice does not catch her, any more than Prejudice wins out in Hamilton's play.

In each image thus far discussed, Justice fights against oppression. This battle is nowhere more evident than in images that directly address forcible feeding and hunger strikes, as in the poster *Undaunted!* (fig. 67) and "The Majesty of the Law" from *The Suffragette* in 1913 (fig. 68). She befriends the militants just as Britannia does. The poster shows a suffragette in prison clothing with a black printed inscription that reads: "Undaunted! Oh, Justice, what crimes are practiced in thy name, to the Law's discredit and the Nation's shame!" Conjectured to be by Osmond Garrick, cartoonist for the short-lived journal, *The Suffragist*, it appeared as a supplement to *The Suffragist* journal as a poster, and was also reprinted in *The Suffragette* and *Votes for Women*.[32]

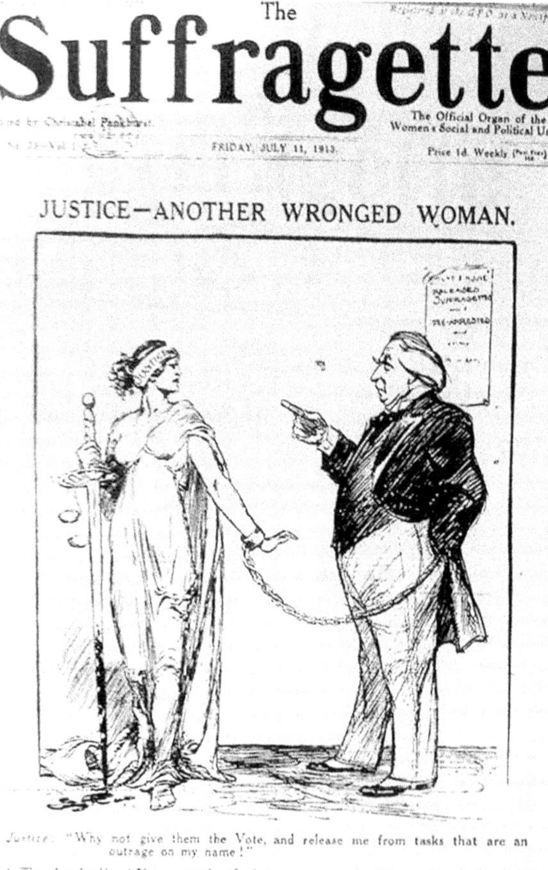

Figure 65. "Justice—Another Wronged Woman," shows a Suffragette chained to "The Leader," from *The Suffragette* (July 11, 1913).

Here the militant woman invokes Justice to help her fight the Law and its unfairness, bringing in the concept of Justice to do battle with forces that are opposed to those that Justice represents: fair-mindedness, reason, wisdom and righteousness. The image from *The Suffragette* goes much further; reproduced from *Punch*, the WSPU voice hurls its barbs in the text that accompanies the image, which is hard hitting; Justice, it seems, has no choice but to be on the side of those oppressed:

> The law is powerless to repress the militant woman. It can no longer protect property nor preserve order. Justice herself is become a Suffragette, and leaving judges and legislators, her accustomed ministers, in the lurch, she befriends the Militants.
>
> For the sake of Justice, the militant women have surrendered all thought of self, and that is why the material force of the law fails to subdue them. The law may imprison, may torture, may kill, but it cannot make women afraid, and it cannot make them surrender.[33]

Justice is blindfolded, holding her scales, and is dressed in a white gown, but here her sword is wrapped in a cloth that

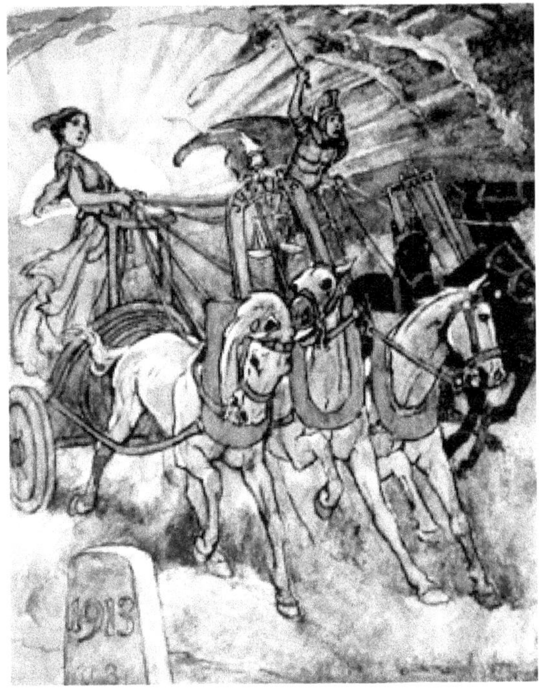

Figure 66. Artists' Suffrage League for NUWSS. Probably designed by Mary Lowndes (1857–1929). *Justice at the Reins of a Chariot with White Horse being pursued by Prejudice at reins of a Black Horse*, 1913. Women's Library, London.

reads "Hunger Strike" and she has a small banner attached to her head that reads "Votes for Women." Behind her a house is engulfed in flames, the smoke billowing out menacingly to frame the figure of Justice herself. The house could refer to militant suffrage activities of burning buildings, or it could equally refer symbolically to the disintegration of the home that is being wrought by keeping women in prison and hence away from their families and their regular duties. Women's militant determination seems to be buoyed up in this case by their ability to invoke Justice's example. Here they align themselves as real women with her and, in turn, align her with them, a coming together of an allegorical representation with real-life women in the same way as in *Undaunted!* and the case that Tickner recognizes, *Justice Demands the Vote*, 1909, published by the Brighton and Hove Society for Women's Suffrage and available from the Artists' Suffrage League for the NUWSS. In this last image, the artist combines Justice with the woman worker, the lady and the mother,[34] as if she, like Britannia and Bodica, is their protector. Tickner argues that Justice's presence here "involves a re-identification of the abstract and allegorical with the concrete (the commonality of voteless women). It reclaims her from being a symbol of the Law, and makes her a symbol of women subject to the operations of the law."[35] But these images show us that the suffrage women, no matter to which group they belonged, sought closer proximity to the ideals that such allegorical imagery implied, not a deified "other" dispensing justice from above. As the editorial states, "Justice herself is become a Suffragette...."

That Justice is on the side of women's suffrage is again apparent in a 1912 poster designed by Mary Lowndes and published by the NUWSS: Justice says, "But I, surely, am not excluded" as she attempts to enter the House of Commons while holding tightly to her scales, her sword hanging from her side, next to a sign that reads "Reform Bill Debate" (fig. 69). In 1912, Asquith introduced a Reform Bill for male suffrage that would not include women and would, effectively, kill the Conciliation Bill on which the suffrage women had been working closely. This decision resulted in resumed militant activity and the NUWSS dividing from the WSPU. The efforts that the NUWSS had made towards the Conciliation Bill, which was a compromise bill that would enfranchise single women householders, and a number of married women occupiers (amounting to around one million women), were brought to an abrupt stop by the militant window-smashing campaign. Thus, this image could be a protest image not only against the government, but also against the militancy of the WSPU. That the NUWSS were vehemently embittered over this blow to the Conciliation Bill is evident in their subsequent decision to shift their sympathies to the Labour Party (they had always been non-partisan but with heavy Liberal leanings), such that, in 1912, they formed the Election Fighting Fund to support raising funds for candidates who would stand in opposition to those who were Liberal Antisuffragists.[36]

This image of Justice at the door of Parliament, then, represents their great frustration at continued exclusion and shows that they, like the militants, align themselves with the forces of good and fairness that Justice symbolizes and defends. That Justice is still being excluded from the houses of government even after their diligent committee work is perhaps the most hard-hitting message they could deliver.

The images shown thus far position Justice in her ancient representation as one of the Virtues, with the exception of Dallas's WSPU *Joan*. But, like the Dallas poster, some suffrage imagery of Justice creates her as a medieval warrior, close to Joan and Britannia, as in the poster *Justice* (fig. 70). Ripa explains that in early medieval examples of Justice, she maintains her tripartite powers as "allegory, judge, and prosecutor."[37] This poster created by the Suffrage Atelier is a bold block print showing a medieval style jouster carrying a lance inscribed with "Votes Votes" while Justice carries a banner that identifies her both as allegorical figure of Justice and as judge and possible prosecutor, standing as she does before the medieval castle turret, representative here perhaps of

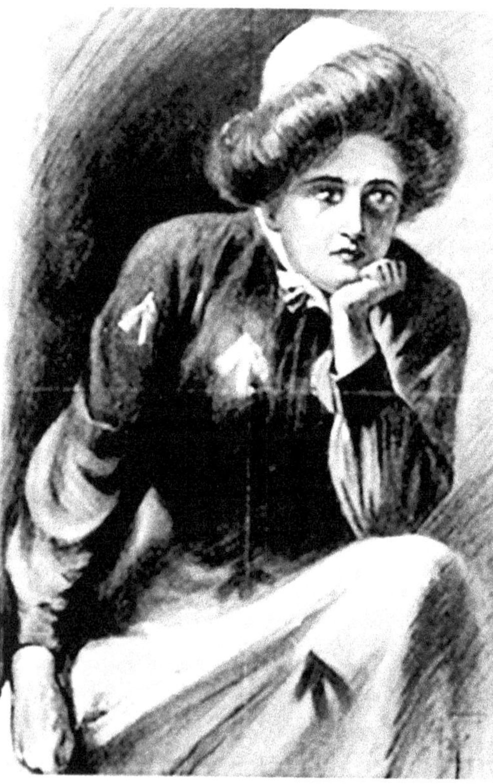

Figure 67. *Undaunted!* Shows suffragette in prison clothing with black printed inscription: "Undaunted! Oh, Justice, what crimes are practiced in thy name, to the Law's discredit and the Nation's shame!" Appeared as a supplement to *The Suffragist*, Oct. 1909, vol. 1, no. 1. Possibly designed by Osmond Garrick (active 1909), cartoonist for *The Suffragist*. Women's Library, London.

British government since it emulates the medieval revival architecture of the Houses of Parliament.

The other images of Justice concentrate on her role as the concept of Justice rather than these other more powerful roles which, as explained earlier, disappeared from conventional representations in the Baroque period. Warner explains that Justice is often presented as a warrior, not unlike Britannia and Liberty, "commonly armed, because the battleground is our most common image for the dialectic between good and evil, partly because memories of Athena, dispenser of justice and warrior, goddess, lingered on."[38] The poster emphatically represents the Suffrage Atelier's alliance with the WSPU and the WFL, the two militant groups, through a printed inscription in the lower right-hand border. Justice here is powerful protector yet, as in "The Majesty of the Law" (fig. 68) she is presented as a suffrage woman, here through her act of holding a banner inscribed "Justice" as so many of them did in their own marches. This poster is not an isolated example of Justice positioned within a medieval context. In the *Votes for Women*'s June 30, 1911, cover, for example, still under the leadership of the WSPU, Justice is mounted on a black horse, with the word Justice inscribed on the horse's blanket as she halts, her flag announcing "Women's Suffrage" at her shoulder, while on her trumpet, which she is sounding, a small flag unfurls that reads "The Vote." She is announcing her presence to "Castle Prejudice" as her horse stomps on another flag that reads "Opposition." In front of the castle, whose gate is drawn down to allow Justice to enter, is the word Injustice. The image, by Poyntz Wright, suggests her multiple roles as defender against prejudice, as bringing decision-making to the table, and as possible prosecutor of the inhabitants of "Castle Prejudice." Her stance is erect and focused, suggesting her power and fearlessness before this "opposition." And, yet, 1911 is still far away from any resolution on women's suffrage as the newspaper makes clear in its opening comments.[39]

We see in the imagery of the NUWSS, the WSPU, the WFL, and splinter groups, their use of allegorical representation but ones which they make concrete, bringing in line Walkowitz's markers of meaning with creators of meaning through each group's alignment of their personal cause with the ideals each allegorical woman embodies, as

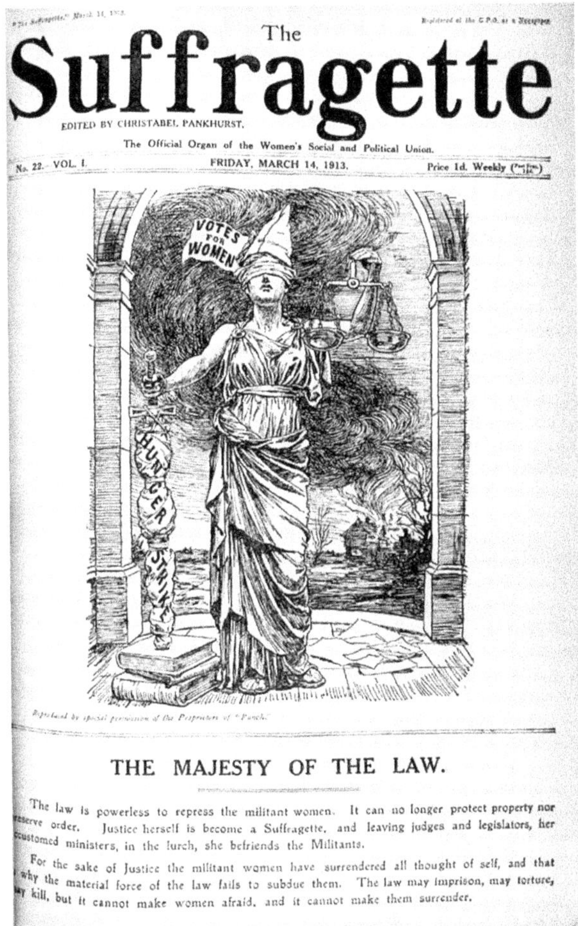

Figure 68. "The Majesty of the Law." Originally published in *Punch*. Reprinted in *The Suffragette* (March 14, 1913).

well as their actual presence in many such images alongside the allegorical figure. They, too, personify the cause and readily identify with Britannia as bringing order to their lives with the passage of women's enfranchisement, allowing them equal freedoms with men for which Liberty so fiercely fights, and ultimately, that these goals are reachable through the name of Justice.

Each of these allegorical figures gave suffrage women a focus for their battle, and each, appropriately, is represented as a warrior, in spirit if not in actual representation. In this regard, we ask today as Christabel Pankhurst asked then, are we making a difference? In a December 22, 1908, speech at the Queen's Hotel, London, following her release from prison, Christabel instilled courage in suffrage women with these words, ones which echo the value of Britannia, Liberty, and Justice:

> [T]he rightness of revolt, the rightness of our militant methods, does not depend upon success. You may resist injustice and fail, or seem to fail, and still you have done right. When you are confronted by oppressions, when you are confronted by the forces of evil, then you must go and do battle against them.[40]

Doing battle against opposing forces is something we will see women protestors continue to do in the closing epilogue, but these are battles that involve their looking closely at this first-wave history.

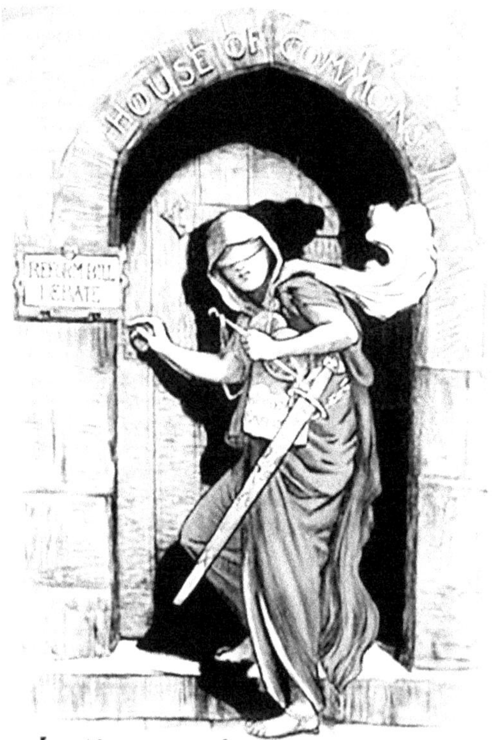

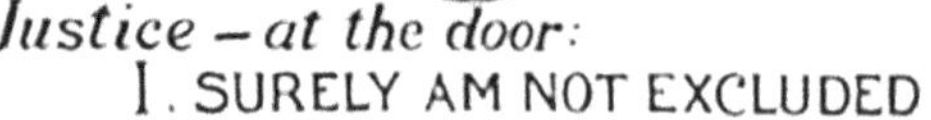

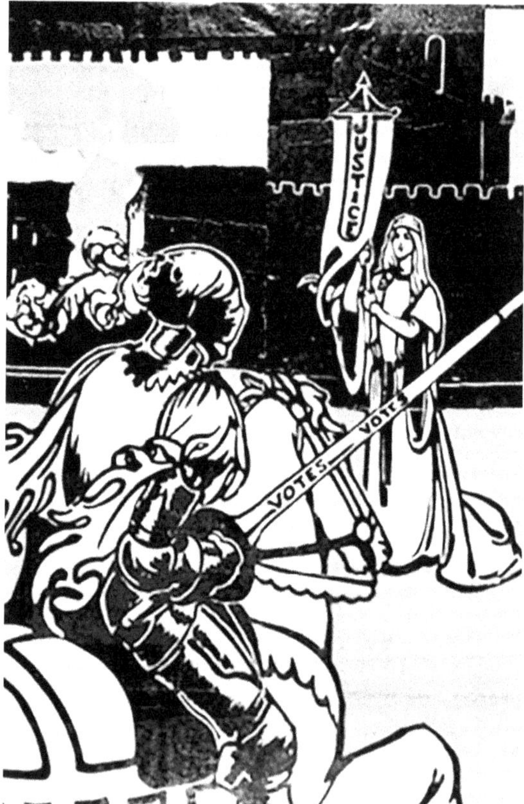

Left: **Figure 69. Artists' Suffrage League for NUWSS,** *Justice at the Door: I, surely, am not excluded.* **Poster designed by Mary Lowndes (1857–1929). Women's Library, London.** *Right:* **Figure 70. Suffrage Atelier,** *Justice Poster,* **before 1914. Women's Library, London.**

Epilogue
From the Hammer to the Fist
March, Process, Progress and Protest

The beautiful suffrage spectacles and the suffragists' efforts to present themselves as respectable women worthy of the vote, were not enough to convince the British government of women's desire for equality under the law. Eventually, they had to push against the government physically. A move from "spectacular activism" to "militant warfare" for the WSPU was necessary and was also a sign of the processions' failure, according to WSPU members, Kitty Marion and Emmeline Pethick-Lawrence.[1] While Martha Vicinus astutely argues that "such huge public events ... asserted the power of women to use public space for political purposes,"[2] the militant WSPU eventually upped the ante by employing aggressive tactics, letting go of such restrained politics of respectability.

In the WSPU leaders' move to more strident actions, they modeled themselves on the tactics of men in the labor movement, particularly in Manchester where Christabel Pankhurst, along with her mother, Emmeline, founded the group in 1903.[3] The WSPU approach represented a new and modern form of politics since they were the first suffrage group to foreground the tactics of militancy and, more broadly, to align themselves with trade-union tactics and other kinds of direct action. It was also the first time that women used these tactics.[4] However, the term "militant" was not equated with WSPU violence until 1908 when certain members started to break windows of government buildings as a form of protest. The next shift came when the 1910 Conciliation Bill failed to pass a bill that would have enfranchised women. Understandably, some 300 women rushed the House of Commons demanding to be heard; this day came to be called Black Friday because of the unprecedented police brutality the women suffered while trying to conduct a peaceful demonstration. The last straw for the WSPU members was when Parliament proposed a Manhood Suffrage Bill in late 1911, excluding women; this final conflict launched their West End window-smashing campaign.

First-wave suffrage women of all groups embraced the public realm, perhaps not always fully cognizant of its dangers, leaving careful records of their lived experiences, both on the streets and in prison, that are filtered through the lens of memory. Activist women's yearnings to push at the boundaries of their respective cultures often means that they meet with violent confrontation, yet these women, historically and today, break on through to the other side, propelled by a need, a desire, that will result in the immanent pleasures and gratifications of being *represented*. It is their public struggles to fulfill their desire for recognition and a place at the table to which I turn in this epilogue which argues that there is a direct link between Edwardian, first-wave activists' visual protests and those of global second, third, and fourth wavers in terms of their transgressions of women's traditional bodily presence and their use of body language.[5] Starting with the toffee hammers that the WSPU suffragettes used in 1912 to smash windows, traditional cultural assumptions about women's bodily possibilities, like the windows themselves, were shattered. What is the bond, then, between the hammer and the raised fist within feminist protest in the quest for social justice? What I will argue in this epilogue with regards to this question is that the suffrage women carved out a new space for themselves and a new body language within that space with which to do battle. Further, I will explore how that space and language continued/continues to reverberate in later women's activist struggles around the world that owe a debt to these first-wave actions.

Evidence of the incredible dangers the first-wave women faced in public life comes from my own experience in London while working on this book in 2013. I attended the Globe's production of Jessica Swale's new play, *Bluestockings* about the 1890s struggles of women at Girton College, Cambridge, to obtain degrees. I was just as shocked as some of my fellow theater-goers to discover the vehement form that male protests took in 1897 when the vote was called to allow women to earn their degrees.

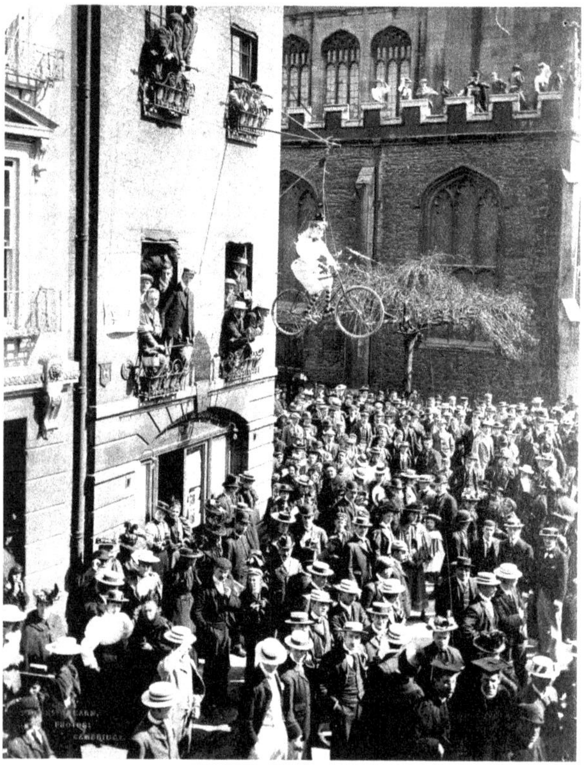

At the time of the vote, suspended above the protestors was an effigy of a Girton Girl on a bicycle in blue stockings (fig. 71); some reports say male students pulled it down and burned it; others that angry male students decapitated it, tore it to bits and stuffed its remains through the gates of Newnham College, the women's college on the main Cambridge campus. Such acts went beyond mere anger to outright violence witnessed most readily in the male students being out of control throughout the night, attacking local shops for lumber to build a bonfire. The level of misogyny was frightening and uncontrollable. Perhaps because of this recent, painful memory, we never see effigies in suffrage marches and protests, yet this event is a constant reminder of just how virulent the tide was set against women's advances in conservative enclaves like Cambridge and Oxford, despite each having women's colleges by this time.

Ironically, the male students were exhibiting the same kind of hysteria they had, until then, projected onto

Figure 71. Thomas Stearn and Sons, *Effigy of Girton Girl outside Bowes and Bowes Bookshop (now Cambridge University Press Bookshop) on Corner of Trinity Street and St. Mary's Street, opposite St. Mary's, Cambridge, England*, 1897. Source: GCPH 9/1/4. The Mistress and Fellows, Girton College, Cambridge.

the female students. During this time period, as part of the gendered politics of modernity, advanced women were represented as radical feminists *and* hysterics. Witness one early example of the shaming of women chartists by the Reverend Francis Close, who criticized the women for crossing the threshold of home into the world of public agitation with all the vitriol he could muster; calling them inhuman like their revolutionary French sisters

> who glutted themselves with blood; and danced like maniacs amidst the most fearful scenes of the Reign of Terror! ... [S]o destitute are they of all sense of female decorum, of female modesty and diffidence, that they become themselves political agitators—female dictators—female mobs—female Chartists![6]

Gail Finney and Elaine Showalter have both addressed the behaviors of feminists and hysterics as a response to such systemic oppression. Showalter argues:

> If we see the hysterical woman as one end of the spectrum of a female avant-garde struggling to redefine women's place in the social order, then we can also see feminism as the other end of the spectrum, the alternative to hysterical silence, and the determination to speak and act for women in the public world.

She reaches this conclusion partly because the women under study (by Sigmund Freud and Jean-Martin Charcot) often lost their voices and even their native language; whereas it is within the feminist movement that women find their voices.[7] Further, the hysterics under observation are the very women we find in our closeted interiors, unhappy with their confinement to home and hearth such that the manifestation of hysteria is their way of coping passively. As Catherine Clément explains, hysteria is tolerated because it poses no threat to the social order; it cannot effect change. It is the more acceptable form of protest than the kind of feminist agitation that necessitates real change in economic and legal rights.[8] To take us back to where we started, Finney argues that the dialogues of modernism were taking place within the domestic realm as evidenced in the struggles of this period's dramatic heroines, such as Henrik Ibsen's character, Hedda Gabler.[9] Rita Felski characterizes Showalter and Finney's analyses within the context of modernism thus: "Just as the feminist expressed a rebellious, emancipatory, and outer-directed response to the condition of female oppression, so ... the hysteric exemplified a rejection of society that was passive, inner-directed, and ultimately self-destructive." Hence, she concludes, "The figure of woman pervades the culture of the *fin de siècle* as a powerful symbol of both the dangers and the promises of the modern age."[10] Such women's *mêlées* were already evident in the tensions we have seen in the women at the windows of London and Parisian homes, a dialogue from within ready to burst forth.

The violence of the male students' response at Cambridge can also be attributed partly to this all-pervasive identification of women's bodies with domestic interiors of the industrial age. It was indeed a violent shift to see women enter the public world of education and radical politics. Perhaps the male students at Cambridge realized the end of an era wherein the sexes were nicely compartmentalized, safe, and organized. The conflation of women's bodies with the domestic interior was eternally broken.[11] These women had moved from the safe confines of respectability to an open space where they might be prone to making spectacles of themselves and many certainly sought to do so in the name of their respective causes. Mary J. Russo characterizes such spectacle within that warning and judgmental phrase, most often uttered about women by other women (sisters, mothers, aunts, friends), "She is making a spectacle of herself," a phrase that is mostly about "a kind of inadvertency and loss of boundaries," the danger of exposure.[12]

Pair this effigy of the woman on a bicycle, suspended (and the liminality of that suspension is apt) with that of John Tenniel's "An Ugly Rush" (fig. 5 in Chapter One) in order to understand the kinds of aggressive body language that men attributed to radical women and you have a more complete picture of what feminists were up against. The lunge forward of the "ugly" radicals was as symbolic as it was real. Tenniel's critique would seem to place them in a liminal space outside of accepted norms. But their body language itself is one of spectacle; not the demure, downcast eyes, pretty features and modest body position of the mother observing the scene close by, but an active engagement in debate reflected in their bodies' postures.

But a study of this campaign, as Elizabeth Crawford argues, "highlights the tension between the 'masculinity' of the political goal and the efforts to achieve it, both the 'feminine' (spectacle and fund-raising, which employed a wide range of womanly skills), and the 'masculine' (from speaking on platforms in public in the 19th-century to terrorism in the 20th)."[13] The political goal in question was to achieve the same rights as men but the women were forced to use methods traditionally associated with both sexes.

As backdrop to such battles were the changing cities of London and Paris themselves. Of London, Judith R. Walkowitz says it was a site for women's and workers' interventions:

> London had become a contested terrain: new commercial spaces and journalist practices, expanding networks of female philanthropy, and a range of public spectacles, from the Hyde Park "Maiden Tribute" demonstration of 1885, to the marches of the unemployed and the matchgirls in the West End, enabled workingmen and women of many classes to challenge the traditional privileges of elite male spectators and to assert their presence in the public domain.[14]

London had become a city of many voices and platforms, the suffrage woman being just one type of protestor in its streets. If we were to set this scene on the London stage, we would have to center ourselves at Trafalgar Square. On center stage would be a woman's body, both physically and emblematically. Just as the London streets became the site of contesting voices, a woman's body became the site of much debate. If she could be burned in effigy, that was only the beginning of her dismemberment. She has been reduced, by the 21st century, to a battle over her right to her own sexuality: birth control, abortion, gay rights, sexuality have all been brought into question and she has been found wanting, judged, brought under government control in the same way that the Girton bluestocking was humiliated and beaten down in effigy. Her body, for the suffrage movement, remained at center, just as it does in our own times. As Walkowitz observes:

> No figure was more equivocal, yet more crucial to the structured public landscape of the male *flâneur*, than the woman in public. In public, women were presumed to be both endangered and a source of danger to those men who congregated in the streets. In the mental map of urban spectators, they lacked autonomy: they were bearers of meaning rather than makers of meaning. As symbols of conspicuous display or of lower-class and sexual disorder, they occupied a multivalent symbolic position....[15]

If our 19th-century women were confined to their homes, destined to observe street life from the safe purview of their living room windows, by the early 1900s they had burst forth onto the public scene, as in this image of women selling *The Suffragette* for the WSPU (fig. 72), in which men lurk nearby, unable to read the women's roles easily. Walkowitz's characterization of the ambiguity of the woman's presence is, again, based on her body and its purpose within the city: either her body is for the *flâneur's* consumption, a symbol of her husband's wealth, or in some way otherwise disorderly. In this photograph, for example, the women are announcing a House of Commons event in relation

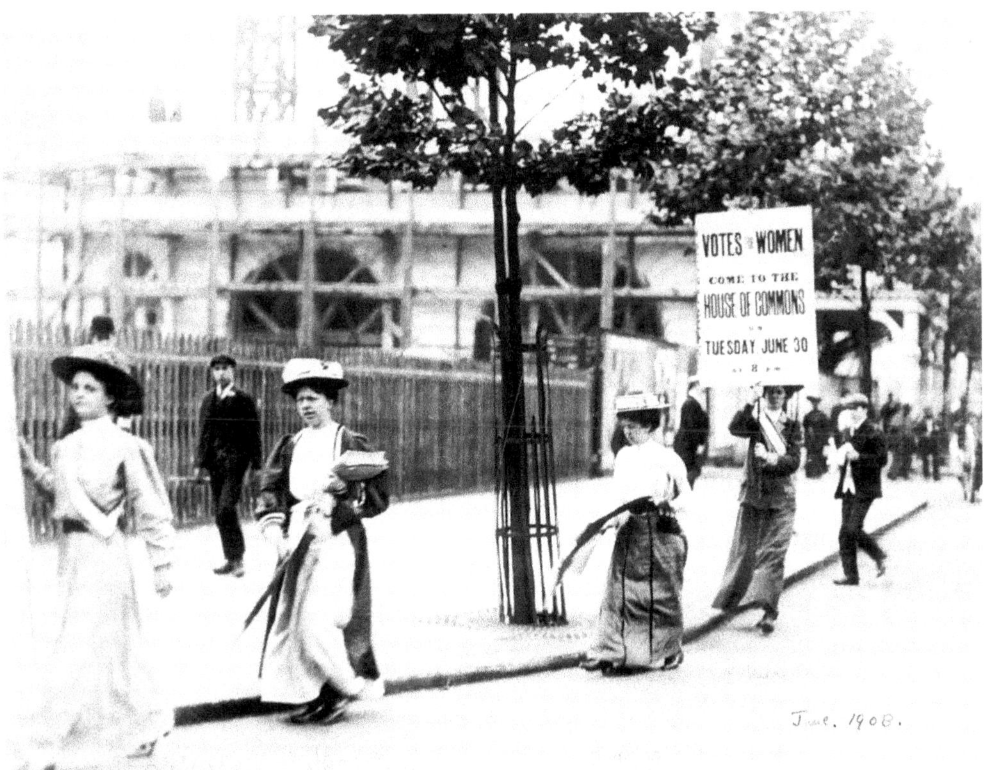

Figure 72. *Suffrage Women Selling The Suffragette and Advertising Meetings,* June 1908. **Museum of London, 50.82/1762.**

to the ongoing agitation for votes for women. Yet these suffragettes could not "make things mean" in a representational way because they were not yet represented as citizens. In this sense, they are not yet part of the dialogue of representation in its two-fold expression: they were not represented by a vote, nor, because they had no voice in government, were they capable of controlling their own representation of self. Their bodies signified what a man could or could not do to them. This is the world into which our suffrage women march and in which they try to negotiate a new space.

Because of this equivocality, it took a transgressive, resistance narrative as in the National Organization for Women (NOW) photograph (fig. 39 in Chapter Two), to do battle in public space. This conceptualization is one that the women have written on their bodies; the woman in the foreground has written her desire for freedom on her t-shirt:"Women's Liberation NOW," both a nod to the request for immediate attention to action and also to the NOW group's central place in the dialogue. Just as her raised fist is a gesture that marks her desire for action, echoed in the body language of the other marchers behind her, in some suffrage demonstrations all the women carry white pennons to symbolize hope for change, their own white garments and hats reiterating that desire fig. 38 in Chapter Two). Yet they speak from a quiet space whereas the NOW image seems noisy, angry and in charge. The NOW women have crossed the line from "bearers of meaning" to "makers of meaning," unlike their suffrage forebears.

Martha Vicinus recognizes this "insistence upon a female presence … in male arenas" as the "most revolutionary aspect of the suffragette movement…." This kind of demand meant political access to the streets, pavements, and hustings, but most of all the House of Commons. The numerous "rushes" on Parliament, carrying petitions to present to the prime minister, were clearly symbolic acts, intended to attract attention to forbidden public places. So too, the decision to sell *Votes for Women* on street corners and to set up soapbox meetings where women spoke to passing crowds were actions only socialist women had undertaken before. Now respectable middle- and upper-class women were refusing to remain at home behind closed doors and were claiming male space for women's purposes.[16]

The incredible shift of women's place from interior to exterior, from circumscribed domestic realm to urbanity necessary to a collective congregation of women is imbricated in a further visual example of this new-found self-possession (fig. 73). In this photograph, suffrage women literally use the street as their canvas/canvass to advertise meetings, by chalking on the street pavement.

Yet, the case was entirely different in France. Hubertine Auclert seems to have been the only suffrage advocate to try and stage protests and demonstrations during the late 19th and early 20th century, with few exceptions. In an example of outward bodily frustration which actually preceded the 1912 WSPU shift to violent action in its window-smashing campaign, Auclert forcibly turned over a ballot box. Illustrations of the event represent her actively rushing the ballot box, her skirts swirling, her arms thrust out as she turns over the box, causing chaos all around her. That event is incredibly important as an example of a woman activist literally and figuratively stepping outside of her expected bodily language and comportment as well as creating an outward expression of her anger at women's lack of inclusion. The British suffragists knew of this event, evidenced in Maud Arncliffe-Sennett's inclusion of *Le Petit Journal*'s color cover image of the event on May 17, 1908, in her scrapbook.[17] Titled *L'Action Feministe* [feminist action], the image placed Auclert's action outside of the confines of feminine respectability; rather

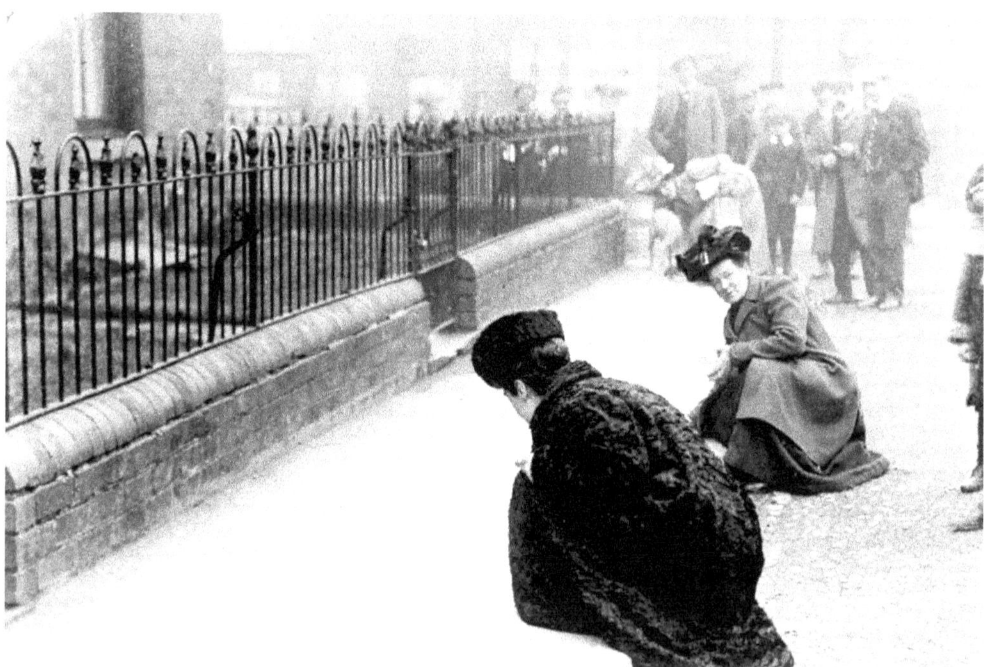

Figure 73. *Suffrage Women Chalking on the Streets,* 1909. Museum of London, 2003.46/19.

in the hands of a radical. That said, Karen Offen discusses the one major French demonstration of French suffragists as a result of Ferdinand Buisson's suffrage proposal that would give the vote to all French women, single or married, at least at the municipal level, as a possible answer to Auclert's angry plea:

> In mid–June 1914, the project of law based on the Buisson report was finally presented to the Chamber of Deputies; in early July French suffragists staged a massive rally on behalf of the proposal at the Condorcet monument in Paris. This was their first—and last—major public demonstration. The timing was terrible; seven days later France was at war. The woman suffrage bill was among the first casualties.[18] Their presence at the Condorcet monument was historically significant since the Marquis de Condorcet had advocated for women's civic rights in the events leading up to the French Revolution.

Thinking back to our examples in Chapter Two of the NOW march in contrast to the orderly first-wave processions also brings us back to the Joan of Arc discussion of the WSPU purity campaign. Vicinus argues that the militant suffrage campaign represented both a radical break with the Victorian women's movement and its culmination. Some scholars have criticized the militant WSPU for its failure to embrace a new sexual ideology which would acknowledge a woman's right to sexual desire and sexual freedom, experimentation and, hence, contraception, but Vicinus says the WSPU made a conscious effort

> to forge a new spirituality, based upon women's traditional idealism and self-sacrifice but intended to reach out and transform not only the position of women but society itself. Women were to become a force in the public sphere, to take over and control the public arena by the strength of their superior morality. This naturally meant a rigorous purity in regard to sexual matters, combined with a strong sense of bodily control; the integrity of the human body—degraded by forced feeding in prison—in turn symbolized the inherent spiritual force of each woman.[19]

Thus, she argues that in terms of the goals of the WSPU at least, in taking charge, they meant to establish themselves in a superior mode to men. The bodily actions they took, which could be read as acting out, were protected, in her view, by their purist stance. Nevertheless, once they transgressed that purest stance with physical, criminal action, they crossed over into a much more multilayered, nuanced representation of the body in public.

The Body Politic and Its Markers

While I will return to this significant shift, here I would like to address the ways that we do see continuity in terms of the usage of visual ephemera and march practice from the first-wave feminists and previous women protestors to more recent times in several events and protests that represent a body politic mentality. In order to represent their ideals and to begin to make things mean something ideological in terms of their goals, suffrage women and other activists made their own banners. Attached to the body, the banner continues to be a prominent visual form of protest. For one, the banner is the main means of communication in such 1980s protests as *Women Against Pit Closures* in England (fig. 74), which includes a banner very similar in its presentation to those of the feminist groups of the first wave. The banner carries the message "Make the Links" and charts how coal, through visual imagery of chain links, creates jobs, generates nuclear power, and brings other benefits to the community. As in the suffrage marches, the marchers all wear buttons announcing their political stance and they have a police escort. Further, in terms of cognizance of how their actions will affect future generations, they include children in their march. Although this group started as a local chapter in Barnsley, similar chapters soon sprung up all over the country to support the Miners' Strike of 1984–85. It is not coincidental that their badge was done up in the WSPU colors. Here, as with the first wave, we see feminism and femininity come together, the women representing themselves as wives and mothers, with a concern for their husbands' or families' ability to survive in the 1980s' economic climate. But, at the same time, they used this moment in the public eye to begin demanding their own political inclusion. Michelle de Larrabeiti reveals that during this strike, the women from the mining communities "became 'conspicuous before the world'" because they

> entered the glare of the public political sphere in all-women support groups. The languages the women used to express their political activity were contradictory in the sense that, in the media at least, the women's actions were seen as emerging out of their "roles" as wives and mothers, as supporters of their men. At the same time the women spoke of their *own* political development, coming from behind the kitchen sink, which led them to consider issues around gender as well as class, and to take part in the most "masculine" aspects of the strike such as picketing.[20]

In this regard, she links tactics used to discredit them as anything other than wives and mothers, with a similar critique launched at the 19th-century British Chartist women who, similarly, have been blamed for holding back early feminist politics in England.[21] The women of the Miners' Strike represent, then, a historical connection to other political wives and mothers who preceded suffrage women. They offer a moment that resists the dominant dialogue of domesticity and family within Chartist rhetoric, asking to be considered "in the multiple languages and selves jostling with each other" as they "managed home, children, work and politics."[22] In this regard, beyond their usage of the visual language of protest, they embody the complicated world of multiple expectations and limitations for women, then as now.

The first wavers were not the first group to use banners as a form of protest, preceded as they were not only by the Chartists but also by other groups who used banners as propagandistic materials necessary to a political cause. For example, the famous Dockers'

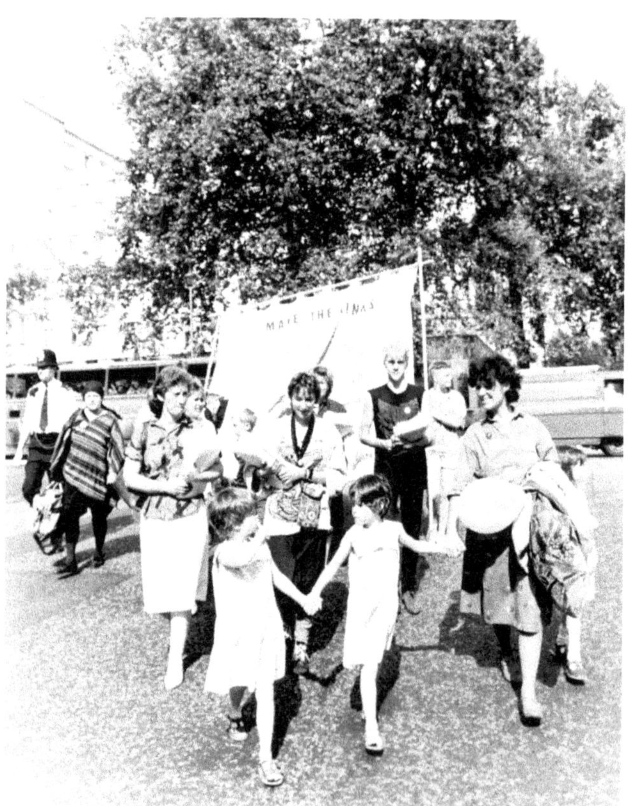

Figure 74. *Women Against Pit Closures.* **Morning Star Photographic Archive: MSPA 6/17/10. Bishopsgate Institute, London.**

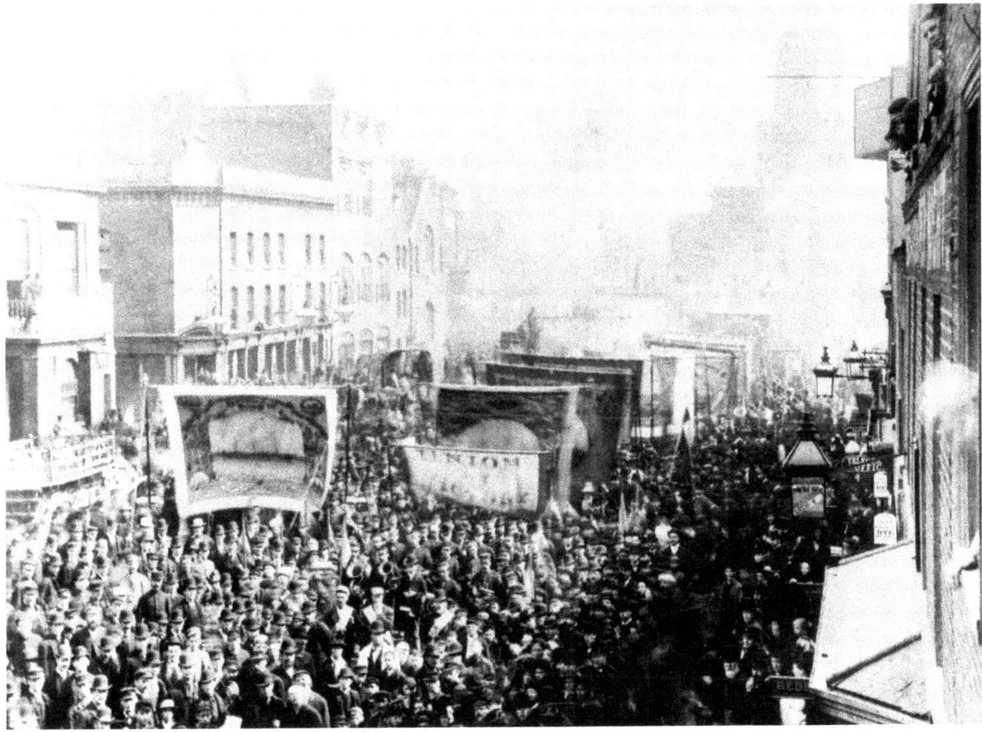

Figure 75. *Dockers' Strike,* London, 1889. London History Workshop Collection LHW 26. Bishopsgate Institute, London.

Strike of 1889 included many large banners that were carried by different constituents of 10,000 strong strikers (fig. 75). Historians have viewed this event as an extremely significant moment since it led to the foundation of the modern trade union movement. The photograph itself shows the incredible swell of workers and their strength in organizing, as revealed through their large banners and their numbers.

The banner has continued to be a prominent form of protest; the joyful articulation of women waving banners, ribbons and sashes triumphantly in suffrage prison releases (fig. 76) reverberates in this 1985 London Gillick ruling march scene (fig. 77), in which under 16s stride alongside older women. They protest the Gillick ruling which would have made it illegal for under 16s to receive medical treatment without parental consent. Their protest contributed to an overruling of that decision; replaced eventually by "Gillick competence," meaning that under 16s could receive treatment without parental consent if they understood the treatment involved.

This protest is similar in its purpose—the control of women's bodies—to a more recent event that my students organized on the University of Wyoming campus for the annual Take Back the Night rally and march (fig. 78) in conjunction with our local domestic violence shelter and advocacy offices, called SAFE Project; our on-campus STOP Violence office; and many recognized student organizations.[23] In this instance, the students purposely emulated the visual rhetoric of suffrage marches; the young women in both photographs emit the same looks of elation, freedom and triumph as they push forward, holding their handmade banners as markers of their ability to become makers of meaning.

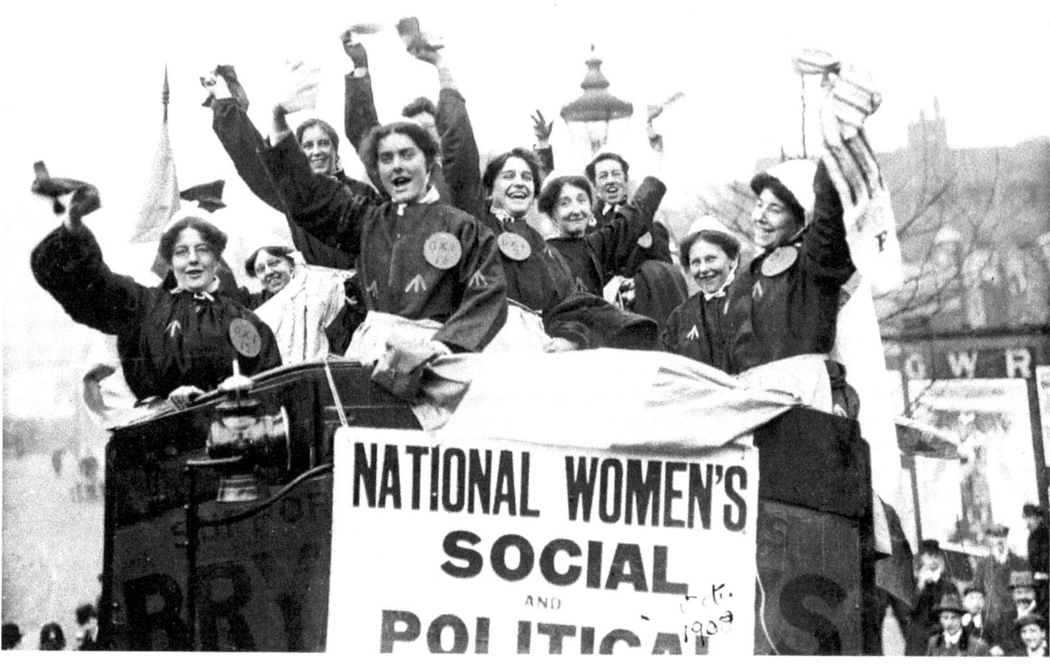

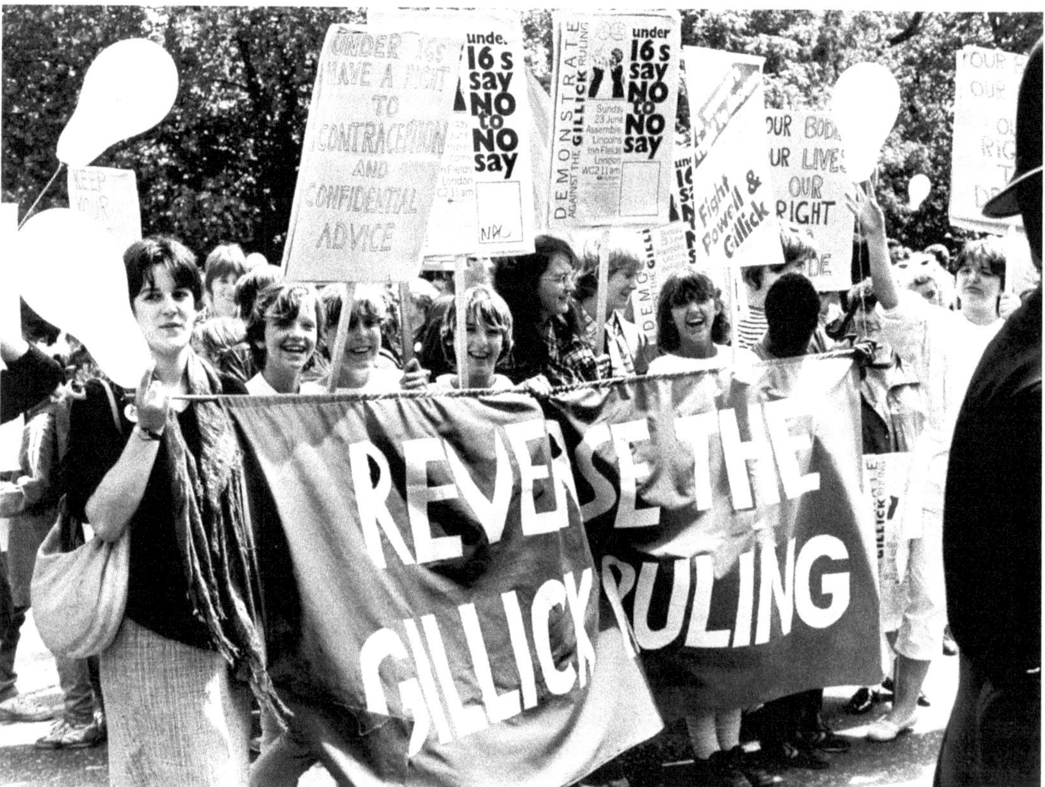

Top: Figure 76. *Release of Prisoners from Holloway Prison,* 1908. Museum of London, 50.82/1508. *Bottom*: Figure 77. *Under 16s Protest the Gillick Ruling,* London, England, 1985. Morning Star Photographic Archive: MSPA 6/17/1. Bishopsgate Institute, London.

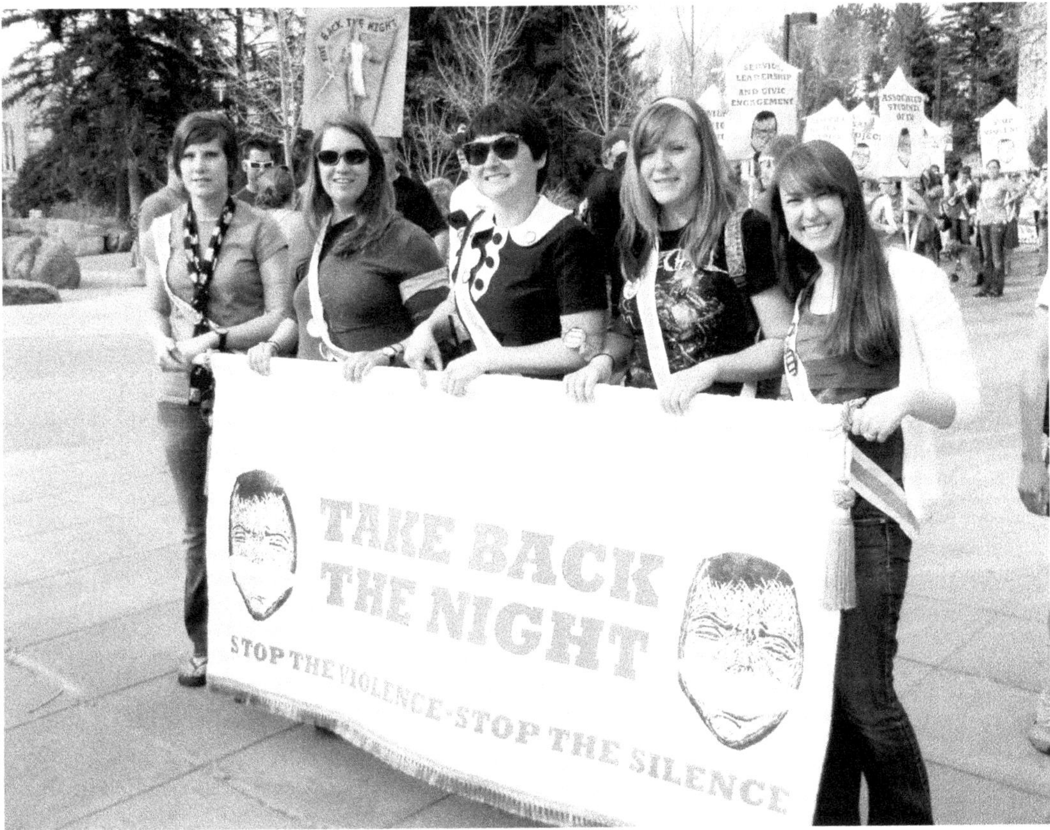

Figure 78. *Take Back the Night Rally and March,* University of Wyoming, Laramie, 2012. Author's photograph.

These young women are writing themselves into the culture, as the suffragette Lady Constance Lytton suggested, when she said of the body politic, "I have decided to write the words 'Votes for Women' on my body."[24] With this statement, Lytton created herself as a visual instance of the body politic in the same way that suffrage women selling newspapers and advertising meetings on their bodies literally embodied the suffrage quest for justice (fig. 79). This act was very bold, forcing the viewer to read their bodies as they read the news. Further, the image shows two women in solidarity, arms linked in a moment of camaraderie and sisterhood.

A similar companionship both in terms of women's bodily language and their protest over control of their own bodies comes in many recent examples from France and, further, around the world for the 2017 Women's March. An example in France in 2016 was reported in *The New York Times* as "French Women Fight Back," and it included a photograph of a group of seventeen French women either currently employed in, or former representatives of, the French government, protesting sexual harassment on the job. They published a "Statement against Sexism" in which they stated: "This happens every day to women using public transportation, on the street, in businesses, in universities" in spite of the fact that France passed a tough sexual harassment law with jail terms of up to two years and extensive fines. Alongside the article is a photograph of the women with arms raised, in the shape of triangles, vocally voicing their protest with mouths agape.[25] We are not far from the pussy hats of the Women's Marches in such protests and their visible message: Our bodies, our rights. The Women's March that I attended made the issue partly about women in Wyoming specifically, the Wyoming Art Party parading with their red banner in bold, Western lettering: "Wild Wombs of the West" (fig. 80).

But, like the suffrage women before them, and the second and third wavers, they are still having to protest the scrutiny of their bodies in public, yet, in this instance and this march worldwide, we saw a fourth-wave move to intersectionality, such that while their body language is still one of subversion, here the banners also acknowledge the sacredness of all women and their vocal protests (including that of yours truly in the white, faux-fur hat!). If these examples do not suffice, women protestors in London as part of their 2017 Women's March donned first-wave suffrage attire and carried a poster that expressed their exasperation over the lack of progress concerning women's bodies that proclaimed "Same Shit, Different Century" (fig. 81). The fact that not only my daughter but also several colleagues made sure I had this image attests to its extreme relevance for this study!

These visible acknowledgments of performative bodies reflect Olive Schreiner's arguments in *Women and Labor* (1911); women were united by a philosophy of a body politic within the suffrage movement, cognizant of "the abiding consciousness of an end to be attained, reaching beyond [their] personal [lives] and individual interests ... [to] bind with the common bond of an impersonal enthusiasm into one solid body."[26] Yet, at the same time, as political theorist Jean Bethke Elstain claims, "When any previously excluded group enters the public sphere ... the terms of that entry will reflect [its] prior privatization," such that, as Mary Jean Corbett argues, their "ethic of personal renunciation" as a body was an extension of Victorian ideologies of womanhood.[27]

As further markers of the body politic, we cannot ignore the sacrifice of the individual body for the cause in the lived experiences and rhetoric surrounding hunger strikes. Corbett argues that "the suffragette's refusal to eat announced her willingness to use her body as a political stake and so to contest the cultural construction of the middle-class feminine body as marginal to the realm of politics."[28] Rather, their prison protests were at the center of the debate and while they were private battles, their public celebration in prison release parades (fig. 76) and portcullis badges of honor, not to men-

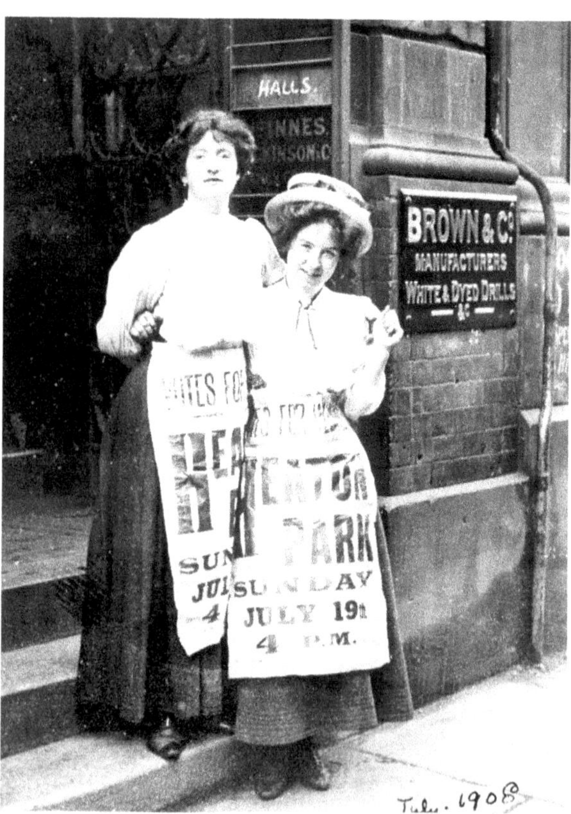

Figure 79. *Suffrage Women advertising meeting: Miss P. Woodlock and Miss Mabel Capper.* **July 1908. Museum of London, NN22779.**

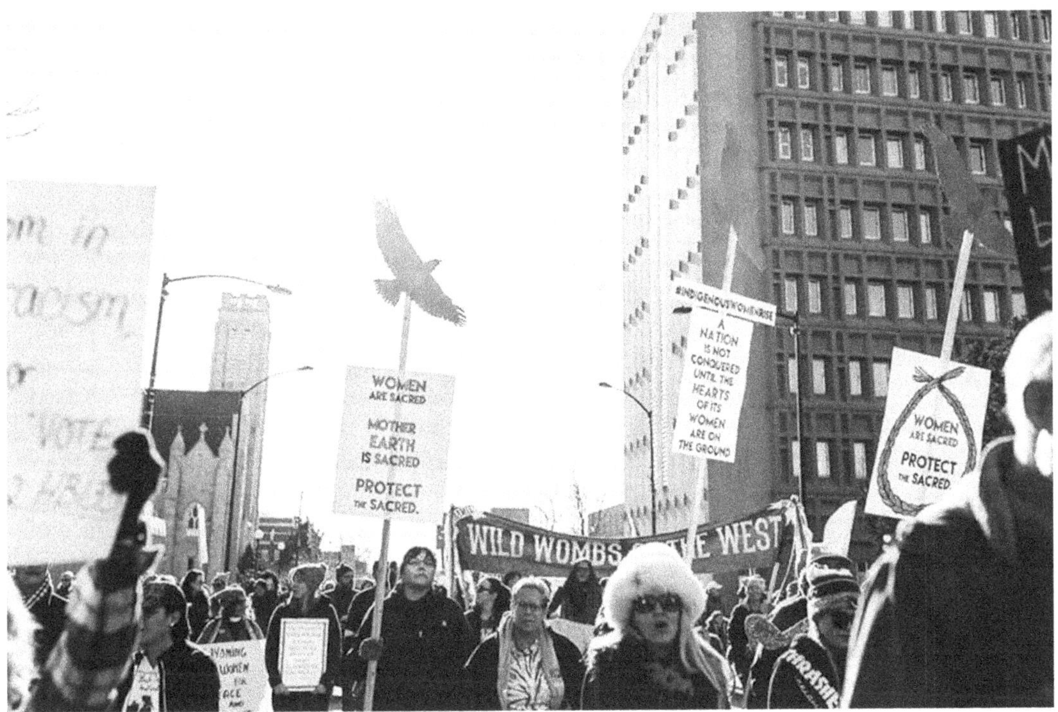

Figure 80. *Women carry Wyoming Art Party banners reading* "Wild Wombs of the West" *and* "Women Are Sacred" *in the Wyoming Women's March, Cheyenne,* 2017. **Colleen Denney marches front and center in the white hat and sunglasses.**

tion the personal, autobiographical prison narratives and the protests the suffrage women mounted in the press, mirror their public placement at the center of London, on platforms, chalking sidewalks, as advertisers of the words that would free their bodies.

Yet, such street action was not confined to the first wave; for example, a 1970s British event demonstrates a practice similar to that of the suffrage women distributing newspapers on the streets of London (fig. 82). The woman shown here is smiling broadly, brandishing a handmade poster that protests the Irish authorities' decision to ban the magazine *Spare Rib* in Ireland due to its supposed pornographic content. The protestors gathered in front of the embassy are inviting passers-by to judge for themselves. Their use of amateur poster design is something we see in the Feminist Library Collection (housed at Bishopsgate Institute, London) repeatedly; Paula Hays Harper proposes that such amateur presentation stems from a long-standing tradition of the broadsheet with crude lettering and readily recognizable imagery to appeal to the masses and that suffrage posters took over the political intent of such broadsheets, if not the look of them. She recognizes that this kind of more direct poster presentation reappears when groups lack "access to public media," instead falling back on these more popular forms of communication.[29] That tradition has continued within feminist protest through today, witness the humorous and hard-hitting posters of the Guerilla Girls, based in New York, who provide stark statistics and attack, as did the *Spare Rib* protestors, societal representations of women. Both groups participate in a kind of guerrilla, underground activity, their visual presentations mirroring their subversive messages, ones which echoed many of the suffrage posters themselves. Images in Washington, D.C., following the Women's

March in 2017, show massive numbers of such handmade posters deposited in front of a Trump building which started a collecting frenzy from museums and archives, anxious to mark what they knew to be an important, historic, grassroots occasion.

Like our suffrage women and our recent women marchers, the *Spare Rib* protestors engage with other people in the urban environment but now they invite a dialogue on a topic that would never have been an option for our first wavers. A woman's body was often on display within the pages of *Spare Rib*; the protestors were certainly playing on the irony of its ban versus the continued acceptance in British culture of London's *Sun* with its page three female nude. Indeed, during this same period there were many protests in front of the newspaper offices of *The Sun* and second wavers also created their own version of page three.[30] *Spare Rib* was at the center of a 1970s dialogue over a woman's right to own her body and to decide how she would use it. Many women artists in the 1970s used their own bodies in their art as a way of fighting back at the objectification of women and were largely responsible for the creation of performance art as a way of using their bodies in an expressive manner that talked back to male objectification.[31] Women on the street, fighting to have the right to publish a women's liberation journal, in the face of total acceptance of the objectification of women on the *Sun*'s page three spoke volumes about the acceptable ways we should see women's bodies in public. If men are in control, then it's acceptable, but if women decide to turn the tables, they suffer repression.

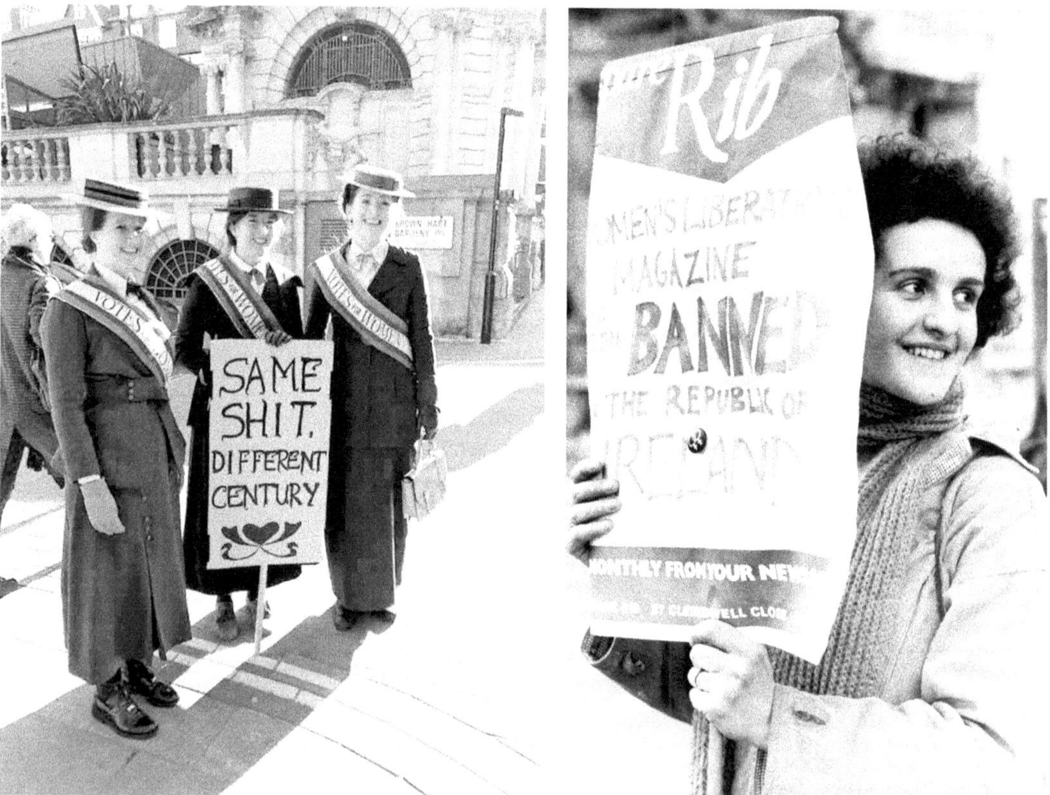

Left: **Figure 81.** *Members of Women's March with Poster,* London, 2017. *Right:* **Figure 82.** *Picket outside the Irish Embassy following the ban on the women's liberation magazine Spare Rib, 1970s.* **Morning Star Photographic Archive: MSPA 6/17/9. Bishopsgate Institute, London.**

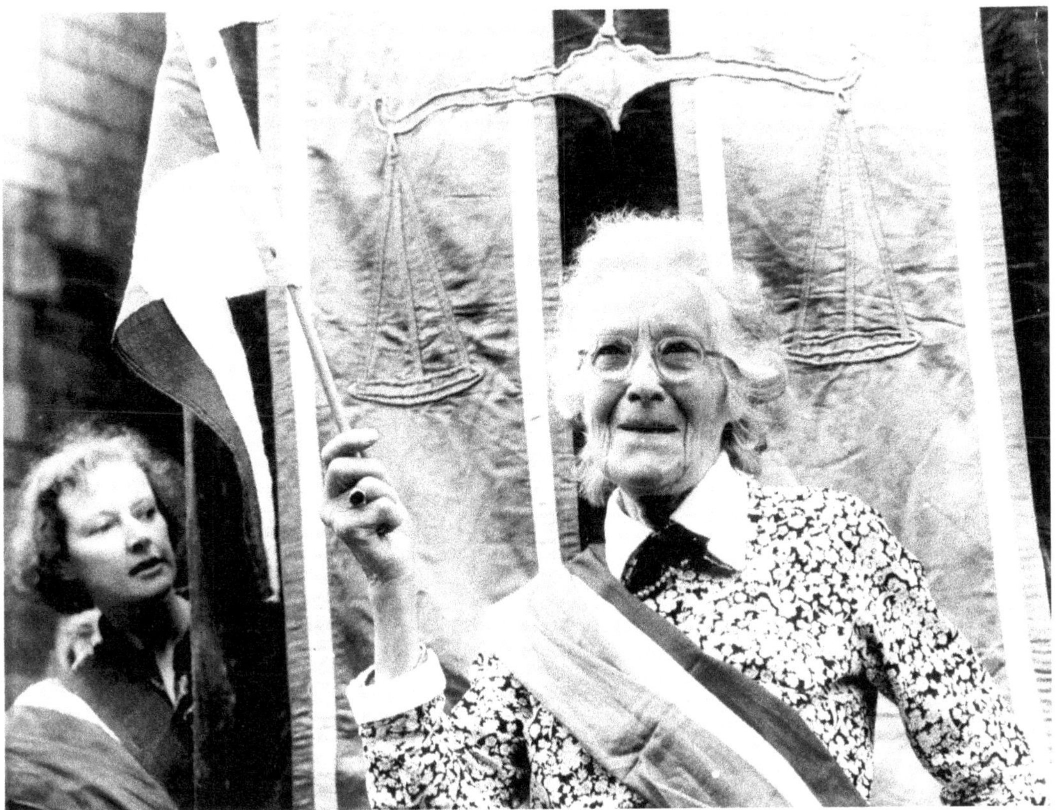

Figure 83. *Dame Margery Corbett Ashby Celebrating 50 Years of Women's Enfranchisement at the "Right to Vote" Exhibition,* **Westminster Hall, London, 1978. Morning Star Photographic Archive: MSPA 6/17/6 552. Bishopsgate Institute, London.**

Another example of such continuity is a purposeful one (fig. 83). Dame Margery Corbett Ashby stands elated in her suffrage sash, in front of an embroidered banner showing the justice scales equalized. This photograph was taken at the opening of "A Right to Vote," an exhibition celebrating voting equality at its fiftieth anniversary in 1978. She had begun campaigning eighty years earlier, in 1889, when she was just sixteen. Thus, the image celebrates a ninety-six-year-old suffrage woman reveling over equal rights with the same symbols of that emancipation she helped to create. She was a member of the NUWSS, holding the position of Secretary and also being on its Executive Committee during the agitation period. She continued to hold positions in feminist groups throughout her life. The key markers of voting equality are present: the sash and the banner and, central to the understanding of equality, the very powerful image of the scales of justice now balanced.

But this image and the event it marks also show us that feminists have not buried suffrage history. With the advent of the 1970s Women's Liberation Movement, women started to ask questions about their own histories. This event is just one of many examples of the resurrection and nod of gratitude we see for the struggles of the suffrage women. Beyond Midge Mackenzie's documentary on the militant suffragettes, *Shoulder to Shoulder* from 1975, some local London examples within the Feminist Library poster collection show further homage to the first wave, such as the Women Artists Slide Library presenting

"A Second Viewing: An exhibition of posters, banners, photographs and text from the Suffragette Movement" in celebration of International Women's Day in 1986. The image that accompanies the poster is from first-wave suffrage, signed JHB, of a woman with a basket of fruit knocking on a locked door with the caption: "Womanhood offers her gifts at her country's door." Similarly, another poster announces a meeting with the Irish Suffragette, Hanna Sheehy Skeffington, along with a historical photograph of her addressing an audience of men and women from a platform.[32]

The look of triumph on Dame Corbett Ashby's face is duplicated in that of other women who have fought for justice. Compare the image of suffragette women returning from prison in a victory parade (fig. 76) with that of women in a 1970s-strike dispute who have won concessions (fig. 84) and you see the same joy, relief, empowerment and sense of accomplishment. The elation of freedom is evident in the faces of all the women in figures 76–81, and 83–84, one that echoes Vicinus' characterization of empowerment, freedom, and a new kind of spirit.

The body politic is not unique then to the first wave; we see a continuity in terms of expressions of solidarity. The photograph of suffrage women advertising meetings (fig. 79) is similar in its comrade-like body language to Martin Jenkinson's *Derbyshire Women Marching in Support of Miners* from Caesterfield, England, 1985 (Bishopsgate Institute, London). In both instances, we see the same body language of women's arms linked, women embracing in sisterhood, as a symbol of their shared purpose. Similarly,

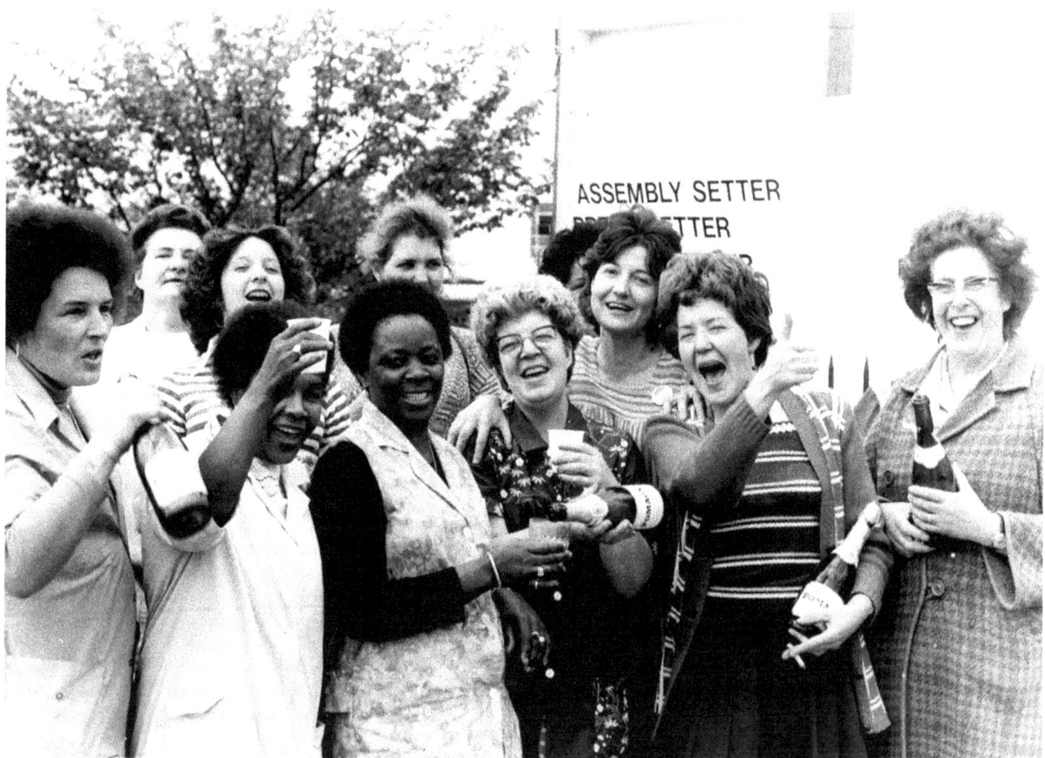

Figure 84. *Women's Dispute Resolution,* c. 1970s, England. Morning Star Photographic Archive: MSPA 6/17/11. Bishopsgate Institute, London.

Midge's 1975 British documentary on suffrage history was called *Shoulder to Shoulder* in order to indicate the bodily group action itself.[33] This kind of camaraderie is certainly also evident in the suffrage marches but a further message is also present there: The impact of great numbers of women, sheer numbers together, was politically marked. Women first began their marches to answer the Liberal Government who said they did not believe that many women desired the vote, that the petitions were full of made-up signatures. The suffrage groups responded with their large, mass demonstrations to prove that there was indeed strength in numbers. Whether we are talking about a struggle for representation, advertising the cause, or supporting a strike, women in numbers sent a powerful message.

The Collective Body

"To lose the personal in the great impersonal is to live!" Christabel Pankhurst, *Unshackled* (1959)

"I believe in the power of individuals and the special power of women together to change things."–Jenny Hiscock, Aged 27, Adelaide, Australia, participant in Women for Survival—Pine Gap Protest (1983)[34]

The body politic, then, is necessarily tied to a collective body. In her study of representation and femininity, Corbett asserts that WSPU members "redefined selflessness as a positive political value and as a counter to the culture of individualism, as an important element of a politicized subjectivity." In this context she argues that "the militant suffragettes forged a collective identity and established an intersubjective model for selfhood through the material practices of hunger-striking and forcible feeding … ."[35] Further, Corbett suggests that shared activities of marching, demonstrating, and selling papers were a way to counter the profound isolation of the forced feeding experience.[36] But not all WSPU women could readily embrace the sudden jolt of freedom from prison into the collective fray. As May Sinclair characterized the situation in her novel, *The Tree of Heaven* (1917), the heroine longs not for the comradeship of the celebratory breakfast but rather to return to her cell: "The singing had threatened her when it began, so that she felt again her old terror of the collective soul. Its massed emotion threatened her. She longed for her white-washed prison-cell, for its hardness, its nakedness, its quiet, its visionary peace." Many women wrote of this dissonance between the public display and the lonely life of the cell.[37]

Attached to this kind of spectrum of inner and outer manifestations of identity, Showalter argues that forced feeding was one arena where the government conflated the hysterical and the suffragette; at the beginning of this chapter I discussed how Showalter characterized the hysteric and the feminist as being at two ends of a spectrum of women's behavior, necessarily attached. In this instance, she states that "the elements of hunger, rebellion, and rage latent in the phenomenon of female nervous disorder became explicit and externalized in the tactics of the suffrage campaigns" specifically in the "hunger strikes of militant women prisoners" which "put the symptomatology of anorexia nervosa to work in the service of the feminist cause." The government responded to their demands by treating them as if they were mental patients, even though the women, upon interview, were seen to be of sound mind.[38] Hence, in this instance we see the conflation of the feminist with the hysteric, a ploy that surfaced repeatedly in the battle over women's bodies in the public arena as a way of discrediting the cause.

Further, Corbett charts differences between suffrage workers as being one of class, but in comparison with the U.S. today, specifically, she asserts that differences arise over race and heterosexism. She states: "While I do not assume that the particular struggles within the suffrage movement and the contemporary feminist one are at all identical, I do see an analogy between the two in that then as now, feminists and others working for social and political change must deal with questions of differences among and within us."[39] At the same time, however, in seeking to define their experience, suffrage women spoke of rising above these differences for the common cause, Emmeline Pethick-Lawrence being a case in point, who said that "women of the upper, middle and working classes [realized] a new comradeship with each other. Neither class, nor wealth, nor education counted any more, only devotion to the common ideal. No longer did women feel loneliness or isolation or inhibition."[40]

Martha A. Ackelsberg and Myrna Margulies Breitbart characterize such collective action within the framing of "the development of a critical consciousness," which they see as

> an active process which involves participation in social struggle and in the design of change. Collective confrontation with structures of authority and/or the creation of some new social-political reality in the interstices of existing power relations often generates changed consciousness and energizes continued action (resistance).[41]

In their analysis of protest, they have hypothesized certain characteristics that are most likely to produce such an altered consciousness:

- It reduces participants' distance from the facts of their lives, enabling them to recognize the significance of the larger social context in which their oppression takes place
- It allows people to learn more about their history, especially if it brings together members of different generations and/or cultures
- It leads to increased confidence: recognizing that one is not alone and can act with others is an empowering process
- It demands changes which cannot be met by mere adjustment and adaptation [which] generates a momentum for continued involvement[42]

The incredible impact of the early processions achieved these collective goals; organized to show the government that women in large numbers did, indeed, desire the vote, these processions grew in size with each event, becoming the largest public demonstrations that the world had seen to date. In this context, Laurence Housman, a suffrage artist, recalled:

> More and more it became difficult to belittle a Movement which could hold up the traffic of London with processions two or three miles long, and decked from end to end with hundreds of banners, some of them of vast size; while in the ranks the most unexpected people were to be seen testifying their support....[43]

What the processions were able to show was a number of important issues about the collective body; for one, women were not all of one type, but diverse in their backgrounds, interests, and pursuits. The press could no longer stereotype them and hence the press could no longer ridicule them. Further, they were incredible organizers and their parades were orderly and with purpose rather than violent. Beyond those reasons, they proved suffrage women right in their refusal to take risks in their appearance; by 1908 the processions persuaded the public, for the most part, that a woman's appearance was not a deadly weapon to be used to beguile men, but rather a mark of her serious endeavor.

One of the most powerful elements of suffrage marches was their dignified silence. From England to the U.S., women marched in orderly lines in white dresses, maintaining their dignity through their silence as a protest in itself against the ways women were silenced as non-citizens in their respective cultures. Similarly, more recent protests, such as that of the *Madres de Plaza de Mayo* from 1977 to 1982, worked to unnerve the Argentinian government. Appearing for the first time in the *Plaza de Mayo* in Buenos Aires on April 30, 1977, fourteen women paraded silently around the monument dedicated to the independence movement of 1810. They repeated this action once a week at the exact same time. Like the suffrage women, their opponents soon labeled them "*las locas* [crazy women] *de Plaza de Mayo*."[44] Their demands were those of mothers, seeking the release, or at least the location, of their children who constituted many of "the disappeared" of the military Junta which had deposed President Maria Estela (Isabel) Peron. But, as with other such peaceful protests, matters soon turned to violence against the protestors. By 1978, one thousand women were expelled from the Plaza, the weekly event having swelled to great numbers and, in a tragic turn of events, some of the *Madres* themselves became "the disappeared."

As with our suffrage women, however, "the actions of the *Madres de Plaza de Mayo* were simultaneously radical and couched in traditional language," evoking the anguish of mothers "in a Catholic country where veneration of the Virgin Mary augmented the respect paid to mothers" while simultaneously, through their visible protest of wearing symbolic diapers of their children, they challenged the government to cease political torture, one that involved unspeakable acts; their knowledge of such activities was traditionally considered a topic unfit for mothers' ears, hence they broke the silence, challenging "the boundaries of public and private as well as prevailing structures of gender."[45] Like the suffrage women before them, they understood the power structures and worked within them.

But Then There Is the Power of the Voting Body

In France, women's rights began to be addressed systematically as a result of the Women's Liberation Movement of the 1970s. These changes included "the complete empowerment of married women with regard to property and personal decisions, rights over children and, for all women, the legalization of contraception and abortion. In the 1980s the French state even undertook sponsorship for programs for family planning," leading to the complete "decolonization" of French women.[46] How do we account for this support of women? Politicians figured out that they represented the swing vote and it was a vote moving increasingly to the left along with French politics.[47] Hence, that fear of the British in 1918 that women would have a significant impact had come true in France.

Body Language

This set of actions and their aftermath, with women moving from a traditional stance to one of increasingly active agitation, is part of an ongoing pattern that Maurice Agulhon characterizes in his study of Marianne imagery, symbol of the French revolutionary forces. Agulhon examines the presentation of reformist tendencies versus revolutionary political tendencies in France, in order to assert that static representations are most often associated with constitutional politics while active representations are most often associated with radical politics.[48] Specifically, the Marianne of Bourgeois Liberalism consists of a "fixed allegory: an image of serenity; seated or standing but immobile posture; orderly hair; covered bosom; a mature, even maternal figure" whereas the Marianne of Popular Revolt is a "live allegory: an image of vehemence; always standing and sometimes on the march; free floating hair; uncovered bosom; youthful figure." While I discussed this framing in relation to representations of Liberty in Chapter Four, here I want to consider the following: If we extrapolate those observations to the imagery of marches, protests and demonstrations, we will see how Agulhon's theory is played out in the bodily representation of the suffrage woman in public and how such imagery either inflects, gives rise to, or counteracts later images of women protestors. The *Madres de Plaza de Mayo*, in relation to the staid early demonstrations of several British suffrage groups, is just one manifestation of the way that Agulhon's construction does not remain fixed. Even orderly processions and silent protest lead to agitation and escalating behaviors, in both cases thrust upon the women by government forces emblematized in police action.

One example from the Edwardian suffrage movement reflects this dichotomy well: Bernard Partridge's 1906 "The Shrieking Sister" (fig. 33 in Chapter Two) shows, as I have argued elsewhere,[49] Millicent Garrett Fawcett putting a calming, precautionary hand on an out-of-control, raging, fist-clenching, arm-waving suffragette who brandishes that weapon of suffragettes, the umbrella, to which she has attached a flag that reads "Female Suffrage." Constitutional reformer and radical suffragette are not in unison here but rather represent the two poles of static and live allegory of Agulhon's construction and in this sense, pin down the two types of body language in which the press insisted these women engaged, whether they reflected reality or not.

These demonstrations sit within the larger umbrella of the politics of transgression. Peter Stallybrass and Allon White explain the structure as a hierarchy in which "the low troubles the high" in the sense that

> the high/low opposition in each of our four symbolic domains—psychic forms, the human body, geographical space and the social order—is a fundamental basis to mechanisms of ordering and sense-making in European cultures. Divisions and discriminations in one domain are continually structured, legitimated and dissolved by reference to the vertical symbolic hierarchy which operates in the other three domains.... [T]ransgressing the rules of hierarchy and order in any one of the domains may have major consequences in the others.[50]

We can also layer over both Agulhon's static and lived allegory, and Stallybrass and Allon's structure, a Bakhtinian analysis of the grotesque body.[51] Let the effigy that opened this chapter stand as the example here, alongside the images of women protestors:

> [T]he grotesque body is the open, protruding, extended, secreting body, the body of becoming, process, and change. The grotesque body is opposed to the Classical body which is monumental, static, closed, and sleek, corresponding to the aspirations of bourgeois individualism; the grotesque body is connected to the rest of the world.[52]

Bakhtin's grotesque corresponds to Agulhon's live allegory whereas the Classical body imaged here corresponds to Agulhon's concept of the fixed allegory. The grotesque body is threatening, always pushing beyond the boundaries; it embraces excess and transgression. The male students of Cambridge could not have found a more fitting representation of it than the female effigy that, in a Bacchanalian kind of frenzy, they then sought to destroy, partly because it existed outside their known "symbolic domains," of social order, geographical space and their patriarchal understanding of the human body. For the young men at Cambridge, Stallybrass and White would see them involved in a "recurring pattern" as a result of this hierarchical structure:

> [T]he "top" attempts to reject and eliminate the "bottom" for reasons of prestige and status, only to discover, not only that it is in some way frequently dependent upon that low-Other [here their example is Hegel's discussion of the relationship between master and slave in his *Phenomenology*], but also that the top *includes* that low symbolically, as a primary eroticized constituent of its own fantasy life. The result is a mobile, conflictual fusion of power, fear and desire in the construction of subjectivity: a psychological dependence upon precisely those Others which are being rigorously opposed and excluded at the social level. It is for this reason that what is *socially* peripheral [here our Girton Girl] is so frequently *symbolically* central (like long hair in the 1960s).[53]

We can liken the actions of the young men of Cambridge to those of some later British male youth on Greenham Common who attacked the homemade tents of the women protestors with excrement and pig's blood. Stallybrass and White argue that these women

> outrage local youths by breaking the norms of women's dependence upon men and by their independent sexual stance and are visited, in consequence, with a "charivari"—a scapegoating carnivalesque ritual, usually carried out by young men against those whom they feel have broken the customs of courtship and sexual duty in the locality: charivari was a rowdy form of crowd behavior often used against "unruly women," and here it is an overt reminder of patriarchal dominance.[54]

This kind of charivari is certainly what the Cambridge boys were performing; it was not at all dissimilar to violence other young men practiced on suffrage women who walked the streets handing out pamphlets, one of whom, on one occasion, met with a group of angry, young, medical students who stripped and tarred her in public; they had also smashed windows at The Women's Press in Charing Cross Road.[55]

This positioning is not to forget that the grotesque body/live allegory is the social body. As Mary Russo interprets it, "The grotesque body is open, protruding, irregular, secreting, multiple, and changing; it is identified with non-official 'low' culture or the carnivalesque, and with social transformation."[56] If we recognize that the public pageants of suffrage come out of a tradition of the carnivalesque, sitting outside of everyday experience as extraordinary and liminal, then it is easy to make the leap to seeing this grotesque body on display as part of that transformative moment. This body, like the live allegory, belongs to the politics of transgression. Russo in fact associates the "shrieking sisterhood" of the first wave and the "bra burners" of the 1960s with the female grotesque,[57] and that's my point. These are important resistant moments that push aside and push past that Classical body; such moments are associated with radical politics and live allegory rather than with something fixed. The ire of the Cambridge male students was partly because they could not suppress this spirit, could not bring it in line, as it existed outside of the norm. And the images themselves are not accurate in their representation. The shrieking sister of the suffrage movement and the bra-burning 1960s feminist are both positioned in the press as hysterical, but neither ever existed anywhere except in the minds of the press. These representations are extremes and hence outlandish, but the fact that such images do in some ways represent the respective activities of the two waves lends evidence to their being included in a grotesque rhetoric.[58]

When we shift to the 1960s in the U.S., we see the feminist phalanx taking on the mantle of active representations associated with radical politics. Their goals during the period of 1968 to 1973 were (1) formal equality for women and (2) self-determination, the latter largely in terms of the then current battles over rights to abortion, yet their goals are still the ones feminist activists seek in today's politically conservative climate; in this sense, feminists of the 1960s and today, continue to fight for a body politic, the woman's body still being at the center of debate over who has the right to control her body. Her body is central to the expanding set of issues around sex, gender, and the family that radical feminism had brought to the forefront, which include

> gay rights, teenage sex and pregnancy, sex education, pornography, sexual and domestic violence, the high rate of divorce and single motherhood, the dilemma of who will care for children and home in place of the vanishing housewife, the demand for recognition of "domestic partnerships," surrogate motherhood and reproductive technology, the future of the sexual revolution in the age of AIDS.[59]

Through these avenues of dialogue, Alice Echols concludes, radical feminism "did exactly what its opponents accuse it of: it played a key role in subverting traditional values and destabilizing the family."[60] In this way, the movement upholds Agulhon's construction of active representations being aligned with radical politics. In this regard, Echols sees radical feminism of the 1960s as being

> distant from the narrow and conservative version of feminism articulated by Alice Paul and her National Women's Party [of the U.S. suffrage fight] in the post-suffrage era [since] the party refused to speak out against labor conditions and black disenfranchisement on the grounds that these were not "purely feminist" issues.... Nor did radical feminists bear much resemblance to 19th-century feminists whose embrace of motherhood and domesticity was antithetical to radical feminism.[61]

What Echols fails to address, however, in this rather glossing contrast, is that the goals of the first wave had to be couched in conservative constructions of womanhood; it was the path they started that had allowed for radical feminism's dialogue. (I address England and the U.S. here, presuming these are the first wavers to which she is referring since, in both England and the U.S., there were both moderate and more radical groups, namely the National American Woman Suffrage Association (NAWSA) in the U.S. and the NUWSS in England versus the National Woman Party (NWP) in the U.S. and the WSPU, WFL and ELF in England.)[62] To suggest that women were going to leave the home in first-wave dialogue would have been their death knell and it was not their goal; rather they sought enfranchisement first, thinking that other rights would follow once their citizenship and representation were no longer in question. In the pages of the NUWSS's mouthpiece, *The Common Cause*, for example, we see arguments that suggest that women's suffrage would lead to higher wages and economic independence; increased job opportunities; improved marriages and child welfare; and legal equality. As Les Garner and Brian Harrison point out, "However limited the value of the vote may now seem, it must be emphasized that the struggle of the suffragists—an active struggle by women, as women—was at the time controversial. It aroused the opposition not only of men who felt that a woman's place was in the home, but also of those frightened of any possible progress towards adult suffrage."[63] Further, many of the first wavers viewed the vote as a gateway to change.[64]

That those same struggles are prevalent among the second wave is clear from a textual poster in the London Feminist Library collection dating from the 1970 to 1980 period on behalf of the National Union of Students which existed

> to fight for the needs and demands of women throughout the UK student movement—for your demands and your needs. The Women's Campaign is part of your Union in your college.... Because

women's work is never done and is underpaid or unpaid or boring or repetitious and we're the first to get the sack and what we look like is more important than what we do and if we get raped it's our fault and if we get bashed we must have provoked it and if we raise our voices we're nagging bitches and if we enjoy sex we're nymphos and if we don't we're frigid and if we love women it's because we can't get a "real" man and if we ask our doctor too many questions we're neurotic and/or pushy and if we expect community care for children we're selfish and if we stand up for our rights we're aggressive and "unfeminine" and if we don't we're typical weak females and if we want to get married we're out to trap a man and if we don't we're unnatural and because we still can't get an adequate safe contraceptive but men can walk on the moon and if we can't cope or don't want a pregnancy we're made to feel guilty about abortion and ... for lots and lots of other reasons we are part of the women's liberation movement.[65]

Further, in relation to this text's discussion of the dilemmas of being sexually active for second wavers, Echols asserts that 19th-century feminists equated sex with danger but she does not discuss the real danger of venereal disease that prompted Christabel Pankhurst's heartfelt cry of "Votes for Women and Chastity for Men." It is hardly fair to condemn this first-wave generation for its ambivalence to sex when to engage in sex, often without any means of protection, might mean eventual insanity and death. So she is somewhat cavalier on this point when she then says that "while 19th-century women's rights activists equated sex with danger, radical feminists believed that sexuality is simultaneously a realm of danger and of pleasure for women."[66] She fails to mention that much has happened between the 19th century and the 1960s in terms of the eradication or at least successful treatment of venereal diseases, along with the advent of the Pill that offered women sexual freedom from reproduction. In any case, the point is that the discussion continues to revolve around a debate over a woman's body and her ability to have access to choices regarding it and her health. Again, the 2017 Women's March around the world and its purpose of protesting for women's reproductive rights brings the conversation to the present moment.

In the 1970s, this point is pressed home to us in two ways by the demands of the British Women's Liberation Movement. For one, Barbara Caine shares that "[t]hese demands were not discussed quietly, but were rather emblazoned on banners, printed on badges and shouted in the streets during mass demonstrations."[67] While these activities speak to a heightening of the first-wave requests in terms of being vocal, their demands were the direct result of first-wave discourse, witness Yeo's observation that

[w]hatever its insensitivity to class and race, the "Four Demands" of the second wave Women's Liberation Movement in Britain tried to base entitlement to human development both on sexual difference, insisting on twenty-four-hour nurseries and contraception and abortion on demand, as well as on equality in education and employment opportunities. None the less feminists still live out motherhood in a society built around domestic ideology, with few social supports for other roles unless they can be privately afforded, in a national situation where women are increasingly more able to find "flexible" (exploitative) employment than men.[68]

This continued dilemma was brought home to a U.S. audience in a recent *New York Times* article entitled "A Feminist's Daughter Finds Love in the Kitchen," in which the feminist mother author does battle with this continued, presumed role of motherhood: "[C]hildren do not stop needing what they need, even when their parents are fighting for justice."[69] The battle is still over women's bodies, both their reproductive choices and their bodily presence in the public world. As Yeo points out, the fight now should be over helping women maintain those dual roles of mother and worker.

Violence and the Female Body as Disorderly and Excessive

The scenes at Black Friday or any number of skirmishes of the Edwardian suffragettes with the police (figs. 85 and 86) were not the first instance of such bodily carnage in the streets of London with regards to the franchise. If, as Richard Sennett has argued, the "civic body" is articulated through a sense of community, nationhood, and civic participation expressed in the public sphere,[70] we cannot ignore its obverse, that the desire to create a civic body is often one that is embattled. For example, the Peterloo Massacre of 1819, prior to any reform bills, was still fresh in the minds of the English, a moment when Henry Hunt, radical orator, was asked by the Manchester Patriotic Union to speak at St. Peter's Fields on his beliefs regarding equal rights, universal suffrage, and a secret ballot. When he stood on the platform, beside him was a woman carrying a banner bearing the legend "Female Reformers of Royston—Let us die like men and not be sold like slaves." His friendly reception prompted the local magistrates to arrest him and to bring in the military, which resulted in fifteen deaths and over six hundred being injured.[71] What is significant for suffrage events is not only that he was vulnerable as a speaker on a platform, subjected to violence in the same ways that women were within the suffrage campaign, but also that the woman present was expressing her view in a banner, a practice in which Chartist women also later engaged. Yeo and Ada Nield Chew explain that such working-class women "from the beginning to the end of the century could mobilise all these political, religious, race, class and gender meanings at the same time, and keep adding to them."[72] While Hunt had clear support from among the sixty-thousand people who had gathered that day, the government was significantly both out of touch with its people's concerns and too invested in control at all costs. Popular images of the Peterloo Massacre paint a picture of the military as the bad guys, thrashing away at the crowds with their swords and tromping people as they ride through the crowds on horseback.

Equally violent events and resulting sympathetic imagery also occurred during the 1887 Bloody Sunday Riot in Trafalgar Square, one particular print detailing the police wrenching the socialists' red flag from the grasp of the socialist leader, Helen Taylor.[73] Although not strictly about enfranchisement, this event was a protest against policies of the Conservative Government with regards to rights of free speech. The event itself was in defiance of a ban on public meetings in Trafalgar Square. We will return to the significance of Trafalgar Square as a site for suffrage in the section below on space, but here it is important to note that such events must have been in the minds of our reforming suffrage women when they took to the streets. Emmeline Pankhurst was in fact present at the Bloody Sunday event alongside her husband, the reformer Richard Pankhurst. The example of Helen Taylor, for one, and the woman banner carrier for another, would seem to indicate that women had long been a voice in the political fray. This situation was doubly true in France, of course, where women took to the barricades during the French Revolution and later fought alongside their male comrades during the Commune, as we have seen in Chapter One.

That women had no other recourse than to act out is evident in Christabel Pankhurst's defense of herself and Annie Kenney following their first arrest after an election meeting at the Manchester Free Trade Hall at which they asked if the Liberal Government would support votes for women. They unfurled a banner that said "Votes for Women." Christabel later reflected:

My conduct in the Free Trade Hall and outside was meant as a protest against the legal position of women today. We cannot make any orderly protest because we have not the means whereby citizens may do such a thing; we have no vote; and so long as we have no vote we must be disorderly. There is no other way whereby we can put forward our claims to political justice.[74]

We could not ask for a more cogent argument, by a trained lawyer no less, one not allowed to practice because of her sex, for Agulhon's active, agitated protestor. And, in addition, for a rationale for a grotesque activity; they literally sit outside of civilization.

Representations of Arrests

When the 1910 Conciliation Bill failed to pass, a bill that would have enfranchised women, some three-hundred women rushed the House of Commons demanding to be heard; this day came to be called Black Friday because of the women's battle with police at an unprecedented level of brutality and violence (fig. 86). Vicinus characterizes this battle as a key moment in this public dialogue:

Black Friday brought into the open the sexual consequences of women's attempting to enter a male domain. In order to protest their public space, men were willing to permit, even encourage, the violation of woman's most intimate space—her body.

Women clearly could not compete physically with men, and indeed, they never wished to do so; the repeated public maulings served to confirm not their weakness, but the brutality of men.[75]

But, also, such events evinced the suffragists' increasing frustration over not being heard and acknowledged. The controlled, conforming, stately, civic-minded marches with their orderly groupings were not enough. They had to push against the government physically which they do in these images (figs. 85 and 86).

Initially, none of the groups had sought violent actions. On one occasion, responding to a remark that the act of women chaining themselves to railings in order to be heard (and not carted off) was just plain silly, Emmeline Pankhurst retorted: "Doing something silly is the women's alternative to doing something cruel. The effect is the same. We use no violence because we can win freedom without it; because we have discovered an alternative."[76] Sadly, it was not to be this easy. Even when the WSPU did resort to violent activities, they argued that it was in response to male reactions over their own attempts at non-violent action, such as sending deputations to Parliament, or street speaking. As Liz Stanley and Ann Morley characterize the opinions of one feminist of the time, Elinor Penn Gaskell, "women's claims were justified and the action they wanted to take was perfectly reasonable; what was unjustified and unreasonable were the reactions of men (who often seized the opportunity to punch and kick and claw and also to sexually assault with impunity)."[77] Harrison characterizes the militant violence as not that shocking in comparison with political violence that has happened since that date; yet, he qualifies this statement by admitting, through the women's voices themselves, how much nerve it took to step outside of their respectable selves to commit such acts.[78]

Even when the militants' violence began, it was in the form of violence to property, not people, yet in the analysis below we will see how the image of the hysteric comes into play again as a conflation of active feminist/sexually-frustrated woman that offers another instance of the collapse of Showalter's construction of the spectrum. In her analysis of the *Daily Mirror's* "The Suffragette Face: New Type Evolved by Militancy" (fig. 85), for example, Caroline J. Howlett determines that, through the decision to show close-ups of the women, the newspaper did not tell the actual story of their anguish in terms of the circumstances of their arrests. By focusing in on the faces, the newspaper elided the actual violence that the police perpetrated upon these women. The press completely erased the acts of violence.

What we see instead, the *Daily Mirror* argues, is a "fanaticism" in the women's facial expressions that the press insisted was typical of all suffrage women. The point was that these women could all be reduced to one recognizable type. For example, the newspaper stated, "Nowadays, indeed, any observant person can pick out a suffragette in a crowd of other women." This commentary appeared alongside the image we see here, where women's faces look exhausted, in pain, tormented. Many of these images were taken from the demonstration outside of Buckingham Palace on May 21, 1914, when the suffrage women appealed directly to the King. Sylvia Pankhurst recalled of the event something very different from what the *Daily Mirror* portrays, stating that women were subject to punches, kicks, bodily assault about the breasts and, worse, struck with truncheons.[79] Howlett discusses that this "elision of the scene of violence" is what Lynn Higgins and Brenda Silver argue "characterizes the male poetics of rape." In this argument, "[t]his elision is associated with the displacement of the violence, which is attributed to the raped woman rather than to the rapist."[80] Howlett concludes of this *Daily Mirror* misrepresentation of the suffragette then, that this erasure of male acts of violence has as its goal to read "the appearance of anguish on the faces … as self-induced: a hysterical symptom."[81] As with many images in the popular press of suffrage women, the journalists create their own image of the suffragette, often reducing her to this kind of type. But to align her with the hysterical woman was also a way to discredit the cause, implying that only unfit, unstable women wanted the vote and that they certainly were not the kind of voters Britain wanted as citizens. They were doubly damned, beaten down by police in many brutal encounters, then the encounter itself used against them to show their lack of credibility.

Rosemary Betterton also discusses this *Daily Mirror* article and page, stating that the layout mimics "the standard format of suffrage programmes for processions and demonstrations in which a central text was surrounded by photographs

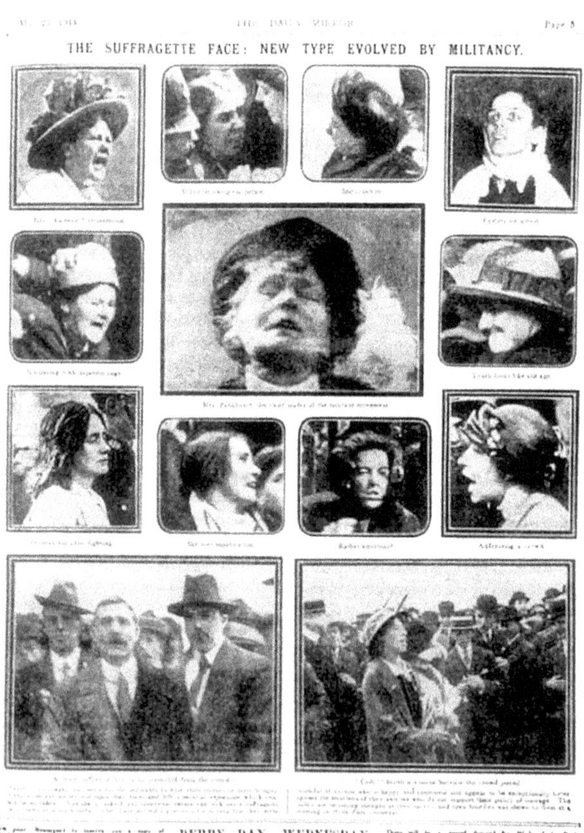

Figure 85. *Daily Mirror front page* "**The Suffragette Face: New Type Evolved by Militancy**" (May 25, 1914).

of the main speakers." Thus, it speaks back to the calm, ordered representation that the suffrage leaders desired to present in a mocking fashion. The titles under the photographs in the *Daily Mirror* page are equally damning: "Dishevelled after fighting" and "screaming with impotent rage," Betterton argues, align themselves as representations with Louis Desnoyers' description of imagery submitted for the competition for the new Republic of France after the 1848 revolutions which consisted of "enraged female devils with disheveled hair" who "hurled abuse." Betterton concludes that "in a collapse of signifier and signified, the visible image of female disorder comes to stand again for militant politics."[82] Hence, her analysis is in line with Agulhon's active construction and Bakhtin's grotesque body.

Betterton's analysis here is also poignant in relation to the actual level of violence of the Black Friday event from which some of the doctored *Daily Mirror*

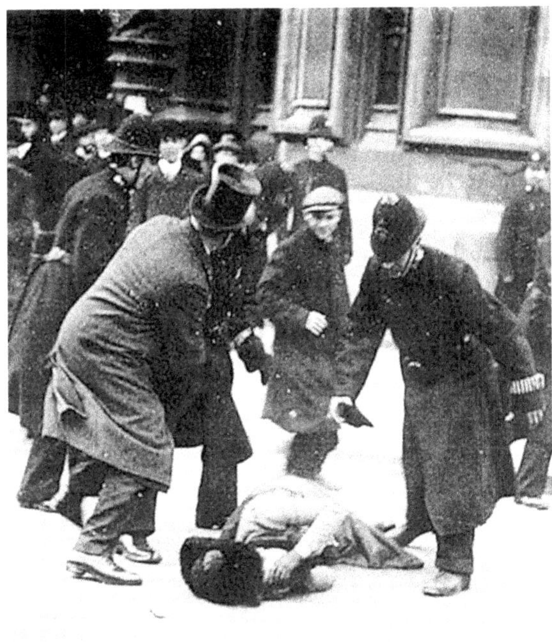

Figure 86. *Black Friday,* rescinded issue of the *Daily Mirror* (November 18, 1910). Museum of London, 2003.46/41.

hysterical images were taken. In the Museum of London suffrage collection, there is a photograph that shows the extreme level of violence of which the police were capable (fig. 86). The commentary that accompanies the image explains:

Black Friday, November 18th, 1910. Ada Wright, her arm twisted to breaking point by a Policeman, is then flung by him to the ground. A supporter of the Suffragettes is seen preventing the Policeman from kicking her as she lay helpless on the ground. This copy of the "Daily Mirror" was called in and circulation immediately stopped and the negative smashed by order of the Liberal Government.

The act of smashing the negative served the same purpose as the published "version" of the "new suffragette": that is, to reduce her to one recognizable and hence conquerable type. The fact that the women had suffered real violence had to be erased from the record.

Betterton determines that the ultimate demonstration that convinced the British public of the suffragette's disorderly and excessive behavior was when Emily Wilding Davison threw herself in front of the King's horse at the Derby on May 25, 1914. There are many points of view about whether she intended to die that day, but the suffragettes treated her as a martyr with an expansive funeral, showing their solidarity with her actions (fig. 37 in Chapter Two). However, as Betterton observes, "she was popularly represented in the press as an unbalanced and hysterical woman who had committed suicide for the vote. Her death was treated as final proof of the 'insanity' of women involved in militant action."[83] She stood for a collection of imagery of the suffrage woman who was imaged, upon arrest, as screaming and fighting, but Betterton argues that these images did not appear often. The *Daily Mirror* page and the many images of women's arrests in the papers would seem to contradict this statement, however. Further, Betterton asserts that prison imagery "tended toward static representations" whereas the actual accounts of women's arrests testify to their poor treatment, subjection to sexual abuse and other forms of physical violence. In this regard Betterton draws a parallel with not only the imagery of Republican France but also with the women arrested during peace protests at Greenham Common in the early 1980s.[84] Our visual evidence suggests, however, that there was a plethora of imagery of women's arrests during the suffrage movement and, further, the women themselves employed artists to create protest imagery about forced feeding that was anything but static, as we have seen in the Joan of Arc chapter. Betterton's point, however, is that the majority of imagery, at the insistence of Emmeline Pankhurst, was to show "calm and restraint even under arrest" and, citing the "Prisoners of War" cartoon from *Votes for Women* and the photograph of *Joan Annan Bryce as Joan of Arc* in the Women's Coronation Procession (figs. 29 and 27 in Chapter Two), she offers up visual evidence of this dominant representation, concluding that "[i]t is within the context of this politics of representation that the WSPU call for bodily control, including both physical decorum and controlled sexuality, must be properly understood."[85] They were fighting back, not only literally but representationally, with imagery of regimented women in orderly, processional marches, and in other forms of representation such as the studio portraits that picture calm, glamorous, well put-together women to counter these destructive types of representation.

Yet, the dominant discourse, as both Howlett and Betterton assert, was that of the hysterical woman. In her review of the debate over hysteria, which includes Jean-Martin Charcot's assertion that hysteria was a psychological disorder manifest in physical symptoms only, a view that remained dominant despite the later work of Freud and Breuer in *Studies of Hysteria* (1895), Betterton observes that "[t]he high profile of debate over the nature of hysteria ensured that it entered into popular consciousness as indelibly linked with female disorder and, moreover, identified with feminism."[86] Thus, the *Daily Mirror's* text brings together the kinds of representations that were used to discredit suffrage women: "fear of female disorder, insanity and sexual power over men" sounded an alarm bell which itself, as Betterton points out, was somewhat hysterical in its high-pitched drama.[87]

Yet a similar construction of women's behavior happened in the U.S. press as a result of the September 20, 1967, Women's Strike for Peace (hereafter WSP) demonstration that gathered in Washington, D.C., in support of young men who were resisting the draft. The narrative moved from one of dignity to swift violence which was a shock to those who knew the representatives who were "overwhelmingly ... middle-class and middle-aged," and who "generally took great pains to project an image of ladylike dignity, dressing for protest actions in knee-length skirts, hats, pearls and, in some cases, white gloves."[88] The disturbance was a result of the police limiting the number of protestors who could picket in front of the White House. Even though the group knew of this limitation ahead of time and had petitioned to have the order rescinded, they were unsuccessful in their plea. The remainder of the group were kept behind a fence in a holding area but many of those women grew angry and knocked down the fence in order to join the demonstration. At that point, the police intervened with violence and the women fought back. As Andrea Estepa characterizes the aftermath, "Anyone who had followed WSP's history to that point could not help but be shocked by the news.... That they could have participated in what was variously described as a 'fracas,' 'clash,' and 'wild melee' threatened to undermine the image of respectability that they had carefully constructed over the previous six years."[89] The representational tables had been turned on these women just as it had on the suffragettes who were brought into conflict with the police on such occasions as Black Friday or the day of the delivery of the petition directly to the King at Buckingham Palace. A peaceful demonstration that embodied Agulhon's fixed allegorical representation of mature womanhood, devolved into a radical event, sliding then from fixed allegory to live allegory and a figure of vehemence. Further, this sequence of events echoes Stallybrass and White's argument, discussed earlier, that "what is socially peripheral is so frequently symbolically central."

Despite the damage control that WSP founder Dagmar Wilson attempted with these words, "We didn't plan to go out and fight policemen. They fought us,"[90] it was no longer possible in 1967 America to remain thus fixed. They stand in line not only with our British suffragettes but also with the silent protests of Alice Paul and the National Woman's Party of the first wave who picketed the White House for suffrage and who suffered similarly poor treatment at the hands of the police. While Agulhon differentiates between the fixed and live allegory of imagery of political representation, the reality was that the two often existed side by side once such women appeared in public. The reality was much messier than the careful representation would allow. But not much had changed even more recently. For example, we have seen the injustice of this brute state force during the Occupy Movement, when silent, peaceable protestors at UC, Davis, were subjected to pepper spray by a police officer, totally unprovoked, just one of many examples of police brutality against what would appear fixed presentations of a political stance.

The Ultimate Break

The ultimate break with the calm image of the orderly suffrage marchers who were convinced that their vast numbers and their own dignity would convince lawmakers of their worthiness for citizenship came about with the 1912 window-smashing campaign. It halted not only any public sympathy for the movement, but also resulted in the NUWSS and other groups distancing themselves from the WSPU; while the WSPU numbers began to dwindle in direct proportion to their increased violence, the numbers in the NUWSS swelled.[91] The WSPU members used toffee hammers and stones wrapped in stockings to smash windows in London's major shopping district in the West End as a protest about not being seen as potential "makers of meaning." As the *Illustrated London News* report announced in "Glass Smashing for Votes! Suffragettes as Window-Smashers" (fig. 87) they were moving outside of their own personal space by swinging their hammers and doing physical damage symbolically to the patriarchy through the destruction of emblems of male power such as the department store front. In this moment, they created the shift to women protesters who dismiss feminine comportment in order to voice their cause, a language which the NOW marchers echo (fig. 39 in Chapter Two).

The window-smashing illustration demonstrates physically, just as does the NOW photograph, the women's desire for change in a threatening way, one not evident in the *From Prison to Citizenship* procession (fig. 38 in Chapter Two). Both groups are transgressive in their bodily presence and in their refusal of feminine body language. Their physical presence in public space creates a talking back to Bentham's Panoptoconic eye, discussed in the introduction as the eye that has framed this entire dialogue, and also a defiance of it, in their corporeal refusal of proper feminine etiquette.

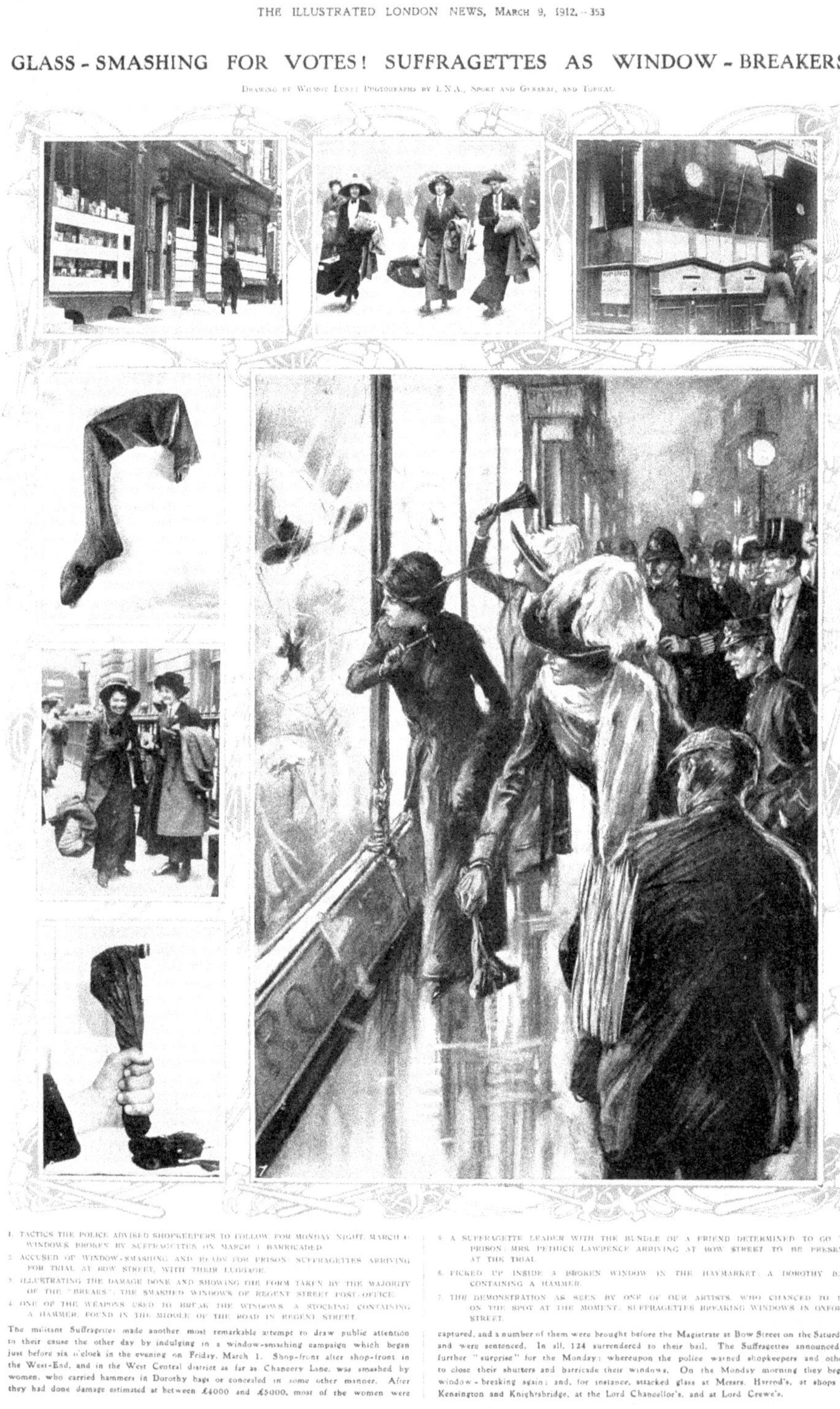

THE ILLUSTRATED LONDON NEWS, MARCH 9, 1912.—353

GLASS-SMASHING FOR VOTES! SUFFRAGETTES AS WINDOW-BREAKERS.

DRAWING BY WILMOT LUNT; PHOTOGRAPHS BY L.N.A., SPORT AND GENERAL, AND TOPICAL.

1. TACTICS THE POLICE ADVISED SHOPKEEPERS TO FOLLOW FOR MONDAY NIGHT, MARCH 4: WINDOWS BROKEN BY SUFFRAGETTES ON MARCH 1 BARRICADED.

2. ACCUSED OF WINDOW-SMASHING AND READY FOR PRISON: SUFFRAGETTES ARRIVING FOR TRIAL AT BOW STREET, WITH THEIR LUGGAGE.

3. ILLUSTRATING THE DAMAGE DONE AND SHOWING THE FORM TAKEN BY THE MAJORITY OF THE "BREAKS": THE SMASHED WINDOWS OF REGENT STREET POST-OFFICE.

4. ONE OF THE WEAPONS USED TO BREAK THE WINDOWS: A STOCKING CONTAINING A HAMMER, FOUND IN THE MIDDLE OF THE ROAD IN REGENT STREET.

5. A SUFFRAGETTE LEADER WITH THE BUNDLE OF A FRIEND DETERMINED TO GO TO PRISON: MRS. PETHICK LAWRENCE ARRIVING AT BOW STREET TO BE PRESENT AT THE TRIAL.

6. PICKED UP INSIDE A BROKEN WINDOW IN THE HAYMARKET: A DOROTHY BAG CONTAINING A HAMMER.

7. THE DEMONSTRATION AS SEEN BY ONE OF OUR ARTISTS, WHO CHANCED TO BE ON THE SPOT AT THE MOMENT: SUFFRAGETTES BREAKING WINDOWS IN OXFORD STREET.

The militant Suffragettes made another most remarkable attempt to draw public attention to their cause the other day by indulging in a window-smashing campaign which began just before six o'clock in the evening on Friday, March 1. Shop-front after shop-front in the West-End, and in the West Central district as far as Chancery Lane, was smashed by women, who carried hammers in Dorothy bags or concealed in some other manner. After they had done damage estimated at between £4000 and £5000, most of the women were captured, and a number of them were brought before the Magistrate at Bow Street on the Saturday and were sentenced. In all, 124 surrendered to their bail. The Suffragettes announced a further "surprise" for the Monday; whereupon the police warned shopkeepers and others to close their shutters and barricade their windows. On the Monday morning they began window-breaking again; and, for instance, attacked glass at Messrs. Harrod's, at shops in Kensington and Knightsbridge, at the Lord Chancellor's, and at Lord Crewe's.

Figure 87. "Glass-Smashing for Votes! Suffragettes as Window-Breakers," *Illustrated London News*, 9 March 1912. Museum of London, 2001.69/79.

What they faced was a desire for political representation which gave rise to and made use of another desire: A body politic; a public, collective body, that is reflective of the first desire to belong to a group of citizens. Hence, in looking again at the window-smashing illustration alongside the NOW photograph, it is apparent that both groups of women are protesting not only for basic rights of equality but also for a banishment of the system of Mulvey's "looked-at-ness," discussed in the introduction, that presumes to keep such women in a limited space for male delectation, a system that is itself responsible for women's oppression. Hence, they are fighting on two fronts: first, to dismiss the patriarchal system of women's objectification for male scopophilic satisfaction in order to be on equal footing with men; second, they are not in a liminal space but rather in the public realm, fighting for their own space within it that will no longer diminish them in relation to patriarchy's desires. They play across this knowledge in both images, the WSPU women slyly pulling small toffee hammers from their purses to do the damage, using the accoutrements of femininity to fight back. More telling, the illustration highlights the fact that they put stones inside dark stockings with which to smash the windows, a symbolic gesture toward the critique of suffrage women as miserable, unloved "blue stockings" who, through education, wore away their femininity. Similarly, the NOW women, many of whom are holding onto their purses as they march, defy such symbols of femininity in their own outward body language.

Despite the divide that this 1912 event caused with other suffrage groups, for many in the public arena, the militant suffragette became *the* image of the suffrage movement. As if in answer to the smashing of the Black Friday *Daily Mirror* negative (fig. 86), women of the WSPU who undertook this strategic window-breaking campaign brought together the various sites of danger of the West End. Aggressive body language came into being with this event. We see a concerted shift in body language that reflects significant and escalating anger on the part of the suffragettes about the lack of progress in the cause. With the smashing of shop windows, traditional cultural assumptions about women's bodily possibilities, like the windows themselves, became shattered and fragmented. This hammer creates a bond with the 20th-century raised fist within feminist protest in its quest for social justice. The strike of the hammer created the ultimate break. Imagine witnessing some one-hundred-and-fifty suffragettes breaking shop and office windows in the Strand, Cockspur Street, Downing Street, Whitehall, Piccadilly, Bond Street and Oxford Circus. Some two-hundred-and-seventy premises were damaged and over two-hundred- and-twenty suffragettes were arrested.[92]

To have been involved in this event was seen as a badge of honor, like going to prison. In fact, the suffrage women created commemorative hammers to be worn as jewelry for those involved in the campaign. In *Votes for Women* the WSPU defended their decision to pursue this new policy:

> Deeds not Words is the motto of this movement, and we are going to prove our love and gratitude to our comrades by continuing the use of the stone as an argument in the further protests that we have to make.... Does not the breaking of glass produce more effect upon the Government?[93]

Hence, bodily force became a political tactic, Emmeline Pankhurst having argued that they should follow the example of the men workers in Manchester who, as a result of rioting, won concessions for themselves and got results.

In response to the outcry over this new tactic, Christabel Pankhurst wrote: "The message of the broken pane is that women are determined that the lives of their sisters shall no longer be broken and that in future those who have to obey the law shall have a voice in saying what that law shall be. Repression cannot break the spirit of liberty." With this event, she envisions women breaking free of that pane, the woman at the window now willing to do battle, a notion made profoundly evident as a battle cry in her closing words: "The time has come when in the interests of the community, a just and reasonable demand must be satisfied and peace secured by the granting of votes for women."[94]

One telling and apparently incongruous image in this regard shows a group of women smiling broadly and somewhat mischievously while they jointly hold up a smashed window. The photo includes Miss Jolly, Miss Joachim, Mrs. Clark, Mrs. Corbett, Mrs. Archdale and Miss Adela Pankhurst, the latter being the youngest daughter of Emmeline Pankhurst (fig. 88). The photograph is displayed in an elegant matt that carries the studio name Martin Studio, Dundee, which shows that it, like the commemorative jewelry, stands as a celebration, here marked by a special studio event.

These women exhibit neither a resemblance to the harridans and hysterical women of the *Daily Mirror*'s 1914 article; nor to *The Times* stereotyping of them as "out with their hammers and their bags full of stones because of dreary, empty lives and high-strung, over-excitable natures."[95] They are, on the contrary, brave soldiers in the fight for freedom using whatever means they can to gain justice. While they manifest no resemblance to the female grotesque, their actions move them beyond the normal boundaries. This moment when the suffrage women created the shift showed their true cognizance of this double-edged dilemma, one which reverberates with the second-wavers of the NOW image.

But in her response to the West End window-smashing event, Garrett Fawcett stated that such violent actions would not help the cause.[96] The WSPU did not heed her warning, however; in fact, they upped the violence by starting a campaign of arson, to their own detriment. As Christine A. Anderson explains:

When the group's militancy turned violent, the press's criticism of the WSPU intensified. The campaign of window-breaking and arson not only went against principles of nonviolence, but also against any established notion of femininity. In the end, it turned public support and even some militants themselves away from the WSPU and confused others about the suffrage campaign's image and even the necessity of women's suffrage.[97]

Further, the WSPU began a campaign of attacking works of art that resulted in police surveillance of key WSPU members. In the "Art Under Attack" exhibit at Tate Britain (2013) a whole room was dedicated to these suffrage events: Mary Richardson slashed Velazquez's *Rokeby*

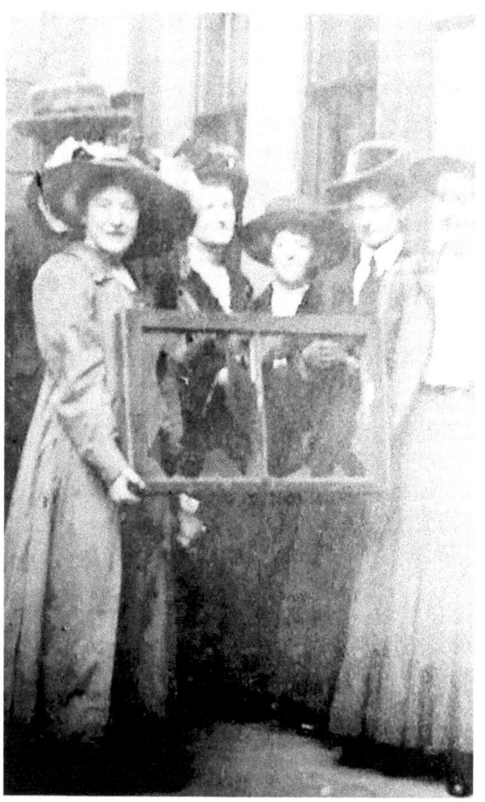

Figure 88. *Women of the WSPU Holding up a Smashed Window*, c. 1912. **Museum of London, 53.140/145.**

Venus at the National Gallery in London[98]; Ivy Bonn destroyed an engraving of a nude woman by Bartolozzi at the Doré Gallery in London, leaving a note that said: "To stop this you must give us justice. We have been too ladylike in the past. Now we are going to fight…."; while Lilian Forester and Evelyn Manesta were arrested in Manchester for attacking Sir Edward Burne-Jones *Sibylla Delphica*. For them, attacking idealized images of women while real women suffered was a symbolic act. At Forest and Manesta's trial, for example, they claimed they were political offenders and were fighting for women's freedom and equal rights.

These events suggest they were following Crawford's framing of suffrage activities under masculine acts of terrorism discussed earlier. The Home Office certainly treated them as terrorists when, in 1913, they commissioned undercover photography of militant suffragettes. Most of the photographs were taken without the women's knowledge while they were exercising in prison yards. The Home Office supplied museum and gallery wardens with such photographs so that they could identify militants who might wish to re-enter these spaces and continue their attacks. Women in prison were literally being subjected to the Panopticonic eye.

The more the WSPU acted out in masculine ways, the less credibility they leant to the cause. Many suffrage scholars admit that these activities damaged the campaign irretrievably. But what it tells us about women's body language in public spaces is multifold: for one, these women sought to bring attention to the glorified female nude and its lack of relationship to their reality, one in which women's bodies were being tortured daily, Richardson's protest specifically geared at the mistreatment of Emmeline Pankhurst who was languishing in prison at the time of Richardson's attack on the *Venus*. For another, women were using male tactics of protest to gain their rights but, while this approach had worked for men, it did not work for women. A patriarchal culture could not stomach women who were not behaving in a feminine fashion; Bonn's statement is telling in this regard when she claimed, "In the past we have been too ladylike," meaning towing the line has produced no results. But to step out of that role was to invoke and take on the mantle of the female grotesque from which all of the suffrage women had fought so hard to distance themselves.

Yet these actions are not that far away from the first public demonstration of the second wave in America: the protest at the 1968 Miss America Pageant in Atlantic City that Robin Morgan orchestrated with her group, New York Radical Women (NYRW). Just as with the harridan and hysterical imagery against which the first wavers

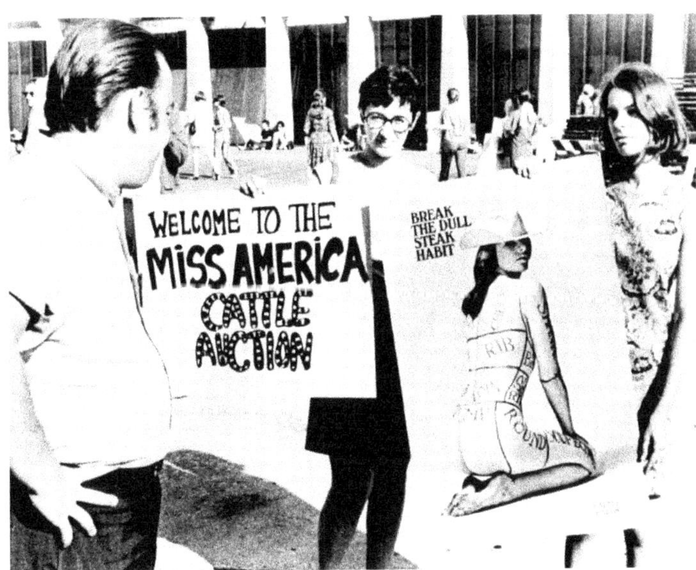

Figure 89. *Cattle Auction, Women's Liberation Movement Protest at 1968 Miss America Pageant.* **Source: AP Images.**

fought, as well as the symbolism of the WSPU's attacks on imagery of nude women, so too these women balked at being "treated like a cross between Pussy Galore and Hazel." Just as with our first wavers, Susan J. Douglas argues, such "media stereotypes were strangling their goals and ambitions. So they singled out the dominant media imagery of women for attack."[99] The event took on a guerrilla theatre flair (fig.89) when the protesters produced a poster of a nude woman sectioned as a side of beef to mark the way the pageant objectified women, reducing them to no more than pieces of meat. The other handmade poster announced: "Welcome to the Miss America Cattle Auction." To drive this point home, they crowned a live sheep as "Miss America." What is most telling in this image is that both women are dressed well and respectably while the man observing their posters with judgmental hands on hips needs a girdle, the very restraints these women were throwing in the nearby *Freedom Trash Can* (fig. 90) along with other such "titillating symbols of female containment"[100] as their bras, and other items of restrictive clothing designed to rein in or augment women's bodies to meet societal expectations. The protesters were not criticizing women for being in the pageant but rather the patriarchal culture that produced such events and sought to control the appearance of women and award them for their conformity to a very narrow and highly sexualized concept of femininity.

In the NYRW subsequent pamphlet about the event, "Why Miss World?" they attest that theirs was the first militant confrontation with the law by feminists since Christabel Pankhurst and Annie Kenney spoke up at the 1905 Free Trade Hall election meeting; similarly, the mass demonstrations of the 1970s were, at the time, hailed as direct descendants of the suffrage processions. Further, the British journal *Spare Rib* took pains to cover this feminist history.[101] But what is perhaps most telling is that, in their pamphlet, one of the women echoes Kitty Marion, loud and clear, and also specifically ties their experience to that of the suffrage women prisoners:

I felt like the event symbolized my daily exploitation. I saw the contestants being judged by men, and I know what it feels like to be judged and scrutinized every day when I am just walking down the street.

She then relays part of the history of British beauty pageants, stating that in order to guard the contestants' reputations, chaperones "rule the girls like Holloway prison warders."[102] While the event brought many more women to the movement, it largely backfired with the media. Margaret Marshment explains:

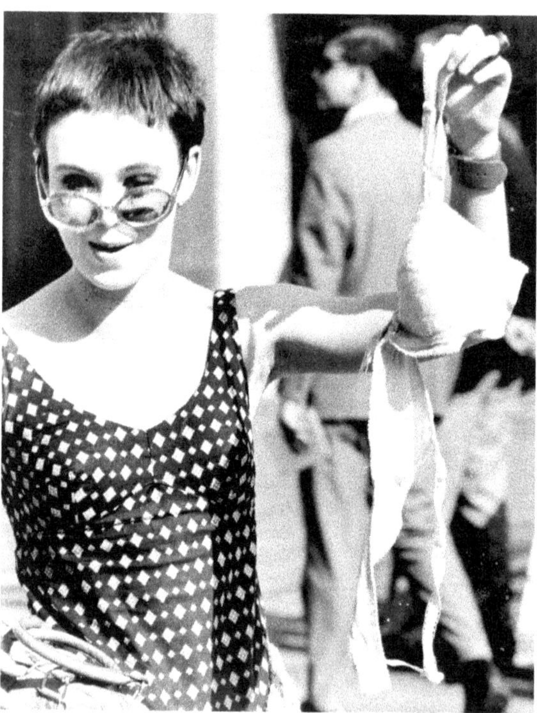

Figure 90. *Freedom Trash Can, Women's Liberation Protest at 1968 Miss America Pageant.* **Source: AP Images.**

This protest was itself the subject of media representation (… mainly by men). The mythic "bra-burning" became for years the dominant cultural signifier of feminism: feminists were "unfeminine," ugly and frustrated, and therefore envious of the truly feminine bathing "beauties." This event encapsulated many of the dilemmas confronted by women in representing their own interests in the context of male domination of institutions and codes of representation. It was directed at male control of definitions of women, but was interpreted as an attack on other women defining themselves; it aimed to attack ideological stereotypes of female beauty, and was interpreted as an attack on beauty itself; it was a protest against the trivialization of women, and was itself trivialized; it aimed to challenge the power of men to define women and was itself defined by men.[103]

The institutional markers that operated to put 1960s feminists in their place were the same ones that functioned to discredit the WSPU militants. These 1960s activities and protests were dismissed as the ravings of unhappy, unfeminine women who could not catch a husband and hence had become hysterical. They belong to the same female grotesque framework as the WSPU women. Further, in the media reporting of the Miss America Pageant, Douglas observes

[h]ow feminists used, or failed to use, their faces and their bodies, and the extent to which their faces and bodies conformed to those in a Max Factor ad, [and] were central features of the coverage. If these girls were out on the streets and swinging bras around, why, they must be closet exhibitionists, narcissists, or simply hysterical....

As Douglas further argues, in an observation as true of the first wave as it is of the second:

The media also paid inordinate attention to the way feminists violated physical and social boundaries, and suggested that, by doing so, they were making spectacles of themselves.... Feminists were cast as unfeminine, unappealing women who were denouncing the importance of the male gaze, yet who secretly coveted that gaze for themselves by protesting in public.[104]

In an article by a female journalist, Charlotte Curtis, she largely missed the point that protestors refused to talk to male journalists and insisted on having women on the beat, this itself a protest against women journalists being relegated to happy family and light stories. As Douglas characterizes her article in the *Times*, "Miss America contestants, beautiful, docile, and compliant, who eagerly sought out and competed for the male gaze, deserved their day in the public spotlight; the demonstrators, unruly, rebellious, excessive, who attacked the institutionalization of male voyeurism, did not."[105]

　　Douglas's analysis would seem at odds with Stanley and Morley's assessment of the first versus later waves of feminists in which they suggest a discontinuity:

It is important to keep in mind that these events took place in Edwardian England. Much of what happened then seems so familiar in feminist terms—like the existence of a feminist community and the development of personal politics—that it's tempting to conclude that these women were just like us, thought like us, and faced similar circumstances with the same kinds of practical, intellectual and other resources—but in fancy dress. Tempting but mistaken. Perhaps *they* were like feminists now; but the social world they lived in was incalculably more rigid, more deeply uncomprehending, more hostile to anything that smacked of an "uppity woman."

　　This was so because they were the trailblazers the authors argue; they "acted in a kind of void in which they had to create 'woman' as a human being."[106] Yet, Douglas would seem to suggest that the category "woman" was still synonymous with the grotesque Other of carnival who had to be brought back in line by patriarchy. The tabula rasa argument is a good one and is probably why we see such a complex mixture of imagery that tries to represent such feminists, but both examples here would seem to suggest that no one can truly grasp her. While she is part of a collective, she is also an individual. She is much more complex than the angel/whore dichotomy (or, more relevant here, the hysteric/activist dichotomy/spectrum) than any of these constructions would allow. She still sits outside the boundaries because she bumps up against the patriarchy, then as now.

Space

The streets and pavements of London received suffrage advertising; Trafalgar Square was the site of incitement to march on Parliament; the West End shopping districts became a target; the main thoroughfares of London were blocked to make way for a series of suffrage processions; and then the cultural heritage, the galleries and museums, became the final target. The suffrage women had certainly entered and made themselves known in the public spaces of London, but to what effect?

Martha A. Ackelsberg discusses the claiming of public space as a moment of transgression that is necessary for any kind of political action, one in which "[t]he transformation of popular forms of opposition into meaningful movements for social change is facilitated when those involved in protest make a concerted effort to reappropriate and transform their physical and social space."[107] Stallybrass and White would characterize such political spaces as not only sites of transgression but also of invention:

> Discursive space is never completely independent of social place and the formation of new kinds of speech can be traced through the emergence of new public sites of discourse and the transformation of old ones.... An utterance is legitimated or disregarded according to its place of production and so, in large part, the history of political struggle has been the history of the attempts made to control significant sites of assembly and spaces of discourse.[108]

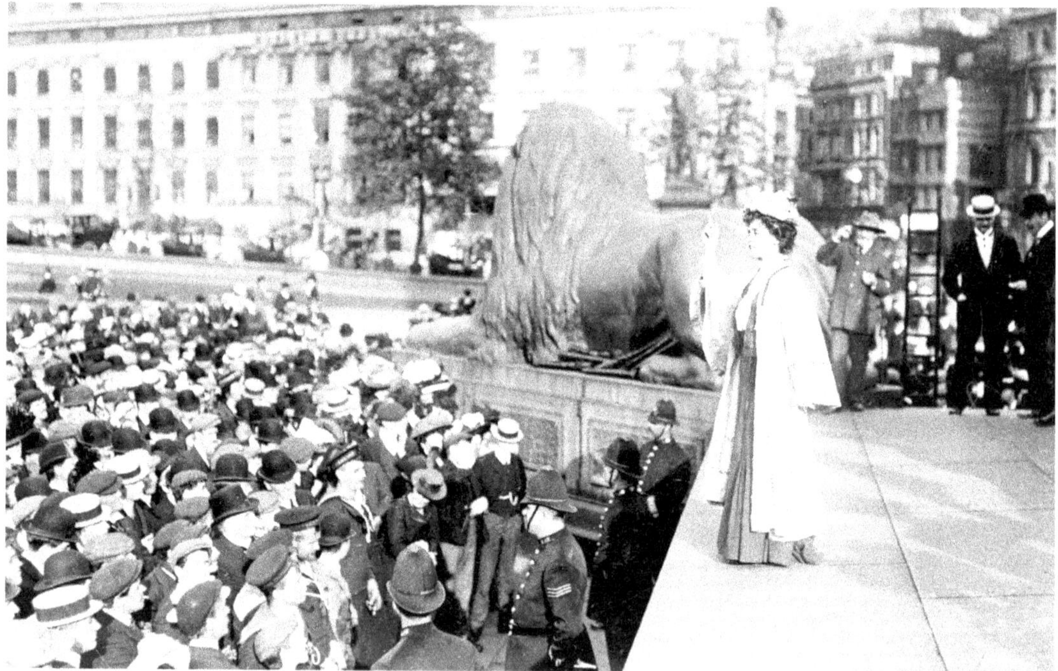

Figure 91. *Emmeline Pankhurst Speaking at Trafalgar Square,* **February 1908. Museum of London, 50/82/1282.**

As Erika Rappaport observes, Trafalgar Square was one such site; it was continuously the epicenter of political activity in 19th- and 20th-century England: "Precisely because the West End represented such a concentration of power, prestige and wealth it had tremendous symbolic importance as a site of political demonstrations and struggle."[109] And intermingling there were different groups of women who were often mistaken for each other. The dangers of the West End were often about the possibility of erroneous identity: "[S]hoppers were often characterized as disorderly figures, as prostitutes, drunkards, debtors and other viragoes. The proximity of feminist, commercial, and illicit spaces in London's West End meant that there had long been a confusion about how to identify shoppers, prostitutes, and feminist activists." But, instead of fearing that danger, particularly in their window-smashing campaign, Rappaport argues, the suffragettes embraced that ambiguity and used it to their advantage.[110]

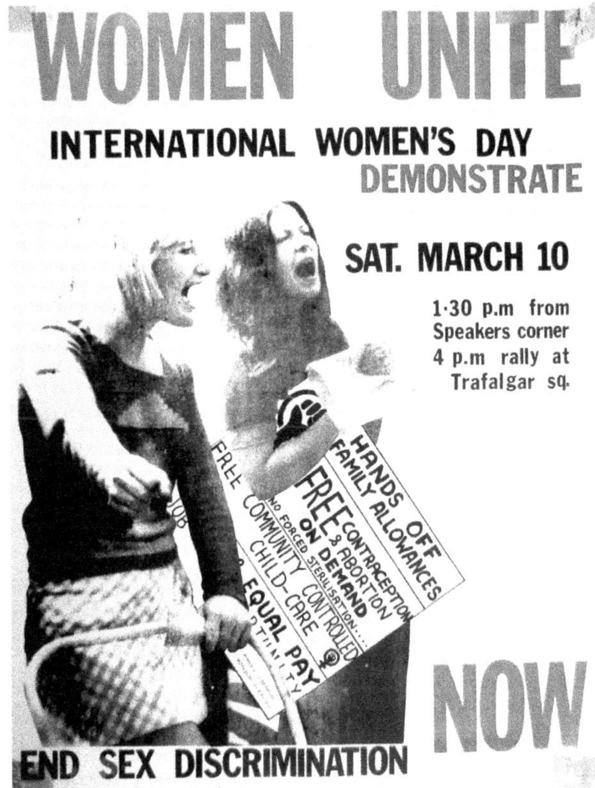

Figure 92. *Women Unite Now!* c. 1975. Feminist Library Poster Collection, Bishopsgate Institute, London.

When suffrage women stepped up on the wide base of Nelson's Column among Sir Edwin Landseer's lions, how many people held a collective memory of Bloody Sunday? Here is a Emmeline Pankhurst speaking at Trafalgar Square in February 1908 (fig. 91). Her body is at the site of political agitation and is itself politically agitated. She has moved from private arena to public stage, the most symbolic public stage, one which witnessed riots, incensed crowds, and large rallies created to march to Parliament to demand women's rights. It was, and remains, a place of engagement, battle, and airing of grievances, a public space in which one came to be heard. It was a space for change. Her raised arm will soon turn into a raised fist, symbol of solidarity, of rage, of battle and hope for triumph and victory.

In this photograph, a woman's body is on center stage, both physically and emblematically. As Walkowitz has observed earlier, such bodies "lacked autonomy: they were bearers of meaning rather than makers of meaning." Her body signified what a man could, or could not, do to her. But it is Emmeline Pankhurst's outward gestures that now separate her from the peaceful suffrage marchers; she both steps into the man's space and challenges it with her body language.

Looking again at the 1970s protesters, like their first wave ancestors, they changed their body language; discarding the outer signs of femininity was both symbolic and real;

they stepped outside of those feminine confines to create a lived allegory of protest, their body language literally embodying their desire for social justice, taking over the language of the presumed hysteric to exhibit their anger, their desire to represent. This ideology is reflected in feminist posters of the 1970s in which Emmeline Pankhurst's gesture that calls all to join her in collective action, is repeated, as in *Women Unite Now!* (fig. 92). Angry faces and clenched fists pervade in actuality and in symbol, women march together with picket signs, voices at high pitch.[111]

Conclusions

The more aggressive postures of the second-, third- and fourth-wave feminists have their roots in the window-smashing campaign of the militant suffragettes, along with the necessary bodily language they used to fight back during police skirmishes. Further, the bodily gestures of the platform in terms of driving home a persuasive argument meant women had to move outside of their former system of bodily restraint.

Within the poster collection of the Feminist Library, all dating from the period of the second wave, we find women in large numbers leading marches; women with fists raised; women singing, linking arms; women chanting; women smiling and marching with picket signs. The body language these women use talks back to imagery of the cloistered, isolated sole woman at the window *and* embraces methods of resistance to violence to women's bodies. Symbolically, then, such bodily expression reflects a now-open window: If the 19th-century woman were bored and soon became frenzied once she crossed the threshold, now she had a support system of women out in force, an arrangement that both Friedan and de Beauvoir called for in their writings. The suffrage activists propelled us beyond the windowsill through their own shift, taking over the hysterical, outwardly focused body, which had, until then, been used against them. Embracing their own agency, they forever admonished the woman at the window waiting wearily for change. Our roots lie with them. What they started with a hammer has since become a determined fist raised high.[112]

Chapter Notes

Preface

1. Margaret Fuller, *Women in the Nineteenth Century* (New York: Greeley and McElrath, 1845).

2. Simone de Beauvoir, *The Second Sex*, trans. H. M. Parshley (London: Jonathan Cape, 1953), was the first English version. On Friedan see Kirsten Fermaglich and Lisa M. Fine, eds., *Betty Friedan: The Feminine Mystique* (New York: W.W. Norton, 2013).

3. Lisa Tickner, *The Spectacle of Women: Imagery of the Suffrage Campaign 1907–14* (London: Chatto and Windus, 1987/Chicago: University of Chicago, 1988).

4. Deborah Cherry, *Beyond the Frame: Feminism and Visual Culture 1850–1900* (London: Routledge, 2000), 1.

Introduction

1. Jill Ker Conway, *When Memory Speaks: The Art of Autobiography* (New York: Vintage, 1998).

2. Ann Snitow, Christine Stanell and Sharon Thompson, eds., *Powers of Desire: The Politics of Sexuality* (New York: Monthly Review, 1983).

3. *SIGNS: Journal of Women in Culture and Society*, paper call for special issue on pleasure and danger; retrieved WMST-L@LISTSERV.UMD.EDU 11/03/14.

4. Barbara Green, *Spectacular Confessions* (New York: St. Martin's Press, 1997), 3.

5. Lisa Tickner, *The Spectacle of Women: Imagery of the Suffrage Campaign 1907–14* (London: Chatto and Windus, 1987/Chicago: University of Chicago Press, 1988), 55–148, gives a detailed chronological history of the processions and pilgrimages.

6. Martha Vicinus, "Male Space and Women's Bodies," *Independent Women: Work and Community for Single Women, 1850–1920* (Chicago: University of Chicago Press, 1985), 266.

7. Green, *Spectacular Confessions*, 5.

8. Vicinus, "Male Space and Women's Bodies," 279–80.

9. Green, *Spectacular Confessions*, 12–15, discusses some personal accounts of the prison experience; her book explores four spaces of the suffrage struggle: the street, the prison, the sickroom, and the archive (23). See also the Suffragette Fellowship Collection (Museum of London; University of Colorado–Boulder).

10. This discussion of visual culture is loosely based on Colleen Denney, *Women, Portraiture and the Crisis of Identity: My Lady Scandalous Reconsidered* (Farnham, Surrey/Burlington, VT: Ashgate, 2009), 8–10. I am working on a separate study of one of the prominent photographers of suffrage women, Lena Connell. For a discreet study of the intertextuality of suffrage cartoon imagery and high art portraits of suffrage women, including paintings and photographs, see Chapters 2 and 3 in the above which address Millicent Garrett Fawcett and Emilia, Lady Dilke.

11. See, for example, the Maud Arncliffe-Sennett Collection, British Library.

12. John Berger, *Ways of Seeing* (London: Penguin/ BBC, 1971); and on Mulvey see n. 34 below.

13. See Paula Hays Harper "Votes for Women? A Graphic Episode in the Battle of the Sexes," in *Art and Architecture in the Service of Politics,* eds., Henry A. Millon and Linda Nochlin (Cambridge: MIT Press, 1978), on some of the exchange of imagery between the U.S. and England. The New Zealand imagery is partly housed in the Alexander Turnbull Library, National Archives, Wellington, New Zealand; and the Auckland Public Library, New Zealand. See Colleen Denney, "Wyoming Women's Suffrage as an Example to the World: A Comparative Look at the Pioneer Spirit of Wyoming and New Zealand," *Wyoming Annals* 18 (Autumn 2016): 2–23. Some key cartoons are also published in Patricia Grimshaw, *Women's Suffrage in New Zealand* (Wellington, NZ: Auckland University Press/Oxford University Press, 1972).

14. Deborah Cherry, *Beyond the Frame: Feminism and Visual Culture 1850–1900* (London: Routledge, 2000), 2.

15. Since the late 1980s many feminist scholars have focused on looking at what the women themselves have to say in order to construct their history from the ground up, instead of looking at it from our end. See, for example, the excellent work of Liz Stanley and Ann Morley, *The Life and Death of Emily Wilding Davison* (London: Women's Press, 1989); Johanna Alberti, *Beyond Suffrage: Feminists in War and Peace* (New York: St. Martin's Press, 1989); Philippa Levine, *Feminist Lives in Victorian Britain* (Oxford: Blackwell, 1990); and Sandra Stanley Holton, "From Anti-Slavery to Suffrage Militancy: The Bright Circle, Elizabeth Cady Stanton and the British Women's Movement," in *Suffrage and Beyond: International Feminist Perspectives,* eds., Caroline Daley and Melanie Nolan (New York: New York University Press, 1994), 213–233.

16. On visual production see Tickner, *Spectacle of Women*, 11–52.

17. Paula Hays Harper, "Votes for Women?" 150.

18. *Ibid.*

19. *Ibid.*

20. See, for example, Norma Broude and Mary Garrard, eds., *The Power of Feminist Art* (New York: Abrams, 1994).

21. Originally published in September 1909, it was reprinted as a pamphlet by the Artists Suffrage League; reprinted in Tickner, "Appendix 5. Banners & Banner-making," in *Spectacle of Women*, 262–64.

22. Hays Harper, "Votes for Women?"150.

23. Quoted in Mary Louise Roberts, "Subversive Copy: Feminist Journalism in Fin-de- Siècle France," in *Making the News*, eds., Dean de la Motte and Jeannene M. Przyblyski (Amherst: University of Massachusetts Press, 308), 325.

24. Hays Harper, "Votes for Women?"156.

25. Tickner, *The Spectacle of Women*.

26. Hays Harper, "Votes for Women?"157.

27. Michel Foucault, *Discipline and Punish: The Birth of the Prison*, trans., Alan Sheridan (New York: Random House, 1991), 200–201.

28. *Ibid.*, 202.

29. Mikhail Bakhtin, *Rabelais and his World*, trans. Helene Iswolsky (Cambridge: MIT Press, 1968), 6–23.

30. Barbara Babcock, "Introduction," in *The Reversible World*, ed., Barbara Babcock (Ithaca: Cornell University Press, 1978), 14.

31. Peter Stallybrass and Allon White, *The Politics and Poetics of Transgression* (Ithaca: Cornell University Press, 1986), 9.

32. *Ibid.*, 19.

33. Rachel Bowlby, "Walking Women and Writing: Virginia Woolf as *Flâneuse*," in *New Feminist Discourses: Critical Essays on Theories and Texts*, ed., Isobel Armstrong (New York: Routledge, 1992), 26–47, responds to Janet Wolff's initial essay which introduced the concept of the *flâneuse* into Baudelarian discourse, in "The Invisible *Flâneuse*: Women and the Literature of Modernity," *Feminine Sentences: Essays on Women and Culture* (Berkeley: University of California Press, 1990), 34–50. For more recent challenges to this view, see the essays in *The Invisible Flâneuse? Gender, Public Space, and Visual Culture in Nineteenth-Century Paris*, eds., Aruna d'Souza and Tom McDonough (Manchester: Manchester University Press, 2006), especially Woolff's revisitation of her own text in "Gender and the Haunting of Cities (or, the Retirement of the Flâneur)," 18–31. I discuss this phenomenon in terms of women professionals' entrance into British public space in *Women, Portraiture and the Crisis of Identity in Victorian England*. See Virginia Woolf, *Mrs. Dalloway* (London: Vintage Classics, 1925).

34. Green, *Spectacular Confessions*, 189 n. 26; and Laura Mulvey, "Visual Pleasure and Narrative Cinema"14–26; and idem, "Afterthoughts on 'Visual Pleasure and Narrative Cinema' Inspired by King Vidor's *Duel in the Sun*," 29–38, in *Visual and Other Pleasures* (Bloomington: Indiana University Press, 1989).

35. Laura M. Nym Mayhall, *The Militant Suffrage Movement: Citizenship and Resistance in Britain, 1860–1930* (Oxford: Oxford University Press, 2003), offers a different slant in reference to surveillance by focusing on the WSPU suffragettes' embodiment of femininity. In her study, she spends a section on their representations of Joan of Arc and Florence Nightingale in order to discuss the literary rhetoric of these two women within the broadening of our understanding of "staging public spectacles of womanliness." Mayhall makes a claim for WSPU women as seeking "to represent themselves politically, not merely visually." She views the two forms of representation as "distinct processes" rather than conflated ones. By contrast, I argue that the two processes *are* intertwined; the media that the suffrage women engage to convey their message mirrors their meta-purpose: one desire (political representation) gives rise and makes use of another desire (a body politic; a public, collective body, reflective of the first desire to belong to a group of citizens). Mayhall misses the point that these demonstrations themselves had many goals, only one of which related to their visual presence, itself acting as a counterargument, as Tickner in *Spectacle of Women* points out, to the visual stereotypes of militant women the press was employing to make light of their desire for political representation.

36. Judith Newton, "History as Usual? Feminism and the 'New Historicism,'" *Cultural Critique* 9 (1988): 93; and Christine Stansell, "Response," *International Labor and Working Class History* 31 (Spring 1987): 28; discussed in Joan W. Scott, "Experience," in *Feminists Theorize the Political*, eds., Judith Butler and Joan W. Scott (New York: Routledge, 1992), 31.

37. See Sandra Stanley Holton, *Feminism and Democracy: Women's Suffrage and Reform Politics in Britain 1900–1918* (Cambridge: Cambridge University Press, 1986), 4, who explains that many militants were also constitutionalists and vice versa, and many constitutionalists learned tactics from the militants when they took to the streets. See also Maroula Joannou and June Purvis, "Introduction: The Writing of the Women's Suffrage Movement," in *The Women's Suffrage Movement: New Feminist Perspectives*, eds., Maroula Joannou and June Purvis (Manchester: Manchester University Press, 1998), 6; and David Rubinstein, *A Different World for Women* Columbus: Ohio University Press, 1991), on Garrett Fawcett's efforts to maintain good partnership with the WSPU. Sandra Stanley Holton brings to light the seeds of the WSPU militancy through a long exchange with American suffragists. She explains that it was not a "rupture" with previous tactics but instead a continuity with tactics used as far back as the abolition movement, for example ("From Anti-Slavery to Suffrage Militancy). Hilda Kean discusses their acknowledgment of a long British history of radicalism in "Public History and Popular Memory: Issues in the Commemoration of the British Militant Suffrage Campaign," *Women's History Review* 14 (2005): 581–602; while Brian Harrison, "The Act of Militancy: Violence and the Suffragettes, 1904–1914," *Peaceable Kingdom: Stability and Change in Modern Britain* (Oxford: Oxford University Press, 1982), 26–81, discusses their debt to Irish radicalism. In turn, the National American Woman Suffrage Association welcomed the use of some of the ASL's posters for its own campaign and the Suffrage Atelier was probably involved in the California campaign in 1911. See Tickner, *Spectacle of Women*, Appendix 7, "The Impact of British Propaganda Techniques in America," 266–67, where she also outlines the crossovers of feminists such as Alice Paul who was a member of the WSPU and imprisoned and forcibly fed in England, before she returned to America in 1912, taking with her knowledge of British suffrage spectacles that influenced her pageants first in Washington D.C., then in New York and Baltimore. She was supported by the Reverend Anna Shaw who had marched with Garrett Fawcett in the NUWSS 13 June 1908 procession.

38. For an analysis of their various feminist proposals, see Les Garner, *Stepping Stones to Women's Liberty* (London: Heinemann, 1984), 28–43.

39. Garner characterizes the split this way in *Stepping Stones*, 44–60, based on a close reading of the official papers of the WSPU and of the correspondence between Christabel and her sister Sylvia at the time.

40. See Elizabeth Crawford, *The Women's Suffrage Movement: A Reference Guide 1860–1928* (London: Routledge, 1999), in which she contextualizes all of the suffrage groups.

41. Jane Marcus, "The Asylum of Antaeus: Women, War and Madness—Is There a Feminist Fetishism?" in *The New Historicism*, ed., H. Aram Veeser (New York: Routledge, 1989), 132–51; and Garner, *Stepping Stones*, 49.

42. Jill Liddington and Jill Norris, *One Hand Tied Behind Us: The Rise of the Women's Suffrage Movement* (London: Virago Press, 1984).

43. Hays Harper, "Votes for Women?"156.

44. Tickner, *Spectacle of Women,* 174–182.

45. *Ibid.,* 100.

46. *Ibid.,* 102.

47. *Sunday Times,* 8 Feb. 1914, 9; quoted in Harrison, "Act of Militancy," 60.

48. This is the argument that Stanley and Morley, *Davison,* put forward, particularly in terms of the actions of the WSPU member, Emily Wilding Davison, which ended in her death on Derby Day, but it also applies to suffrage workers in general.

49. Tickner, *Spectacle of Women,* ix.

50. Stanley and Morley, *Davison,* 84–85, disband this mythology through a careful analysis of the feminist papers and identification of the various groups to which women belonged. The suffrage women were not by any means exclusive and there was considerable overlap of Labour and suffrage sentiments.

51. Garner, *Stepping Stones,* 24; 45.

52. *Ibid.,* 16.

53. Vicinus, *Independent Women,* 359 n. 1; and see Leslie Parker Hume, *The National Union of Women's Suffrage Societies, 1897–1914* (New York: Garland, 1982), Chapter 5.

54. On this time period, see, for example, Angela K. Smith, *Suffrage Discourse in Britain during the First World War* (Aldershot, England/Burlington, VT: Ashgate, 2005); and Jo Vellacott, *Pacifists, Patriots and the Vote* (Houndsmill, England: Palgrave Macmillan, 2007).

55. Holton, *Feminism and Democracy.*

56. The traditional argument for giving women the vote in 1918 was in way of gratitude for their war efforts. However, Holton, *Feminism and Democracy,* has been able to show that, indeed, it was the persistence of the NUWSS and their repositioning within the political parties that brought about even this limited vote. But as to why it was limited in 1918, the argument, generally, was because of the devastating losses during World War I; with fewer men returning from the war, there was a fear that women would outnumber men at the voting polls. Further, politicians were not certain that women were as capable as men of exercising their citizenship. But only women over the age of 30 who were occupiers or the wives of occupiers were enfranchised in 1918, along with occupiers of property of £5 or more annual value, and university graduates. Martin Pugh characterizes the situation by saying, "It is scarcely surprising that hopes and fears should have been high. The reforms of 1918 had created 8.47 million female voters or, approximately 40 per cent of the total. The equal suffrage legislation introduced by Stanley Baldwin in 1928 abolished the 30-year age limit and gave women a simple residential qualification, thereby boosting women votes to 15.19 million or 52.7 per cent of the entire population" ("The Impact of Women's Enfranchisement in Britain," in *Suffrage and Beyond,* 313).

57. David Mitchell, *Queen Christabel: A Biography of Christabel Pankhurst* (London: MacDonald and Jane, 1977), 258.

58. See Andrew Rosen, *Rise Up Women! The Militant Campaign of the Women's Social and Political Union, 1903–1914* (London: Routledge and Kegan Paul, 1974), 266–69.

59. Garner, *Stepping Stones,* 102–103.

60. Susan Kingsley Kent, *Sex and Suffrage in Great Britain, 1860–1914* (Princeton: Princeton University Press, 1987), argues that the vote was not an end in itself but rather a means to an end, that of redirecting society to be inclusive of women's rights and issues particularly related to their protection.

61. Winifred Holtby, *Women and a Changing Civilisation* (London: John Lane, 1934), 52–53.

62. Millicent Garrett Fawcett, "What the Vote has Done," *National Union for the Society of Equal Citizenship* (October 1927); discussed in Garner, *Stepping Stones,* 110.

63. Garner, *Stepping Stones,* 110–111.

64. Cicely Hamilton, Foreword to 1948 reprint for The Suffragette Fellowship, in *A Pageant of Great Women* 1909; quoted in Tickner, *Spectacle of Women,* xii.

Chapter One

1. Linda Nochlin, *Realism* (London: Penguin, 1971).

2. *The Complete Writings of Alfred de Musset* (New York: Edwin C. Hill, 1905), 1–39.

3. Charles Rice, *The Emergence of the Interior: Architecture, Modernity, Domesticity* (London: Routledge, 2007), 2–3.

4. Despite the more rapid progression towards women's rights in England, Karen Offen explains in *European Feminisms, 1700–1950* (Stanford: Stanford University Press, 2000), 19: "The first self-proclaimed *feminist* was the French women's suffrage advocate Hubertine Auclert, who beginning in 1882 used the term in her periodical, *La Citoyenne* (The Woman Citizen), to describe herself and her associates. The words gained currency following discussion in the French press of the first 'feminist' congress in Paris, sponsored in May 1892 by Eugénie Pontonié-Pierre and her colleagues from the women's group *Solidarité,* who shortly thereafter juxtaposed *feminisme* with *masculinisme,* by which they meant something analogous to what we now call male chauvinism. By 1894–95 the terms 'feminism' and 'feminist' had crossed the Channel to Great Britain, and before 1900 they were appearing in Belgian, French, Spanish, Italian, German, Greek, and Russian publications" And, yet, by the end of the nineteenth century feminists in other countries found France "woefully backward" with regards to advances in women's rights (Frederic Lees, "The Progress of Woman in France," *The Humanitarian* (February 1901): 88).

5. Offen, *European Feminisms,* 79–83.

6. Reprint, Charleston, SC: BiblioLife, 2008.

7. Henrik Ibsen, *The Doll's House,* trans. William C. Archer (London: T. Fisher Unwin, 1889).

8. Offen, *European Feminisms,* 170.

9. John Ruskin, *Sesame and Lilies* (London: Smith, Elder & Co., 1862); Adolphe Monod, *Woman: Her Mission in Life,* trans. and ed. Constance R. Walker (Vestavia, AL: Solid Ground Christian Books, 2011).

10. Beverly Gordon examines the phenomenon of women's confluence with the interior in 19th-century

America in terms of the advance of the interior design and dress movements, arguing that there is a "conflationary metaphoric relationship" in terms of "the arrangement and outfitting of both the interior and the body" ("Woman's Domestic Body: The Conceptual Conflation of Women and Interiors," *Winterthur Portfolio* 31 (Winter 1996): 28).

11. See Lorenz Eitner, "The Open Window and the Storm-Tossed Boat: An Essay in the Iconography of Romanticism," *Art Bulletin* 37 (Dec. 1955): 281–90. See also Sabine Rewald, *Rooms with a View: The Open Window in the 19th Century* (New York: Metropolitan Museum of Art/New Haven: Yale University Press, 2011).

12. Elaine Shefer, "The Woman at the Window in Victorian Art and Christina Rossetti as the Subject of Millais's *Mariana*," *Journal of Pre-Raphaelite Studies* 4 (Nov. 1983): 14–24; and idem, "The Woman at the Window," in *Birds, Cages and Women in Victorian and Pre-Raphaelite Art* (New York: Peter Lang, 1990), 127–150.

13. Shefer, "The Woman at the Window in Victorian Art."

14. Pamela Gerrish Nunn, "Trouble in Paradise," in *Problem Pictures: Women and Men in Victorian Painting* (Aldershot, England: Scolar Press; Brookfield, VT: Ashgate, 1995), 49–71. One particularly pointed example is Jane Bowkett's 1860s painting, *Preparing for Dinner*, which shows a young wife laying the table while minding the children and looking out the window at the evening train which carries her husband home. This image reflects the idea of the window as a sign of waiting, the woman's existence dependent on the implied male presence, as Nunn argues. On the French situation see Deborah Silverman, "*Amazone, Femme Nouvelle,* and the Threat to the Bourgeois Family," *Art Nouveau in Fin-de-Siécle France: Politics, Psychology and Style* (Berkeley: University of California Press, 1989), 63–74.

15. Mark Wigley, "Untitled: The Housing of Gender," in *Sexuality and Space: Volume 1: Princeton Papers on Architecture*, eds., Beatriz Colomina and Jennifer Bloomer (New York: Princeton Architectural Press, 1992), 337.

16. Susan Sidlauskas, "Psyche and Sympathy: Staging Interiority in the Early Modern Home," in *Not at Home: The Suppression of Domesticity in Modern Art and Architecture*, ed., Christopher Reed (London: Thames and Hudson, 1996): 65, 80.

17. Kathryn Brown, *Women Readers in French Painting 1870–1890: A Space for the Imagination* (Farnham, Surrey; Burlington, VT: Ashgate, 2012), xv.

18. Geneviève Fraisse, "A Philosophical History of Sexual Difference," in *A History of Women in the West. Volume IV: Emerging Feminism from Revolution to World War*, eds., Geneviève Fraisse and Michelle Perrot (Cambridge: Harvard University Press/London: Belknap Press, 1993), 49.

19. See Sidlauskas, "Psyche and Sympathy," 65.

20. Griselda Pollock wrote one of the definitive studies of women Impressionist painters in which she began this kind of analysis of the spaces women could inhabit in the nineteenth century. Her goal was to show how limited the women painters were in terms of their access to the public spaces of Paris which, in turn, affected the subjects they could paint. While they did interior scenes, their paintings were more often of congenial family groupings or portraits of family and friends over tea or at the seaside. She does, however, discuss some "barrier" imagery, in which women are kept from the outside world through visual frames of fences and balconies. I will address some of that imagery here

(Griselda Pollock, "Modernity and the Spaces of Femininity," in *The Expanding Discourse: Feminism and Art History*, eds., Norma Broude and Mary Garrard (New York: HarperCollins, 1992), 244–67). More recently, scholars have begun to expand on her observations, addressing ways that women may, in fact, be seen in the public space. See Sidsel Maria Søndergaard, "Women in Impressionism: An Introduction," in *Women in Impressionism: From Mythical Feminine to Modern Woman*, ed., Sidsel Maria Søndergaard (Milan, Italy: SKIRA, 2006), 11–97.

21. See Søndergaard, "Women in Impressionism," 94 n. 27, where she discusses the construction of woman in the etiquette books versus the woman's real experience in French culture. That does not negate the fact that if an artist represented her alone in public, or if she were traversing the city alone, she would be considered suspect and of doubtful reputation.

22. In a study of the Boston school of male artists at the turn of the twentieth century, Bernice Kramer Leader argues that they were either "unable or unwilling to face the complex realities of the Boston woman's expanded sphere of influence" and hence these Bostonians "portrayed her as a beautiful dreamer instead of an energetic reformer, and thus turned the real Boston lady into an idealized work of art" ("Antifeminism in the Paintings of the Boston School," *Arts Magazine* 56 (Jan.-March 1982): 112–119). Hence, the imagery does not show women as in any way agitated or discontent as I am suggesting here of the British works/situation.

23. In recent literature, we also see a challenge to men only in public spheres. See, for example, Temma Balducci, Heather Belknap Jensen and Pamela J. Warner, eds., *Interior Portraiture and Masculine Identity in France, 1789–1914* (Farnham, Surrey/Burlington, VT: Ashgate, 2011), particularly Pamela J. Warner, "The Competing Dialectics of the *Cabinet de Travail*: Masculinity at the Threshold," 159–176, in which she discusses the necessity of a man having a private study for intellectual contemplation within the home environment that revealed the sitter's class standing and secured his masculine, active purpose within society.

24. Lynn Nead, "The Magdalen in Modern Times: The Mythology of the Fallen Woman in Pre- Raphaelite Painting," *Oxford Art Journal* 7 (1984): 26. On revisions to the separate sphere ideology, see for example, Amanda Vickery, "Golden Age to Separate Spheres? A Review of the Categories and Chronology of English Women's History," *The Historical Journal* 36 (June 1993): 383–414.

25. Nead, "Magdalen," 27–28.

26. Harriet Martineau, *Edinburgh Review* (1859): 294; quoted in Donald E. Hall, "From Margin to Center: Agency and Authority in the Novels of Wilkie Collins," *Fixing Patriarchy: Feminism and Mid-Victorian Male Novelists* (New York: New York University Press, 1996), 151.

27. Hall, "From Margin to Center," 155, and n. 2, 219.

28. *Ibid.,* 151.

29. Pierre Bourdieu, *Outline of a Theory of Practice* (Cambridge: Cambridge University Press, 1977); discussed in Daphne Spain, *Gendered Spaces* (Chapel Hill: University of North Carolina Press, 1992), 7.

30. See Deborah Cherry, *Beyond the Frame: Feminism and Visual Culture, Britain 1850–1900* (London: Routledge, 2000), 39–47; Susan Casteras, "The Necessity of a Name," in *Gender and Discourse in Victorian Art and Literature*, eds., Anthony H. Harrison and Beverley Taylor (DeKalb: Northern Illinois University Press, 1992),

207–32; and Colleen Denney, *Women, Portraiture and the Crisis of Identity in Victorian England: My Lady Scandalous Reconsidered* (Burlington, VT/ Farnham, Surrey: Ashgate, 2009), 22–24.

31. Cherry, *Beyond the Frame*, 47.

32. Patricia Hollis, comp., *Women in Public, 1850–1900: Documents of the Victorian Women's Movement* (London: G. Allen & Unwin, 1979), 53. Martha Vicinus, "Appendix A: Gross Population Figures," *Independent Women: Work and Community for Single Women 1850–1920* (Chicago: University of Chicago Press, 1985), 294, lists for England and Wales, in 1861, the number of unmarried women between 20–44 as 1,312,050 and for women 45 and over, 225,183, making up roughly one fifth of the entire female population, the remaining 5,517,152 being married or widowed. By 1901 those figures had increased to 2,520,184 and 3,962,042, respectively, those numbers of single women increasing to roughly one fourth of the overall female population. Vicinus' study demonstrates, however, the ways that women created their own communities in nineteenth-century England, either out of necessity or desire, or both. The populations she considers include Sisterhoods, the nursing profession, women's colleges, boarding schools, settlement houses, and the suffrage movement. Her study thus indicates that women were not idol, contradicting the reality upon which these interior scenes seem to insist.

33. Lynda Nead, "Seduction, Prostitution, Suicide: *On the Brink* by Alfred Elmore," *Art History* 5 (Sept. 1982): 309–22.

34. Linda Nochlin, "Women, Art, and Power," in *Visual Theory: Painting and Interpretation*, eds. Norman Bryson et al. (New York: HarperCollins, 1991), 13–46.

35. Offen, *European Feminisms*, 87.

36. Hall, "From Margin to Center," 151–152.

37. "A Fear for the Future," *Fraser's* (1859), 215–216; quoted in Hall, "From Margin to Center," 152.

38. Hall, "From Margin to Center," 153.

39. Jill Ker Conway, "Feminist Plots," *Exploring the Art of Autobiography: When Memory Speaks* (New York: Vintage Books, 1999), 87.

40. Carolyn Heilbrun, *Writing a Woman's Life* (New York: Dutton, 1988); cited in Elaine Showalter, *Inventing Herself: Claiming a Female Intellectual Heritage* (New York: Scribner, 2001), 19.

41. See Gay L. Gullickson, *Unruly Women of Paris: Images of the Commune* (Ithaca: Cornell University Press, 1996).

42. Annie Kenney, *Memories of a Militant* (London: Edward Arnold, 1924), 110.

43. Andreas Huyssen, *After the Great Divide: Modernism, Mass Culture, Postmodernism* (Bloomington: Indiana University Press, 1986), 47 and 52; Gullickson, *Unruly Women of Paris*; and Susanna Barrows, *Distorting Mirrors: Visions of the Crowd in Late Nineteenth-Century France* (New Haven: Yale University Press, 1981); the latter discussed in Mary Louise Roberts, "Subversive Copy: Feminist Journalism in Fin-de-Siècle France," in *Making the News*, eds., Dean de la Motte and Jeannene M. Przyblyski (Amherst: University of Massachusetts Press, 1999), 302–350.

44. Emmeline Pethick-Lawrence, *My Part in a Changing World* (1938. Reprint, Westport, CT: Hyperion Press, 1976), 188.

45. Peter Toohey, *Boredom: A Lively History* (New Haven: Yale University Press, 2011), 176.

46. George Gissing, *The Odd Women*, with introduction by Elaine Showalter (London: Penguin, 1994).

47. Claire Goldberg Moses, *French Feminism in the 19th Century* (Albany: State University of New York Press, 1984), ix, x, 151, 209.

48. See Offen, *European Feminisms*, 108–143; and John Stuart Mill, *The Subjection of Women*, with an introduction by Patricia M. Ulbrich (New York: Barnes and Noble, 2005).

49. Offen, *European Feminisms*, 122. See also idem, "Women, Citizenship, and Suffrage With a French Twist," in *Suffrage and Beyond: International Feminist Perspectives*, eds., Caroline Daley and Melanie Nolan (New York: New York University Press, 1994), 151–170.

50. See Charles Sowerwine, "Revising the Sexual Contract: Women's Citizenship and Republicanism in France, 1789–1944," 19–42; and Karen Offen, "Is the 'Woman Question' Really the 'Man Problem'?," 43–62, in *Confronting Modernity in Fin-de-Siècle France: Bodies, Minds and Gender*, eds., Christopher E. Forth and Elinor Accampo (Houndmills: Palgrave Macmillan/New York: St. Martin's Press, 2010).

51. Goldberg Moses, *French Feminism*, ix, x, 151, 209.

52. Sowerwine, "Revising the Sexual Contract,"19–42.

53. See, for example, Jules Simon, *L'Ouvrière* (Paris, 1861).

54. Patrick Kay Bidelman, *Pariahs Stand Up! The Founding of the Liberal Feminist Movement in France, 1858–1889* (Westport, CT: Greenwood Press, 1982), xvi.

55. Silverman, "*Amazone*," 63.

56. Bidelman, *Pariahs Stand Up!*, 12–13.

57. Mary Louise Roberts, *Discursive Acts: The New Woman in Fin-de-Siècle France* (Chicago: University of Chicago Press, 2002), 3, 22–24. See also Denney, *Women, Portraiture and the Crisis of Identity*, chapters three, four and five, on how British feminists fought to dissociate themselves from what the culture perceived as the loose morals often associated with the New Woman.

58. See Jennifer Waelti-Walters, *Feminist Novelists of the Belle Epoque: Love as a Lifestyle* (Bloomington: Indiana University Press, 1990), 178.

59. Silverman, "*Amazone*," 65. See also Bidelman, *Pariahs Stand Up!*, xvii–xix.

60. Silverman, "*Amazone*," 65.

61. Adeline Daumard, *Les Bourgeois de Paris au XIXe siècle* (Paris: Flammarion, 1970), 196–197; quoted in Goldberg Moses, *French Feminism*, 36.

62. Stephen Hause with Anne R. Kenney, *Women's Suffrage and Social Politics in the French Third Republic* (Princeton: Princeton University Press, 1984), 19–20.

63. Jennifer Waelti-Walters and Stephen C. Hause, "Introduction," in *Feminisms of the Belle Epoque*, eds., Jennifer Waelti-Walter and Stephen C. Hause (Lincoln: University of Nebraska Press, 1994), 2.

64. Silverman, "*Amazone*," 66.

65. Offen, "Women, Citizenship, and Suffrage with a French Twist," 163. In England there was also a desire to keep up the birthrate, particularly in the years leading up to the First World War; however, as early as the 1860s the eugenicists, such as Francis Galton in *Hereditary Genius* (1869), argued for early marriage for those who represented "the strong strains" and later marriage for "the weak strains" in an effort to fortify the population. But this concern seems less about fear over declining birthrates than it does about healthier offspring who would be ready to fight. See Brian Harrison, "Women's Health and the Women's Movement," in *Biology, Medicine and Society 1840–1940*, ed. Charles Webster (Cam-

bridge: Cambridge University Press, 1981), 61, where he discusses the philosophy of the early twentieth century birth control campaign not to prevent pregnancy, but rather to help women have healthier babies. Nonetheless, Harrison points out that in the early twentieth century there was a fear that "the entry of women into political life would undermine Britain's international standing by causing the birth-rate to fall. Acutely conscious of military threats from abroad, anti-feminists wanted citizenship linked to fighting capacity." Gerry Holloway, "'Let the Women Be Alive!' The Construction of the Married Working Woman in the Industrial Women's Movement, 1890–1914," in *Radical Femininity: Women's Self-Representation in the Public Sphere*, ed., Eileen Janes Yeo (Manchester: Manchester University Press/New York: St. Martin's Press, 1998), 172–195, also discusses eugenics pressures on women who either chose to work out of a desire for independence or had to work out of financial necessity. These desires worked against the eugenics' stance of elevating women to the status of mothers of the race. The irony here is that suffrage women argued, in part, that women needed the vote because they were mothers. As Eileen Janes Yeo explains, the argument went, "[I]f men's claim to citizenship on the basis of their humanity rather than property rested on their willingness to die for their country, then women made an equally important contribution by creating the lives that might be sacrificed" ("Some Paradoxes of Empowerment," 15).

66. Offen, *European Feminisms*, 236.

67. Silverman, *"Amazone,"* 74, argues specifically for the identification of the French woman with the home in terms of the goals of the Art Nouveau movement in France: "[T]he craft officials united in forging a specifically cultural route to contain and interiorize women. By celebrating women as queens and artists of the interior, they developed a powerful antidote to the *femme nouvelle* [new woman], who threatened to relinquish her role as decorative object and decorative artist."

68. Ruth Iskin, "Was There a New Woman in Impressionist Painting?" in *Women in Impressionism,* 202.

69. See Erna Olafson Hellerstein, Leslie Parker Hume, and Karen M. Offen, eds., *Victorian Women: A Documentary Account of Women's Lives in Nineteenth-Century England, France, and the United States* (Stanford: Stanford University Press, 1981), 273, 282.

70. Badelman, *Pariahs Stand Up!,* 10.

71. See Søndergaard, "Women in Impressionism," 97 n. 118.

72. On the 1860s struggles of French women which, nonetheless, called for equal treatment of women in the home as did the later agitation of French feminists in the 1890s, see Tamar Garb, *Sisters of the Brush: Women's Artistic Culture in Late Nineteenth-Century Paris* (New Haven: Yale University Press, 1994). Women were granted suffrage in Finland in 1906, Norway in 1913, Denmark and Iceland in 1915, in the USSR and Netherlands in 1917, in Austria, Czechoslovakia, Poland, and Sweden in 1918, Germany and Luxembourg in 1919, Spain in 1931, Belgium, Italy, Romania and Yugoslavia in 1946, Switzerland in 1971, and Lichtenstein in 1984. Characterizing the situation in France, Karen Offen writes, "The ultimate irony of the French campaign was that woman suffrage was finally achieved in April 1944— not by the magnanimity of the legislators of the parliamentary republic but by decree of General Charles de Gaulle. The political enfranchisement of women was accorded as a 'paternal gift' of the Liberation and the new provisional government" ("Women, Citizenship and Suffrage with a French Twist," 161; where she cites Michelle Perot with coining the phrase "paternal gift.")

73. On this debate in France see Roberts, *Discursive Acts*.

74. Kathleen Adler and Tamar Garb, "Introduction," in *Berthe Morisot: The Correspondence with her family and her friends Manet, Puvis de Chavannes, Degas, Monet, Renoir and Mallarmé*, ed., Denis Rouart; trans. Betty W. Hubbard (New York: Moyer Bell/ London: Camden Press, 1987), 9.

75. Toohey, *Boredom,* 185.

76. See Iskin, "Was There a New Woman in Impressionist Painting?" 189–223.

77. *Ibid.,* 202–204.

78. Lee Holcombe, *Victorian Ladies at Work: Middle-Class Working Women in England and Wales, 1850–1914* (Hamden, CT: Archon Books, 1973), 107.

79. See Søndergaard, "Women in Impressionism"; and the following essays in the same volume, *Women in Impressionism*: John House, "Women Out of Doors," 156–87; and Iskin, "Was There a New Woman in Impressionist Painting?" 189–223.

80. See Bidelman, *Pariahs Stand Up!,* 20–21.

81. Søndergaaard, "Women in Impressionism," 56, 58.

82. See Joan Wallach Scott, "'L'Ouvriere! Mot impie, sordide. . .' Women workers in the discourse of political economy, 1849–1860," *Gender and the Politics of History* (New York: Columbia University Press, 1988), 139–62; and James F. McMillan, *France and Women 1789–1914* (London: Routledge, 2000), 112–114.

83. Angelique Richardson and Chris Willis, *The New Woman in Fact and Fiction: Fin de Siècle Feminisms*, foreword by Lynn Pykett (Houndmills: Palgrave, Macmillian, 2001), 28.

84. John House, "New Material on Monet and Pissarro in London in 1870–71," *Burlington Magazine* 120 (October 1978): 638–641. According to House's examination of the catalogues of the exhibit, Monet showed the painting in London at the International Exhibition at South Kensington in 1871 under its English title, *Repose* (no. 1273). Mary Mathews Gedo, *Monet and His Muse: Camille Monet in the Artist's Life* (Chicago: University of Chicago Press, 2010), 108–109, explains that Camille is dressed in mourning for Monet's father, Adolphe, although she may also be dressed so due to the death of their dear friend, the painter Frédéric Bazille, but it is unclear when they became aware of his death. Comparing the painting with Albrecht Dürer's 1514 print *Melancholy*, she notes that the painting could also be called *Melancholy*, based on the similar attribute of the preoccupied figure holding a book. In the print, the angel's melancholia relates to his cognizance of the brief span of human life. Such a reading of this portrait of Camille does not preclude, but rather enhances a reading of it as an image of despair, of time running out but of an anguish over how to fill that time.

85. Petra ten-Doeschatte Chu, "The Lu(c)re of London: French Artists and Art Dealers in the British Capital, 1859–1914," in *Monet's London: Artists' Reflections on the Thames* (St. Petersburg, FL: Museum of Fine Arts/Ghent, Belgium: Shoeck, 2005), 50.

86. See Denys Sutton, *Nocturne: The Art of James McNeill Whistler* (London: Country Life, 1964), 40; and Elizabeth Broun, "Thoughts that Began with the Gods: The Content of Whistler's Art," *Arts Magazine* 62 (October 1987): 39; and Gary Tinterow and Henri Loyrette, *Origins of Impressionism* (New York: Metropolitan Museum of Art/Harry Abrams, 1995), 465–66.

87. Aileen Tsui, "The Phantasm of Aesthetic Autonomy in Whistler's Work: Titling *The White* Girl," *Art History* 29 (June 2006): 464–65.

88. See David Park Curry, *James McNeill Whistler: Uneasy Pieces* (Richmond: Virginia Museum of Fine Arts/New York: Quantuck Lane Press, 2004), 114 and 397 n. 2.

89. Similar situations appear elsewhere in nineteenth-century paintings; for example, the abundance of peasant imagery we find in the latter half of the century corresponds with the literal disappearance of the peasant working the fields, this figure as equally diminished by the Industrial Revolution as our bored leisured women. Robert L. Herbert has argued that the images are then nostalgic, picturing a lost world never to return since most workers were forced into an urban environment to find work, displaced by the machinery of the Revolution ("City vs. Country: The Rural Image in French Painting," *Artforum* 5 (Feb. 1970): 44–55).

90. The woman at the mirror as iconographic emblem has received considerable attention from art historians. See, for example, Anne Higonnet, *Berthe Morisot's Images of Women* (Cambridge: Harvard University Press, 1992). The woman reader represents another thread of this discourse on women in interiors, particularly in relation to concepts of boredom. See Spacks, *Boredom*, 1–30; and Kate Flint, *The Woman Reader 1837–1914* (Oxford: Clarendon Press, 1995), for literary analysis of the phenomenon; and Laure Adler and Stefan Bollmann, *Les femmes qui lisent sont dangereuses* (Paris: Flammarion, 2006); and Brown, *Women Readers*, for an art historical examination.

91. Park Curry, *James McNeill Whistler*, 88. See also Sidlauskas, "Psyche and Sympathy," 67, where she offers up Whistler's *Harmony* as an example of "disequilibrium."

92. On this debate see Tamar Garb, "Portraiture and the New Woman," in *The Body in Time: Figures of Femininity in late Nineteenth-Century France* (Seattle: Spencer Museum of Art in association with University of Washington Press, 2008), 39–78. As discussed in the introduction, the nineteenth-century French writer, Charles Baudelaire, laid the groundwork for this attitude that men beheld women while women offered themselves up as delectable visions. See Charles Baudelaire, *The Painter of Modern Life and other essays*, ed. and trans. Jonathan Mayne (London: Phaidon, 1964).

93. From "Exposition Universelle de 1867," in Théophile Thoré, *Les Salons de W. Bürger 1861–1868*, Vol. 2 (Paris 1870), 380; quoted in Søndergaard, "Women in Impressionism," 94 n. 30.

94. Liana F. Piehler suggests somewhat the same predicament for the women pictured in Margaret Carpenter's 1839 painting *The Sisters*, in which one of the sisters is fingering the pages of a book. Piehler says the space "implies an extension to the world beyond the small glimpse we receive through the open window. The open window—through its rectangular shape and hazy natural view—seems to operate as an extension of the book suggesting a link between these worlds" (*Spatial Dynamics and Female Development in Victorian Art* (New York: Peter Lane, 2003), 11–12).

95. This phenomenon appears across Europe and Scandinavia and hence suggests that the woman in the interior is an iconic image of a zeitgeist. The Danish artist, Vilhelm Hammershoi's works, in particular, are disturbingly chilling, such as his *Interior with a Lady*, 1901, or his *Resting*, 1901. This should not surprise us since many of the feminist plays came from the hands of his fellow Scandinavian Henrik Ibsen. *The Doll's House* (1879) and *Hedda Gabler* (1891) are both examples of women's struggles for selfhood and frustrations with the patriarchal system in a culture that left them with little recourse other than escape, through abandonment of home and hearth.

96. An adverse example that suggests a Beidermeir smugness rather than the angst of Astruc's woman, is Adolph Menzel's 1843 *Sleeping Seamstress by the Window*, an image of industry. Markedly, the window is open to the early spring day and she is asleep from exhaustion rather than ennui. Significantly the birdcage, that symbol of a woman's confinement, sits outside on the window sill suggesting that while the seamstress is still caught in the cage, she has purpose (reproduced in Rewald, *Rooms with a View*, 168).

97. Sidlauskas, *Body, Place, and Self*, 1.

98. Edmond and Jules de Goncourt, 18 November 1860, in *Journal: Mémoires de la vie littéraire*, ed. |R. Ricatte, vol. 1 (Paris, 1989), 835; quoted in Iskin, "Was There a New Woman in Impressionist Painting?" 202.

99. Rodolphe Rapetti, "Paris Seen from a Window," in *Gustave Caillebotte: Urban Impressionist*, eds., Anne Distel et al. (New York: Abbeville Press, 1995), 144–45.

100. On the issue of the use of formal devices to signify the confinement of women, see Pollock, "Modernity and the Spaces of Femininity."

101. Garb, "Portraiture and the New Woman," 44.

102. Jennifer Schuessler, "Our Boredom, Ourselves," *The New York Times Book Review* (January 24, 2010): 23; and Charles Dickens, *Bleak House* (London: Penguin, 2003).

103. Patricia Meyer Spacks, *Boredom: The Literary History of a State of Mind* (Chicago: University of Chicago Press, 1995), x.

104. Haskell Bernstein, "Boredom and the Ready-Made Life," *Social Research* 42 (1975): 515.

105. Spacks, *Boredom*, 191.

106. Sarah Stickney Ellis, *The Daughters of England* (London, 1842), 48.

107. Spacks, *Boredom*. Testimony to the obverse, a lack of boredom gave New Zealand colonial women great happiness; many Englishwomen went to New Zealand to marry and be helpmeets to colonial men who valued their labor, Raewyn Dalziel arguing that this domestic purpose attributed to the early passage of the vote for women in New Zealand in 1893 ("The Colonial Helpmeet: Women's Role and the Vote in Nineteenth-Century New Zealand," *New Zealand Journal of History* 11 (October 1977): 112–23); and, for an assessment of this study and other analyses of New Zealand women's suffrage, see Patricia Grimshaw, "Women's Suffrage in New Zealand Revisited: Writing From the Margins," in *Suffrage and Beyond*, 25–41.

108. Spacks, *Boredom*, 13.

109. Brown, *Women Readers*, 7. This phenomenon is not unique to the nineteenth century, however. Janice A. Radway, in her study of twentieth-century women's reading of romance novels, notes one of the chief objections within the household was that women were not available to perform their normal domestic tasks. Families often resented such escapism (*Reading the Romance* [Chapel Hill: University of North Carolina Press, 1984; reprint 1991]). See also Norbert Jonard, *L'Ennui dans la littérature Européenne* (Paris: Honoré Champion, 1998), 16–67.

110. Brown, *Women Readers*, argues this case more

generally for the motif of reading in nineteenth-century French painting, but I am arguing that it is applicable to *Madame Bovary* in particular.

111. Brown, *Women Readers*, 61.

112. Quoted in Moses, *French Feminism*, 36.

113. Brown, *Women Readers*, 12.

114. *Ibid.*, 17.

115. Spacks, *Boredom*; discussed in Sidlauskas, *Body, Place, and Self*, 143. Sidlauskas applies this analysis to a painting by Walter Sickert, called *Ennui*, c. 1914 (Tate Britain, London), which she determines reflects the artist's anxieties about the First World War and his own displacement.

116. Toohey, *Boredom*, 4–5.

117. Londey, cited in Toohey, *Boredom*, 4.

118. Quoted in Toohey, *Boredom*, 16.

119. See Toohey, *Boredom*, 150, who debates this view, citing Spacks, *Boredom*, in particular.

120. Tooley, *Boredom*, 29.

121. Spacks, *Boredom*, presents this shift as her argument for the rise of boredom in conjunction with the rise of modernity but Toohey is skeptical, partly because Spacks limits herself to boredom's manifestation in literature; he cites the necessity, for example, of entertainments in Ancient Roman culture, to appease an otherwise restless populous. However, he views the situation as more complex than that, stating that some cultures seem to be more prone to boredom than others but that the phenomenon is not confined to the modern period.

122. Toohey, *Boredom*, 77.

123. *Ibid.*, 36–37, employs this interpretation in his discussion of Mariana's dreariness, for example.

124. Toohey, *Boredom*, 47.

125. Quoted in Toohey, *Boredom*, 63.

126. See Piehler, *Spatial Dynamics*, 24–28 for an interpretation of Siddal's drawing along these lines. For interpretations of these images in terms of issues of a woman's awakened sexuality see Elizabeth Nelson, "Tennyson and the Ladies of Shalott" in *Ladies of Shalott: A Victorian Masterpiece and Its Contexts* (Providence: Bell Gallery/Brown University, 1985), 4–16. For a study that focuses on the Siddal drawing as a self-portrait of the artist, see Elaine Shefer, "Elizabeth Siddal's 'Lady of Shalott.'" *Woman's Art Journal* 9 (Spring-Summer 1988): 21–29.

127. Piehler, *Spatial Dynamics*, 15–16.

128. Hilde Heynen, *Negotiating Domesticity: Spatial Productions of Gender in Modern Architecture*, eds., Hilde Heynen and Gülsüm Bayder (London: Routledge, 2005), 1.

129. John Ruskin, *"Awakening Conscience,"* in *The Art Criticism of John Ruskin*, ed., Robert Herbert (New York: Anchor Books/Doubleday, 1964), 399.

130. See Nead, "Seduction," 309–322, where she argues that the woman's only choices are between virtue and vice.

131. On this historical shift, see Patricia Mainardi, *Husbands, Wives, and Lovers: Marriage and Its Discontents in Nineteenth-Century France* (New Haven: Yale University Press, 2003), 110, where she reproduces both states of the print.

132. Janet Wolff, "The Invisible *Flâneuse*: Women and the Literature of Modernity," *Feminine Sentences* (Berkeley: University of California Press, 1990), 34–49; reconsidered in idem, "Gender and the Haunting of Cities (or, the Retirement of the *Flâneur*)," in *The Invisible Flâneuse? Gender, Public Space, and Visual Culture in Nineteenth-Century Paris*, eds., Aruna d'Souza and Tom McDonough (Manchester: Manchester University Press, 2006), 18–31.

133. Aruna D'Souza and Tom McDonough, "Introduction," in *The Invisible Flâneuse*, 2.

134. Wolff, "Gender and the Haunting of Cities," 24–25.

135. Norma Broude and Mary Garrard, "Introduction," in *Reclaiming Female Agency: Feminist Art History after Postmodernism*, eds., Norma Broude and Mary Garrard (Berkeley: University of California Press, 2005), 22.

136. On Victorian's women's public roles in terms of craft artisanship, writing, and performing, see Patricia Zakreski, *Representing Female Artistic Labour, 1848–1890* (Burlington, VT: Ashgate, 2006).

137. Mary P. Ryan, *Women in Public: Between Ballots and Banners, 1825–1880* (Baltimore, MD: John Hopkins UP, 1990), 13.

138. Bidelman, *Pariahs Stand Up!*, 18.

139. Heynen, *Negotiating Domesticity*, 2. See also Reed, ed., *Not at Home*.

140. See Erika Rappaport, *Shopping for Pleasure: Women in the Making of London's West End* (Princeton: Princeton University Press, 2000), 122–126; where she cites Dorothy Constance Peel, *Life's Enchanted Cup: An Autobiography, 1872–1933* (London: John Lane and the Bodley Head, 1933), 105–6, who confesses that she was daily accosted by men while waiting for the omnibus. And, despite women's move into the public realm today, they still face such dangers on a daily basis. That this is so is reflected in the recent "Hollaback" activism in which women take charge of the public space by literally hollering back at their harassers. See also Judith R. Walkowitz, "Going Public: Shopping, Street Harassment, and Streetwalking in Late Victorian London," *Representations* 62 (Spring 1998): 1–30.

141. Hollis Clayson, "Threshold space: Parisian modernism betwixt and between 1869 to 1891," in *Impressionist Interiors*, ed. Janet McLean (Dublin, Ireland: National Gallery of Ireland, 2008), 15–29.

142. Griselda Pollock, *Mary Cassatt: Painter of Modern Women* (London: Thames and Hudson, 1998), 169.

143. *Ibid.*

144. *Ibid.*, 172. Linda Nochlin and Ruth E. Iskin make similar arguments in terms of issues of firmly establishing the bourgeois family as the central piece, although they do not discuss the class issue as Pollock does. See Nochlin, *Representing Women* (London: Thames and Hudson, 1999), 208; and Iskin, "Was There a New Woman in Impressionist Painting?" 201–202.

145. Heyne, *Negotiating Domesticity*, 2.

146. Kate Krueger Henderson, "Conveying Femininity: The New Woman and the Omnibus in Evelyn Sharp's 'In Dull Brown,'" 22nd Annual Interdisciplinary Nineteenth Century Studies Conference, University of Missouri–Kansas City, MO, April 2007.

147. Ana Pareja Vadillo, "Phenomena in Flux: The Aesthetics and Politics of Travelling in Modernity," in *Women's Experience of Modernity*, eds., Ann Ardis and Leslie W. Lewis (Baltimore: John Hopkins University Press, 2003), 212.

148. Henderson, "Conveying Femininity," 3.

149. *Ibid.*, 4.

150. Clayson, "Threshold Space," 27.

151. This short story and the young man's mistake reflect my earlier refutation of Iskin's argument that we can find the New Woman in representations of the shop girl. His assumption is also an insult to the shop girl who, while she might be hardworking and the subject of the public gaze, is not necessarily sexually available.

152. Henderson, "Conveying Femininity."

153. Camille Mauclair, "Les Femmes devant les peintres moderns," *La Nouvelle* Revue, 2d ser., I (1899): 212–213; quoted in Silverman, *"Amazone,"* 69.

154. Clayson, "Threshold Space," 17.

155. Higonnet, *Berthe Morisot's Images of Women*, 116.

156. Adler and Garb, "Introduction," 9–10.

157. *Ibid.,* 10.

158. 1869 letters to Edmé Pontillion; quoted in *Berthe Morisot: The Correspondence*, 34–35.

159. 1869 letter to Madame Morisot; quoted in *Berthe Morisot: The Correspondence*, 19.

160. 1869 letter to Edmé Pontillion; quoted in *Berthe Morisot: The Correspondence*, 33.

161. *Ibid.,* 36.

162. *Ibid.*

163. Clayson, "Threshold Space," 19, notes that Renoir's *Portrait of Rapha Maître*, 1871 (Private Collection) "marks allegorically the weight of the gulf between those hiding from the Commune and the April 1871 street fighting between the insurrectionary Communards and federal army troops."

164. Many French artists went to England or sent work there to take advantage of its freer art market. Edgar Degas did purposeful genre scenes which he hoped to sell in London, such as the controversial *L'Interieur (Interior)*, 1868 or 1869 (Philadelphia Museum of Art) which he called "my genre picture." Many scholars think he was influenced in this decision and in the treatment of this painting by his French friend, James Tissot, who lived in London from the early 1870s until 1882. See Chu, "The Lu(c)re of London," 40–54; and Tinterow and Loyrette, *Origins of Impressionism*, 375–76.

165. Distel et al., *Gustave Caillebotte: Urban Impressionist*, 66. While Clayson' "Threshold Space," 22, argues astutely that the Caillebotte painting shows "a vexed female response to her containment within a contemporary, shared urban apartment interior," she considers the woman's view of the woman neighbor opposite only in the context of a woman's nosiness about the "equivalent, inquisitive female prisoner of the interior directly across the way."

166. See Søndergaard, "Women in Impressionism," 61; Madame Romieu (Marie Sincère), *La Femme au XIXe siècle* (Paris, 1858); and Monseigneur Dupanloup, *La femme studieuse* (Paris, 1869).

167. Garb, "Portraiture and the New Woman," 66.

168. *Ibid.,* 61.

169. Søndergaard, "Women in Impressionism," 41.

170. Kenneth McConkey, "New English *Intimisme*: The Painting of the Edwardian Interior," in *The Edwardians: Secrets and Desires,* ed. Anne Gray (Canberra: National Gallery of Australia/Seattle: University of Washington Press, 2004).

171. *Ibid.,* 93.

172. Orpen creates an even more shocking update of the woman at the window in *An Eastern Gown*, 1906 (The Atkinson, Merseyside, England) in which a young model reclines on a couch in the same arrangement as Monet' Camille, with a significant difference: Her naked body, barely dressed in a transparent gown, is highlighted by the sun coming through the window. She partakes in her own beauty symbolized, as in so many *vanitas* images, by the mirror she holds up to reflect her scantily-clad body. In this painting, Orpen has taken the restless maiden or married woman, and turned her into a courtesan. While she may still be bored, she has crossed over the threshold of respectability.

173. Hause and Kenney, *Women's Suffrage and Social Politics*, 28, enumerate that the French started to make key advances in the period 1896–1901 through a series of women's congresses that increased dialogue and awareness; through the galvanizing feminist journal *La Fronde* which had a much wider circulation than previous feminist journals; and French feminists' efforts to create an international presence through the establishment of the *Conseil national des femmes françaises (CNFF)*. Yet, despite such efforts, French groups continued to be divided.

174. Quoted in Les Garner, *Stepping Stones to Women's Liberty: Feminist Ideas in the Women's Suffrage Movement 1900–1918* (London: Heinemann, 1984), 65.

175. Richard Harding Davis, "A General Election in England," *Harper's New Monthly Magazine* 87 (Sept. 1893): 503.

176. Olive Schreiner, *Women and Labor*, 7th ed. (New York: Frederick A. Stokes, 1911), 128.

177. Mary Jean Corbett, "Representation and Subjectivity in the Edwardian Suffrage Movement," in *Representing Femininity* (New York: Oxford University Press, 1992), 158.

178. Margaret Haig [Viscountess Rhondda], *This Way My World* (London: Macmillan, 1933), 132.

179. The Museum of London houses an example of a pin made in the shape of a toffee hammer which was the commemorative jewelry the suffragettes created for this window-smashing campaign. Women who were arrested (some 270 by some reports) were awarded this pendant. For an analysis of this campaign, see Rappaport, "The Politics of Plate Glass," *Shopping for Pleasure*, 215–22. See also Walkowitz, "Going Public."

180. Rappaport, "Politics of Plate Glass," 220.

181. *Ibid.*

182. Edmond de Goncourt, "Preface," in Edmond and Jules de Goncourt, *La Maison d'un artiste*, 1880; discussed in Pamela Todd, *The Impressionists at Home* (London: Thames and Hudson, 2005), 44.

183. Vicinus, "Male Space and Women's Bodies," 265–66.

184. *Punch* also published an article in which Asquith explained his turnabout. See Diane Atkinson, *Funny Girls: Cartooning for Equality* (London: Penguin, 1997), 19, where she comments: "Asquith had 'missed the bus' politically on several occasions before the outbreak of the First World War in 1914, and he is drawn as an elderly man who is struggling (he was sixty-five years old, and had another eleven years to live). He needs the help of this strong, young, forgiving suffragette-ish figure. The women's suffrage movement had rallied round and encouraged women to fight the war on the 'home front.'"

185. "Female Labor Force Participation Trends in the Twentieth Century," in *Betty Friedan: The Feminine Mystique: A Norton Critical Edition*, eds., Kirsten Fermaglich and Lisa M. Fine (New York: Norton, 2013), 361.

186. Eva Moskowitz, "'It's Good to Blow Your Top': Women's Magazines and a Discourse of Discontent, 1945–1965," *Journal of Women's History* 8 (Fall 1996): reproduced in Fermaglich and Fine, *Betty Friedan: The Feminine Mystique*, 483–484.

187. Many feminist scholars today, and many feminists historically, criticized Friedan's NOW institution for its exclusion of all but middle-class, straight white women. See, for example, excerpt from Sandra Dijkstra, "Simone de Beauvoir and Betty Friedan: The Politics of

Omission," *Feminist Studies* 6 (Summer 1980); reproduced in *Betty Friedan: The Feminine Mystique*, 444.

188. Quoted in Susan Douglas, *Where the Girls Are* (New York: Times Books, 1994), 141.

189. Excerpt from Jennifer Scanlon, *Bad Girls Go Everywhere: The Life of Helen Gurley Brown* (New York: Oxford University Press, 2009); reproduced in *Betty Friedan: The Feminine Mystique*, 502.

190. Scanlon, *Bad Girls*, in *Betty Friedan: The Feminine Mystique,* 502–503.

191. Discussed in Lisa Tickner, *The Spectacle of Women: Imagery of the Suffrage Campaign 1907–14* (London: Chatto and Windus, 1987/Chicago: University of Chicago Press, 1988), 67.

Chapter Two

1. *Letters of Constance Lytton. Selected and Arranged by Betty Balfour* (London: William Heinemann, 1925), 130.

2. V. N. Volosinov, *Marxism and the Philosophy of Language,* trans., L. Matejka and I. Titunik (Cambridge: Harvard University Press, 1929; reprint 1986), 23; discussed in Eileen Janes Yeo, "Some Paradoxes of Empowerment," in *Radical Femininity: Women's Self-Representation in the Public Sphere,* ed., Eileen Janes Yeo (New York: St. Martin's Press; Manchester: Manchester University Press, 1998), 6.

3. Laura M. Nym Mayhall argues that, ironically, the WFL's more democratic leadership ended up crippling their efforts ("Defining Militancy: Radical Protest, the Constitutional Idiom, and Women's Suffrage in Britain, 1908–1909," *Journal of British Studies* 39 (July 2000): 340–71). See also Claire Eustance, "Meanings of Militancy: The Ideas and Practice of Political Resistance in the Women's Freedom League, 1907–14," in *The Women's Suffrage Movement: New Feminist Perspectives,* eds., Maroula Joannou and June Purvis (Manchester: Manchester University Press, 1998), 51–64; and Elizabeth Crawford, *The Women's Suffrage Movement: A Reference Guide 1866–1928* (London: Routledge, 2001), 720–24.

4. In a related study Sheila Stowell has argued that George Bernard Shaw was inspired both by Garrett Fawcett's writings on Joan of Arc and by the pageantry and rhetoric of the WSPU as he formulated his play *Saint Joan* (1923). See Sheila Stowell, "Dame Joan, Saint Christabel," *Modern Drama* 37 (1994): 421–36. He also had a series of portraits of himself done by the suffrage photographer Lena Connell; she was known for her portraits of suffrage campaigners, many men among them, so this set of photographs further aligned Bernard Shaw with the cause (located at the British Library).

5. I use this approach in Colleen Denney, "'Voiceless London': Millicent Garrett Fawcett's Embodiment of the Common Cause, or, Resistance to the Scandal of the Platform," *Women, Portraiture and the Crisis of Identity in Victorian England: My Lady Scandalous Reconsidered* (Farnham, Surrey/Burlington, VT: Ashgate, 2009), 125–178. See Linda Gordon, "What is Women's History?" in *What is History Today?,* ed., Juliet Gardiner (Basingstoke: Macmillan, 1988), 91. See also Maroula Joannou and June Purvis, "Introduction: The Writing of the Women's Suffrage Movement," in *The Women's Suffrage Movement,* 1–14. In terms of establishing that the campaigns, while pushing for the vote, ultimately also spoke to women's desire to not only be included as citizens, but also to have their demands as women addressed, Linda Gordon defines feminism as "a critique of male supremacy, formed and offered in the light of a will to change it. ..." arguing that this definition "suggests both the historical continuum in which such a struggle has necessarily operated and the breadth of vision which can successfully think about a movement with sites in more than one arena" ("What's New in Women's History," in *Feminist Studies/Critical Studies,* ed., Teresa de Laurentis (Bloomington: Indiana University Press, 1986), 29). This stance is especially important for understanding the debates on moral purity and women's sexuality in relation to regulations of prostitution and the discourse on venereal disease.

6. Nora Heimann, *Joan of Arc in French Art and Culture (1700–1855): From Satire to Sanctity* (Aldershot, England/Burlington, VT: Ashgate, 2005).

7. Lisa Tickner, *The Spectacle of Women: Imagery of the Suffrage Campaign, 1907–14* (London: Chatto and Windus, 1987; Chicago: University of Chicago Press, 1988); and Rosemary Betterton, "'A Perfect Woman': The Political Body of Suffrage," *An Intimate Distance: Women, Artists and the Body* (London: Routledge, 1996), 46–78, where she also argues that the idea of "the perfect woman" fueled the debate and that interpretations of her differed greatly from group to group of "different political constituencies and factions"(48).

8. See Hilda Kean, "Public History and Popular Memory: Issues in the Commemoration of the British Militant Suffrage Campaign," *Women's History Review* 14 (2005): 581–602.

9. Marina Warner, *Joan of Arc: The Image of the Heroine* (New York: Knopf, 1981), 9.

10. Maurice Agulhon, *Marianne into Battle: Republican Imagery and Symbolism in France, 1789–1880* (Cambridge: Cambridge University Press/Paris: Maison des Sciences de l'Homme, 1981), 66.

11. I will discuss imagery of Justice in chapter four at greater length but here it should be noted that Joan's judges, during her trial, asked her if there were any representations of Justice, Peace and Unity in her host's house in Orleans. Warner, *Joan of Arc,* suggests, "they believed either that she had modeled herself on such Virtues or, more plausibly, since the question follows immediately upon another about portraits and images painted of her, that she had already been identified with such Virtues in her lifetime" (233). See Daniel Hobbins, ed., *The Trial of Joan of Arc,* trans., Daniel Hobbins (Cambridge: Harvard University Press, 2005), 81.

12. Betterton, "Perfect Woman," and Tickner, *Spectacle of Women.* In Denney, "'Voiceless London,'" 125–78, I assert that Garrett Fawcett carefully constructs her own image to counter this damaging stereotype and that she strategically employs one of the WSPU photographers, Lena Connell, to aid her in this endeavor.

13. Tickner, *Spectacle of Women;* and Betterton, "Perfect Woman."

14. Barbara Caine, "Millicent Garrett Fawcett," *Victorian Feminists* (Oxford: Oxford University Press, 1992), 238.

15. This argument is culled from Denney, "Voiceless London," 174 n. 24. See also Marysa Demoor, *Their Fair Share: Women, Power and Criticism in the Athenaeum, From Millicent Garrett Fawcett to Katherine Mansfield, 1870–1920* (Aldershot, England: Ashgate, 2000), 63, who links Garrett Fawcett's political activities with her self-perceived larger role as protector of women's rights.

16. See Denney, "'Voiceless London,'" 153.

17. Michelle Cliff, "The Resonance of Interruption," *Chrysalis* 8 (1979): 29; quoted in Dale Spender, "Introduction," in *Feminist Theorists: Three Centuries of Women's Intellectual Traditions*, ed., Dale Spender (London: The Women's Press, 1983), 3.

18. Ann Oakley, "Millicent Garrett Fawcett: Duty and Determination," in Spender, *Feminist Theorists*, 198.

19. Betterton, "Perfect Woman," 74.

20. *Ibid.*

21. Christabel Pankhurst, *The Great Scourge and How to End It* (London: E. Pankhurst, Lincoln's Inn,1913); discussed in Betterton, "Perfect Woman," 74.

22. Martha Vicinus, "Male Space and Women's Bodies," *Independent Women: Work and Community for Single Women, 1850–1920* (Chicago: University of Chicago Press, 1985), 278. Many early historians follow the arguably slanted history put forth by Sylvia Pankhurst, who, because she had been forced to split from the WSPU by her sister, Christabel, presented a somewhat bitter appraisal of the WSPU in E. Sylvia Pankhurst, *The Suffragette Movement. An Intimate Account of Persons and Ideals* (London: Longmans, 1931), where she puts forth that, with the publication of *The Great Scourge*, Christabel launched a sex war; many try to dismiss Christabel's alarm by arguing that Christabel's statistics were inaccurate. But she was a university-educated scholar and took her information from the work of reputed authorities. On more positive readings of *The Great Scourge*, that position it as I do here within the context of feminist polemics and an alternate narrative for women, see Linda Martz, "An AIDS-Era Reassessment of Christabel Pankhurst's *The Great Scourge and How to End It*," *Women's History Review* 14 (2005): 435–46; and June Purvis, "Fighting the Double Moral Standard in Edwardian Britain: Suffragette Militancy, Sexuality and the Nation in the Writings of the Early Twentieth-Century British Feminist Christabel Pankhurst," in *Women's Activism: Global Perspectives from the 1890s to the Present*, eds., Francisca de Hann et al. (London: Routledge, 2013), 120–135. Christabel's statistics may have been inaccurate (see Les Garner, *Stepping Stones to Women's Liberty* (London: Heinemann, 1984, for example), but that is not to negate the impact and comfort her stance had for many women in the movement.

23. See Martz, "An AIDS-Era Reassessment," 436–37, where she discusses the Royal Commission on Venereal Disease which many feminists feared would bring back the oppressive measures used under the Contagious Diseases Acts. Further, the White Slavery Act did not penalize seducers who were, in fact, the ones responsible for luring women and children into sex work. See also Purvis, "Fighting the Double Moral Standard,"128–130, where she also discusses the violation of women's bodies in relation to the Prisoners Temporary Discharge for Ill-Health Act passed in April 1913, popularly known as the "Cat and Mouse Act," which discharged women on hunger strike who were in poor health, only to re-arrest them once they had regained their health. Purvis explains, "The Government was not acting because it felt compassionate towards the women, Christabel, thundered, but because it was afraid of being responsible for a prisoner's death" (131).

24. Christabel Pankhurst, *The Great Scourge*; discussed in E. Sylvia Pankhurst, *The Suffragette Movement. An Intimate Account of Persons and Ideals* (London: Longmans, 1931); in *A Sylvia Pankhurst Reader*, ed., Kathryn Dodd (Manchester: Manchester University Press, 1993), 179–86.

25. E. Sylvia Pankhurst, *Suffragette Movement*; quoted in Dodd, *Sylvia Pankhurst Reader*, 185.

26. Elisabeth Sarah, "Christabel Pankhurst: Reclaiming Her Power," in Spender, *Feminist Theorists*; Susan Kingsley Kent, *Sex and Suffrage in Britain 1860–1914* (Princeton: Princeton University Press, 1987); and Margaret Jackson, *The Real Facts of Life: Feminism and the Politics of Sexuality c. 1850–1940* (London: Taylor & Francis, 1994), 44–49.

27. Andrew Rosen, *Rise Up Women! The Militant Campaign of the Women's Social and Political Union, 1903–1914* (London: Routledge, 1974), 140. Brian Harrison, "The Act of Militancy: Violence and the Suffragettes, 1904–1914," *Peaceable Kingdom: Stability and Change in Modern Britain* (Oxford: Oxford University Press, 1982), 64, argues that because the majority were single (63 percent by 1912–14), they were ideal candidates for militancy since they had no one to worry over them; in addition, as younger members, many of them were more physically fit and hence more able to weather the physical demands of militancy than older members.

28. Purvis, "Fighting the Double Moral Standard," 132.

29. *Ibid.*, 131, where she discusses Jane Marcus, "Introduction," in *Suffrage and the Pankhursts*, ed., Jane Marcus (London: Routledge, 1987), 14.

30. David Rubinstein, "Millicent Garrett Fawcett and the Meaning of Women's Emancipation, 1886–99," *Victorian Studies* 35 (spring 1991): 369.

31. Millicent (Garrett) Fawcett, *Five Famous Women* (London: Cassell and Co., 1905).

32. *Ibid.*, 30.

33. *Ibid.*

34. Discussed in Purvis, "Fighting the Double Moral Standard," 122. See Louisa Martindale, *Under the Surface* (Brighton: Southern Publishing Company, 1908); and Olive Banks, *The Biographical Dictionary of British Feminists*. Vol. 2 (New York: New York University Press, 1990), 151.

35. Sally Ledger, "The New Woman and the Crisis of Victorianism," in *Cultural Politics at the Fin de Siècle*, eds., Sally Ledger and Scott McCracken (Cambridge: Cambridge University Press, 1995), 23–24.

36. Millicent Garrett Fawcett, "The Woman Who Did," *Contemporary Review* 67 (1895): 630. For a complete discussion of Garrett Fawcett and the New Woman, see Denney, "Voiceless London," 148–55.

37. Rene de Cériziers, *Jeanne d'Arc, ou L'Innocence affigée* (Paris, 1639), 176–77; quoted in Warner, *Joan of Arc*, 18.

38. See Denney, "Voiceless London," 155–57.

39. Warner, *Joan of Arc*, 19.

40. Garrett Fawcett quoted in Ray Strachey, *Millicent Garrett Fawcett* (London: John Murray, 1931), 232.

41. Millicent Garrett Fawcett, *The Women's Victory—and After: Personal Reminiscences, 1911–1918* (London: Sidgwick & Jackson, 1920), 157.

42. Jane Marcus, "Introduction," *Suffrage and the Pankhursts*, 14. She criticizes Christabel's model, however, since it puts blame on a group of women—prostitutes—for infecting men when, in fact, suffrage was supposed to save such women.

43. David Mitchell, *Queen Christabel: A Biography of Christabel Pankhurst* (London: MacDonald and Jane's, 1977), 319–20; and Susan Douglas, *Where the Girls Are* (New York: Times Books, 1994), 141.

44. Quoted in Douglas, *Where the Girls Are*, 141.

45. Rebecca West, "On Mentioning the Unmentionable," *Clarion* (26 Sept. 1913); discussed in Marcus, "Introduction," 15.

46. Christabel Pankhurst, *The Great Scourge*, viii; which Purvis discusses over this point in "Fighting the Double Moral Standard," 130.

47. Mitchell, *Queen Christabel*, 320; Purvis, "Fighting the Double Moral Standard," cites specifically David Mitchell and Martin Pugh.

48. Garner, *Stepping Stones*, 54.

49. Lesley A. Hall, "Suffrage, Sex and Science," in Joannou and Purvis, *The Women's Suffrage Movement*, 188–200.

50. Mary Poovey, *Uneven Developments: The Ideological Work of Gender in Victorian England* (Chicago: University of Chicago Press, 1988. Reprint, London: Virago, 1989), 11.

51. This examination thus conflates femininity and leadership as dual goals of representation of the main suffrage groups. Laura M. Nym Mayhall argues for this kind of interpretation of Joan for the WSPU in her discussion of the literary rhetoric surrounding their campaign. See her "The Militant Campaign: Embodying Citizenship, 1908–1914," in *The Militant Suffrage Movement: Citizenship and Resistance in Britain, 1860–1930* (Oxford: Oxford University Press, 2003), 84–87.

52. *The Suffragette* (9 May 1913): 501.

53. Sandra Stanley Holton, "The Political Protest of Male Suffragists and the Gendering of the 'Suffragette' Identity," in *The Men's Share?: Masculinities, Male Support and Women's Suffrage in Britain, 1890–1920*, eds., A.V. John and C. Eustance (London: Routledge, 1997), 110.

54. Christabel Pankhurst, "Why the Union is Strong," *The Suffragette* (27 December 1912): 160.

55. Harrison, "Act of Militancy," 44–45.

56. For Joan's inspiration for Third Republic Catholic spirituality, see Denise L. Despres, "*Le Triomphe de l'Humilité: Thérèse of Liseux and 'La Nouvelle Jeanne*,'" in *Joan of Arc and Spirituality*, eds., Ann W. Astell and Bonnie Wheeler (New York: Palgrave Macmillan, 2003), 249–265.

57. Cheryl R. Jorgensen-Earp, *The Transfiguring Sword: The Just War of the Women's Social and Political Union* (Tuscaloosa: University of Alabama Press, 1997), particularly 89–95.

58. Colleen Denney, "The Princess, Globally and Locally," *Representing Diana, Princess of Wales: Cultural Memory and Fairy Tales Revisited* (Madison: Associated University Press, 2005), 153–59.

59. See Papers of Millicent Garrett Fawcett, M50/2/1/6, Women's Suffrage Collection, Manchester Central Library, Manchester Archives and Local Studies, fol. 92. On Wyoming and New Zealand as suffrage pioneers see Colleen Denney, "Wyoming Women's Suffrage as an Example to the World: A Comparative Look at the Pioneer Spirit of Wyoming and New Zealand," *Annals of Wyoming* 18 (Autumn 2016): 2–23.

60. Betterton, "Perfect Woman," 52.

61. Agulhon, *Marianne into Battle*, 65.

62. Tickner, *Spectacle of Women*, 210. See Christabel Pankhurst, *The Suffragette* (9 May 1913).

63. Emmeline Pethick-Lawrence, "Welcome Christabel Pankhurst!" *Votes for Women* 2 (December 17, 1908): 200.

64. Quoted in Christabel Pankhurst, *The Militant Methods of the N.W.S.P.U* (2nd ed. Women's Press, n.d.), 14; in Harrison, "Act of Militancy," 35.

65. Emmeline Pankhurst, *Why We Are Militant; A Speech Delivered in New York, Oct. 21, 1913* (London: Women's Social and Political Union, 1913), 11, and 2.

66. Jorgensen-Earp, *The Transfiguring Sword*, 94.

67. Harrison, "Act of Militancy," 48; *Votes for Women* (7 June 1912): 584; (14 April 1911): 460.

68. Harrison, "Act of Militancy," 48.

69. Fawcett, *Five Famous Women*, 21.

70. *Ibid.*, 30.

71. Jorgensen-Earp, *The Transfiguring Sword*, 98.

72. See Diane Atkinson, *Suffragettes in the Purple, White and Green. London 1906–1914* (London: Museum of London, 1992).

73. For the WSPU the parallel with military paraphernalia goes even further; for example, women who went on hunger strike in Holloway Prison earned medals "for valour" with the colors of the WSPU on the ribbon and, among other items, prisoners received badges of honor shaped like the portcullis with the prisoner's arrow superimposed on them.

74. Cicely Hamilton, *Life Errant: Autobiographical Reminiscences* (London: J. M. Dent, 1935), 75–76.

75. A later commentary on the obsessive dress of soldiers comes in the political cartoon by Arthur Horner about letting women into the Royal Tournament, known as an event that was an important recruiting locale for the armed forces (*News Chronicle* 8 June 1951, with the caption: "Dammit, now they're letting women in, the Tournament will become just a fashion parade." The joke is that the male soldiers are totally overdressed in retro military attire whereas the woman walking past them is in practical riding gear. See Diane Atkinson, *Funny Girls: Cartooning for Equality* (London: Penguin, 1997), 53).

76. Vicinus, "Male Space and Women's Bodies," 278.

77. Included in Fawcett Library Scrapbooks: "Votes for Women: A Picturebook of the Campaign in Recent Years," 10/4/1, 6–7. Women's Library, London School of Economics.

78. Elaine Showalter, *Sexual Anarchy: Gender and Culture at the Fin de Siècle* (London: Virago, 1990. Reprint, 2001), 21.

79. Kent, *Sex and Suffrage in Britain*, 13; quoted in Showalter, *Sexual Anarchy*, 21.

80. Showalter, *Sexual Anarchy*, 21–22.

81. Purvis, "Fighting the Double Moral Standard," 131, where, however, she is strictly talking about religious communities. My point here is that Joan was seen as a spiritual guide for these women, part of an alternative religion to which many women dedicated themselves, replacing religion with the cause for which they took on the role of martyr.

82. See, for example, Sheila Jeffrys, *The Spinster and her Enemies: Feminism and Sexuality 1880–1930* (London: Pandora, 1985); and Hall, "Suffrage, Sex and Science."

83. Hall, "Suffrage, Sex and Science," 188–200.

84. Showalter, *Sexual Anarchy*, 21–22.

85. Warner, *Joan of Arc*, 23.

86. Tickner, *Spectacle of Women*, 122.

87. See Liz Stanley and Ann Morley, *The Life and Death of Emily Wilding Davison* (London: The Women's Press, 1988), who debate the suicide issue.

88. Quoted in Fawcett, *Five Famous Women*, 20.

89. Tickner, *Spectacle of Women*, 128.

90. Quoted in Dodd, "Introduction," *Sylvia Pankhurst Reader*, 15; who also discusses Tickner's stance of characterizing the imagery of militant women in this way (*Spectacle of Women*, 205–13).

91. Mary Phillips, "A Typical Suffragist," *Votes for Women* 1 (Dec. 1907): 35; included in Papers of Millicent Garrett Fawcett, GB/106/7/RMB/B3150/7MGF/2, Women's Library, London School of Economics.

92. Included in Papers of Millicent Garrett Fawcett, GB/106/7/RMB/B3150/7/MGF/2, Women's Library, London School of Economics.

93. Vicinus, "Male Space and Women's Bodies," 267–68.

94. See Michel Foucault, *The History of Sexuality*, vol. 1, *An Introduction*, trans., Robert Hurley (New York: Pantheon Books, 1978), especially 17–35.

95. Tickner, *Spectacle of Women*, 211.

96. Showalter, *Sexual Anarchy*, 29.

97. Leslie Feinberg, *Transgender Warriors: Making History from Joan of Arc to Dennis Rodman* (Boston: Beacon Press, 1996), 68–69; and Heimann, *Joan of Arc*, 9.

98. See, for example, Daniel Hobbins, "Introduction," in *The Trial of Joan of Arc*, 24–26.

99. Feinberg, *Transgender Warriors*, 9.

100. *Ibid.*, xi. See also Susan Schibanoff, "True Lies: Transvestism and Idolatry in the Trial of Joan of Arc," in *Fresh Verdicts on Joan of Arc*, eds., Bonnie Wheeler and Charles T. Wood (New York: Garland, 1996), 31–60.

101. Feinberg, *Transgender Warriors*, 78–79.

102. Warner, *Joan of Arc*, 145–46.

103. *Ibid.*, 147.

104. Harrison, "Act of Militancy," 45.

105. Schibanoff, "True Lies," 53.

106. See Sandra Stanley Holton, "Free Love and Victorian Feminism: The Divers Matrimonials of Elizabeth Wolstenholme and Ben Elmy," *Victorian Studies* 37 (1994): 199–223.

107. Sophia Phoca and Rebecca Wright, *Introducing Postfeminism*, ed., Richard Appignanesi (London: Icon Books; New York: Totem Books, 1990).

108. Phoca and Wright, *Introducing Postfeminism*, 170.

109. Warner, *Joan of Arc*, 155.

110. Vicinus, "Male Space and Women's Bodies," 264.

111. This idea of the power of silent marches has not left us, however. Just as one example, in June 2009, angry Iranians marched by the thousands in the streets in complete silence to protest their objections to the new regime. I will return to this discussion in the epilogue. A very impacting silent march, much closer to home, was that of a group of protesters for gay rights during the Homecoming Parade at the University of Wyoming in 1998, immediately after the murder of gay student, Matthew Shepard, in a hate crime.

112. "The New Woman," *The Woman's Signal* (December 26, 1895): 407; cited in Michelle Elizabeth Tusan, "Inventing the New Woman: Print Culture and Identity Politics during the Fin-de-Siècle," *Victorian Periodicals Review* 31 (summer 1998): 176, argues that feminists tried to produce a counter-image of the upright, womanly, feminist suffragist to resist the loose woman of easy virtue with which the New Woman had become associated in the press.

113. "The Anti-Suffragist," *Votes for Women* 1 (November 1907): 13.

114. Vicinus, "Male Space and Women's Bodies," 257.

115. Cicely Hamilton, *Daily Mail*, 15 June 1908.

116. Tickner, *Spectacle of Women*, 81.

117. See June Purvis, "'Deeds, not Words': Daily Life in the Women's Social and Political Union in Edwardian Britain," in *Votes for Women*, eds., June Purvis and Sandra Stanley Holton (London: Routledge, 2000), 153 n. 10 on the problematics of reclaiming women's lived experiences.

118. S. Bulan, "A 'Doll House' Revisited," *Votes for Women* 4 (February 17, 1911), 323.

119. Will Dyson was Australian and still fresh in his mind when he moved to England was the enfranchisement of women in his home province of South Australia in 1894; hence, his political cartoons were heavily on the side of the women in the conflict.

120. Martha Vicinus, "Male Space and Women's Bodies," 269.

121. Barbara Green, *Spectacular Confessions* (New York: St. Martin's Press, 1997), 82.

122. Betterton, "Perfect Woman," 56.

123. See J. F. Geddes, "Culpable Complicity: The Medical Profession and the Forcible Feeding of Suffragettes, 1909–1914," *Women's History Review* 17 (2008): 79–94; and June Purvis, "The Prison Experiences of the Suffragettes in Edwardian Britain," *Women's History Review* 4 (1995): 103–133.

124. Quoted in Strachey, *Millicent Garrett Fawcett*, 240.

125. Brian Harrison uses the battle of forcible feeding as just one of many instances "to illustrate the difficulties involved in mounting effective feminist pressure on the medical profession" ("Women's Health and the Women's Movement," in *Biology, Medicine and Society 1840–1940*, ed., Charles Webster (Cambridge: Cambridge University Press, 1981), 47–50).

126. June Purvis, "'Deeds, not Words,'" 149.

127. Suffragette Fellowship Collection, Museum of London.

128. John Mercer, "Media and Militancy: Propaganda in the Women's Social and Political Union's Campaign," *Women's History Review* 14 (2005): 475. While this characterization is apt for the posters, it is not true of the banners, a type of artwork Mercer does not cover in his study. See, for example, Tickner, "A Note on the WSPU Silk Banners unfurled 17 June 1908," *Spectacle of Women*, 261.

129. Mercer, "Media and Militancy," 475.

130. Caroline J. Howlett, "Writing on the Body? Representation and Resistance in British Suffragette Accounts of Forcible Feeding," in *Bodies of Writing, Bodies in Performance*, eds., Thomas Foster, Carol Siegel and Ellen E. Berry (New York: New York University Press, 1996), 14. She discusses the misogynist treatment of women in two anti-suffrage images, *The Prevention of Hunger Strikes* and *Feeding a Suffragette by Force*, both reproduced in Tickner, *Spectacle of Women*, 107.

131. Elaine Showalter, *The Female Malady: Women, Madness, and English Culture* (New York: Pantheon Books, 1985), 163–64.

132. Betterton, "Perfect Woman," 58.

133. *Ibid.*, 69. Tickner, *Spectacle of Women*, 211, makes this same argument.

134. Betterton, "Perfect Woman," 202 n. 16.

135. Michel Foucault, *Discipline and Punish: The Birth of the Prison*, trans., Alan Sheridan (New York: Vintage Books/Random House, 1991).

136. Green, *Spectacular Confessions*, 83.

137. Foucault, *Discipline and Punish*, 201.

138. *Ibid.*, 232.

139. Betterton, 72. See Jeffrey Weeks who argues that suffragism, while it cultivated intimate relations between women, could not bank on supporting the issue of lesbianism (*Sex, Politics and Society: The Regulation of Sexuality Since 1800* [London: Longman, 1981], 164).

140. Barbara Caine, *English Feminism 1780–1980* (Oxford: Oxford University Press, 1997. Reprint, 1999), 43.

141. Frederick Pethick-Lawrence, *Fate Has Been Kind*, 74; quoted in Harrison, "Act of Militancy," 46.

142. Val Williams, *The Other Observers: Women Photographers in Britain, 1900 to the Present* (London: Virago Press, 1986. Reprint, 1991), 93.

143. Showalter, *Sexual Anarchy*, 23.

144. Williams, *Other Observers*, 24.

145. E. Sylvia Pankhurst, *The Suffragette Movement*, 194; and Mary Richardson, *Laugh a Defiance*, 12; discussed in Harrison, "Act of Militancy," 47.

146. Green, *Spectacular Confessions*, 75. For further information on these two organizations see Crawford, *The Women's Suffrage Movement*, 4–5; 712–713.

147. Katharine Cockin, "Cicely Hamilton's Warriors: Dramatic Reinventions of Militancy in the British Women's Suffrage Movement," *Women's History Review* 14 (2005): 527–542, where one of her goals is to detail the ways the productions themselves promoted women's ability to make history, and further, to create certain messages that were dependent on staging in an active manner rather than the static message of the published play. Laura E. Nym Marshall argues for plural forms of militancy, and considers the work of the WFL in this regard in "Defining Militancy: Radical Protest, The Constitutional Idiom, and Women's Suffrage in Britain, 1908–1909," *Journal of British Studies* 39 (July 2000): 340–371.

148. Cockin, "Cicely Hamilton's Warriors," 530.

149. Nym Mayhall addresses this lack with a focus on WFL types of militancy in "Defining Militancy." Yet, in her "Embodying Citizenship 1908–1914," 85, she asserts that the WFL was not responsible for the *Pageant* productions, giving credit instead to the WSPU. This miscalculation then leads her to assert that the WFL did not employ Joan imagery, when, in fact, she was a key player in the *Pageant* itself.

150. TWL.2004.335, TWL.2004.336, and TWL.2004.337, Box 6, Visual Resources Materials, Women's Library, London School of Economics. Cockin, "Cicely Hamilton's Warriors," Appendix 1, 538, lists many productions of the pageant and their dates but she does not list this similar event in Edinburgh.

151. Cockin, "Cicely Hamilton's Warriors," 535.

152. *Ibid.*, 534.

153. Nym Mayhall, "Defining Militancy," 357–369. On Muriel Matters see Crawford, *The Women's Suffrage Movement*, 392–93, and 721.

154. Nym Mayhall, "Defining Militancy," 344.

155. Green, *Spectacular Confessions*, 75.

156. This discussion of the Watts poster is based on Tickner, *Spectacle of Women*, 211–212. Sophia Andres discusses it in the context of Tracey Chevalier's *Falling Angels* (New York: Dutton, 2001) arguing that for the main character, Kitty, Chevalier conjures up images of Joan of Arc as the *Bugler Girl* that act as a "clarion call" for her to join the movement. Later in the novel, Kitty acts as the pageboy who leads Joan of Arc on her horse in the 1911 Coronation Procession and, as Andres notes, Kitty's funeral echoes that of Emily Wilding Davison. See Sophia Andres, "From Camelot to Hyde Park: The Lady of Shalott's Pre-Raphaelite Postmodernism in A. S. Byatt and Tracy Chevalier," *Victorian Institute Journal* 34 (2006): 26–32.

157. *Common Cause* 5 (November 7, 1913).

158. Tickner, *Spectacle of Women*, 211–212.

159. *Common Cause* 5 (November 28, 1913).

160. Garner, *Stepping Stones*, after page 60, points out this shift.

161. Betterton, n. 39, 205; Joan became the symbol of the extreme right-wing *Action Française* group founded in 1899. Further, she cites a more recent evocation of Joan in 1995 for the French Presidential elections during which the extreme right-wing candidate, Jean-Marie Le Pen, used the image of Joan of Arc in his election rallies.

162. Nadia Margolis, "The 'Joan Phenomenon' and the French Right," in *Fresh Verdicts on Joan*, 266.

163. For a study of Joan's imaging in the period prior to suffrage in France, see Heimann, *Joan of Arc*. On reconsiderations of her representation during her lifetime, see *Fresh Verdicts on Joan of Arc*.

164. Heimann, *Joan of Arc*, 5–6.

165. *Ibid.*, 175.

166. Gay L. Gullickson, *Unruly Women of Paris: Images of the Commune* (Ithaca and London: Cornell UP, 1996), 86–88.

167. Heimann, *Joan of Arc*, 175.

168. *Ibid.*

169. Nora M. Heimann, "Joan of Arc: From Medieval Maiden to Modern Saint," in Nora M. Heimann and Laura Coyle, *Joan of Arc: Her Image in France and America* (Washington, D.C.: Corcoran Gallery of Art, in association with London: D. Giles, 2006), 15–51. On the American reception of Joan of Arc see, in this same volume, Laura Coyle, "A Universal Patriot: Joan of Arc in America during the Gilded Age and the Great War," 53–73. See Boutet de Monvel's illustrated *Jeanne d'Arc* (Paris,1896), which exists also in many American editions.

170. Heimann, "Joan of Arc," 48–49. Caroline Igra, "Measuring the Temper of Her Time: Joan of Arc in the 1870s and 1880s," *Konsthistorik tidskrift* 68 (1999): 117–125, argues that we see a shift in Joan imagery in France between the 1870s to the 1880s, from Joan as militant leader to Joan as spiritual leader, but spiritual imagery, in sculptural form exists alongside militant works. Henri Chapu's *Joan Listening to Her Voices*, 1872, a sculpture exhibited at the first Paris Salon to follow the Franco-Prussian War, for one, is very close to Bastien-Lepage's painted version. It is probably truer to say that both types of representations existed side by side to meet different aspects of Joan's appeal to a suffering and recovering nation.

171. Karen Offen, "Women, Citizenship, and Suffrage with a French Twist, 1789–1993," in *Suffrage and Beyond: International Feminist Perspectives*, eds. Caroline Daley and Melanie Nolan (New York: New York University Press, 1994), 159.

172. Martha Hanna, "Iconology and Ideology: Images of Joan of Arc in the Idiom of the *Action française*, 1908–1931," *French Historical Studies* 14 (Autumn 1985): 215–239.

173. This discussion of French feminism is based on James F. McMillan, *France and Women 1789–1914: Gender, Society and Politics* (London: Routledge, 2000).

174. McMillan, *France and Women*, 218.

175. Christabel Pankhurst, "An Anti-Militant on Joan of Arc," *The Suffragette* (26 June 1914), discussed in Tickner, *Spectacle of Women*, 317 n. 224.

176. Garrett Fawcett, *The Women's Victory*.

177. *Ibid.*, v.

178. Advertisement included in 7AMP/D FL594 Box A. Muriel Pierotti Papers, Women's Library.

Chapter Three

1. "Women's Suffrage Bill"; speech delivered by Sir Julius Vogel in the New Zealand House of Representatives, May 12, 1887," MS-Papers-2072 Sir Julius Vogel, 1835–1899, Alexander Turnbull Library, National Archives, Wellington, New Zealand.

2. Joan Wallach Scott, "Introduction," in *Feminism and History*, ed., Joan Wallach Scott (Oxford: Oxford University Press, 1996), 2.

3. Wallach Scott, "Introduction," 2.

4. Marguerite Johnson, "Boadicea and British Suffrage Feminists," *Outskirts: Crawley* 31 (November 2014)(online journal). Retrieved 6/30/17; from proquest.com.libproxy.uwyo.edu. While she argues at the beginning of her article that Bodica was different from Joan of Arc in being a mother, she does not pursue this representation as a theme. Further, she erroneously argues that Bodica's presence in monuments (she discusses only Thomas Thornycroft's statue) "was more tangible" than that of Joan of Arc. However, many statues of Joan of Arc were extant by the time of the Edwardian suffrage movement and many more were erected in her honor during the campaign in England.

5. See Sharon Macdonald, Pat Holden and Shirley Ardener, eds., *Images of Women in Peace and War: Cross-Cultural and Historical Perspectives* (Madison: University of Wisconsin Press, 1988).

6. Eileen Janes Yeo, "Some Paradoxes of Empowerment," in *Radical Femininity: Women's Self-Representation in the Public Sphere*, ed., Eileen Janes Yeo (Manchester: Manchester University Press, 1998), 6.

7. Karl Marx, "The Eighteenth Brumaire of Louis Bonaparte," in Karl Marx and Friedrich Engels, *Selected Works*, Vol. 1 (Moscow: Foreign Languages Publishing House, [1869], 1962), 247; cited in Yeo, "Some Paradoxes of Empowerment," 6.

8. On Despard see A. Linklater, *An Unhusbanded Life: Charlotte Despard: Suffragette, Socialist and Sinn Feiner* (London: Hutchinson, 1980); and M. Mulvihill, *Charlotte Despard: A Biography* (London: Pandora, 1989).

9. Reproduced in Elizabeth Crawford, *The Women's Suffrage Movement* (London: Routledge, 2001), 506; and 303, where she lists other portrait photographs of suffrage women wearing Bodica brooches created for and sold by the WSPU. The Bodica brooch was advertised in *Votes for Women* (19 November 1908)).

10. Samantha Freénée-Hutchins, *Boudica's Odyssey in Early Modern England* (Burlington, VT: Ashgate, 2014), 186.

11. Richard Hingley and Christina Unwin, *Boudica: Iron Age Warrior Queen* (London: Hambledon Continuum, 2005), 150.

12. It is fitting also that the Emmeline Pankhurst statue in Victoria Tower Gardens was the result of a fundraising campaign initiated by the former militant suffragette Viscountess Rhonnda. See Hilda Kean, "Public History and Popular Memory: Issues in the Commemoration of the British Militant Suffrage Campaign," *Women's History Review* 14 (2005): 587–588.

13. Quoted from *The Mrs. Pankhurst Memorial Fund Raising Leaflet*. Memorial Material SC 35, Suffragette Fellowship Collection, Museum of London.

14. Maud Arncliffe-Sennett, *The State and the Woman*, vol. 2 (London: Women's Franchise League, 1908), 252. She reproduces the illustration in Maud Arncliffe- Sennett Collection, vol. 1 (1907–1908) (British Library, London).

15. See V. Irene Cockroft, *New Dawn Women: Women in the Arts & Crafts and Suffrage Movements at the Dawn of the 20th Century* (Compton, Surrey, England: Watts Gallery, 2005), 10–11.

16. *Votes for Women* (Sept. 2, 1910).

17. For some of the history of the Pankhurst household in terms of radical politics while they lived in Manchester, see Kean, "Public History and Popular Memory."

18. Lisa Tickner, *The Spectacle of Women: Imagery of the Suffrage Movement* (London: Chatto and Windus, 1987/Chicago: University of Chicago Press, 1988), 60.

19. Ellen Carol Dubois, "Introduction," in *Feminist Theorists*, ed., Dale Spender (New York: Pantheon Books, 1983), 4.

20. Included as Item 65, "Modern Postcards," Box 6, Postcard Collection, Women's Library, London.

21. Records tell us that there were thousands of banners created for the various processions. Tickner provides us with a list of the extant ones in "Appendix 4. A Checklist of Surviving Banners," in *Spectacle of Women*, 254–61. For a comparative analysis of suffrage and trade union banners see idem, 63–66.

22. Quoted in Tickner, *Spectacle of Women*, 126.

23. Tickner, *Spectacle of Women*, 126.

24. Cited in Tickner, *Spectacle of Women*, "Appendix 4: A Checklist of Surviving Banners," 254.

25. Julia Kristeva, "Stabat Mater," in *The Kristeva Reader*, ed., Toril Moi (New York: Columbia University Press, 1986), 160–186.

26. Tickner, *Spectacle of Women*, 218. The latter quotation is from Mrs. Gerald Paget, "Good Motherhood," *Votes for Women* (13 January 1911), in which she calls for putting the interest of the mother first, not last, in the state; lightening of the working mother's burden; protecting young girls; and for the necessity for women's voices in issues related to the home and nursery. Garrett Fawcett voiced her opinion in the *Daily Graphic* (undated letter cutting in her scrapbook, Women's Library, London); and Pankhurst's Mother's Day appearance is recorded in the Museum of London pamphlet, "Mother's Day Sunday May 14th Normal Park Presbyterian Church, Chicago."

27. Tickner, *Spectacle of Women*, 100.

28. *Ibid.*

29. Paula Hays Harper, "Votes for Women? A Graphic Episode in the Battle of the Sexes." In *Art and Architecture in the Service of Politics*, eds., Henry A. Millon and Linda Nochlin (Cambridge: MIT Press, 1978), 156.

30. Hays Harper, "Votes for Women?" 157.

31. *Ibid.*, 151.

32. Tickner, *Spectacle of Women*, x.

33. Sharon Macdonald, "Boadicea: Warrior, Mother and Myth," in *Images of Women in Peace and War*, 55.

34. Joan Wallach Scott, *The Fantasy of Feminist History* (Durham: Duke University Press, 2011), 59.

35. Wallach Scott, *Fantasy*, 59.

36. Quoted in Wallach Scott, *Fantasy*, 59–60.

37. Geraldine Lennox, "The Suffragette Spirit," originally published by the Suffragette Fellowship (London: Allen and Donaldson, 1932); included in 7VJH/1/5/10, Vera (Jack) Holmes Papers, Box 1, Campaign for Women's Suffrage 1908–1962 (Women's Library, London).

38. Lennox, "The Suffragette Spirit."

39. Tickner, *Spectacle of Women*, 207.

40. *Ibid.*, 208.

41. Dora Montefiore, *From Victorian to Modern*

(London: E. Archer, 1927), 109; quoted in Macdonald, "Boadicea: Warrior, Mother and Myth," 55.

42. Hingley and Unwin, *Boudica: Iron Age Warrior Queen*, 176.

43. Cicely Hamilton, *A Pageant of Great Women* (Liverpool: A.W. Duncan, 1912).

44. Katherine Cockin, "Cicely Hamilton's Warriors: Dramatic Reinventions of Militancy in the British Women's Suffrage Movement," *Women's History Review* 14 (2005): 527.

45. Lennox, "The Suffragette Spirit."

46. *Britannia* 6 (June 22, 1917).

Chapter Four

1. I discuss this issue at length in the epilogue. The designation comes from Judith Walkowitz, *City of Dreadful Delight: Narratives of Sexual Danger in Late Victorian London* (Chicago: University of Chicago Press, 1992).

2. Lisa Tickner, *The Spectacle of Women: Imagery of the Suffrage Campaign 1907–14* (London: Chatto and Windus, 1987/Chicago: University of Chicago Press, 1988), 209.

3. Marina Warner, *Monuments and Maidens: The Allegory of the Female Form* (New York: Atheneum, 1985), xx.

4. Gay L. Gullickson, *Unruly Women of Paris: Images of the Commune* (Ithaca: Cornell University Press, 1996), 6.

5. Tickner, *Spectacle of Women*, 209.

6. *Ibid.*

7. Warner, *Monuments and Maidens*, xx.

8. Maud Arncliffe-Sennett Collection, Vol. 3, 53 and 1, respectively (British Library).

9. Warner, *Monuments and Maidens*, 87.

10. *Ibid.*, 250–251.

11. "The Suffrage Atelier," *Women's Franchise* 2, no. 53 (July 1, 1909): 658. The *Women's Franchise* journal was non-partisan; it represented all of the major tendencies within the suffrage movement but when the NUWSS withdrew funding in 1909 because they did not agree with the journal's continued support of the now openly militant WSPU, the journal effectively folded. See David Dougan and Denise Sanchez, *Feminist Periodicals 1855–1984* (London: Harvester Press, 1987), 24–25.

12. Elizabeth Crawford, *The Women's Suffrage Movement: A Reference Guide 1866–1928* (London: Routledge, 2001), 721.

13. Gullickson, *Unruly Women of Paris*, 6.

14. www.australia.gov.au/about-australia/australilanstory/austn-suffragettes The image from the banner was later used in the commemorative one dollar Australian coin, minted in 2003, to celebrate a century of women's suffrage in Australia. The banner is on display in Parliament House, Canberra. The British presented it in 1988 as a bicentennial gift to the women of Australia.

15. See *Encyclopedia of Comparative Iconography*, vol. 1, ed., Helene Roberts (Chicago: Fitzroy Dearborn, 1998), 54.

16. Warner, *Monuments and Maidens*, 13.

17. Gullickson, *Unruly Women of Paris*, 8.

18. *Ibid.*, 9.

19. Maurice Agulhon, *Marianne into Battle: Republican Imagery and Symbolism in France, 1789–1880* (Cambridge: Cambridge University Press, 1979), 11.

20. Maud Arncliffe-Sennett Collection, vol. 27 (1916), 2.

21. Agulhon, *Marianne into Battle*, 16.

22. *Ibid.*, 88.

23. Brian Harrison, "The Act of Militancy: Violence and the Suffragettes," *Peaceable Kingdom: Stability and Change in Modern Britain* (Oxford: Clarendon Press, 1982), 32.

24. Gina Strumwasser, "Justice," in *Encyclopedia of Comparative Iconography*, 465.

25. *Ibid.*

26. Cited in *Ibid.*, 467.

27. Warner, *Monuments and Maidens*, 160.

28. Cited in Strumwasser, "Justice," 467.

29. Cited in *Ibid.*

30. TWL.2002.509.PR/028 (Women's Library, London).

31. Cicely Hamilton, *A Pageant of Great Women* (Liverpool: A. W. Duncan, 1912), 6, 12.

32. TWL.1999.3.1 (Women's Library, London). According to Crawford, *The Women's Suffrage Movement*, 460, *The Suffragist* only existed in this one 1909 publication from the address of the Suffragists' Vigilance League and was pro-militant.

33. *The Suffragette* (March 14, 1913), cover page.

34. Tickner, *Spectacle of Women*, 38.

35. *Ibid.*, 39.

36. *Ibid.*, 133, discusses this definitive shift for the NUWSS.

37. Cited in Strumwasser, "Justice," 467.

38. Warner, *Monuments and Maidens*, 259.

39. "The Outlook," *Votes for Women* 4 (1911): 200.

40. Quoted in *Votes for Women* 1 (1908): 234.

Epilogue

1. Barbara Green, *Spectacular Confessions* (New York: St. Martin's Press, 1997), 3; Kitty Marion and Emmeline Pethick-Lawrence, quoted in idem, *Spectacular Confessions*, 71. A version of this chapter was published as Colleen Denney, "From the Hammer to the Fist: The Pleasures and Dangers of March, Progress and Protest in Creating Social Justice from the First Wave to the Present," *Journal of International Women's Studies* 18 (January 2017); http://vc.bridgew.edu/jiws/.

2. Martha Vicinus, "Male Space and Women's Bodies," *Independent Women: Work and Community for Single Women, 1850–1920* (Chicago: University of Chicago Press, 1985), 266.

3. Brian Harrison, "The Act of Militancy: Violence and the Suffragettes," *Peaceable Kingdom: Stability and Change in Modern Britain* (Oxford: Clarendon Press, 1983), 36–38.

4. Suzanne Romaine, *Communicating Gender* (Mahwah, NJ: Lawrence Erlbaum Associates, 1999), 143.

5. Miranda Outman-Kramer and Susana Galán, eds., "Comparative Perspectives Symposium. Gendered Bodies in the Protest Sphere." *Signs* 40 (2014): 1–79, http://www.jstor.org/stable/10.1086/673741 present a series of articles that address contemporary, global, gendered protests of women in the streets. The present study seeks to situate the back history that allows for such public activism and its outward bodily expression, employing Foucaultian theoretical constructs as well as Bahktinian theories of the grotesque. See also Wendy Parkins, "Protesting like a Girl: Embodiment, Dissent and Feminist Agency," *Feminist Theory* 1 (2000): 59–78, in which she discusses the militant suffragettes' efforts to embody citizenship in order to gain it, focusing particularly on the militant career of Mary Leigh and framing her experience through the theoretical lens of

Maurice Merleau-Ponty's phenomenological account of the body subject. She does not, however, engage in an examination of the visual culture surrounding such a phenomenon nor does she focus, as I do here, on the relationship between such bodily protest then and now.

6. Revd. F. Close, *A Sermon Addressed to the Female Chartists of Cheltenham 25 Aug. 1839* (London: Hamilton, Adams, 1839), 16, 13); discussed in Eileen Janes Yeo, "Some Paradoxes of Empowerment," in *Radical Femininity: Women's Self-Representation in the Public Sphere*, ed., Eileen Janes Yeo (Manchester: Manchester University Press, 1998), 3.

7. Elaine Showalter, *The Female Malady: Women, Madness, and English Culture, 1830–1980* (London: Virago, 1987), 161.

8. See Hélène Cixous and Catherine Clément, *La Jeune Née* (Paris: Union Générale d'Editions, 1975), 271–296; Catherine Clément, "Enclave Esclave," trans. Marilyn R. Shuster, in *New French Feminism*, eds. Isabelle de Courtivron and Elaine Marks (Amherst: University of Massachusetts Press, 1981), 133; and Jane Gallop, *The Daughter's Seduction: Feminism and Psychoanalysis* (Ithaca: Cornell University Press, 1982), 132–50, where an exchange between Cixous and Clement is analyzed; discussed in Showalter, *Female Malady*, 161.

9. Gail Finney, *Women in Modern Drama: Freud, Feminism, and European Theater at the Turn of the Century* (Ithaca: Cornell University Press, 1989), 13; discussed in Rita Felski, *The Gender of Modernity* (Cambridge: Harvard University Press, 1995), 3. *Hedda Gabler* was first produced in Norway in 1890. Its first London performance was at the Vaudeville Theatre in 1891.

10. Finney, *Women in Modern Drama*; and Showalter, *Female Malady*; discussed in Felski, *Gender of Modernity*, 3.

11. See Beverly Gordon, "Woman's Domestic Body: The Conceptual Conflation of Women and Interiors in the Industrial Age," *Winterthur Portfolio* 31 (Winter 1996): 281–301; and Colleen Denney, "'Sex, Money and Dirt': Mary Elizabeth Braddon, William Powell Frith, and the Business of Respectability," *Women, Portraiture and the Crisis of Identity in Victorian England: My Lady Scandalous Reconsidered* (Farnham, Surrey/Burlington, VT: Ashgate, 2009), particularly 58–63.

12. Mary J. Russo, *The Female Grotesque: Risk, Excess, and Modernity* (New York: Routledge, 1995), 53.

13. Elizabeth Crawford, "Introduction," *The Women's Suffrage Movement: A Reference Guide 1866–1928* (London: Routledge, 1999), ix.

14. Judith R. Walkowitz, *City of Dreadful Delight: Narratives of Sexual Danger in Late-Victorian London* (Chicago: University of Chicago Press, 1992), 11.

15. Walkowitz, *Dreadful Delight*, 21.

16. Vicinus, "Male Space and Women's Bodies," 264.

17. Maud Arncliffe-Sennett Collection, vol. 3, reel 1 (1908)(British Library, London).

18. Karen Offen, "Women, Citizenship, and Suffrage with a French Twist," in *Suffrage and Beyond: International Feminist Perspectives*, eds., Caroline Daley and Melanie Nolan (New York: New York University Press, 1994), 160.

19. Vicinus, "Male Space and Women's Bodies," 252.

20. Michelle de Larrabeiti, "Conspicuous Before the World: The Political Rhetoric of the Chartist Women," in *Radical Femininity*, 106.

21. De Larrabeiti, "Conspicuous Before the World," 107.

22. *Ibid.*, 108.

23. See Colleen Denney, "Raise Your Banner High! Mounting a 'Take Back the Night' Event: Visual Culture, Community Engagement, and Feminist Practices on a University Campus," in *Women, Power and Inequality in the 21st Century*, ed., Brittany C. Slatton (forthcoming from New York: Routledge).

24. Constance Lytton, *Prisons and Prisoners* (London: W. Heinemann, 1914); excerpted in Suffragette Fellowship Collection, Museum of London.

25. "French Women Fight Back," *The New York Times* (May 20, 2016); retrieved 1/18/17; https:///www.nytimes.com/2016/05/20/opinion/french-women-fight-back.html.

26. Olive Schreiner, *Women and Labor*, 7th ed. (New York: Frederick A. Stokes, 1911), 128.

27. Jean Methke Elshtain, *Public Man, Private Woman* (Princeton: Princeton University Press, 1981), 176; discussed in Mary Jean Corbett, *Representing Femininity: Middle-Class Subjectivity in Victorian and Edwardian Women's Autobiographies* (New York: Oxford University Press, 1992), 158.

28. Corbett, *Representing Femininity*, 163.

29. Paula Hays Harper, "Votes for Women? A Graphic Episode in the Battle of the Sexes," in *Art and Architecture in the Service of Politics*, eds., Henry A. Millon and Linda Nochlin (Cambridge: MIT Press, 1978), 150–151.

30. This information is on a poster in the Feminist Library Poster Collection (Bishopsgate Institute, London). The poster advertises a march and rally to stop page three of *The Sun* organized by Women's Self-Reliance Movement, 1986. It includes a cartoon of young lads buying *The Sun* for a look at page three, but instead of the nude image, they find "Sun Page 3 Great Women Series Part I: Caroline Herschel Astronomer 1780–1840" with a picture of her holding her telescope and underneath it says "Elevate the Dignity of Women." This idea of honoring women's history was already in place, as we have seen in this study, with the first wave. But, further, this particular event addresses the ongoing dialogue about the proper place of women's bodies in a public space and who has control over them.

31. For an example that itself consciously emulates suffrage women's tactics, see the work of Suzanne Lacy, particularly her protest piece *Three Weeks in May*, 1977; discussed in Jeff Kelley, "The Body Politics of Suzanne Lacy." In *But is it Art?*, ed., Nina Felshin (Seattle, WA: Bay Press, 1995), 221–249.

32. See Midge Mackenzie, *Shoulder to Shoulder* (London: Allen/New York: Knopf, 1975); "A Second Viewing," Battersea Arts Center, Old Town Hall, Lavender Hill, 1986; "Reminiscences of an Irish Suffragette," Tabard Theatre, Turnham Green, no date listed (Feminist Library Poster Collection, Bishopsgate Institute, London).

33. Mackenzie, *Shoulder to Shoulder*.

34. Women for Survival—Pine Gap, Nov. 11–29, 1983. Pamphlet (Feminist Library Pamphlet Collection. Bishopsgate Institute, London).

35. Corbett, "Representation and Subjectivity in the Edwardian Suffrage Movement," in *Representing Femininity*, 150.

36. Corbett, "Representation and Subjectivity," 165.

37. May Sinclair, *The Tree of Heaven* (London: Cassell, 1917); and on other women's voices see the Suffragette Fellowship Collection, Museum of London.

38. Showalter, *Female Malady*, 162.

39. Corbett, "Representation and Subjectivity," 151.

40. Quoted in Corbett, "Representation and Subjectivity," 160.

41. Martha A. Ackelsberg and Myrna Margulies Breitbart, "Terrains of Protest: Striking City Women," *Resisting Citizenship: Feminist Essays on Politics, Community, and Democracy* (New York: Routledge, 2010), 52.

42. Ackelsberg and Margulies Breitbart, "Terrains of Protest," 52.

43. Laurence Housman, *The Unexpected Years* (London: Cape, 1937), 235.

44. Martha A. Ackelsberg and Mary Lyndon Shanley, "Gender, Resistance, and Citizenship: Women's Struggle with/in the State," in *Resisting Citizenship*, 92–93; a political situation made widely known in the traveling art exhibition curated by Laurel Reuter, Director of the North Dakota Museum of Art (2006) called "The Disappeared" ("*Los Desaparecidos*") which gave a special place within the exhibit to these mothers (and grandmothers). See the exhibition catalog by the same title (Milano: Charta; Grand Forks, North Dakota: North Dakota Museum of Art, 2006).

45. Ackelsberg and Shanley, "Gender, Resistance, and Citizenship," 94.

46. Offen, "Women, Citizenship and Suffrage with a French Twist," 164. She cites "Decolonization" as the term Mariette Sineau uses in "Droit et démocratie," in *Histoire des femmes*, vol. 5, ed., Françoise Thébaud (Paris: Plon, 1992), 481.

47. Offen, "Women, Citizenship, and Suffrage with a French Twist," 164.

48. Maurice Agulhon, *Marianne into Battle: Republican Imagery and Symbolism in France, 1789–1880* (Cambridge: Cambridge University Press/Paris: Maison des Sciences de l'Homme, 1981), 88.

49. Denney, *Women, Portraiture and the Crisis of Identity*, 153.

50. Peter Stallybrass and Allon White, *The Politics and Poetics of Transgression* (Ithaca: Cornell University Press, 1986), 3. One second-wave demonstration which they code in this way, is the Greenham Common protest of the nuclear missile base near Newbury. Seated at the roadside entrance to a mass military base (hence on the periphery) the protesting women "occupy a very powerful *symbolic* domain *despite and because* of their actual social marginalization" (24).

51. Stallybrass and White, *Transgression*, conflate their hierarchical order with Mikhail Bakhtin's "world turned upside down" theories as presented in his *Rabelais and his World*, trans. Helene Iswolsky (Cambridge, MA: MIT Press, 1968), 6–23.

52. Bakhtin, *Rabelais and his World*; discussed in Russo, *Female Grotesque*, 62–63.

53. Stallybrass and White, *Transgression*, 5.

54. *Ibid.*, 24.

55. Marie Mulvey Roberts, "Introduction," in *The Militants: Suffragette Activism*, ed., Marie Mulvey Roberts and Tamae Mizuta (London: Routledge/Thoemmes Press, 1994), xiii–xiv.

56. Russo, *Female Grotesque*, 8.

57. *Ibid.*, 14.

58. Barbara Green, "From Visible *Flâneuse* to Spectacular Suffragette," *Spectacular Confessions*, discusses a similar phenomenon in the writings of suffrage women, exploring "the ways in which the spectacular activism of the suffragettes was haunted by the specter of an unruly feminine crowd and by the crowd's representative, the 'other woman'—the working woman, the imprisoned woman, the 'grotesque woman,' the loosely defined 'woman of the street' (31). She examines two suffrage texts, Lady Constance Lytton's confessional auto-

biography, *Prisons and Prisoners* (1914) and Elizabeth Robins' novel, *The Convert* (1907).

59. Alice Echols, *Daring to Be Bad: Radical Feminism in America, 1967–1975* (Minneapolis: University of Minnesota Press, 1989), ix.

60. Echols, *Daring to Be Bad*, xi.

61. *Ibid.*, 12. Juliet Mitchell, *Women's Estate* (London: Harmondsworth, 1971), 36; discussed in Barbara Caine, *English Feminism 1780–1980* (Oxford: Oxford University Press, 1997. [Reprint, 1999]), voices the same criticism of the first wave; that it did not embrace the wide-reaching reformism of Women's Liberation which now included a dialogue with civil rights, student rights, hippie rights; the first wavers were, by contrast, too narrow in their thinking (but she wrongly states that they did not embrace the ideals of working-class women).

62. For a considered examination of the multifaceted dialogue around liberal and radical feminism in the Women's Liberation Movement, see Stephanie Gilmore, *Groundswell: Grassroots Feminist Activism in Postwar America* (New York: Routledge, 2013).

63. Les Garner, *Stepping Stones to Women's Liberty* (London: Heinemann, 1984), 12; and Brian Harrison, *Separate Spheres: The Opposition to Women's Suffrage* (London: Croom Helm, 1978), 33. *The Common Cause* discusses these issues between 1909 and 1911.

64. Liz Stanley and Ann Morley, *The Life and Death of Emily Wilding Davison* (London: The Women's Press, 1988), 83–84.

65. Published by the National Union of Students, 461 Holloway Road, London; poster in Feminist Library Poster Collection (Bishopsgate Institute, London).

66. Echols, *Daring to Be Bad*, 14.

67. Caine, *English Feminism*, 256.

68. Yeo, "Some Paradoxes of Empowerment," 20. Caine, *English Feminism*, notes that they continued the same demands of other groups back to the nineteenth century, the only new addition being the request for 24 hour nurseries (257).

69. Janet Benton, "A Feminist's Daughter Finds Love in the Kitchen," *New York Times Sunday Styles Section* (Oct. 6, 2013): 6.

70. Richard Sennett, *Flesh and Stone: The Body and the City in Western Civilization* (New York: W.W. Norton, 1994).

71. Molly Housego and Neil R. Storey, *The Women's Suffrage Movement* (Oxford: Shire Publications, 2012), 5.

72. Yeo, "Some Paradoxes of Empowerment," 11; and Ada Nield Chew, "'Let the Women Be Alive!" *Freewoman* 13 (18 April 1912); discussed in Gerry Holloway, "'Let the Women Be Alive!' The Construction of the Married Working Woman in the Industrial Women's Movement, 1890–1914," in *Radical Femininity*, 172–195. On Chartist women see de Larrabeiti, "Conspicuous Before the World," 106–126.

73. Reproduced in Housgo and Storey, *Women's Suffrage Movement*, 7.

74. Quoted in Housego and Storey, *Women's Suffrage Movement*, 16.

75. Vicinus, "Male Space and Women's Bodies," 265.

76. Emmeline Pankhurst, *Votes for Women* (8 March 1908): 82; quoted in Stanley and Morley, *Davison*, 150.

77. Stanley and Morley, *Davison*, 151.

78. Harrison, "Act of Militancy," 26–27; and passim.

79. Caroline J. Howlett, "Writing on the Body? Representation and Resistance in British Suffragette Accounts of Forcible Feeding," in *Bodies of Writing, Bodies in Performance*, eds., Thomas Foster, Carol Siegel,

and Ellen E. Berry (New York: New York University Press, 1996), 8–9.

80. Lynn A. Higgins and Brenda Silver, "Rereading Rape," in *Rape and Representation*, eds., Lynn A. Higgins and Brenda Silver (New York: Columbia University Press, 1991), 5; discussed in Howlett, "Writing on the Body?" 11–12.

81. Howlett, "Writing on the Body?" 12.

82. Rosemary Betterton, "'A Perfect Woman,' The political body of suffrage," *An Intimate Distance: Women, Artists and the Body* (London: Routledge, 1996), 65; Desnoyes is discussed in Agulhon, *Marianne into Battle*, 77.

83. Betterton, "A Perfect Woman," 65. On Davison see Stanley and Morley, *Davison*, particularly 147–55.

84. Betterton, "A Perfect Woman," n. 21, 202.

85. *Ibid.*, 64–65.

86. *Ibid.*, 67.

87. *Ibid.*, 69.

88. Andrea Estepa, "Taking the White Gloves Off: Women Strike for Peace and 'the Movement,' 1967–73," in *Feminist Coalitions: Historical Perspectives on Second-Wave Feminism in the United States,* ed., Stephanie Gilmore (Urbana: University of Illinois Press, 2008), 85.

89. Estepa, "Taking the White Gloves Off," *Feminist Coalitions*, 84–85.

90. "Minutes, WSP National Conference, September 22, 1967," WSP Papers, series A.1, box 3, Swarthmore College Peack Collection; quoted in Estepa, 85.

91. Harrison, "Act of Militancy," 60.

92. As with other militant acts, window smashing started as the act of a few isolated individuals who were then supported by the WSPU leaders. Edith New and Mary Leigh in 1908; in 1909, thirteen women hurled stones "(wrapped in brown paper with string attached, so as to avoid injuring people inside the buildings)" at government buildings without official authorization, but they all received "retrospective justification" from the leaders (Harrison, "Act of Militancy," 51).

93. *Votes for Women* (February 23, 1912).

94. Christabel Pankhurst, *Broken Windows* (London: Women's Social and Political Union, 1912); reprinted in *The Militants: Suffragette Activism*, 2–6.

95. *The Times* (1912); quoted in Harrison, "Act of Militancy," 32–33.

96. Mrs. Henry Fawcett, "Broken Windows—and After," March 9, 1912, in *The Militants: Suffragette Activism*, 1–2.

97. Christine A. Anderson, response to Christabel Pankhurst, "Broken Windows," in *The Militants: Suffragette Activism*, 443.

98. On Mary Richardson's actions and their feminist implications in relationship to the female nude see Lynda Nead, *Myths of Sexuality: Representations of Women in Victorian England* (Oxford: B. Blackwell, 1988).

99. Susan J. Douglas, *Where the Girls Are: Growing up Female with the Mass Media* (New York: Times Books/Random House, 1994), 151.

100. Douglas, *Where the Girls Are*, 139.

101. Caine, *English Feminism*, 259–260; New York Radical Women, reprinted as "Miss World," in *The Body Politic: Writings from the Women's Liberation Movement in Britain, 1969-1972*, comp., Michelene Wandor (London: Stage 1, 1972), 254.

102. New York Radical Women, "Miss World," 249–250.

103. Margaret Marshment, "The Picture is Political: Representation of Women in Contemporary Popular Culture," in *Introducing Women's Studies: Feminist Theory and Practice*, eds., Victoria Robinson and Diane Richardson (New York: New York University Press, 1997), 127.

104. Douglas, *Where the Girls Are*, 156.

105. *Ibid.*, 159.

106. Stanley and Morley, *Davison*, 154.

107. Ackelsberg, *Resisting Citizenship*, 53.

108. Stallybrass and White, *Transgression*, 80.

109. Erika Rappaport, *Shopping for Pleasure: Women in the Making of London's West End* (Princeton: Princeton University Press, 2000), 218.

110. Rappaport, *Shopping for Pleasure*, 218.

111. Feminist Library Pamphlet Collection (Bishopsgate Institute, London).

112. Other posters in the Feminist Library Poster Collection also address the move outward from the domestic interior, one specifically addressing Ibsen's *Doll's House*. It is a poster announcing "Out of the Doll's House: The exhibition, National Theatre," from 1988. The exhibition was based on a BBC television series which traced the people and the events during the twentieth century who challenged the traditional idea that a woman's place was in the home. The accompanying photograph, ironically, shows women on the means streets of Liverpool in 1954 outside their respective doors on a long, gloomy street, all positioned on their knees, scrubbing their front stoops (Hulton Picture Library).

Bibliography

Archives

A. Muriel Pierotti Papers, Women's Library, London School of Economics.

Auckland Public Library Archives, Auckland, New Zealand.

Feminist Library Pamphlet Collection, Bishopsgate Institute, London.

Feminist Library Poster Collection, Bishopsgate Institute, London.

Manchester Archives and Local Studies, Manchester, England.

Maud Arncliffe-Sennett Collection, British Library, London.

Millicent Garrett Fawcett Papers, Women's Library, London School of Economics.

Millicent Garrett Fawcett Papers, Women's Suffrage Collection, Manchester Central Library,

Postcard Collection, Women's Library, London School of Economics.

Sir Julius Vogel Papers, Alexander Turnbull Library, National Archives, Wellington, New Zealand.

Suffragette Fellowship Collection, Museum of London.

Vera (Jack) Holmes Papers, Women's Library, London School of Economics.

Visual Resources Materials, Women's Library, London School of Economics.

Historical Periodicals

Britannia
The Common Cause
Punch
The Suffragette
The Vote
Votes for Women

Articles

Andres, Sophia. "From Camelot to Hyde Park: The Lady of Shalott's Pre-Raphaelite Postmodernism in A.S. Byatt and Tracy Chevalier." *Victorian Institute Journal* 34 (2006): 26–32.

Benton, Janet. "A Feminist's Daughter Finds Love in the Kitchen." *New York Times Sunday Styles Section* (Oct. 6, 2013): 6.

Bernstein, Haskell. "Boredom and the Ready-Made Life." *Social Research* 42 (1975): 512–537.

Broun, Elizabeth. "Thoughts That Began with the Gods: The Content of Whistler's Art." *Arts Magazine* 62 (October 1987): 35–42.

Bulan, S. "A 'Doll House' Revisited." *Votes for Women* 4 (February 17, 1911): 323.

Cockin, Katharine. "Cicely Hamilton's Warriors: Dramatic Reinventions of Militancy in the British Women's Suffrage Movement." *Women's History Review* 14 (2005): 527–542.

Dalziel, Raewyn. "The Colonial Helpmeet: Women's Role and the Vote in Nineteenth-Century New Zealand." *New Zealand Journal of History* 11 (October 1977): 112–23.

Davis, Richard Harding. "A General Election in England." *Harper's New Monthly Magazine* 87 (Sept. 1893): 489–506.

Denney, Colleen. "Wyoming Women's Suffrage as an Example to the World: A Comparative Look at the Pioneer Spirit of Wyoming and New Zealand." *Wyoming Annals* 18 (Autumn 2016): 2–23.

Eitner, Lorenz. "The Open Window and the Storm-Tossed Boat: An Essay in the Iconography of Romanticism." *Art Bulletin* 37 (Dec. 1955): 281–90.

Fawcett, Millicent Garrett. "The Woman Who Did." *Contemporary Review* 67 (1895): 630.

"French Women Fight Back." *New York Times* (May 20, 2016); retrieved 18 January 2017; https:///www.nytimes.com/2016/05/20/opinion/french-women-fight-back.html.

Geddes, J.F. "Culpable Complicity: The Medical Profession and the Forcible Feeding of Suffragettes, 1909–1914." *Women's History Review* 17 (2008): 79–94.

Gordon, Beverly. "Woman's Domestic Body: The Conceptual Conflation of Women and Interiors." *Winterthur Portfolio* 31 (Winter 1996): 281–301.

Hanna, Martha. "Iconology and Ideology: Images of Joan of Arc in the Idiom of the *Action Française*, 1908–1931." *French Historical Studies* 14 (Autumn 1985): 215–239.

Herbert, Robert L. "City Vs. Country: The Rural Image in French Painting." *Artforum* 5 (Feb. 1970): 44–55.

Holton, Sandra Stanley. "Free Love and Victorian Feminism: The Divers Matrimonials of Elizabeth Wolstenholme and Ben Elmy." *Victorian Studies* 37 (1994): 199–223.

House, John. "New Material on Monet and Pissarro in London in 1870–71." *Burlington Magazine* 120 (October 1978): 638–641.

Igra, Caroline. "Measuring the Temper of Her Time: Joan of Arc in the 1870s and 1880s." *Konsthistorik Tidskrift* 68 (1999): 117–125.

Johnson, Marguerite. "Boadicea and British Suffrage Feminists." *Outskirts: Crawley* 31 (November 2014) (online journal). Retrieved 30 June 2017; from proquest.com.libproxy.uwyo.edu.

Kean, Hilda. "Public History and Popular Memory: Issues

in the Commemoration of the British Militant Suffrage Campaign." *Women's History Review* 14 (2005): 581–602.

Leader, Bernice Kramer. "Antifeminism in the Paintings of the Boston School." *Arts Magazine* 56 (Jan.-March 1982): 112–119.

Lees, Frederic. "The Progress of Woman in France." *The Humanitarian* (February 1901): 88.

Marshall, Laura M. Nym. "Defining Militancy: Radical Protest, the Constitutional Idiom, and Women's Suffrage in Britain, 1908–1909." *Journal of British Studies* 39 (July 2000): 340–71.

Martz, Linda. "An AIDS-Era Reassessment of Christabel Pankhurst's *The Great Scourge and How to End It*." *Women's History Review* 14 (2005): 435–46.

Mercer, John. "Media and Militancy: Propaganda in the Women's Social and Political Union's Campaign." *Women's History Review* 14 (2005): 471–486.

Nead, Lynn. "The Magdalen in Modern Times: The Mythology of the Fallen Woman in Pre-Raphaelite Painting." *Oxford Art Journal* 7 (1984): 26–37.

_____. "Seduction, Prostitution, Suicide: On the *Brink* by Alfred Elmore." *Art History* 5 (Sept. 1982): 309–22.

Outman-Kramer, Miranda and Susana Galán, eds. "Comparative Perspectives Symposium. Gendered Bodies in the Protest Sphere." *Signs* 40 (2014): 1–79; http://www.jstor.org/stable/10.1086/673741

Parkins, Wendy. "Protesting Like a Girl: Embodiment, Dissent and Feminist Agency." *Feminist Theory* 1 (2000): 59–78.

Purvis, June. "The Prison Experiences of the Suffragettes in Edwardian Britain." *Women's History Review* 4 (1995): 103–133.

Rubinstein, David. "Millicent Garrett Fawcett and the Meaning of Women's Emancipation, 1886–99." *Victorian Studies* 35 (spring 1991): 365–380.

Schuessler, Jennifer. "Our Boredom, Ourselves." *New York Times Book Review* (January 24, 2010): 23.

Shefer, Elaine. "Elizabeth Siddal's 'Lady of Shalott.'" *Woman's Art Journal* 9 (Spring-Summer 1988): 21–29.

_____. "The Woman at the Window in Victorian Art and Christina Rossetti as the Subject of Millais's *Marian*." *Journal of Pre-Raphaelite Studies* 4 (Nov. 1983): 14–24.

Stowell, Sheila. "Dame Joan, Saint Christabel." *Modern Drama* 37 (1994): 421–36.

"The Suffrage Atelier." *Women's Franchise* 2 (July 1, 1909): 658. www.australia.gov.au/about-australia/australian-story/austn-suffragettes

Tsui, Aileen. "The Phantasm of Aesthetic Autonomy in Whistler's Work: Titling *The White Girl*." *Art History* 29 (June 2006): 444–475.

Tusan, Michelle Elizabeth. "Inventing the New Woman: Print Culture and Identity Politics During the Fin-De-Siècle." *Victorian Periodicals Review* 31 (summer 1998): 169–182.

Vickery, Amanda. "Golden Age to Separate Spheres? A Review of the Categories and Chronology of English Women's History." *The Historical Journal* 36 (June 1993): 383–414.

Walkowitz, Judith R. "Going Public: Shopping, Street Harassment, and Streetwalking in Late Victorian London." *Representations* 62 (Spring 1998): 1–30.

Books

Ackelsberg, Martha A., and Myrna Margulies Breitbart. "Terrains of Protest: Striking City Women." *Resisting Citizenship: Feminist Essays on Politics, Community, and Democracy*, 39–55. New York: Routledge, 2010.

Ackelsberg, Martha A., and Mary Lyndon Shanley. "Gender, Resistance, and Citizenship: Women's Struggle With/In the State." *Resisting Citizenship: Feminist Essays on Politics Community, and Democracy*, 86–100. New York: Routledge, 2010.

Adler, Laure, and Stefan Bollmann. *Les Femmes Qui Lisent Sont Dangereuses*. Paris: Flammarion, 2006.

Agulhon, Maurice. *Marianne into Battle: Republican Imagery and Symbolism in France, 1789–1880*. Cambridge: Cambridge University Press/Paris: Maison des Sciences de l'Homme, 1981.

Alberti, Johanna. *Beyond Suffrage: Feminists in War and Peace*. New York: St. Martin's Press, 1989.

Arncliffe Sennett, Maud. *The State and the Woman*. Vol. 2. London: Women's Franchise League, 1908.

Atkinson, Diane. *Funny Girls: Cartooning for Equality*. London: Penguin, 1997.

_____. *Suffragettes in the Purple, White and Green. London 1906–1914*. London: Museum of London, 1992.

Babcock, Barbara, ed. *The Reversible World*. Ithaca: Cornell University Press, 1978.

Bakhtin, Mikhail. *Rabelais and His World*, translated by Helene Iswolsky. Cambridge: MIT Press, 1968.

Balducci, Temma, Heather Belknap Jensen and Pamela J. Warner, eds. *Interior Portraiture and Masculine Identity in France, 1789–1914*. Farnham, Surrey/Burlington, VT: Ashgate, 2011.

Banks, Olive. *The Biographical Dictionary of British Feminists*. Vol. 2. New York: New York University Press, 1990.

Baudelaire, Charles. *The Painter of Modern Life and Other Essays*, edited and translated by Jonathan Mayne. London: Phaidon, 1964.

Betterton, Rosemary. "'A perfect woman': The Political Body of Suffrage." In *An Intimate Distance: Women, Artists and the Body*, 46–78. London: Routledge, 1996.

Berger, John. *Ways of Seeing*. London: BBC/Penguin, 1971.

Bidelman, Patrick Kay. *Pariahs Stand Up! The Founding of the Liberal Feminist Movement in France, 1858–1889*. Westport, CT: Greenwood Press, 1982.

Bowlby, Rachel. "Walking Women and Writing: Virginia Woolf as *Flâneuse*." In *New Feminist Discourses: Critical Essays on Theories and Texts*, edited by Isobel Armstrong, 26–47. New York: Routledge, 1992.

Broude, Norma, and Mary Garrard, eds. *The Power of Feminist Art*. New York: Abrams, 1994.

_____. *Reclaiming Female Agency: Feminist Art History After Postmodernism*. Berkeley: University of California Press, 2005.

Brown, Kathryn. *Women Readers in French Painting 1870–1890: A Space for the Imagination*. Farnham, Surrey; Burlington, VT: Ashgate, 2012.

Caine, Barbara. *English Feminism 1780–1980*. Oxford: Oxford University Press, 1997. Reprint 1999.

_____. *Victorian Feminists*. Oxford: Oxford University Press, 1992.

Casteras, Susan. "The Necessity of a Name." In *Gender and Discourse in Victorian Art and Literature*, edited by Anthony H. Harrison and Beverley Taylor, 207–232. DeKalb: Northern Illinois University Press, 1992.

Cherry, Deborah. *Beyond the Frame: Feminism and Visual Culture 1850–1900*. London: Routledge, 2000.

Chevalier, Tracey. *Falling Angels*. New York: Dutton, 2001.

Clayson, Hollis. "Threshold Space: Parisian Modernism Betwixt and Between 1869 to 1891." In *Impressionist*

Interiors, edited by Janet McLean, 15–29. Dublin, Ireland: National Gallery of Ireland, 2008.

Cockroft, V. Irene. *New Dawn Women: Women in the Arts & Crafts and Suffrage Movements at the Dawn of the 20th Century.* Compton, Surrey: Watts Gallery, 2005.

The Complete Writings of Alfred de Musset. New York: Edwin C. Hill, 1905.

Corbett, Mary Jean. "Representation and Subjectivity in the Edwardian Suffrage Movement." In *Representing Femininity*, 150–179. New York: Oxford University Press, 1992.

Cott, Nancy. *The Grounding of Modern Feminism.* New Haven: Yale University Press, 1987.

Coyle, Laura. "A Universal Patriot: Joan of Arc in America During the Gilded Age and the Great War." In *Joan of Arc: Her Image in France and America*, edited by Nora M. Heimann and Laura Coyle, 53–73. Washington, D.C.: Corcoran Gallery of Art, in association with London: D. Giles, 2006.

Crawford, Elizabeth. *The Women's Suffrage Movement: A Reference Guide 1860–1928.* London: Routledge, 1999.

Curry, David Park. *James McNeill Whistler: Uneasy Pieces.* Richmond: Virginia Museum of Fine Arts/ New York: Quantuck Lane Press, 2004.

De Beauvoir, Simone. *The Second Sex*, translated by H.M. Parshley. London: Jonathan Cape, 1953.

Demoor, Marysa. *Their Fair Share: Women, Power and Criticism in the Athenaeum, from Millicent Garrett Fawcett to Katherine Mansfield, 1870–1920.* Aldershot, England: Ashgate, 2000.

Denney, Colleen. "The Princess, Globally and Locally." In *Representing Diana, Princess of Wales: Cultural Memory and Fairy Tales Revisited*, 153–159. Madison: Associated University Press, 2005.

______."Raise Your Banner High! Mounting a 'Take Back the Night' Event: Visual Culture, Community Engagement, and Feminist Practices on a University Campus." In *Women, Power and Inequality in the 21st Century*, edited by Brittany C. Slatton (forthcoming from New York: Routledge).

______. *Women, Portraiture and the Crisis of Identity: My Lady Scandalous Reconsidered.* Burlington, VT: Ashgate, 2009.

Despres, Denise L. "*Le Triomphe De L'humilité: Thérèse of Liseux and 'La Nouvelle Jeanne.'*" In *Joan of Arc and Spirituality*, edited by Ann W. Astell and Bonnie Wheeler, 249–265. New York: Palgrave Macmillan, 2003.

Dickens, Charles. *Bleak House.* London: Penguin, 2003.

Distel, Anne, et al. *Gustave Caillebotte: Urban Impressionist.* New York: Abbeville Press, 1995.

Dodd, Kathryn, ed. *A Sylvia Pankhurst Reader.* Manchester: Manchester University Press, 1993.

Dougan, David, and Denise Sanchez. *Feminist Periodicals 1855–1984.* London: Harvester Press, 1987.

Douglas, Susan. *Where the Girls Are.* New York: Times Books, 1994.

D'Souza, Aruna, and Tom McDonough, eds. *The Invisible Flâneuse? Gender, Public Space, and Visual Culture in Nineteenth-Century Paris.* Manchester: Manchester University Press, 2006.

Dubois, Ellen Carol. "Introduction." In *Feminist Theorists: Three Centuries of Women's Intellectual Traditions*, edited by Dale Spender, ix–xiii. London: The Women's Press, 1983.

Dupanloup, Monseigneur. *La Femme Studieuse.* Paris, 1869.

Echols, Alice. *Daring to Be Bad: Radical Feminism in America, 1967–1975.* Minneapolis: University of Minnesota Press, 1989.

Ellis, Sarah Stickney. *The Daughters of England.* London, 1842.

Estepa, Andrea. "Taking the White Gloves Off: Women Strike for Peace and 'The Movement,' 1967–73." In *Feminist Coalitions: Historical Perspectives on Second-Wave Feminism in the United States*, edited by Stephanie Gilmore, 84–112. Urbana: University of Illinois Press, 2008.

Eustance, Claire. "Meanings of Militancy: The Ideas and Practice of Political Resistance in the Women's Freedom League, 1907–14." In *The Women's Suffrage Movement: New Feminist Perspectives*, edited by Maroula Joannou and June Purvis, 51–64. Manchester: Manchester University Press, 1998.

Fawcett, Mrs. Henry. "Broken Windows—And After, March 9, 1912." In *The Militants: Suffragette Activism*, edited by Marie Mulvey Roberts and Tamae Mizuta, 1–2. London: Routledge/Thoemmes Press, 1994.

Fawcett, Millicent (Garrett). *Five Famous Women.* London: Cassell and Co., 1905.

Fawcett, Millicent Garrett. *The Women's Victory—And After: Personal Reminiscences, 1911–1918.* London: Sidgwick & Jackson, 1920.

Feinberg, Leslie. *Transgender Warriors: Making History from Joan of Arc to Dennis Rodman.* Boston: Beacon Press, 1996.

Felski, Rita. *The Gender of Modernity.* Cambridge: Harvard University Press, 1995.

Fermaglich, Kirsten, and Lisa M. Fine, eds. *Betty Friedan: The Feminine Mystique: A Norton Critical Edition.* New York: Norton, 2013.

Flaubert, Gustave. *Madame Bovary.* Trans. and ed. Geoffrey Wall. London: Penguin, 2002.

Flint, Kate. *The Woman Reader 1837–1914.* Oxford: Clarendon Press, 1995.

Foucault, Michel. *Discipline and Punish: The Birth of the Prison*, translated by Alan Sheridan New York: Random House, 1991.

______. *The History of Sexuality. Volume 1. an Introduction*, translated by Robert Hurley. New York: Pantheon Books, 1978.

Fraisse, Geneviève. "A Philosophical History of Sexual Difference." In *A History of Women in the West. Volume IV: Emerging Feminism from Revolution to World War*, edited by Geneviève Fraisse and Michelle Perrot, 48–79. Cambridge: Harvard University Press/ London: Belknap Press, 1993.

Freénée-Hutchins, Samantha. *Boudica's Odyssey in Early Modern England.* Burlington, VT: Ashgate, 2014.

Fuller, Margaret. *Women in the Nineteenth Century.* New York: Greeley and McElrath, 1845.

Garb, Tamar. "Portraiture and the New Woman." In *The Body in Time: Figures of Femininity in Late Nineteenth-Century France*, 39–78. Seattle: Spencer Museum of Art in association with University of Washington Press, 2008.

______. *Sisters of the Brush: Women's Artistic Culture in Late Nineteenth-Century Paris.* New Haven: Yale University Press, 1994.

Garner, Les. *Stepping Stones to Women's Liberty.* London: Heinemann, 1984.

Gedo, Mary Mathews. *Monet and His Muse: Camille Monet in the Artist's Life.* Chicago: University of Chicago Press, 2010.

Gissing, George. *The Odd Women.* Introduction by Elaine Showalter. London: Penguin, 1994.

Green, Barbara. *Spectacular Confessions*. New York: St. Martin's Press, 1997.

Gilmore, Stephanie. *Groundswell: Grassroots Feminist Activism in Postwar America*. New York: Routledge, 2013.

Grimshaw, Patricia. *Women's Suffrage in New Zealand*. Wellington, NZ: Auckland University Press/Oxford University Press, 1972.

______. "Women's Suffrage in New Zealand Revisited: Writing from the Margins." In *Suffrage and Beyond: International Feminist Perspectives*, edited by Caroline Daley and Melanie Nolan, 25–41. New York: New York University Press, 1994.

Gordon, Linda. "What Is Women's History?" In *What Is History Today?*, edited by Juliet Gardiner, 91–93. Basingstoke, England: Macmillan, 1988.

______. "What's New in Women's History." In *Feminist Studies/Critical Studies*, edited by Teresa de Laurentis, 20–30. Bloomington: Indiana University Press, 1986.

Gullickson, Gay L. *Unruly Women of Paris: Images of the Commune*. Ithaca: Cornell University Press, 1996.

Haig, Margaret [Viscountess Rhondda]. *This Way My World*. London: Macmillan, 1933.

Hall, Donald E. "From Margin to Center: Agency and Authority in the Novels of Wilkie Collins." In *Fixing Patriarchy: Feminism and Mid-Victorian Male Novelists*, 151–174. New York: New York University Press, 1996.

Hall, Leslie A. "Suffrage, Sex and Science." In *The Women's Suffrage Movement: New Feminist Perspectives*, edited by Maroula Joannou and June Purvis, 188–200. Manchester: Manchester University Press, 1998.

Hamilton, Cicely. *Life Errant: Autobiographical Reminiscences*. London: J.M. Dent, 1935.

______. *A Pageant of Great Women*. Liverpool: A.W. Duncan, 1912.

Harper, Paula Hays. "Votes for Women? A Graphic Episode in the Battle of the Sexes." In *Art and Architecture in the Service of Politics*, edited by Henry A. Millon and Linda Nochlin, 150–156. Cambridge: MIT Press, 1978.

Harrison, Brian. "The Act of Militancy: Violence and the Suffragettes, 1904–1914." In *Peaceable Kingdom: Stability and Change in Modern Britain*, 26–81. Oxford: Oxford University Press, 1982.

______. *Separate Spheres: The Opposition to Women's Suffrage*. London: Croom Helm, 1978.

______. "Women's Health and the Women's Movement." In *Biology, Medicine and Society 1840–1940*, edited by Charles Webster, 15–71. Cambridge: Cambridge University Press, 1981.

Hause, Stephen, with Anne R. Kenney. *Women's Suffrage and Social Politics in the French Third Republic*. Princeton: Princeton University Press, 1984.

Hebert, Robert L., ed. *The Art Criticism of John Ruskin*. New York: Anchor Books/Doubleday, 1964.

Heimann, Nora M. "Joan of Arc: From Medieval Maiden to Modern Saint." In *Joan of Arc: Her Image in France and America*, edited by Nora M. Heimann and Laura Coyle, 15–51. Washington, D.C.: Corcoran Gallery of Art, in association with London: D. Giles, 2006.

______. *Joan of Arc in French Art and Culture (1700–1855): From Satire to Sanctity*. Burlington, VT: Ashgate, 2005.

Hellerstein, Erna Olafson, Leslie Parker Hume and Karen M. Offen, eds. *Victorian Women: A Documentary Account of Women's Lives in Nineteenth-Century England, France, and the United States*. Stanford: Stanford University Press, 1981.

Heynen, Hilde, and Gülsüm Bader, eds. *Negotiating Domesticity: Spatial Productions of Gender in Modern Architecture*. London: Routledge, 2005.

Higonnet, Anne. *Berthe Morisot's Images of Women*. Cambridge: Harvard University Press, 1992.

Hingley, Richard, and Christina Unwin. *Boudica: Iron Age Warrior Queen*. London: Hambledon Continuum, 2005.

Hobbins, Daniel, ed. and trans. *The Trial of Joan of Arc*. Cambridge: Harvard University Press, 2005.

Hollis, Patricia, comp. *Women in Public, 1850–1900: Documents of the Victorian Women's Movement*. Boston: G. Allen & Unwin, 1979.

Holloway, Gerry. "'Let the women be alive!' The Construction of the Married Working Woman in the Industrial Women's Movement, 1890–1914." In *Radical Femininity: Women's Self-Representation in the Public Sphere*, edited by Eileen Janes Yeo, 172–195. Manchester: Manchester University Press/New York: St. Martin's Press, 1998.

Holtby, Winifred. *Women and a Changing Civilisation*. London: John Lane, 1934.

Holton, Sandra Stanley. *Feminism and Democracy: Women's Suffrage and Reform Politics in Britain 1900–1918*. Cambridge: Cambridge University Press, 1986.

______. "From Anti-Slavery to Suffrage Militancy: The Bright Circle, Elizabeth Cady Stanton and the British Women's Movement." In *Suffrage and Beyond: International Feminist Perspectives*, edited by Caroline Daley and Melanie Nolan, 213–233. New York: New York University Press, 1994.

______. ""The Political Protest of Male Suffragists and the Gendering of the 'Suffragette' Identity." In *The Men's Share?: Masculinities, Male Support and Women's Suffrage in Britain, 1890–1920*, edited by A.V. John and C. Eustance, 110–134. New York: Routledge, 1997.

Holcombe, Lee. *Victorian Ladies at Work: Middle-Class Working Women in England and Wales, 1850–1914*. Hamden, CT: Archon Books, 1973.

House, John. "Women Out of Doors." In *Women in Impressionism: From Mythical Feminine to Modern Woman*, edited by Sidsel Maria Søndergaard, 156–187. Milan, Italy: SKIRA, 2006.

House, John, Petra ten-Doeschatte Chu, and Jennifer Hardin. *Monet's London: Artists' Reflections on the Thames*. St. Petersburg, FL: Museum of Fine Arts/Ghent, Belgium: Shoeck, 2005.

Housego, Molly, and Neil R. Storey. *The Women's Suffrage Movement*. Oxford: Shire Publications, 2012.

Housman, Laurence. *The Unexpected Years*. London: Cape, 1937.

Howlett, Caroline J. "Writing on the Body? Representation and Resistance in British Suffragette Accounts of Forcible Feeding." In *Bodies of Writing, Bodies in Performance*, edited by Thomas Foster, Carol Siegel and Ellen E. Berry, 3–41. New York: New York University Press, 1996.

Hume, Leslie Parker. *The National Union of Women's Suffrage Societies, 1897–1914*. New York: Garland, 1982.

Huyssen, Andreas. *After the Great Divide: Modernism, Mass Culture, Postmodernism*. Bloomington: Indiana University Press, 1986.

Ibsen, Henrik. *Doll's House*. Trans. William C. Archer. London: T. Fisher Unwin, 1889.

Iskin, Ruth. "Was There a New Woman in Impressionist Painting?" In *Women in Impressionism: From Mythical Feminine to Modern Woman*, edited by Sidsel Maria Søndergaard, 189–223. Milan, Italy: SKIRA, 2006.

Jackson, Margaret. *The Real Facts of Life: Feminism and*

the Politics of Sexuality c. 1850–1940. London: Taylor & Francis, 1994.

Jeffrys, Sheila. *The Spinster and Her Enemies: Feminism and Sexuality 1880–1930*. London: Pandora, 1985.

Joannou, Maroula, and June Purvis, eds. *The Women's Suffrage Movement: New Feminist Perspectives*. Manchester: Manchester University Press, 1998.

Jonard, Norbert. *L'Ennui Dans La Littérature Européenne*. Paris: Honoré Champion, 1998.

Jorgensen-Earp, Cheryl R. *The Transfiguring Sword: The Just War of the Women's Social and Political Union*. Tuscaloosa: University of Alabama Press, 1997.

Kelley, Jeff. "The Body Politics of Suzanne Lacy." In *But Is It Art?*, edited by Nina Felshin, 221–249. Seattle: Bay Press, 1995.

Kenney, Annie. *Memories of a Militant*. London: Edward Arnold, 1924.

Kent, Susan Kingsley. *Sex and Suffrage in Great Britain, 1860–1914*. Princeton: Princeton University Press, 1987.

Ker Conway, Jill. *When Memory Speaks: The Art of Autobiography*. New York: Vintage, 1998.

Kristeva, Julia. "Stabat Mater." In *The Kristeva Reader*, edited by Toril Moi, 160–186. New York: Columbia University Press, 1986.

Larrabeiti, Michelle de. "Conspicuous Before the World: The Political Rhetoric of the Chartist Women." In *Radical Femininity Women's Self-Representation in the Public Sphere*, edited by Eileen Janes Yeo, 106–126. Manchester: Manchester University Press/New York: St. Martin's Press, 1998.

Ledger, Sally. "The New Woman and the Crisis of Victorianism." In *Cultural Politics at the Fin De Siècle*, edited by Sally Ledger and Scott McCracken, 22–44. Cambridge: Cambridge University Press, 1995.

Letters of Constance Lytton. Selected and Arranged by Betty Balfour. London: William Heinemann, 1925.

Levine, Philippa. *Feminist Lives in Victorian Britain*. Oxford: Blackwell, 1990.

Liddington, Jill, and Jill Norris. *One Hand Tied Behind Us: The Rise of the Women's Suffrage Movement*. London: Virago Press, 1984.

Linklater, A. *An Unhusbanded Life: Charlotte Despard: Suffragette, Socialist and Sinn Feiner*. London: Hutchinson, 1980.

Macdonald, Sharon. "Boadicea: Warrior, Mother and Myth." In *Images of Women in Peace and War: Cross-Cultural and Historical Perspectives*, edited by Sharon Macdonald, Pat Holden, and Shirley Ardener, 40–61. Madison: University of Wisconsin Press, 1988.

Macdonald, Sharon, Pat Holden and Shirley Ardener, eds. *Images of Women in Peace and War: Cross-Cultural and Historical Perspectives*. Madison: University of Wisconsin Press, 1988.

Mackenzie, Midge. *Shoulder to Shoulder*. London: Allen/New York: Knopf, 1975.

Mainardi, Patricia. *Husbands, Wives, and Lovers: Marriage and Its Discontents in Nineteenth-Century France*. New Haven: Yale University Press, 2003.

Marcus, Jane. "The Asylum of Antaeus: Women, War and Madness—Is There a Feminist Fetishism?" In *The New Historicism*, edited by H. Aram Veeser, 132–151. New York: Routledge, 1989.

_____. "Introduction." In *Suffrage and the Pankhursts*, edited by Jane Marcus, 1–17. London: Routledge, 1987.

Margolis, Nadia. "The 'Joan Phenomenon' and the French Right." In *Fresh Verdicts on Joan of Arc*, edited by Bonnie Wheeler and Charles T. Wood, 265–287. New York: Garland, 1996.

Marshment, Margaret. "The Picture Is Political: Representation of Women in Contemporary Popular Culture." In *Introducing Women's Studies: Feminist Theory and Practice*, edited by Victoria Robinson and Diane Richardson, 124–151. New York: New York University Press, 1997.

Martindale, Louisa. *Under the Surface*. Brighton: Southern Publishing Company, 1908.

Mayhall, Laura E. Nym. *The Militant Suffrage Movement: Citizenship and Resistance in Britain, 1860–1930*. Oxford: Oxford University Press, 2003.

McConkey, Kenneth. "New English *Intimisme*: The Painting of the Edwardian Interior." In *The Edwardians: Secrets and Desires*, edited by Anne Gray, 89–106. Canberra: National Gallery of Australia/Seattle: University of Washington Press, 2004.

McMillan, James F. *France and Women 1789–1914: Gender, Society and Politics*. London: Routledge, 2000.

Mill, John Stuart. *The Subjection of Women*. Introduction by Patricia M. Ulbrich. New York: Barnes and Noble, 2005.

Mitchell, David. *Queen Christabel: A Biography of Christabel Pankhurst*. London: MacDonald and Jane, 1977.

Monod, Adolphe. *Woman: Her Mission in Life*. Edited and translated. Constance K. Walker. Vestovia, AL: Solid Ground Christian Books, 2011.

Moses, Claire Goldberg. *French Feminism in the 19th Century*. Albany: State University of New York Press, 1984.

Mulvey, Laura. *Visual and Other Pleasures*. Bloomington: Indiana University Press, 1989.

Mulvihill, M. *Charlotte Despard: A Biography*. London: Pandora, 1989.

Nead, Lynda. *Myths of Sexuality: Representations of Women in Victorian England*. Oxford: B. Blackwell, 1988.

Nelson, Elizabeth. "Tennyson and the Ladies of Shalott." In *Ladies of Shalott: A Victorian Masterpiece and Its Contexts*, 4–16. Providence: Bell Gallery/Brown University, 1985.

New York Radical Women. "Miss World." In *The Body Politic: Writings from the Women's Liberation Movement in Britain, 1969–1972*, compiled by Michelene Wandor, 249–260. London: Stage 1, 1972.

Nochlin, Linda. *Realism*. London: Penguin, 1971

_____. *Representing Women*. New York: Thames and Hudson, 1999.

_____. "Women, Art, and Power." In *Visual Theory: Painting and Interpretation*, edited by Norman Bryson et al., 13–46. New York: Harper Collins, 1991.

Nunn, Pamela Gerrish. "Trouble in Paradise." In *Problem Pictures: Women and Men in Victorian Painting*, 49–71. Aldershot, England: Scolar Press; Brookfield, VT: Ashgate, 1995.

Oakley, Ann. "Millicent Garrett Fawcett: Duty and Determination." In *Feminist Theorists: Three Centuries of Women's Intellectual Traditions*, edited by Dale Spender, 184–202. London: The Women's Press, 1983.

Offen, Karen. *European Feminisms, 1700–1950*. Stanford: Stanford University Press, 2000.

_____. "Is the 'Woman Question' Really the 'Man Problem'?" In *Confronting Modernity in Fin-De-Siècle France: Bodies, Minds and Gender*, edited by Christopher E. Forth and Elinor Accampo, 43–62. Houndmills: Palgrave Macmillan/New York: St. Martin's Press, 2010.

_____. "Women, Citizenship, and Suffrage with a French Twist." In *Suffrage and Beyond: International Feminist Perspectives*, edited by Caroline Daley and Melanie

Nolan, 151–170. New York: New York University Press, 1994.

Pankhurst, Christabel. "Broken Windows." In *The Militants: Suffragette Activism*, edited by Marie Mulvey Roberts and Tamae Mizuta, 1–6. London: Routledge/Thoemmes Press, 1994.

Pankhurst, E. Sylvia. *The Suffragette Movement. an Intimate Account of Persons and Ideals*. London: Longmans, 1931.

Pankhurst, Emmeline. *Why We Are Militant; a Speech Delivered in New York, Oct. 21, 1913*. London: Women's Social and Political Union, 1913.

Pethick-Lawrence, Emmeline. *My Part in a Changing World*. 1938. Reprint: Westport, CT: Hyperion Press, 1976.

Phoca, Sophia, and Rebecca Wright. *Introducing Postfeminism*, edited by Richard Appignanesi. London: Icon Books/New York: Totem Books, 1990.

Piehler, Liana F. *Spatial Dynamics and Female Development in Victorian Art*. New York: Peter Lane, 2003.

Pollock, Griselda. *Mary Cassatt: Painter of Modern Women*. London: Thames and Hudson, 1998.

______. "Modernity and the Spaces of Femininity." In *The Expanding Discourse: Feminism and Art History*, edited by Norma Broude and Mary Garrard, 244–267. New York: HarperCollins, 1992.

Poovey, Mary. *Uneven Developments: The Ideological Work of Gender in Victorian England*. Chicago: University of Chicago Press, 1988. Reprint: London: Virago, 1989.

Pugh, Martin. "The Impact of Women's Enfranchisement in Britain." In *Suffrage and Beyond: International Feminist Perspectives*, edited by Caroline Daley and Melanie Nolan, 313–328. New York: New York University Press, 1994.

Purvis, June. "'Deeds, not words': Daily Life in the Women's Social and Political Union in Edwardian Britain." In *Votes for Women*, edited by June Purvis and Sandra Stanley Holton, 135–158. London: Routledge, 2000.

______. "Fighting the Double Moral Standard in Edwardian Britain: Suffragette Militancy, Sexuality and the Nation in the Writings of the Early Twentieth-Century British Feminist Christabel Pankhurst." In *Women's Activism: Global Perspectives from the 1890s to the Present*, edited by Francisca de Hann et al., 120–135. London: Routledge, 2013.

Radway, Janice A. *Reading the Romance*. Chapel Hill: University of North Carolina Press, 1984; reprint 1991.

Rappaport, Erica. *Shopping for Pleasure: Women in the Making of London's West End*. Princeton: Princeton University Press, 2000.

Reed, Christopher, ed. *Not at Home: The Suppression of Domesticity in Modern Art and Architecture*. London: Thames and Hudson, 1996.

Reuter, Laurel. *"The Disappeared" ("Los Desaparecidos")*. Milano: North Dakota Museum of Art, 2006.

Rewald, Sabine. *Rooms with a View: The Open Window in the 19th Century*. New York: Metropolitan Museum of Art/New Haven: Yale University Press, 2011.

Rice, Charles. *The Emergence of the Interior: Architecture, Modernity, Domesticity*. London: Routledge, 2007.

Richardson, Angelique and Chris Willis. *The New Woman in Fact and Fiction: Fin De Siècle Feminisms*. Foreword by Lynn Pykett. Houndmills, New York: Palgrave, 2001.

Roberts, Helene, ed. *Encyclopedia of Comparative Iconography*. Vol. 1. Chicago: Fitzroy Dearborn, 1998.

Roberts, Marie Mulvey. "Introduction." In *The Militants: Suffragette Activism*, edited by Marie Mulvey Roberts and Tamae Mizuta, xiii-xiv. London: Routledge/Thoemmes Press, 1994.

Roberts, Mary Louise. *Discursive Acts: The New Woman in Fin-De-Siècle France*. Chicago: University of Chicago Press, 2002.

______. "Subversive Copy: Feminist Journalism in Fin-De-Siècle France." In *Making the News*, edited by Dean de la Motte and Jeannene M. Przyblyski, 302–350. Amherst: University of Massachusetts Press, 1999.

Romaine, Suzanne. *Communicating Gender*. Mahwah, NJ: Lawrence Erlbaum Associates, 1999.

Romieu, Madame (Marie Sincère). *La Femme Au XIXe Siècle*. Paris, 1858.

Rosen, Andrew. *Rise Up Women! The Militant Campaign of the Women's Social and Political Union, 1903–1914*. London: Routledge and Kegan Paul, 1974.

Rouart, Denis, ed. *Berthe Morisot: The Correspondence with Her Family and Her Friends Manet, Puvis De Chavannes, Degas, Monet, Renoir and Mallarmé*. Translated by Betty W. Hubbard. New York: Moyer Bell/London: Camden Press, 1987.

Rubinstein, David. *A Different World for Women*. Columbus: Ohio University Press, 1991.

Ruskin, John. *Sesame and Lilies*. London: Smith, Elder, & Co., 1862.

Russo, Mary J. *The Female Grotesque: Risk, Excess, and Modernity*. New York: Routledge, 1995.

Ryan, Mary P. *Women in Public: Between Ballots and Banners, 1825–1880*. Baltimore: Johns Hopkins University Press, 1990.

Sarah, Elizabeth. "Christabel Pankhurst: Reclaiming Her Power." In *Feminist Theorists: Three Centuries of Women's Intellectual Traditions*, edited by Dale Spender, 256–284. London: The Women's Press, 1983.

Schibanoff, Susan. "True Lies: Transvestism and Idolatry in the Trial of Joan of Arc." In *Fresh Verdicts on Joan of Arc*, edited by Bonnie Wheeler and Charles T. Wood, 31–60. New York: Garland, 1996.

Schreiner, Olive. *Women and Labor*. 7th ed. New York: Frederick A. Stokes, 1911.

Scott, Joan Wallach. "Experience." In *Feminists Theorize the Political*, edited by Judith Butler and Joan Wallach Scott, 29–35. New York: Routledge, 1992.

______. *The Fantasy of Feminist History*. Durham: Duke University Press, 2011.

______. "'L'ouvriere! Mot impie, sordide..' Women Workers in the Discourse of Political Economy, 1849–1860." In *Gender and the Politics of History*, 139–162. New York: Columbia University Press, 1988.

Scott, Joan Wallach, ed. *Feminism and History*. Oxford: Oxford University Press, 1996.

Sennett, Richard. *Flesh and Stone: The Body and the City in Western Civilization*. New York: W.W. Norton, 1994.

Shefer, Elaine. "The Woman at the Window." In *Birds, Cages and Women in Victorian and Pre-Raphaelite Art*, 127–150. New York: Peter Lang, 1990.

Showalter, Elaine. *The Female Malady: Women, Madness, and English Culture*. New York: Pantheon Books, 1985.

______. *Inventing Herself: Claiming a Female Intellectual Heritage*. New York: Scribner's, 2001.

______. *Sexual Anarchy: Gender and Culture at the Fin De Siècle*. London: Virago, 1990. Reprint: 2001.

Sidlauskas, Susan. "Psyche and Sympathy: Staging Interiority in the Early Modern Home." In *Not at Home:*

The Suppression of Domesticity in Modern Art and Architecture, edited by Christopher Reed, 65–80. London: Thames and Hudson, 1996.

Silverman, Deborah. "Amazone, *Femme Nouvelle*, and the Threat to the Bourgeois Family." In *Art Nouveau in Fin-De-Siécle France: Politics, Psychology and Style*, 63–74. Berkeley: University of California Press, 1989.

Simon, Jules. *L'Ouvrière*. Paris, 1861.

Smith, Angela K. *Suffrage Discourse in Britain During the First World War*. Burlington, VT: Ashgate, 2005.

Snitow, Ann, Christine Stansell and Sharon Thompson, eds. *Powers of Desire: The Politics of Sexuality*. New York: Monthly Review, 1983.

Søndergaard, Sidsel Maria. "Women in Impressionism: An Introduction." In *Women in Impressionism: From Mythical Feminine to Modern Woman*, edited by Sidsel Maria Søndergaard, 11–97. Milan, Italy: SKIRA, 2006.

Sowerwine, Charles. "Revising the Sexual Contract: Women's Citizenship and Republicanism in France, 1789–1944." In *Confronting Modernity in Fin-De-Siècle France: Bodies, Minds and Gender*, edited by Christopher E. Forth and Elinor Accampo, 19–42. Houndmills: Palgrave Macmillan/New York: St. Martin's Press, 2010.

Spacks, Patricia Meyer. *Boredom: The Literary History of a State of Mind*. Chicago: University of Chicago Press, 1995.

Spain, Daphne. *Gendered Spaces*. Chapel Hill: University of North Carolina Press, 1992.

Spender, Dale. "Foreword." In *Feminist Theorists: Three Centuries of Women's Intellectual Traditions*, edited by Dale Spender, 1–7. London: The Women's Press, 1983.

Stallybrass, Peter, and Allon White. *The Politics and Poetics of Transgression*. Ithaca: Cornell University Press, 1986.

Stanley, Liz, and Ann Morley. *The Life and Death of Emily Wilding Davison*. London: Women's Press, 1989.

Stanton, Theodore, and Frances Power Cobbe. *The Woman Question in Europe: A Series of Original Essays*. Reprint. Charleston, SC: BiblioLife, 2008.

Strachey, Ray. *Millicent Garrett Fawcett*. London: John Murray, 1931.

Strumwasser, Gina. "Justice." In *Encyclopedia of Comparative Iconography*. Vol. 1. Edited by Helene Roberts, 465–467. Chicago: Fitzroy Dearborn, 1998.

Sutton, Denys. *Nocturne: The Art of James McNeill Whistler*. London: Country Life, 1964.

Tickner, Lisa. *The Spectacle of Women: Imagery of the Suffrage Campaign 1907–14*. London: Chatto and Windus, 1987. Chicago: University of Chicago Press, 1988.

Tinterow, Gary and Henri Loyrette. *Origins of Impressionism*. New York: Metropolitan Museum of Art/Harry Abrams, 1995.

Todd, Pamela. *The Impressionists at Home*. London: Thames and Hudson, 2005.

Toohey, Peter. *Boredom: A Lively History*. New Haven, CT: Yale University Press, 2011.

Vadillo, Ana Pareja. "Phenomena in Flux: The Aesthetics and Politics of Travelling in Modernity." In *Women's Experience of Modernity*, edited by Ann Ardis and Leslie W. Lewis, 205–222. Baltimore: Johns Hopkins University Press, 2003.

Vellacott, Jo. *Pacifists, Patriots and the Vote*. Houndsmill, England: Palgrave Macmillan, 2007.

Vicinus, Martha. *Independent Women: Work and Community for Single Women, 1850–1920* Chicago: University of Chicago Press, 1985.

Waelti-Walters, Jennifer. *Feminist Novelists of the Belle Epoque: Love as a Lifestyle*. Bloomington: Indiana University Press, 1990.

Waelti-Walters, Jennifer, and Stephen C. Hause. "Introduction." In *Feminisms of the Belle Epoque*, edited by Jennifer Waelti-Walter and Stephen C. Hause, 2–10. Lincoln: University of Nebraska Press, 1994.

Walkowitz, Judith. *City of Dreadful Delight: Narratives of Sexual Danger in Late Victorian London*. Chicago: University of Chicago Press, 1992.

Warner, Marina. *Joan of Arc: The Image of the Heroine*. New York: Knopf, 1981

_____. *Monuments and Maidens: The Allegory of the Female Form*. New York: Atheneum, 1985.

Weeks, Jeffrey. *Sex, Politics and Society: The Regulation of Sexuality Since 1800*. London: Longman, 1981.

Wigley, Mark. "Untitled: The Housing of Gender." In *Sexuality and Space: Volume 1: Princeton Papers on Architecture*, edited by Beatriz Colomina and Jennifer Bloomer, 331–348. New York: Princeton Architectural Press, 1992.

Williams, Val. *The Other Observers: Women Photographers in Britain, 1900 to the Present*. London: Virago Press, 1986. Reprint, 1991.

Wolff, Janet. *Feminine Sentences: Essays on Women and Culture*. Berkeley: University of California Press, 1990.

Woolf, Virginia. *Mrs. Dalloway*. London: Vintage Classics, 1925.

Yeo, Eileen Janes. "Some Paradoxes of Empowerment." In *Radical Femininity: Women's Self-Representation in the Public Sphere*, edited by Eileen Janes Yeo, 1–24. Manchester: Manchester University Press/New York: St. Martin's Press, 1998.

Zakreski, Patricia. *Representing Female Artistic Labour, 1848–1890*. Burlington, VT: Ashgate, 2006.

Conference Papers

Henderson, Kate Krueger. "Conveying Femininity: The New Woman and the Omnibus in Evelyn Sharp's 'In Dull Brown.'" 22nd Annual Interdisciplinary Nineteenth Century Studies Conference, University of Missouri—Kansas City, MO, April 2007.

Index

Numbers in *bold italics* indicate pages with illustrations

9 781476 671376